Swift Development with Cocoa

*Jonathon Manning, Paris Buttfield-Addison,
and Tim Nugent*

Beijing · Cambridge · Farnham · Köln · Sebastopol · Tokyo

Swift Development with Cocoa

by Jonathon Manning, Paris Buttfield-Addison, and Tim Nugent

Printed in the United States of America.

Published by O'Reilly Media, Inc., 1005 Gravenstein Highway North, Sebastopol, CA 95472.

O'Reilly books may be purchased for educational, business, or sales promotional use. Online editions are also available for most titles (*http://safaribooksonline.com*). For more information, contact our corporate/institutional sales department: 800-998-9938 or *corporate@oreilly.com*.

Editor: Rachel Roumeliotis
Production Editor: Matthew Hacker
Copyeditor: Jasmine Kwityn
Proofreader: Charles Roumeliotis

Indexer: Wendy Catalano
Cover Designer: Ellie Volckhausen
Interior Designer: David Futato
Illustrator: Rebecca Demarest

December 2014:   First Edition

Revision History for the First Edition:

2014-12-08:   First release

2014-12-19:   Second release

See *http://oreilly.com/catalog/errata.csp?isbn=9781491908945* for release details.

ISBN: 978-1-491-90894-5

[LSI]

Table of Contents

Preface

We've been developing for the Cocoa framework since Mac first supported it. In that time, we've seen the ecosystem evolve from a small programming niche to one of the most important and influential development environments in the world. In our earlier books—which focused on Apple's other programming language, Objective-C—with each revised edition, we'd boast about how Objective-C was climbing the language charts, hovering around the third most popular programming language in the TIOBE index (*http://www.tiobe.com/index.php/content/paperinfo/tpci/index.html*).

We can't yet boast that Swift, the language used in this book, has reached the top five languages (or even the top ten), but it's definitely climbing the charts, and will almost certainly ascend to similarly lofty heights in the future.

When Apple announced Swift during its Worldwide Developers Conference (WWDC) in June 2014, we were amazed and quite excited. Because Apple keynotes take place in the middle of the night, Australian time, we hurriedly organized a 6 a.m. Skype meeting with our ever-patient editor, Rachel, and kicked off planning for this book. In the months that followed, we built a number of projects in Swift, to become familiar with the language and the way it was designed to be used.

Over the years, we've built a lot of large, complex iOS and OS X software, shipping it to millions upon millions of users along the way. We've picked up a deep understanding of the toolset, frameworks, and programming language—an understanding that is crucial to building the best possible software for iOS and OS X. Becoming familiar with the Swift way of doing things with Cocoa and Cocoa Touch was important, so we took a few months to work it all out. We wanted to make sure the book didn't just explain Swift, but explained how to do things the right way with Swift and Cocoa/Cocoa Touch.

Apple constantly changes things, as evidenced by Swift, as well as the recent introduction of the powerful iPhone 6 and 6 Plus, and the ever-increasing power of iPads. This book will give you the knowledge, confidence, and appreciation for iOS and OS X development with Cocoa, Cocoa Touch, and Swift, and the current way things work.

Objective-C to Swift

The original Macintosh computers were mostly programmed in C, using a library called Toolbox. When Apple acquired NeXT Computer, Inc., and replaced its operating system with Mac OS X, Toolbox was replaced with Cocoa, which was written using the Objective-C programming language.

Objective-C was designed around the same time as its chief competitor, C++. Both languages are descendants of the C programming language, and are *object-oriented* programming languages. This means that, while C has separate functions and data structures, object-oriented languages like C++ and Objective-C combine related functions and data into *objects*. For example, an object named Car might contain information about its color, its speed, and the number of doors; it might also contain functions like drive, stop, and openDoor. This close connection of data to functions that work with that data lets you think about your software as a collection of modular tools, rather than thinking about the software as a single large entity.

Objective-C is a very powerful language. Its primary difference from C++ is that it is a *dynamic* language. In any object-oriented language, the binding of functions to the specific data that they work with needs to either happen when the code is compiled (*static* binding), or at runtime (*dynamic* binding). C++ uses static binding, which makes runtime performance faster, but reduces flexibility. Objective-C uses dynamic binding, which is slightly slower, but dramatically increases the flexibility of the language.

However, Objective-C has its own problems. Because it's based on C, it inherited a number of quirks from its parent language, such as the preprocessor and pointer arithmetic (to name only a couple examples). These features, though powerful, tend to make code less readable and safe. Apple has done a good job of keeping the language up to date, but even die-hard fans of the language (which your humble authors consider themselves to be) see the language as getting a bit rusty.

This is where Swift comes in. Swift is a new language, designed to make programming iOS and Mac applications easier, faster, and safer. It's designed to be easier to learn and more resilient to programmer error than Objective-C; indeed, Apple described it as "Objective-C without the C." Because Swift is built and compiled with LLVM (the same toolset used by Objective-C), and uses the Objective-C runtime, you can write an app that uses C, Objective-C, and Swift.

Swift has a lot of very modern programming language features, including things like generics, type inference, type safety, closures, tuples, and automatic memory management. Swift is an evolving language, and will change over time, but it is the future of software development for Apple's platforms! In this book, you'll learn how to use Swift in real-world situations, and take advantage of the features in iOS and OS X to make your apps amazing.

Audience

This book is solely focused on Swift, and does not cover the use of Objective-C. We might mention it occasionally, but we don't expect you to know how to use it.

We assume that you're a reasonably capable programmer, but we don't assume you've ever developed for iOS or OS X, or used Swift or Objective-C before. We assume that you're fairly comfortable navigating OS X and iOS as a user, though.

Organization of This Book

In this book, we'll be talking about Cocoa and Cocoa Touch, the frameworks used on OS X and iOS, respectively. Along the way, we'll also be covering Swift, including its syntax and features.

Pretty much every chapter contains practical exercises that you can follow along with. The early chapters cover general topics, such as setting up a development environment and coming to grips with the Swift language, while later chapters cover specific features of Cocoa and Cocoa Touch.

Here is a concise breakdown of the material each chapter covers:

Chapter 1, Cocoa Development Tools
> This chapter introduces Cocoa and Cocoa Touch, the frameworks used on OS X and iOS. It introduces Xcode, the integrated development environment (IDE) that you'll be using while coding for these platforms. This chapter also covers the Apple Developer Programs, which are necessary if you want to distribute software on the Mac or iTunes App Stores.

Chapter 2, Programming with Swift
> This chapter introduces and explores the Swift programming language, the features of the language, and the design patterns used for Swift development with Cocoa and Cocoa Touch. It also explores the basic data types (like strings, arrays, and dictionaries).

Chapter 3, Applications on OS X and iOS
> This chapter discusses how applications are assembled and operate on Mac and iOS devices. In this chapter, we'll talk about the application life cycle on both platforms, as well as how sandboxing affects application access to data and resources.

Chapter 4, Graphical User Interfaces
> This chapter demonstrates how user interfaces are loaded and presented to the user. It introduces two of the most powerful concepts provided by Cocoa, *nibs* and *storyboards*, which are predesigned and preconfigured user interfaces, and which can be directly connected to your code. This chapter also touches on Core

Animation, the animation system used on OS X and iOS, and UI Dynamics, used for adding physics to your user interfaces.

Chapter 5, Closures and Operation Queues
This chapter introduces closures, which are an incredibly powerful feature of the Swift language that allows you to store code in variables. Closures are functions that can be stored in variables and passed around like values. This makes things like callbacks very simple to implement. This chapter also introduces operation queues, which are a straightforward way to work with concurrency without having to deal with threads.

Chapter 6, Drawing Graphics in Views
In this chapter, you'll learn about the drawing system used on both OS X and iOS, as well as how to draw custom graphics. We'll also cover the Retina display, and how view geometry works.

Chapter 7, SpriteKit
This chapter explores SpriteKit, a framework available on both iOS and OS X that is designed for making fast and efficient 2D games and graphics.

Chapter 8, SceneKit
This chapter explores SceneKit, a framework available on both iOS and OS X that is designed for making fast and efficient 3D scenes and graphics. You'll learn about materials, constraints, physics, camera, and lights.

Chapter 9, Audio and Video
This chapter covers audio and video playback using AVFoundation, the audio and video engine. You'll also learn how to use speech synthesis, access the iOS photo library, and get access to the user's photos.

Chapter 10, iCloud and Data Storage
This chapter covers a range of data storage options available on OS X and iOS. The filesystem, preferences, and iCloud are all covered. In addition, you'll learn how to make security-scoped bookmarks, which allow sandboxed apps to retain access to locations that the user has granted your apps permission to use.

Chapter 11, Cocoa Bindings
This chapter covers Cocoa bindings, a tremendously powerful system that allows you to connect your application's user interface to an application's data without the need for intermediary glue code. Bindings are an OS X-only feature.

Chapter 12, Table Views and Collection Views
This chapter covers table views (an effective way to display multiple rows of data to your user) and collection views, which allow you to display a collection of items to the user.

Chapter 13, Document-Based Applications

This chapter discusses the document systems on both iOS and OS X, which are instrumental in creating applications that work with multiple documents. Here we discuss the differences in how the two platforms handle documents.

Chapter 14, Networking

Cocoa and Cocoa Touch provide straightforward tools for accessing networked resources, and this chapter demonstrates how to retrieve information from the Internet while keeping the application responsive. This chapter also covers the network service discovery system, Bonjour, and multipeer connectivity.

Chapter 15, Working with the Real World

This chapter covers a variety of technologies used to work with the physical world: Core Location, for getting access to the GPS; Core Motion, for learning about how the hardware is moving and oriented; and the printing systems on both iOS and OS X. Beacons, game controllers, and maps are also discussed.

Chapter 16, EventKit

This chapter discusses the calendaring system used on iOS and OS X, and demonstrates how to get access to the user's calendar. We also discuss considerations for user privacy.

Chapter 17, Instruments and the Debugger

This chapter covers Instruments, the profiler and analysis tool for Mac and iOS applications. An example of a crashing application is discussed, and the cause of the crash is diagnosed and fixed using the application. Additionally, this chapter covers Xcode's built-in debugger.

Chapter 18, Sharing and Notifications

This chapter discusses how applications can share text, images, and other content with various services like Twitter and Facebook, using the built-in sharing systems (which don't require your application to deal with authenticating to these services). Additionally, we'll cover both push notifications and local notifications, which allow your application to display information to the user without running.

Chapter 19, Nonstandard Apps

Not every program you write will be an app that sits on the user's home screen, and this chapter tells you how to write four different kinds of nontraditional apps: command-line tools, menu bar apps, multiscreen iOS apps, and preference panes.

Chapter 20, Working with Text

This chapter covers TextKit, as well as the string localization system available on iOS and OS X. Here we also discuss data extraction from text using the built-in data detectors.

Conventions Used in This Book

The following typographical conventions are used in this book:

Italic

> Indicates new terms, URLs, email addresses, filenames, and file extensions.

`Constant width`

> Used for program listings, as well as within paragraphs to refer to program elements such as variable or function names, databases, data types, environment variables, statements, and keywords.

`Constant width bold`

> Shows commands or other text that should be typed literally by the user.

`Constant width italic`

> Shows text that should be replaced with user-supplied values or by values determined by context.

 This element signifies a tip or suggestion.

 This element signifies a general note.

 This element indicates a warning or caution.

Using Code Examples

Supplemental material (code examples, exercises, errata, etc.) is available for download at *http://www.secretlab.com.au/books/swift-development-with-cocoa*.

This book is here to help you get your job done. In general, if example code is offered with this book, you may use it in your programs and documentation. You do not need to contact us for permission unless you're reproducing a significant portion of the code. For example, writing a program that uses several chunks of code from this book does not require permission. Selling or distributing a CD-ROM of examples from O'Reilly books does require permission. Answering a question by citing this book and quoting example code does not require permission. Incorporating a significant amount of example code from this book into your product's documentation does require permission.

We appreciate, but do not require, attribution. An attribution usually includes the title, author, publisher, and ISBN. For example: "*Swift Development with Cocoa* by Jonathon Manning, Paris Buttfield-Addison, and Tim Nugent (O'Reilly). Copyright 2015 Secret Lab, 978-1-491-90894-5."

If you feel your use of code examples falls outside fair use or the permission given above, feel free to contact us at *permissions@oreilly.com*.

Safari® Books Online

 Safari Books Online is an on-demand digital library that delivers expert content in both book and video form from the world's leading authors in technology and business.

Technology professionals, software developers, web designers, and business and creative professionals use Safari Books Online as their primary resource for research, problem solving, learning, and certification training.

Safari Books Online offers a range of plans and pricing for enterprise, government agencies, education, and individuals. Members have access to thousands of books, training videos, and prepublication manuscripts in one fully searchable database from publishers like O'Reilly Media, Prentice Hall Professional, Addison-Wesley Professional, Microsoft Press, Sams, Que, Peachpit Press, Focal Press, Cisco Press, John Wiley & Sons, Syngress, Morgan Kaufmann, IBM Redbooks, Packt, Adobe Press, FT Press, Apress, Manning, New Riders, McGraw-Hill, Jones & Bartlett, Course Technology, and dozens more. For more information about Safari Books Online, please visit us online.

How to Contact Us

Please address comments and questions concerning this book to the publisher:

O'Reilly Media, Inc.
1005 Gravenstein Highway North
Sebastopol, CA 95472
800-998-9938 (in the United States or Canada)
707-829-0515 (international or local)
707-829-0104 (fax)

We have a web page for this book, where we list errata, examples, and any additional information. You can access this page at *http://bit.ly/swift_dev_with_cocoa*.

To comment or ask technical questions about this book, send email to *bookques tions@oreilly.com*.

For more information about our books, courses, conferences, and news, see our website at *http://www.oreilly.com*.

Find us on Facebook: *http://facebook.com/oreilly*

Follow us on Twitter: *http://twitter.com/oreillymedia*

Watch us on YouTube: *http://www.youtube.com/oreillymedia*

Acknowledgments

Jon thanks his mother, father, and the rest of his crazily extended family for their tremendous support.

Paris thanks his mother, without whom he wouldn't be doing anything nearly as interesting, let alone writing books.

Tim thanks his parents and family for putting up with his rather lackluster approach to life.

We'd all like to thank our editors, Brian Jepson and Rachel Roumeliotis—their skill and advice were invaluable to completing the book. Likewise, all the O'Reilly Media staff we've interacted with over the course of writing the book have been the absolute gurus of their fields.

A huge thank you to Tony Gray and the Apple University Consortium (AUC) (*http://www.auc.edu.au*) for the monumental boost they gave us and others listed on this page. We wouldn't be writing this book if it weren't for them.

Thanks also to Neal Goldstein, who deserves full credit and/or blame for getting us into the whole book-writing racket.

We're thankful for the support of the goons at MacLab (who know who they are and continue to stand watch for Admiral Dolphin's inevitable apotheosis), as well as Professor Christopher Lueg, Dr. Leonie Ellis, and the rest of the staff at the University of Tasmania for putting up with us.

Additional thanks to Nic W., Andrew B., Jess L., and Ash J., for a wide variety of reasons. Finally, very special thanks to Steve Jobs, without whom this book (and many others like it) would not have reason to exist.

CHAPTER 1

Cocoa Development Tools

Developing applications using Cocoa and Cocoa Touch involves using a set of tools developed by Apple. In this chapter, you'll learn about these tools, where to get them, how to use them, how they work together, and what they can do.

These development tools have a long and storied history. Originally a set of standalone application tools for the NeXTSTEP OS, they were eventually adopted by Apple for use as the official OS X tools. Later, Apple largely consolidated them into one application, known as Xcode, though some of the applications (such as Instruments and the iOS Simulator) remain somewhat separate, owing to their relatively peripheral role in the development process.

In addition to the development applications, Apple offers memberships in its Developer Programs (*https://developer.apple.com/programs/*) (formerly Apple Developer Connection), which provide resources and support for developers. The programs allow access to online developer forums and specialized technical support for those interested in talking to the framework engineers.

Now, with the introduction of Apple's curated application storefronts for OS X and iOS, these developer programs have become the official way for developers to provide their credentials when submitting applications to the Mac App Store or iTunes App Store—in essence, they are your ticket to selling apps through Apple. In this chapter, you'll learn how to sign up for these programs, as well as how to use Xcode, the development tool used to build apps for OS X and iOS.

The Mac and iOS Developer Programs

Apple runs two developer programs, one for each of the two platforms you can write apps on: iOS and OS X.

You need to have a paid membership to the iOS Developer Program (*https://develop er.apple.com/programs/ios/*) if you want to run code on your iOS devices, because signing up is the only way to obtain the necessary code-signing certificates. (At the time of writing, membership in this program costs $99 USD per year.) It isn't as necessary to be a member of the Mac Developer Program if you don't intend to submit apps to the Mac App Store (you may, for example, prefer to sell your apps yourself). However, the Mac Developer Program includes useful things like early access to the next version of the OS, so it's worth your while if you're serious about making apps. Downloading Xcode is free, even if you aren't a member of either developer program.

Both programs provide the following, among a host of other smaller features:

- Access to the Apple Developer Forums (*https://developer.apple.com/devforums/*), which are frequented by Apple engineers and designed to allow you to ask questions of your fellow developers and the people who wrote the OS.

- Access to beta versions of the OS before they are released to the public, which enables you to test your applications on the next version of OS X and iOS and make necessary changes ahead of time. You also receive beta versions of the development tools.

- A digital signing certificate (one each for OS X and iOS) used to identify you to the App Stores. Without this, you cannot submit apps to the App Store, making the programs mandatory for anyone who wants to release software either for free or for sale via the App Store.

As a developer, you can register for one or both of the developer programs. They don't depend on each other.

Finally, registering for a developer program isn't necessary to view the documentation or to download the current version of the developer tools, so you can play around with writing apps without opening your wallet.

Registering for a Developer Program

To register for one of the developer programs, you'll first need an Apple ID. It's quite likely that you already have one, as the majority of Apple's online services require one to identify you. If you've ever used iCloud, the iTunes store (for music or for apps), MobileMe, or Apple's support and repair service, you already have an ID. You might even have more than one (one of the authors of this book has four). If you don't yet have an ID, you'll create one as part of the registration process. When you register for a program, it gets added to your Apple ID.

To get started, visit the Apple site for the program you want to join.

- For the Mac program, go to *http://developer.apple.com/programs/mac/*.

- For the iOS program, go to *http://developer.apple.com/programs/ios/*.

Simply click through the steps to enroll.

You can choose to register as an individual or as a company. If you register as an individual, your apps will be sold under your name. If you register as a company, your apps will be sold under your company's legal name. Choose carefully, as it's very difficult to convince Apple to change your program's type.

If you're registering as an individual, you'll just need your credit card. If you're registering as a company, you'll need your credit card as well as documentation that proves you have authority to bind your company to Apple's terms and conditions.

 For information on code signing, and using Xcode to test and run your apps on your own physical devices, see Apple's App Distribution Guide (*http://bit.ly/app_dist_guide*).

Apple usually takes about 24 hours to activate an account for individuals, and longer for companies. Once you've received confirmation from Apple, you'll be emailed a link to activate your account; when that's done, you're a full-fledged developer!

Downloading Xcode

To develop apps for either platform, you'll use Xcode, Apple's integrated development environment. Xcode combines a source code editor, debugger, compiler, profiler, iPhone and iPad simulator, and more into one package, and it's where you'll spend the majority of your time when developing applications.

 Xcode is only available for Mac.

You can get Xcode from the Mac App Store. Simply open the App Store application and search for "Xcode," and it'll pop up. It's a free download, though it's rather large (several gigabytes at the time of writing).

Once you've downloaded Xcode, it's straightforward enough to install it. The Mac App Store gives you an installer to double-click. Follow the prompts to install.

Swift is only available if you're using Xcode 6 or later. Make sure you're using the latest version of Xcode.

Creating Your First Project with Xcode

Xcode is designed around a single window. Each of your projects will have one window, which adapts to show what you're working on.

To start exploring Xcode, you'll first need to create a project by following these steps:

1. Launch Xcode. You can find it by opening Spotlight (by pressing ⌘-Spacebar) and typing Xcode. You can also find it by opening the Finder, going to your hard drive, and opening the Applications directory. If you had any projects open previously, Xcode will open them for you. Otherwise, the Welcome to Xcode screen appears (see Figure 1-1).

Figure 1-1. The Welcome to Xcode screen

2. Create a new project. Do this simply by clicking "Create a new Xcode project" or go to File→New→Project.

   You'll be asked what kind of application to create. The template selector is divided into two areas. On the lefthand side, you'll find a collection of categories that applications can be in. You can choose to create an iOS or Mac project template, which sets up a project directory that will get you started in the right direction.

Because we're just poking around Xcode at the moment, it doesn't really matter, so choose Application under the iOS header and select Single View Application. This creates an empty iOS application.

3. Enter information about the project. Depending on the kind of project template you select, you'll be asked to provide different information about how the new project should be configured.

At a minimum, you'll be asked for the following information, no matter which platform and template you choose:

The product's name
> This is the name of the project and is visible to the user. You can change this later.

Your organization identifier
> This is used to generate a *bundle ID*, a string that looks like a reverse domain name (e.g., if O'Reilly made an application named MyUsefulApplication, the bundle ID would be *com.oreilly.MyUsefulApplication*).

> Bundle IDs are the unique identifier for an application, and are used to identify that app to the system and to the App Store. Because each bundle ID must be unique, the same ID can't be used for more than one application in either of the iOS or Mac App Stores. That's why the format is based on domain names—if you own the site *usefulsoftware.com*, all of your bundle IDs would begin with *com.usefulsoftware*, and you won't accidentally use a bundle ID that someone else is using or wants to use because nobody else owns the same domain name.

If you don't have a domain name, enter anything you like, as long as it looks like a backwards domain name (e.g., *com.mycompany* will work).

> If you plan on releasing your app, either to the App Store or elsewhere, it's very important to use a company identifier that matches a domain name you own. The App Store requires it, and the fact that the operating system uses the bundle ID that it generates from the company identifier means that using a domain name that you own eliminates the possibility of accidentally creating a bundle ID that conflicts with someone else's.

If you're writing an application for the Mac App Store, you'll also be prompted for the App Store category (whether it's a game, an educational app, a social networking app, or something else).

Depending on the template, you may also be asked for other information (e.g., the file extension for your documents if you are creating a document-aware application, such as a Mac app). You'll also be asked which language you want to use; because this book is about Swift, you should probably choose Swift! The additional information needed for this project is in the following steps.

4. Name the application. Enter "HelloCocoa" in the Product Name section.

5. Make the application run on the iPhone. Choose iPhone from the Devices drop-down list.

 iOS applications can run on the iPad, iPhone, or both. Applications that run on both are called "universal" applications and run the same binary but have different user interfaces. For this exercise, just choose iPhone.

6. Click Next to create the project. Leave the rest of the settings as shown in Figure 1-2.

Figure 1-2. The project settings

7. Choose where to save the project. You'll be asked where to save the project. Select a location that suits you.

Once you've done this, Xcode will open the project and you can now start using the entire Xcode interface, as shown in Figure 1-3.

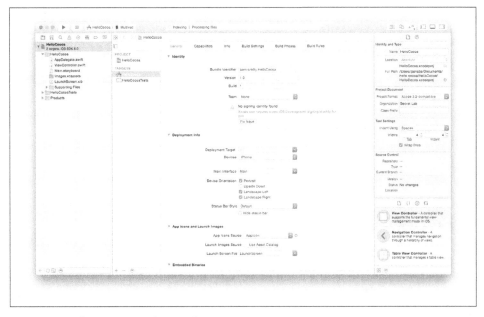

Figure 1-3. The entire Xcode interface

The Xcode Interface

As mentioned, Xcode shows your entire project in a single window, which is divided into a number of sections. You can open and close each section at will, depending on what you want to see.

Let's take a look at each of these sections and examine what they do.

The editor

The Xcode editor (Figure 1-4) is where you'll be spending most of your time. All source code editing, interface design, and project configuration take place in this section of the application, which changes depending on which file you currently have open.

If you're editing source code, the editor is a text editor, with code completion, syntax highlighting, and all the usual features that developers have come to expect from an integrated development environment. If you're modifying a user interface, the editor becomes a visual editor, allowing you to drag around the components of your interface. Other kinds of files have their own specialized editors as well.

Figure 1-4. Xcode's editor

The editor can also be split into a *main editor* and an *assistant editor*. The assistant shows files that are related to the file currently open in the main editor. It will continue to show files that have that relationship to whatever is open, even if you open different files.

For example, if you open an interface file and then open the assistant, the assistant will, by default, show related code for the interface you're editing. If you open another interface file, the assistant will show the code for the newly opened files.

You can also jump directly from one file in the editor to its counterpart—for example, from an interface file to the corresponding implementation file. To do this, hit Control-⌘-Up Arrow to open the current file's counterpart in the current editor. You can also hit Control-⌘-Option-Up Arrow to open the current file's counterpart in an assistant pane.

The toolbar

The Xcode toolbar (Figure 1-5) acts as mission control for the entire interface. It's the only part of Xcode that doesn't significantly change as you develop your applications, and it serves as the place where you can control what your code is doing.

Figure 1-5. Xcode's toolbar

From left to right, after the OS X window controls, the toolbar features the following items:

Run button
Clicking this button instructs Xcode to compile and run the application. Depending on the kind of application you're running and your currently selected settings, this button will have different effects:

- If you're creating a Mac application, the new app will appear in the Dock and will run on your machine.

- If you're creating an iOS application, the new app will launch in either the iOS Simulator or on a connected iOS device, such as an iPhone or iPad. Additionally, if you click and hold this button, you can change it from Run to another action, such as Test, Profile, or Analyze. The Test action runs any unit tests that you have set up; the Profile action runs the application Instruments (see Chapter 17); and the Analyze action checks your code and points out potential problems and bugs.

Stop button
Clicking this button stops any task that Xcode is currently doing—if it's building your application, it stops, and if your application is currently running in the debugger, it quits it.

Scheme selector
Schemes are what Xcode calls build configurations—that is, what's being built and how. Your project can contain multiple *targets*, which are the final build products created by your application. Targets can share resources like code, sound, and images, allowing you to more easily manage a task like building an iOS version of a Mac application. You don't need to create two projects, but rather have one project with two targets that can share as much code as you prefer. To select a target, click on the lefthand side of the scheme selector. You can also choose where the application will run. If you are building a Mac application, you will almost always want to run the application on your current Mac. If you're building an iOS application, however, you have the option of running the application on an iPhone simulator

or an iPad simulator. (These are in fact the same application; it simply changes shape depending on the application that is run inside it.) You can also choose to run the application on a connected iOS device if it has been set up for development.

Status display

The status display shows what Xcode is currently doing—building your application, downloading documentation, installing an application on an iOS device, and so on. If there is more than one task currently in progress, a small button will appear on the lefthand side, which cycles through the current tasks when clicked.

Editor selector

The editor selector determines how the editor is laid out. You can choose to display either a single editor, the editor with the assistant, or the versions editor, which allows you to compare different versions of a file if you're using a revision control system like Git or Subversion.

 We don't have anywhere near the space needed to talk about using version control in your projects in this book, but it's an important topic. We recommend Jon Loeliger and Matthew McCullough's *Version Control with Git, 2nd Edition* (O'Reilly).

View selector

The view selector controls whether the navigator, debug, and detail views appear on screen. If you're pressed for screen space or simply want less clutter, you can quickly summon and dismiss these parts of the screen by clicking each of the elements.

The navigator

The lefthand side of the Xcode window is the *navigator*, which presents information about your project (Figure 1-6).

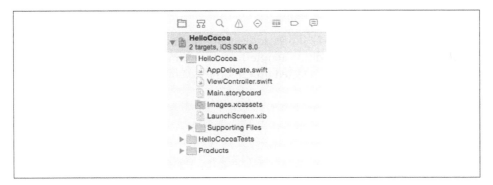

Figure 1-6. The navigator pane

The navigator is divided into eight tabs, from left to right:

- The *project navigator* gives you a list of all the files that make up your project. This is the most commonly used navigator, as it determines what is shown in the editor. Whatever is selected in the project navigator is opened in the editor.

- The *symbol navigator* lists all the classes and functions that exist in your project. If you're looking for a quick summary of a class or want to jump directly to a method in that class, the symbol navigator is a handy tool.

- The *search navigator* allows you to perform searches across your project if you're looking for specific text. (The shortcut is ⌘-Shift-F. Press ⌘-F to search the current open document.)

- The *issue navigator* lists all the problems that Xcode has noticed in your code. This includes warnings, compilation errors, and issues that the built-in code analyzer has spotted.

- The *test navigator* shows all the unit tests associated with your project. Unit tests used to be an optional component of Xcode, but are now built into Xcode directly. Unit tests are discussed in "The Testing Framework" on page 383.

- The *debug navigator* is activated when you're debugging a program, and it allows you to examine the state of the various threads that make up your program.

- The *breakpoint navigator* lists all of the breakpoints that you've currently set for use while debugging.

- The *report navigator* lists all the activity that Xcode has done with your project (such as building, debugging, and analyzing). You can go back and view previous build reports from earlier in your Xcode session, too.

Utilities

The Utilities pane (Figure 1-7) shows additional information related to what you're doing in the editor. If you're editing an interface, for example, the Utilities pane allows you to configure the currently selected user interface element.

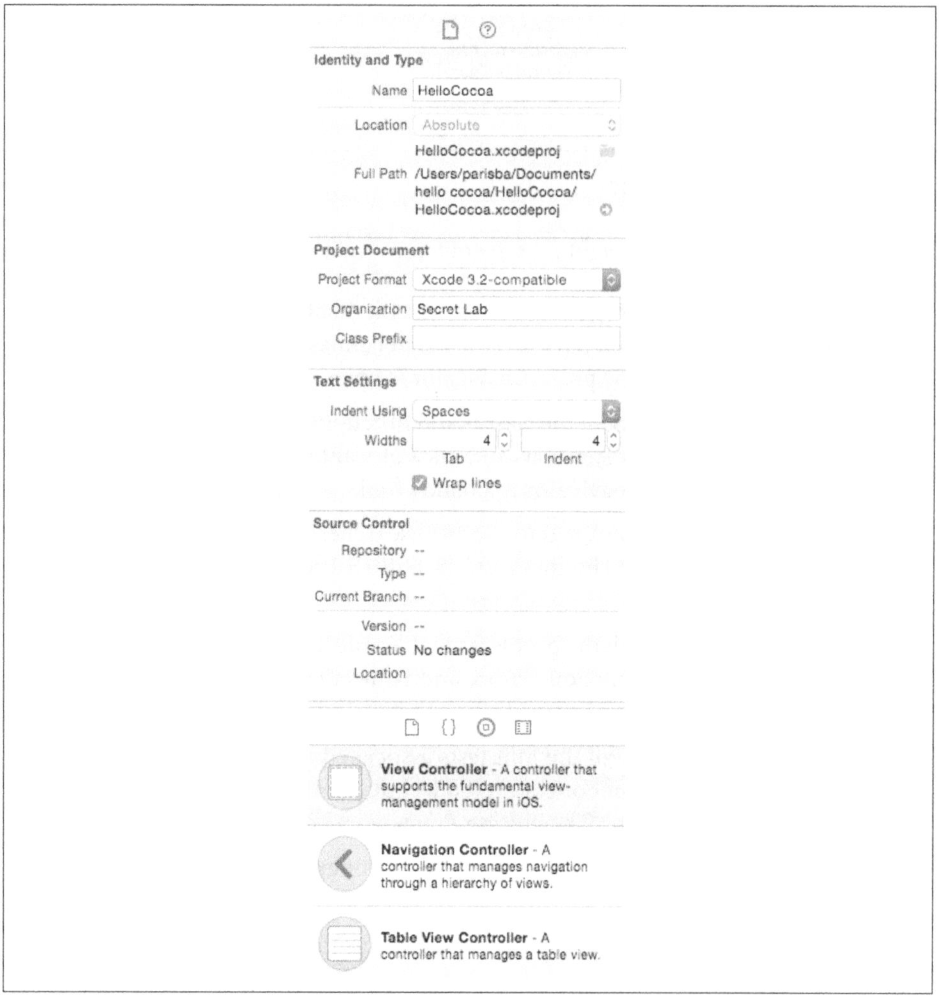

Figure 1-7. The Utilities pane

The Utilities pane is split into two sections: the inspector, which shows extra details and settings for the currently selected item, and the library, which is a collection of items that you can add to your project. The inspector and the library are most heavily used when building user interfaces; however, the library also contains a number of useful items such as file templates and code snippets, which you can drag and drop into place.

The debug area

The debug area (Figure 1-8) shows information reported by the debugger when the program is running. Whenever you want to see what the application is reporting while running, you can view it in the debug area.

Figure 1-8. The debug area

The area is split into two sections: the lefthand side shows the values of local variables when the application is paused; the righthand side shows the ongoing log from the debugger, which includes any logging that comes from the debugged application.

Developing a Simple Swift Application

Let's jump right into working with Xcode. We'll begin by creating a simple iOS application and then connect it together. If you're more interested in Mac development, don't worry—the same techniques apply.

This sample application will display a single button that, when tapped, will pop up an alert and change the button's label to "Test!" We're going to build on the project we created earlier, so make sure you have that project open.

It's generally a good practice to design the interface first and then add code. This means that your code is written with an understanding of how it maps to what the user sees.

To that end, we'll start by designing the interface for the application.

Designing the Interface

When building an application's interface using Cocoa and Cocoa Touch, you have two options. You can either design your application's screens in a *storyboard*, which shows how all the screens link together, or you can design each screen in isolation. This book covers storyboards in more detail later; for now, this first application has only one screen, so it doesn't matter much either way.

Start by opening the interface file and adding a button. These are the steps you'll need to follow:

1. First, open the main storyboard. Because newly created projects use storyboards by default, your app's interface is stored in the *Main.storyboard* file.

   Open it by selecting it in the project navigator. The editor will change to show the application's single, blank screen.

2. Next, drag in a button. We're going to add a single button to the screen. All user interface controls are kept in the *object library*, which is at the bottom of the Utilities pane on the righthand side of the screen.

   To find the button, you can either scroll through the list until you find Button, or type "button" in the search field at the bottom of the library.

   Once you've located it, drag it into the screen.

3. At this point, we need to configure the button. Every item that you add to an interface can be configured. For now, we'll only change the label.

   Select the new button by clicking it, and select the Attributes Inspector, which is the third tab from the right at the top of the Utilities pane. You can also reach it by pressing ⌘-Option-4.

   Change the button's Title to "Hello!"

 You can also change the button's title by double-clicking it in the interface.

Our simple interface is now complete (Figure 1-9). The only thing left is to connect it to code.

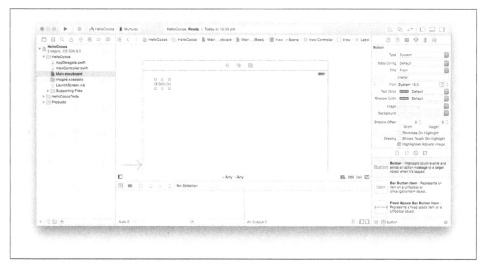

Figure 1-9. Our completed simple interface

Connecting the Code

Applications aren't just interfaces—as a developer, you also need to write code. To work with the interface you've designed, you need to create connections between your code and your interface.

There are two kinds of connections that you can make:

- *Outlets* are variables that refer to objects in the interface. Using outlets, you can instruct a button to change color or size, or hide itself. There are also *outlet collections*, which allow you to create an array of outlets and choose which objects it contains in the Interface Builder.

- *Actions* are methods in your code that are run in response to the user interacting with an object. These interactions include the user touching a finger to an object, dragging a finger, and so on.

To make the application behave as we've just described—tapping the button displays a label and changes the button's text—we'll need to use both an outlet and an action. The action will run when the button is tapped, and will use the outlet connection to the button to modify its label.

To create actions and outlets, you need to have both the interface editor and its corresponding code open. Then hold down the Control key and drag from an object in the interface editor to your code (or to another object in the interface editor, if you want to make a connection between two objects in your interface).

We'll now create the necessary connections:

1. First, open the assistant. To do this, select the second tab in the editor selector in the toolbar.

   The assistant should show the corresponding code for interface *View-Controller.swift*. If it doesn't, click the interwining circles icon (which represents the assistant) and navigate to Automatic→ViewController.swift.

    If you're using OS X 10.9 Mavericks, the assistant button looks like a tuxedo, and not a pair of circles.

2. Create the button's outlet. Hold down the Control key and drag from the button into the space below the first { in the code.

   A pop-up window will appear. Leave everything as the default, but change the Name to "helloButton." Click Connect.

   A new line of code will appear: Xcode has created the connection for you, which appears in your code as a property in your class.

3. Create the button's action. Hold down the Control key, and again drag from the button into the space below the line of code we just created. A pop-up window will again appear.

   This time, change the Connection from Outlet to Action. Set the Name to showA lert. Click Connect.

   A second new line of code will appear. Xcode has created the connection, which is a method inside the ViewController class.

4. In the showAlert method you just created, add in the new code:

```
@IBAction func showAlert(sender: AnyObject) {
    var alert = UIAlertController(title: "Hello!", message: "Hello, world!",
        preferredStyle: UIAlertControllerStyle.Alert)
    alert.addAction(UIAlertAction(title: "Close",
        style: UIAlertActionStyle.Default, handler: nil))
    self.presentViewController(alert, animated: true, completion: nil)
    self.helloButton.setTitle("Clicked", forState: UIControlState.Normal)
}
```

This code creates a UIAlertController, which displays a message to the user in a pop-up window. It prepares it by setting its title to "Hello!" and the text inside the window to "Hello, world!" The alert is then shown to the user. Finally, an action (doing nothing but dismissing the alert in this case) is added with the text "Click." It then sets the title of the button to "Clicked."

The application is now ready to run. Click the Run button in the upper-left corner. The application will launch in the iPhone simulator.

 If you happen to have an iPhone or iPad connected to your computer, Xcode will by default try to launch the application on the device rather than in the simulator. To make Xcode use the simulator, go to the Scheme menu in the upper left corner of the window and change the currently selected scheme to the simulator.

When the app finishes launching in the simulator, tap the button. An alert will appear; when you close it, you'll notice that the button's text has changed.

Using the iOS Simulator

The iOS Simulator (Figure 1-10) allows you to test out iOS applications without having to mess around with devices. It's a useful tool, but keep in mind that the simulator behaves very differently compared to a real device.

For one thing, the simulator is a lot faster than a real device and has a lot more memory. That's because the simulator makes use of your computer's resources—if your Mac has 8 GB of RAM, so will the simulator, and if you're building a processor-intensive application, it will run much more smoothly on the simulator than on a real device.

The iOS Simulator can simulate many different kinds of devices: everything from the iPad 2 to the latest iPads, and from the Retina display 3.5- and 4-inch iPhone-sized devices to the latest 4.7-inch and 5.5-inch iPhones.

To change the device, open the Hardware menu, choose Device, and select the device you want to simulate. You can also change which simulator to use via the scheme selector in Xcode.

You can also simulate hardware events, such as the home button being pressed or the iPhone being locked. To simulate pressing the home button, you can either click the virtual button underneath the screen, choose Hardware→Home, or press ⌘-Shift-H. To lock the device, press ⌘-L or choose Hardware→Lock.

Figure 1-10. The iOS Simulator

If there's no room on the screen, the simulator won't show the virtual hardware buttons. So if you want to simulate the home button being pressed, you need to use the keyboard shortcut ⌘-Shift-H.

There are a number of additional features in the simulator, which we'll examine more closely as they become relevant to the various parts of iOS we'll be discussing.

Testing iOS Apps with TestFlight

TestFlight is a service operated by Apple that allows you to send copies of your app to people for testing. Using TestFlight, you can send builds of your app to people in your organization and up to 1,000 external testers.

TestFlight allows you to submit testing builds to up to 25 people who are members of your Developer Program account. Additionally, you can send the app to up to a thousand additional people for testing, once the app is given a preliminary review by Apple.

To use TestFlight, you configure the application in iTunes Connect by providing information like the app's name, icon, and description. You also create a list of users who should receive the application. You then upload a build of the app through Xcode, and Apple emails them a link to download and test it.

For more information on how to use TestFlight, see the iTunes Connect documentation (*http://bit.ly/testing_w_testflight*).

CHAPTER 2

Programming with Swift

The Swift programming language is a new language for writing software for both iOS and OS X. Introduced in June 2014 at Apple's Worldwide Developers Conference (WWDC), Swift was a surprise to everyone: Apple had managed to develop an entire language (as well as all of the supporting libraries, developer tools, and documentation), *and* made it work seamlessly with the existing Objective-C language. And on top of that, it's a really good language.

Swift draws upon an extensive history of language design, and has a number of very cool design features that make developing software easier, simpler, and safer.

In this chapter, you'll learn how to code in Swift.

The Swift Programming Language

The Swift programming language aims for the following goals:

Safety
> Swift is designed to be a safe language. Many of the pitfalls of C, such as accidentally working with null pointers, are much harder to encounter. Swift is very strongly typed, and objects aren't allowed to be null except under very specific circumstances.

Modernity
> Swift contains a large number of modern language features designed to make it easy to express the logic of your code. These include features like pattern-matching switch statements (see "Switches" on page 33), closures ("Closures" on page 39), and the concept of all values being objects that you can attach properties and functions to ("Extensions" on page 47).

Power
> Swift has access to the entire Objective-C runtime, and is seamlessly bridged to Objective-C's classes. This means that you can use Swift right away to write full iOS

and OS X apps—you don't need to wait for anyone to port any features from Objective-C to Swift.

So, what does Swift look like? Here's an example:

```
func sumNumbers(numbers: Int...) -> Int { ❶
    var total = 0 ❷
    for number in numbers { ❸
        total += number ❹
    }
    return total ❺
}
let sum = sumNumbers(2,3,4,5) ❻
println(sum) ❼
```

This code snippet does the following things:

❶ First, a function called sumNumbers is defined. This function takes one or more Int values, which are integers (whole numbers), and returns a single Int. The ... denotes that the function takes a variable number of Int values.

❷ Inside the function, the variable total is declared. Note that the type isn't given—the compiler knows that it stores an Int, because it's being set to the integer value of zero.

❸ Next, a for-in loop starts up, which loops over every number that was sent to the method. Notice again that the type of the number variable isn't defined—the compiler infers that, given that numbers is an array of Int values, number should itself be an Int.

❹ The value of number is added to total.

❺ When the loop is complete, total is returned.

❻ The function sumNumbers is called with a collection of integers, and the result is stored in the new variable sum. This variable is *constant*: by defining it with the let keyword, the compiler is being told that its value never changes. Attempting to change the value of a constant is an error.

❼ Finally, the value is displayed using the println function, which prints values out to the console.

There are a few interesting things to note here:

- You usually don't need to define the type of variables. The compiler will do that for you, based on what values you're using.

- Even though the `sumNumbers` function takes a variable number of parameters, there's no weird syntax to deal with it (if you're a C or C++ programmer, you might remember struggling with `va_start` and friends).

- Variables that are declared with the `let` keyword are constants. The language is designed so that any variables that can be a constant should be one, in order to prevent accidental changes later. Importantly, constants in Swift don't have to be known at compile time. Instead, you can think of them as variables that are only set once.

Playgrounds

The easiest way to learn Swift is to use a *playground*. Playgrounds are environments that let you write Swift code, and see its results instantly. You don't need to build and run your code to see the results, and the code doesn't need to be a part of a larger app. This means that if you want to play around with the language, a function, or even with a piece of a larger app, you don't need to make it part of an entire app.

 A lot of this book is written assuming that the code is being run in a playground. You should get used to working in one if you want to follow along!

To start using a playground, you can create one from the "Welcome to Xcode" screen that appears when Xcode starts up (see Figure 2-1).

You can also choose File → New → New Playground and create a new playground from there.

When you create a playground, you'll end up seeing something that looks like Figure 2-2. On the lefthand side of the window, you can type Swift code. On the righthand side of the window, the result of each line of code that you write will appear.

Figure 2-1. The Welcome to Xcode screen (click "Get started with a playground" to create a new playground)

Figure 2-2. An empty playground

Variables and Constants

You define a variable in Swift using either the let or var keywords:

```
var myVariable = 123
let myConstantVariable = 123
```

 Comments in Swift are nonexecutable text. You can use comments as a note or reminder to yourself. We use comments often in sample code in this book. They are ignored by the compiler. You can begin a single-line comment with two forward slashes (//), or open a multi-line comment using a forward slash and an asterisk (/*) and close it using an asterisk followed by a foward slash (*/).

When you define a variable using var, you're allowed to change its value. If you define one using let, it's never allowed to change. Swift encourages you to use constants as much as possible, because they're safer—if you know that a value can never change, it won't cause a bug by changing without you knowing about it:

```
myVariable += 5

// (ERROR: can't change a constant variable)
myConstantVariable += 2
```

In addition to letting the compiler infer the type of your variables, you can also explicitly tell the compiler what value it should have:

```
// Explicit type of integer
let anExplicitInteger : Int = 2
```

Constants in Swift are required to have values. If you define a constant, but don't give it a value at the time it's created, the compiler will give you an error:

```
let someConstant : Int
// ERROR: constants must contain values when they're declared
```

Variables (the nonconstant kind, that is) are allowed to not have a value, as long as you never try to access it. In other words, if you create a variable and don't give it a value, the only thing you can do with it is to give it a value. After that, you can use it as normal:

```
var someVariable : Int
someVariable += 2
// ERROR: someVariable doesn't have a value, so can't add 2 to it
someVariable = 2
someVariable += 2
// WORKS, because someVariable has a value to add to
```

Unlike many popular languages, Swift doesn't require that you end your lines of code with a semicolon. However, if you want to, that's totally OK.

You can also break your lines of code over multiple lines without problems, like this:

```
var someVariable =
    "Yes"
```

The single exception to the rule of not needing to use semicolons is when you want to put multiple statements on a single line. In those cases, you separate the statements with a semicolon:

```
someVariable = "No"; println(someVariable)
```

Types

You don't need to define what type the variable is. Swift will infer its type from its initial value. This means that when you define a variable and set it to the value 2, that variable will be an `Int`:

```
// Implicit type of integer
var anInteger = 2
```

Most types can't be combined, because the compiler doesn't know what the result would be. For example, you can't add a `String` to an `Int` value, because the result is meaningless:

```
// ERROR: Can't add a string to an integer
anInteger += "Yes"
```

It's often very useful to have variables that can sometimes have no value. For example, you might have a variable that stores a number to display to the user, but you don't know what that number is yet. As we've seen already, Swift variables need to have a value. One solution might be to use the number zero to represent "no value"; indeed, many languages, including C, C++, Java, and Objective-C do just this. However, this creates a problem: there is no way to distinguish between the value zero and no value at all. What if the value you want to show is actually zero?

To deal with this issue, Swift makes a very clear distinction between "no value" and all other values. "No value" is referred to as `nil`, and is a different type to all others.

In Objective-C, `nil` is actually defined as a `void` pointer to 0. This makes it technically a number, which means you can do things like this:

```
int i = (int)(nil)+2;
// equals 2 (because 0 + 2 = 2)
```

This isn't allowed in Swift, because `nil` and `Int` are different types.

However, recall that all variables in Swift are required to have values. If you want a variable to be allowed to *sometimes* be nil, you make it an *optional* variable. Optional variables are defined by using a question mark (?) as part of their type:

```
// Optional integer, allowed to be nil
var anOptionalInteger : Int? = nil
anOptionalInteger = 42
```

Only optional variables are allowed to be set to nil. If a variable isn't defined as nil, it's not allowed to be set to the nil value:

```
// Nonoptional (regular), NOT allowed to be nil
var aNonOptionalInteger = 42

aNonOptionalInteger = nil
// ERROR: only optional values can be nil
```

You can check to see if an optional variable has a value, by using an if statement:

```
if anOptionalInteger != nil {
    println("It has a value!")
} else {
    println("It has no value!")
}
```

When you have an optional variable, you can *unwrap* it to get at its value. You do this using the ! character.

Note that if you unwrap an optional variable, and it has no value, your program will throw a runtime error, and the program will crash:

```
// Optional types must be unwrapped using !
anOptionalInteger = 2
1 + anOptionalInteger! // = 3

anOptionalInteger = nil
1 + anOptionalInteger!
// CRASH: anOptionalInteger = nil, can't use nil data
```

If you don't want to unwrap your optional variables every time you want to use them, you can declare them as unwrapped, like this:

```
var unwrappedOptionalInteger : Int!
unwrappedOptionalInteger = 1
1 + unwrappedOptionalInteger // = 2
```

This lets you use their values directly, but can be unsafe (because it lets you get away with not unwrapping them when needed, which can make you forget that they can sometimes be nil). Use this with caution.

You can convert between different types in Swift. For example, to convert an Int to a String, you do this:

```
let aString = String(anInteger)
// = "2"
```

Note that not all types can be converted to other types. It depends on the specific types you're trying to convert between, and the precise value of the thing you're trying to convert. For example, the string "2" can be converted to an Int, but the string "Hello" can't.

You also can't convert types by directly assigning variables—you must explicitly cast. Attempting to assign a value of one type to a variable with another produces an error:

```
// ERROR: Can't directly convert between types
let aString = anInteger
```

Tuples

A *tuple* is a simple collection of data. Tuples let you bundle multiple values together into a single value:

```
let aTuple = (1, "Yes")
```

Once you have a tuple, you can get values out of it:

```
let theNumber = aTuple.0 // = 1
```

In addition to using numbers to get the values out of a tuple, you can also apply labels to values inside tuples:

```
let anotherTuple = (aNumber: 1, aString: "Yes")

let theOtherNumber = anotherTuple.aNumber // = 1
```

Arrays

Arrays are very easy in Swift. To create an array, you use square brackets ([and]):

```
// Array of integers
let arrayOfIntegers : [Int] = [1,2,3]
```

Swift can also infer the type of the array:

```
// Type of array is implied
let implicitArrayOfIntegers = [1,2,3]
```

You can create an empty array as well, though you need to manually specify its type if you do this:

```
// You can also create an empty array, but you must provide the type
let anotherArray = [Int]()
```

If you define an array with the `let` keyword, its contents become *immutable* (i.e., it's not allowed to change its contents):

```
let immutableArray = [42,24]
```

Once you have an array, you can work with its contents. For example, you can append objects to the end of the array using the `append` function:

```
var myArray = [1,2,3]
myArray.append(4)
// = [1,2,3,4]
```

In addition to appending to the end of the array, you can also insert objects at any point in the array:

```
myArray.insert(5, atIndex: 0)
// = [5,1,2,3,4]
```

You can't insert items into an array beyond its bounds. For example, if you tried to insert an item at element 99, it wouldn't work, and would throw a runtime error (i.e., your program would crash).

You can also remove items from an array. To do this, you indicate the index of the item that should be removed. In Swift, arrays start at index 0, which means that removing the fifth element from the array looks like this:

```
myArray.removeAtIndex(4)
// = [5,1,2,3]
```

You can also quickly reverse the contents of an array using the `reverse` function.

```
myArray.reverse()
// = [3,2,1,5]
```

Finally, it's often useful to know how many items are in an array. You can work this out using the array's `count` property:

```
myArray.count
// = 4
```

Dictionaries

A *dictionary* is a type that maps *keys* to *values*. Dictionaries are useful for when you want to represent a collection of related information.

In a dictionary, you associate a key with a related value. For example, to store information about the crew of the USS Enterprise-D, you could use a dictionary like this:

```
var crew = [
    "Captain": "Jean-Luc Picard",
    "First Officer": "William Riker",
    "Second Officer": "Data"
];
```

When you have a dictionary, you can access its contents through *subscripting*. Subscripting is where you use square brackets ([and]) after a variable's name to describe what you want to get at the contents of that variable. For example, to get the "Captain" value from the crew variable, you do this:

```
crew["Captain"]
// = "Jean-Luc Picard"
```

You can also set values in a dictionary using subscripting. For example, to register the fact that "Wesley Crusher" is the ship's intern:

```
crew["Intern"] = "Wesley Crusher"
```

In the previous example, we've been talking about a dictionary that uses String values for both its keys and its values. However, it doesn't have to be set up this way—dictionaries can actually contain almost any value. For example, you can make a dictionary use Int values for both keys and values:

```
// This dictionary uses integers for both keys and values
var aNumberDictionary = [1: 2]
aNumberDictionary[21] = 23
```

 If you mix and match different types in your arrays and dictionaries (e.g., if you make a dictionary that contains both strings and integers as values), then Swift will handle it.

Control Flow

In every program you write, you'll want control over what code gets executed and when. For this, we'll make use of if statements, loops, and so on. The syntax for this in Swift is very straightforward, and includes some handy additional features as well.

if statements in Swift are pretty much the same as in any other language, though in Swift there's no need to wrap the expression you're checking in parentheses:

```
if 1+1 == 2 {
    println("The math checks out")
}
// Prints "The math checks out", which is a relief
```

In Swift, the body of all `if` statements—as well as all loops—is *required* to be put between two braces ({ and }). In C, C++, Java, and Objective-C, you can omit these braces if you just want to have a single statement in your loop or `if` statement, like this:

```
if (something)
    do_something();
```

However, this has led to all kinds of bugs and security problems caused by programmers forgetting to include braces. So, in Swift, they're mandatory.

When you have a collection of items, such as an array, you can use a `for-in` loop to iterate over every item:

```
let loopingArray = [1,2,3,4,5]
var loopSum = 0
for number in loopingArray {
    loopSum += number
}
loopSum // = 15
```

The `number` variable used in the `for-in` loop is implicitly created. You don't need to define a variable called `number` to make it work.

You can also use a `for-in` loop to iterate over a range of values. For example:

```
var firstCounter = 0
for index in 1 ..< 10 {
    firstCounter++
}
// Loops 9 times
```

Note the `..<` operator on the first line. This is a *range* operator, which Swift uses to describe a range of numbers from one value to another. There are actually two range operators: two dots and a left-angle-backet (`..<`) means a range that starts at the first value, and goes up to but does not include the last value. For example, the range `5..<9` contains the numbers 5, 6, 7, and 8.

If you want to create a range that *does* include the last number, you use *three* dots and no angle bracket (`...`). The range `5...9` contains the numbers 5, 6, 7, 8, and 9. You can use an inclusive range operator in `for-in` loops like so:

```
var secondCounter = 0
for index in 1 ... 10 { // note the three dots, not two
    secondCounter++
```

```
}
// Loops 10 times
```

Finally, `for` loops can be used in the same way as other languages—that is, you create an initial state, a condition to test against, and an increment:

```
var sum = 0
for var i = 0; i < 3; i++ {
    sum += 1
}
sum // = 3
```

A `while` loop lets you repeatedly run code while a certain condition remains true. For example:

```
var countDown = 5
while countDown > 0 {
    countDown--
}
countDown // = 0
```

`while` loops check to see if the condition at the start of the loop evaluates to `true`, and if it does, runs the code (and then returns to the start). In addition to `while` loops, the do-while loop runs the code at least once, and *then* checks the condition:

```
var countUp = 0
do {
    countUp++
} while countUp < 5
countUp // = 5
```

When working with optional values (see "Types" on page 26 for more on this), you can use an `if-let` statement to check to see if an optional variable has a value, and if it does, assign that value to a constant variable, and then run some code. This can save you quite a few lines of code, while preserving the safety of first checking to see if an optional variable actually has a value to work with.

An `if-let` statement looks like this:

```
var conditionalString : String? = "a string"

if let theString = conditionalString? {
    println("The string is '\(theString)'")
} else {
    println("The string is nil")
}
// Prints "The string is 'a string'"
```

You can include the values of variables in strings by using the following syntax:

```
let myNumber = 3
let myString = "My number is \(myNumber)"
// = "My number is 3"
```

You can also include the results of expressions, as well:

```
let myOtherString = "My number plus one is \(myNumber + 1)"
// = "My number plus one is 4"
```

Switches

A *switch* is a powerful way to run code depending on the value of a variable. Switches exist in other languages, but Swift kicks them into high gear.

To run different code based on the value of an integer, you can use a `switch` statement like this:

```
let integerSwitch = 3

switch integerSwitch {
case 0:
    println("It's 0")
case 1:
    println("It's 1")
case 2:
    println("It's 2")
default: // note: default is mandatory if not all
        // cases are covered (or can be covered)
    println("It's something else")
}
// Prints "it's something else"
```

In Swift, you can use the `switch` statement to handle more than just integers. You can switch on many things, including `String` values:

```
let stringSwitch = "Hello"

switch stringSwitch {
case "Hello":
    println("A greeting")
case "Goodbye":
    println("A farewell")
default:
    println("Something else")
}
// Prints "A greeting"
```

You can also switch on tuples. This is especially powerful, as you can write cases that run when only one of the components matches your condition:

```
let tupleSwitch = ("Yes", 123)

switch tupleSwitch {
case ("Yes", 123):
    println("Tuple contains 'Yes' and '123'")
case ("Yes", _):
    println("Tuple contains 'Yes' and something else")
default:
    break
}
// Prints "Tuple contains 'Yes' and '123'"
```

Finally, you can also use ranges in switches, to create code that runs when the value you're testing falls between certain ranges:

```
var someNumber = 15

switch someNumber {
case 0...10:
    println("Number is between 0 and 10")
case 11...20:
    println("Number is between 11 and 20")
default:
    println("Number is something else")
}
// Prints "Number is between 11 and 20"
```

Switches in Swift work a little differently to switches in C and Objective-C. In Swift, the execution of a section in a switch statement doesn't automatically "fall through" into the next section, which means you don't need to include a break keyword at the end of your section.

Additionally, switch statements are required to be *exhaustive*. This means that the switch statement must cover all possible values. If you're switching using a Bool type, which can either be true or false, you *must* provide handlers for both values. If you don't, it's a compiler error.

However, it's sometimes not possible to cover all cases. In the case of integers, for example, it's impossible to write a case for all possible numbers. In these cases, you provide a default case, which is shorthand for "every other possible value." So, to recap: in Swift, you either provide a case for all possible values, or you provide a default case.

Functions and Closures

In Swift, you define *functions* to perform tasks with data. Functions let you organize your code into small, repeatable chunks:

```
func firstFunction() {
    println("Hello")
}
firstFunction()
```

Functions can return a value to the code that calls them. When you define a function that returns a type, you must indicate the type of the data that it returns, by using the arrow (->) symbol:

```
func secondFunction() -> Int {
    return 123
}
secondFunction()
```

You can pass *parameters* to a function, which it's able to use to do work. When you define parameters for a function, it is also necessary to define the type of those parameters:

```
func thirdFunction(firstValue: Int, secondValue: Int) -> Int {
    return firstValue + secondValue
}
thirdFunction(1, 2)
```

A function can return a single value, as we've already seen, but they can also return *multiple* values, in the form of a tuple. In addition, you can attach names to the values in the tuple, making it easier to work with the returned value:

```
func fourthFunction(firstValue: Int, secondValue: Int)
    -> (doubled: Int, quadrupled: Int) {
    return (firstValue * 2, secondValue * 4)
}
fourthFunction(2, 4)
```

When you call a function that returns a tuple, you can access its value by number, or by name (if it has them):

```
// Accessing by number:
fourthFunction(2, 4).1 // = 16
// Same thing but with names:
fourthFunction(2, 4).quadrupled // = 16
```

When defining a function, you can give names to the parameters. This is very useful when it might not be immediately obvious what each parameter is meant to be used for. To define parameter names, you do this:

```
func addNumbers(firstNumber num1 : Int, toSecondNumber num2: Int) -> Int {
    return num1 + num2
}
```

```
addNumbers(firstNumber: 2, toSecondNumber: 3) // = 5
```

When you create names for parameters, you define an *external* name for the parameter, as well as an *internal* name. The internal name is how the function refers to the parameter, and the external name is used by the code that calls the function. If you make a function that doesn't have named parameters, each parameter only has an internal name.

You'll often find situations where the internal name of a parameter should be the same as the external one. There's nothing stopping you from typing the same name out twice, but there's a shorthand that you can use to define a parameter with an external name that's the same as its internal name—simply place a pound sign (#) in front of the parameter name:

```
func multiplyNumbers(#firstNumber: Int, #multiplier: Int) -> Int {
    return firstNumber * multiplier
}
multiplyNumbers(firstNumber: 2, multiplier: 3) // = 6
```

 When you define an external name for a function parameter, you must use that external name when calling the function. Your code will fail to compile if you don't.

You can also create functions whose parameters have *default* values. This means that you can call these functions and omit certain parameters; if you do, those parameters will use the value used in the function's definition:

```
func multiplyNumbers2 (firstNumber: Int, multiplier: Int = 2) -> Int {
    return firstNumber * multiplier;
}
// Parameters with default values can be omitted
multiplyNumbers2(2) // = 4
```

Sometimes, you'll want to use functions with a *variable* number of parameters. A parameter with a variable number of values is called a *variadic* parameter. In these cases, you want a function to handle any number of parameters, ranging from 0 to an unlimited number. To do this, use three dots (...) to indicate that a parameter has a variable number of values. Inside the body of the function, the variadic parameter becomes an array, which you can use like any other:

```
func sumNumbers(numbers: Int...) -> Int {
    // in this function, 'numbers' is an array of Ints
    var total = 0
    for number in numbers {
        total += number
    }
    return total
```

```
}
sumNumbers(2,3,4,5) // = 14
```

 When using variable parameters, you can have as many non-variadic parameters as you like. However, note that only the very last parameter in the list can be variadic.

Normally, functions use parameters as input by value, and return values as output. However, if you define a parameter with the inout keyword, you can pass the parameter by reference, and directly change the value that's stored in the variable. You can use this to swap two variables using a function, like so:

```
func swapValues(inout firstValue: Int, inout secondValue: Int) {
    let tempValue = firstValue
    firstValue = secondValue
    secondValue = tempValue
}

var swap1 = 2
var swap2 = 3
swapValues(&swap1, &swap2)
swap1 // = 3
swap2 // = 2
```

When you pass in a variable as an inout parameter, you preface it with an ampersand (&). This is done so that you're reminded that its value is going to change when you call the function.

Using Functions as Variables

Functions can be stored in variables. To do this, you first declare a variable as capable of storing a function that takes certain parameters, and returns a value. Once that's done, you can store *any* function that takes those types of parameters and returns the same type of value in the variable:

```
var numbersFunc: (Int, Int) -> Int;
// numbersFunc can now store any function that takes two ints and returns an int

// Using the 'addNumbers' function from before, which takes two numbers
// and adds them
numbersFunc = addNumbers
numbersFunc(2, 3) // = 5
```

Functions can also receive other functions as parameters, and use them. This means that you can combine functions together:

```
func timesThree(number: Int) -> Int {
    return number * 3
```

```
    }

    func doSomethingToNumber(aNumber: Int, thingToDo: (Int)->Int) -> Int {
        // we've received some function as a parameter, which we refer to as
        // 'thingToDo' inside this function.

        // call the function 'thingToDo' using 'aNumber', and return the result
        return thingToDo(aNumber);
    }

    // Give the 'timesThree' function to use as 'thingToDo'
    doSomethingToNumber(4, timesThree) // = 12
```

Functions can also return *other functions*. This means that you can use a function that creates a new function, which you can use in your code:

```
    func createAdder(numberToAdd: Int) -> (Int) -> Int {
        func adder(number: Int) -> Int {
            return number + numberToAdd
        }
        return adder
    }
    var addTwo = createAdder(2)
    addTwo(2) // = 4
```

A function can also "capture" a value, and use it multiple times. This is a tricky concept, so we'll go into it in a bit of detail. Consider the following example code:

```
    func createIncrementor(incrementAmount: Int) -> () -> Int {   ❶
        var amount = 0   ❷
        func incrementor() -> Int {   ❸
            amount += incrementAmount   ❹
            return amount
        }
        return incrementor   ❺
    }

    var incrementByTen = createIncrementor(10)   ❻
    incrementByTen() // = 10   ❼
    incrementByTen() // = 20

    var incrementByFifteen = createIncrementor(15)   ❽
    incrementByFifteen() // = 15   ❾
```

This example does the following things:

❶   The createIncrementor function takes an Int parameter, and returns a function that takes no parameters and returns an Int.

❷   Inside the function, a variable called amount is created and set to 0.

❸   A new function is created inside the createIncrementor function, which takes no parameters and returns an Int.

❹   Inside this new function, the `amount` variable has the `incrementAmount` parameter added to it, and then returned. Notice that the `amount` variable is outside of this function.

❺   The `incrementor` function is then returned.

❻   The `createIncrementor` function can then be used to create a new incrementor function. In the first example, one is created with the `incremementAmount` parameter set to 10.

❼   Each time this function is called, it will return a value that's 10 higher than the last time it was called. The reason it's doing this is because the function that `createIncrementor` returned *captured* the variable `amount`; every time it's called, that variable goes up by `incrementAmount`.

❽   The `amount` variable is not shared between individual functions, however. When a new incrementor is created, it has its own separate `amount` variable.

❾   The second function goes up by 15.

This feature of Swift allows you to create functions that act as *generators*—functions that return different values each time they're called.

Closures

Another feature of Swift is that of *closures*—small, anonymous chunks of code that you can use like functions. Closures are great for passing to other functions in order to tell them how they should carry out a certain task.

To give you can example of how closures work, consider the built-in `sorted` function. This function takes an array and a closure, and uses that closure to determine how two individual elements of that array should be ordered (i.e., which one should go first in the array).

In addition to the `sorted` function, which takes an array and returns a sorted version of that same array, there's also a `sort` function, which takes an array and changes it into a sorted version:

```
var sortingInline = [2, 5, 98, 2, 13]
sort(&sortingInline)
sortingInline // = [2, 2, 5, 13, 98]
```

Note that the variable has an ampersand (&) in front of it.

To sort an array so that small numbers go before large numbers, you can do this:

```
var numbers = [2,1,56,32,120,13]

var numbersSorted = sorted(numbers, { (n1: Int, n2: Int) -> Bool in
    // Sort so that small numbers go before large numbers
```

```
    return n2 > n1
}) // = [1, 2, 13, 32, 56, 120]
```

A closure, like a function, takes parameters. In the preceding example, the closure specifies the name and type of the parameters that it works with. However, you don't need to be quite so verbose—the compiler can infer the type of the parameters for you, much like how it can with variables. Notice the lack of types in the parameters for the closure:

```
var numbersSortedReverse = sorted(numbers, {n1, n2 in
    return n1 > n2
}) // = [120, 56, 32, 13, 2, 1]
```

You can make it even more terse, if you don't especially care what names the parameters should have. If you omit the parameter names, you can just refer to each parameter by number (the first parameter is called $0, the second is called $1, etc.).

Additionally, if your closure only contains a single line of code, you can omit the return keyword:

```
var numbersSortedAgain = sorted(numbers, {
    $1 > $0
}) // = [1, 2, 13, 32, 56, 120]
```

Finally, if a closure is the last parameter in a function call, you can put it outside the parentheses. This is purely something that improves readibility, and doesn't change how the closure works:

```
var numbersSortedReversedAgain = sorted(numbers) {
    $0 > $1
} // = [120, 56, 32, 13, 2, 1]
```

 The line breaks in this code are optional, too. You could also do this:

```
var numbersSortedReversedOneMoreTime = sorted(numbers) { $0 > $1 }
// = [120, 56, 32, 13, 2, 1]
```

Just like functions, closures can be stored in variables. Once you do that, you can call them, just like a function:

```
var comparator = {(a: Int, b:Int) in a < b}
comparator(1,2) // = true
```

Objects

In Swift, as with Objective-C, Java, and C++, you define *classes* as the templates for your object. Classes in Swift look like this:

```
class Vehicle {

    var color: String?
    var maxSpeed = 80

    func description() -> String {
        return "A \(self.color) vehicle"
    }

    func travel() {
        println("Traveling at \(maxSpeed) kph")
    }
}
```

Classes contain both *properties* and *methods*. Properties are variables that are part of a class, and methods are functions that are part of a class.

The Vehicle class in this example contains two properties: an optional String called color, and an Int called maxSpeed. Property declarations look the same as variable declarations do in other code:

```
var color: String?
var maxSpeed = 80
```

Methods in a class look the same as functions anywhere else. Code that's in a method can access the properties of a class by using the self keyword, which refers to the object that's currently running the code:

```
func description() -> String {
    return "A \(self.color) vehicle"
}

func travel() {
    println("Traveling at \(maxSpeed) kph")
}
```

When you've defined a class, you can create instances of the class to work with. Instances have their own copies of the class's properties and functions to work with.

For example, to define an instance of the Vehicle class, you define a variable and call the class's initializer. Once that's done, you can work with the class's functions and properties:

```
var redVehicle = Vehicle()
redVehicle.color = "Red"
redVehicle.maxSpeed = 90
redVehicle.travel() // prints "Traveling at 90 kph"
redVehicle.description() // = "A Red vehicle"
```

Inheritance

When you define a class, you can create one that *inherits* from another. When a class inherits from another (called the *parent* class), it incorporates all of its parent's functions and properties.

 In Swift, classes are allowed to have only a single parent class. This is the same as Objective-C, but is different to C++, which allows classes to have multiple parents (known as *multiple inheritance*).

To create a class that inherits from another, you put the name of the class you're inheriting from after the name of the class you're creating, like so:

```
class Car: Vehicle {
    // Inherited classes can override functions
        override func description() -> String  {
            var description = super.description()
            return description + ", which is a car"
        }
}
```

Classes that inherit from other classes can *override* functions in their parent class. This means that you can create subclasses that inherit most of their functionality, but can specialize in certain areas.

To override a function, you re-declare it in your subclass and add the `override` keyword to let the compiler know that you aren't accidentally creating a method with the same name as one in the parent class.

In an overridden function, it's often very useful to call back to the parent class's version of that function. You can do this through the `super` keyword, which lets you get access to the superclass's functions:

```
override func description() -> String  {
    var description = super.description()
    return description + ", which is a car"
}
```

Initialization and Deinitialization

When you create an object in Swift, a special method known as its *initializer* is called. The initializer is the method that you use to set up the initial state of an object.

In addition to initializers, you can run code when an object is going away, in a method called its *deinitializer*. This runs when the retain count of an object drops to zero (see "Memory Management" on page 54), and is called right before the object is removed from memory. This is your object's final opportunity to do any necessary cleanup before it goes away forever:

```
class InitAndDeinitExample {
    // Designated (i.e., main) initializer
    init () {
        println("I've been created!")
    }
    // Convenience initializer, required to call the
    // designated initializer (above)
    convenience init (text: String) {
        self.init() // this is mandatory
        println("I was called with the convenience initializer!")
    }
    // Deinitializer
    deinit {
        println("I'm going away!")
    }
}

var example : InitAndDeinitExample?

// using the designated initializer
example = InitAndDeinitExample() // prints "I've been created!"
example = nil // prints "I'm going away"

// using the convenience initializer
example = InitAndDeinitExample(text: "Hello")
// prints "I've been created!" and then
//   "I was called with the convenience initializer"
```

An initializer can also return nil. This can be useful when your initializer isn't able to usefully construct an object. For example, the NSURL class has an initializer that takes a string and converts it into a URL; if the string isn't a valid URL, the initializer returns nil.

To create an initializer that can return nil—also known as a *failable initializer*—put a question mark after the init keyword, and return nil if the initializer decides that it can't successfully construct the object:

```
// This is a convenience initializer that can sometimes fail, returning nil
// Note the ? after the word 'init'
convenience init? (value: Int) {
    self.init()

    if value > 5 {
        // We can't initialize this object; return nil to indicate failure
        return nil
    }

}
```

When you use a failable initializer, any variable you store the result in will be optional:

```
let failableExample = InitAndDeinitExample(value: 6)
// = nil
```

Properties

Classes store their data in *properties*. Properties, as previously mentioned, are variables or constants that are attached to instances of classes. Any property that you've added to a class can be accessed:

```
class Counter {
    var number: Int = 0
}
let myCounter = Counter()
myCounter.number = 2
```

In the previous example, the property is a simple value stored in the object. This is known in Swift as a *stored property*. However, you can do more with properties, including creating properties that use code to figure out their value. These are known as *computed properties*, and you can use them to provide a simpler interface to information stored in your classes.

For example, consider a class that represents a rectangle, which has both a width and a height property. It'd be useful to have an additional property that contains the area, but you don't want that to be a third stored property. Instead, you can use a computed property, which looks like a regular property from the outside, but on the inside is really a function that figures out the value when needed.

To define a computed property, you declare a variable in the same way as you do for a stored property, but add braces ({ and }) after it. Inside these braces, you provide a get section, and optionally a set section:

```
class Rectangle {
    var width: Double = 0.0
    var height: Double = 0.0
    var area : Double {
        // computed getter
        get {
            return width * height
        }

        // computed setter
        set {
            // Assume equal dimensions (i.e., a square)
            width = sqrt(newValue)
            height = sqrt(newValue)
        }
    }
}
```

In the previous example, the area is computed by multiplying the width and height together. The property is also settable—if you set the area of the rectangle, the code assumes that you want to create a square, and updates the width and height to both the square root of the area.

Working with computed properties looks identical to working with stored properties:

```
var rect = Rectangle()
rect.width = 3.0
rect.height = 4.5
rect.area // = 13.5
rect.area = 9 // width & height now both 3.0
```

When working with properties, you often want to run some code whenever a property changes. To support this, Swift properties let you add *observers* to your properties. These are small chunks of code that can run just before or after a property's value changes. To create a property observer, add braces after your property (much like you do with computed properties), and include willSet and didSet blocks. These blocks each get passed a parameter—willSet, which is called before the property's value changes, is given the value that is about to be set, and didSet is given the old value:

```
class PropertyObserverExample {
    var number : Int = 0 {
        willSet(newNumber) {
            println("About to change to \(newNumber)")
        }
        didSet(oldNumber) {
            println("Just changed from \(oldNumber) to \(self.number)!")
        }
    }
}
```

Property observers don't change anything about how you actually work with the property—they just add additional behavior before and after the property changes:

```
var observer = PropertyObserverExample()
observer.number = 4
// prints "About to change to 4", then "Just changed from 0 to 4!"
```

You can also make a property *lazy*. A lazy property is one that doesn't get set up until the first time it's accessed. This lets you defer some of the more time-consuming work of setting up a class to later on, when it's actually needed. To define a property as lazy, you put the lazy keyword in front of it.

You can see lazy properties in action in the following example. In this code, there are two properties, both of the same type, but one of them is lazy:

```
class SomeExpensiveClass {
    init(id : Int) {
        println("Expensive class \(id) created!")
    }
```

```
}

class LazyPropertyExample {
    var expensiveClass1 = SomeExpensiveClass(id: 1)
    // note that we're actually constructing a class,
    // but it's labeled as lazy
    lazy var expensiveClass2 = SomeExpensiveClass(id: 2)


    init() {
        println("First class created!")
    }
}

var lazyExample = LazyPropertyExample()
// prints "Expensive class 1 created", then "First class created!"

lazyExample.expensiveClass1 // prints nothing, it's already created
lazyExample.expensiveClass2 // prints "Expensive class 2 created!"
```

In this example, when the lazyExample variable is created, it immediately creates the first instance of SomeExpensiveClass. However, the second instance isn't created until it's actually used by the code.

Protocols

A *protocol* can be thought of as a list of requirements for a class. When you define a protocol, you're creating a list of properties and methods that classes can declare that they have.

A protocol looks very much like a class, with the exception that you don't provide any actual code—you just define what kinds of properties and functions exist, and how they can be accessed.

For example, if you wanted to create a protocol that describes any object that can blink on and off, you could use this:

```
protocol Blinking {

    // This property must be (at least) gettable
    var isBlinking : Bool { get }

    // This property must be gettable and settable
    var blinkSpeed: Double { get set }

    // This function must exist, but what it does is up to the implementor
    func startBlinking(blinkSpeed: Double) -> Void
}
```

Once you have a protocol, you can create classes that *conform* to a protocol. When a class conforms to a protocol, it's effectively promising to the compiler that it implements

---

all of the properties and methods listed in that protocol. It's allowed to have more stuff besides that, and it's also allowed to conform to multiple protocols.

To continue this example, you could create a specific class called Light that implements the Blinking protocol. Remember, all a protocol does is specify *what* a class can do—the class itself is responsible for determining *how* it does it:

```
class Light : Blinking {
    var isBlinking: Bool = false

    var blinkSpeed : Double = 0.0

    func startBlinking(blinkSpeed : Double) {
        println("I am now blinking")
        isBlinking = true

        // We say self.blinkSpeed here to help the compiler tell
        // the difference between the parameter 'blinkSpeed' and the property
        self.blinkSpeed = blinkSpeed
    }
}
```

The advantage of using protocols is that you can use Swift's type system to refer to any object that conforms to a given protocol. This is useful, because you get to specify that you only care about whether an object conforms to the protocol—the specific type of the class doesn't matter:

```
var aBlinkingThing : Blinking?
// can be ANY object that has the Blinking protocol

aBlinkingThing = Light()

// Using ? after the variable name checks to see
// if aBlinkingThing has a value before trying to work with it
aBlinkingThing?.startBlinking(4.0) // prints "I am now blinking"
aBlinkingThing?.blinkSpeed // = 4.0
```

Extensions

In Swift, you can *extend* existing types, and add additional methods and computed properties. This is very useful in two situations:

- You're working with a type that someone else wrote, and you want to add funcitonality to it but either don't have access to its source code or don't want to mess around with it.

- You're working with a type that you wrote, and you want to divide up its functionality into different sections, for readability.

Extensions let you do both with ease. In Swift, you can extend *any* type—that is, you can extend both classes that you write, as well as built-in types like Int and String.

To create an extension, you use the extension keyword, followed by the name of the type you want to extend. For example, to add methods and properties to the built-in Int type, you can do this:

```
extension Int {
    var doubled : Int {
        return self * 2
    }
    func multiplyWith(anotherNumber: Int) -> Int {
        return self * anotherNumber
    }
}
```

Once you extend a type, you can call the additional functions and properties that you've added. Note that when you extend a type, the functions and properties you define in the extension are added to *every* instance of that type:

```
2.doubled // = 4
4.multiplyWith(32) // = 128
```

 You can only add computed properties in an extension. You can't add your own stored properties.

You can also use extensions to make a type conform to a protocol. For example, you can make the Int type conform to the Blinking protocol described earlier:

```
extension Int : Blinking {
    var isBlinking : Bool {
        return false;
    }

    var blinkSpeed : Double {
        get {
            return 0.0;
        }
        set {
            // Do nothing
        }
    }

    func startBlinking(blinkSpeed : Double) {
        println("I am the integer \(self). I do not blink.")
    }
}
```

```
2.isBlinking // = false
2.startBlinking(2.0) // prints "I am the integer 2. I do not blink."
```

Access Control

Swift defines three levels of access control, which determines what information is accessible to which parts of the application:

Public

Public classes, methods, and properties are accessible by any part of the app. For example, all of the classes in UIKit that you use to build iOS apps are public.

Internal

Internal data is only accessible to the *module* in which they're defined. A module is an application, library, or framework. This is why you can't access the inner workings of UIKit—it's defined as internal to the UIKit framework. Internal is the default level of access control: if you don't specify the access control level, it's assumed to be internal.

Private

Private data is only accessible to the file in which it's declared. This means that you can create classes that hide their inner workings from other classes in the same module, which helps to keep the amount of surface area that those classes expose to each other to a minimum.

The kind of access control that a method or property can have depends on the access level of the class that it's contained in. You can't make a method more accessible than the class in which it's contained. For example, you can't define a private class that has a public method:

```
public class AccessControl {
```

By default, all properties and methods are `internal`. You can explicity define a member as `internal` if you want, but it isn't necessary:

```
// Accessible to this module only
// 'internal' here is the default and can be omitted
internal var internalProperty = 123
```

> The exception is for classes defined as `private`—if you don't declare an access control level for a member, it's set as `private`, not `internal`.

When you declare a method or property as `public`, it becomes visible to everyone in your app:

```
// Accessible to everyone
public var publicProperty = 123
```

If you declare a method or property as `private`, it's only accessible from within the source file in which it's declared:

```
// Only accessible in this source file
private var privateProperty = 123
```

Finally, you can render a property as read-only by declaring that its setter is private. This means that you can freely read and write the property's value within the source file that it's declared in, but other files can only read its value:

```
// The setter is private, so other files can't modify it
private(set) var privateSetterProperty = 123
```

Operators

When you add two integers together in Swift using the + symbol, you're using an *operator*. There are a wide variety of different operators built into Swift, and the most common ones are the arithmetic operators (+, -, /, *, etc.). An operator is actually a function that takes one or two values, and returns a value. For example, you could represent the + function like this:

```
func +(left: Int, right: Int) -> Int {
    return left + right
}
```

 The preceding example actually calls itself in an infinitely recursive way, which hangs your app.

Swift lets you define new operators, and overload existing ones for your new types. This means that, if you have a new type of data, you can operate on that data using both existing operators, as well as new ones you invent yourself.

For example, imagine you have an object called `Vector2D`, which stores two floating-point numbers:

```
class Vector2D {
    var x : Float = 0.0
    var y : Float = 0.0

    init (x : Float, y: Float) {
        self.x = x
        self.y = y
    }
}
```

If you want to allow adding these two objects together using the + operator, all you need to do is provide an implementation of the + function:

```
func +(left : Vector2D, right: Vector2D) -> Vector2D {
    let result = Vector2D(x: left.x + right.x, y: left.y + right.y)

    return result
}
```

You can then use it as you'd expect:

```
let first = Vector2D(x: 2, y: 2)
let second = Vector2D(x: 4, y: 1)

let result = first + second
// = (x:6, y:3)
```

 For information on how to create your own custom operators, see the "Advanced Operators" (*https://developer.apple.com/library/ios/docu mentation/Swift/Conceptual/Swift_Programming_Language/Advan cedOperators.html*) section of *The Swift Programming Language*.

Generics

Swift is a statically typed language. This means that the Swift compiler needs to definitively know what type of information your code is dealing with. This means that you can't pass a string to code that expects to deal with a date, which is something that can happen in Objective-C.

However, this rigidity means that you lose some flexibility. It's annoying to have to write a chunk of code that does some work with strings, and another that works with dates.

This is where *generics* come in. Generics allow you to write code that doesn't need to know precisely *what* information it's dealing with. An example of this kind of use is in arrays: they don't actually do any work with the data they store, but instead just store it in an ordered collection. Arrays are, in fact, generics.

To create a generic type, you name your object as normal, and then specify any generic types between angle brackets. T is traditionally the term used, but you can put anything you like. For example, to create a generic Tree object, which contains a value and any number of child Tree objects, you'd do the following:

```
class Tree <T> {

    // 'T' can now be used as a type
    var value : T

    var children : [Tree <T>] = []
```

```
    init(value : T) {
        self.value = value
    }

    func addChild(value : T) -> Tree <T> {
        let newChild = Tree<T>(value: value)
        children.append(newChild)
        return newChild
    }
}
```

Once a generic type is defined, you can create a specific, nongeneric type from it. For example, the Tree generic type just defined can be used to create a version that works with Ints and one that works with Strings:

```
// Tree of integers
let integerTree = Tree<Int>(value: 5)

// Can add children that contain Ints
integerTree.addChild(10)
integerTree.addChild(5)

// Tree of strings
let stringTree = Tree<String>(value: "Hello")

stringTree.addChild("Yes")
stringTree.addChild("Internets")
```

Interoperating with Objective-C

Fortunately, this is very easy to do. For example, to use the UIView class (which is the main focus of Chapter 4), which is written in Objective-C, you can construct an instance just like any other Swift class:

```
var view = UIView(frame: CGRect(x: 0,y: 0,width: 100,height: 100))
```

Accessing the properties of an object that's defined in Objective-C is easy, and works the same way as a Swift object:

```
view.bounds
```

Methods in Objective-C get translated from their original form into Swift:

```
view.pointInside(CGPoint(x: 20, y: 20), withEvent:nil) // = true
```

Using Objective-C and Swift in the Same Project

If you're making a new project from scratch, you'll likely have the opportunity to write all of your code in Swift. However, if you have an existing project written in Objective-C, and want to write code in Swift, you need a way to bridge the two. The same thing applies in reverse, for when you have a project written in Swift and need to add some Objective-C code.

Using Swift Objects in Objective-C

To make objects written in Swift available in Objective-C, you need to add the `@objc` tag in front of them. For example, if you have a class written in Swift called `Cat`, you write the class as normal, and prepend `@objc` in front of its name:

```
@objc class Cat : NSObject {
    var name : String = ""

    func speak() -> String {
        return "Meow"
    }
}
```

In your Objective-C code, you import an Xcode-generated header file that makes all of your `@objc`-tagged Swift code available to Objective-C:

```
#import "MyAppName-Swift.h"
```

Once it's imported, you can use the class as if it had originally been written in Objective-C:

```
Cat* myCat = [[Cat alloc] init];
myCat.name = "Fluffy";
[myCat speak];
```

Using Objective-C Objects in Swift

To use classes and other code written in Objective-C in your Swift code, you fill out a *bridging header*. When you add an Objective-C file to a project containing Swift files, or vice versa, Xcode will offer to create and add a bridging header to your project.

Inside this header, you add `#import` statements for all of the Objective-C files you want to export to Swift. Then, inside your Swift code, you can use the Objective-C classes as if they had been originally written in Swift.

 This method is actually how your code accesses the majority of the Cocoa and Cocoa Touch APIs, which are mostly written in Objective-C.

For example, consider a class written in Objective-C, like so:

```
@interface Elevator
```

```
- (void) moveUp;
- (void) moveDown;

@property NSString* modelName;

@end
```

All you need to do is import the class's header file into the bridging header that Xcode generates for you:

```
#import "Elevator.h"
```

Once that's done, you can use the class in Swift as if it was originally written in Swift:

```
let theElevator = Elevator()

theElevator.moveUp()
theElevator.moveDown()

theElevator.modelName = "The Great Glass Elevator"
```

 Interoperation between Swift and Objective-C is a large and complex topic, and there are several details that you should know if you plan on making the two work together. Apple's written an entire book on the topic, *Using Swift with Cocoa and Objective-C* (*https:// itunes.apple.com/us/book/usingswift-cocoa-objective/id888894773? mt=11*), which is available for free both online and on the iBooks Store.

Modules

In Swift, just like in Objective-C, code is grouped into *modules*. When you define a framework or application, all of the code that's added to it is placed within that target's module. To get access to the code, you use the `import` keyword:

```
import AVFoundation
```

Memory Management

Objects in Swift are *memory managed*. When an object is being used, Swift keeps it in memory; when it's no longer being used, it's removed from memory.

The technique that Swift uses to keep track of which objects are being used and which are not is called *reference counting*. When an object is assigned to a variable, a counter called the *retain count* goes up by 1. When the object is no longer assigned to that variable, the retain count goes down. If the retain count ever reaches 0, that means that no variables are referring to that object, and the object is then removed from memory.

The nice thing about Swift is that this all happens at the compiler level. As the compiler reads your code, it keeps track of when objects get assigned to variables, and adds code that increments and decrements the retain count.

However, this automatic memory management has one potential snag that you need to keep an eye out for: *retain cycles*.

A retain cycle is where you have two objects that refer to each other, but are otherwise not referred to by any other part of the application. Because those objects refer to each other, their retain count is not zero, which means they stay in memory; however, because no variable in the rest of the application refers to them, they're inaccessible (and consequently useless).

Swift solves this using the concept of *weak* references. A weak reference is a variable that refers to an object, but doesn't change the retain count of that object. You use weak references when you don't particularly care whether an object stays in memory or not (i.e., your code isn't the *owner* of that object).

To declare a weak reference in Swift, you use the `weak` keyword, like so:

```
class Class1 {
    init() {
        println("Class 1 being created!")
    }

    deinit {
        println("Class 1 going away!")
    }
}

class Class2 {
    // Weak vars are implicitly optional
    weak var weakRef : Class1?
}
```

Working with Strings

In Swift, strings are sequences of Unicode characters. This means that they're able to store pretty much any character that has ever been a part of a human language, which is great news for making your app translatable to other languages.

Creating a string in Swift is easy. Creating an empty string can be done by creating a string literal with nothing in it:

```
let emptyString = ""
```

You can also create an empty string by using the `String` type's initializer:

```
let anotherEmptyString = String()
```

Checking to see if a string is empty can be done using the `isEmpty` property:

```
emptyString.isEmpty // = true
```

Strings can be combined together, using the + and += operators:

```
var composingAString = "Hello"
composingAString += ", World!" // = "Hello, World!"
```

A string is actually a sequence of `Character` objects, each representing a Unicode character. To loop over every character in a string, you can use a `for-in` loop:

```
var reversedString = ""
for character in "Hello" {
    reversedString = String(character) + reversedString
}
reversedString // = "olleH"
```

To work out how many characters are in a string, you use the `countElements` function:

```
countElements("Hello") // = 5
```

The `countElements` function actually works on any collection, including arrays and dictionaries.

Note that the number of characters in a `String` is *not* the same as the number of bytes. Unicode characters can range in size from 1 byte to 4 bytes, depending on their type (emoji, for example, are 4 bytes).

Comparing Strings

To compare two different strings, you just use the == operator. This operator checks the contents of two strings to see if they contain the same characters:

```
let string1 : String = "Hello"
let string2 : String = "Hel" + "lo"

if string1 == string2 {
    println("The strings are equal")
}
```

In other languages like C and Objective-C, the == operator checks to see if two values are equal, or if two variables refer to the same location in memory. If you really do want to see if two string variables refer to the same object, you use the === operator (note that it's three equals signs, instead of two):

```
if string1 as AnyObject === string2 as AnyObject {
    println("The strings are the same object")
}
```

To change the case of a string, you use the `uppercaseString` and `lowercaseString` properties, which return modified versions of the original string:

```
string1.uppercaseString // = "HELLO"
string2.lowercaseString // = "hello"
```

Searching Strings

You can check to see if a string has a given suffix or prefix by using the `hasPrefix` and `hasSuffix` methods:

```
if string1.hasPrefix("H") {
    println("String begins with an H")
}
if string1.hasSuffix("llo") {
    println("String ends in 'llo'")
}
```

Data

In Cocoa, you'll frequently find yourself working with chunks of arbitrary data that you need to save to or load from disk, or that you've downloaded from the network. Cocoa represents these as `NSData` objects.

You can get an `NSData` object in a variety of ways. For example, if you have a string that you want to convert to an `NSData`, you can use the string's `dataUsingEncoding` method, like so:

```
let stringToConvert = "Hello, Swift"
let data = stringToConvert.dataUsingEncoding(NSUTF8StringEncoding)
```

Loading Data from Files and URLs

You can also load data from a URL or from a file location on disk. If the file is one of the resources built into your project, you first need to work out where on disk it's being stored; once you have that, you can load its contents into memory.

To get the location of a built-in file, you first use the `NSBundle` class to determine where a given file is being stored on disk. Once you've done that, you construct an `NSData` object by providing it either a URL or a file path:

```
// Loading from URL
if let fileURL = NSBundle.mainBundle()
    .URLForResource("SomeFile", withExtension: "txt") {
    let loadedDataFromURL = NSData(contentsOfURL:fileURL)
}

// Loading from a file
if let filePath = NSBundle.mainBundle()
```

```
        .pathForResource("SomeFile", ofType: "txt") {
        let loadedDataFromPath = NSData(contentsOfFile:filePath)
}
```

Serialization and Deserialization

You can also convert an object to data. To do this, you first make an object conform to
the NSObject and NSCoding protocols, and then add two methods: encodeWithCoder,
and an initializer that takes an NSCoder:

```
class SerializableObject : NSObject, NSCoding {

    var name : String?

    func encodeWithCoder(aCoder: NSCoder) {
        aCoder.encodeObject(name!, forKey:"name")
    }
    override init() {
        self.name = "My Object"
    }
    required init(coder aDecoder: NSCoder)  {
        self.name = aDecoder.decodeObjectForKey("name") as? String
    }
}
```

An object that conforms to NSCoding can be converted to an NSData object, and also be
loaded from one, via the NSKeyedArchiver and NSKeyedUnarchiver classes. The trick
to it is in the encodeWithCoder method, and in the special initializer: in the encode
WithCoder method, you take the NSCoder that's passed in as a parameter, and store any
values that you want to keep in it. Later, in the initializer, you pull those values out.

Converting these objects to and from data is very straightforward, and looks like this:

```
let anObject = SerializableObject()

anObject.name = "My Thing That I'm Saving"

// Converting it to data
let objectConvertedToData =
    NSKeyedArchiver.archivedDataWithRootObject(anObject)

// Converting it back
// Note that the conversion might fail, so 'unarchiveObjectWithData' returns
// an optional value. So, use 'as?' to check to see if it worked.
let loadedObject =
    NSKeyedUnarchiver.unarchiveObjectWithData(objectConvertedToData)
        as? SerializableObject

loadedObject?.name
// = "My Thing That I'm Saving"
```

Design Patterns in Cocoa

Cocoa is built around a number of design patterns, whose purpose is to make your life as a developer more consistent and (one hopes) more productive. Three key patterns are the model-view-controller (MVC) pattern, upon which most of Cocoa and Cocoa Touch is built; the delegation pattern, which allows both your code and Cocoa to be highly flexible in determining what code gets run by whom; and notifications, which allow your code to watch for important events that happen within your app.

Model-View-Controller

The model-view-controller design pattern is one of the fundamental design patterns in Cocoa. Let's take a look at what each of these parts mean:

- *Models* are objects that contain data or otherwise coordinate the storing, management, and delivery of data to other objects. Models can be as simple as a string or as complicated as an entire database—their purpose is to store data and provide it to other objects. They don't care what happens to the data once they give it to someone else; their only concern is managing how the data is stored.

- *Views* are objects that work directly with the user, providing information to them and receiving input back. Views do not manage the data that they display—they only show it to the user. Views are also responsible for informing other objects when the user interacts with them. Likewise with data and models, views do not care what happens next—their responsibility ends with informing the rest of the application.

- *Controllers* are objects that mediate between models and views, and contain the bulk of what some call the "business logic" of an application—the actual logic that defines what the application is and how it responds to user input. At a minimum, the controller is responsible for retrieving information from the model and providing it to the view; it is also responsible for providing information to the model when it is informed by the view that the user has interacted with it.

For an illustration of the model-view-controller design pattern in action, imagine a simple text editor. In this example, the application loads a text file from disk and presents its contents to the user in a text field. The user makes changes in the text field and saves those changes back to disk.

We can break this application down into model, view, and controller objects:

- The model is an object that is responsible for loading the text file from disk and writing it back out to disk. It is also responsible for providing the text as a string to any object that asks for it.

- The view is the text field, which asks another object for a string to display, and then displays the text. It also accepts keyboard input from the user; whenever the user types, it informs another object that the text has changed. It is also able to tell another object when the user has told it to save changes.

- The controller is the object responsible for instructing the model object to load a file from disk, and passes the text to the view. It receives updates from the view object when the text has changed, and passes those changes to the model. Finally, it can be told by the view that the user has asked to save the changes; when that happens, it instructs the model to do the work of actually writing the file out to disk.

By breaking the application into these areas of responsibility, it becomes easier to make changes to the application.

For example, if the developer decides that the next version of the application should add the ability to upload the text file to the Internet whenever the file is saved, the only thing that must be changed is the model class—the controller can stay the same, and the view never changes.

Likewise, by clearly defining which objects are responsible for which features, it's easier to make changes to an application while maintaining a clear structure in the project. If the developer decides to add a spellchecking feature to the application, that code should clearly be added to the controller, as it has nothing to do with how the text is presented to the user or stored on disk. (You could, of course, add some features to the view that would allow it to indicate which words are misspelled, but the bulk of the code would need to be added in the controller.)

The majority of the classes described in this chapter, such as NSData, arrays, and dictionaries, are model classes; all they do is store and present information to other classes. NSKeyedArchiver is a controller class; it takes information and performs logical operations on it. NSButton and UITextField are examples of view objects; they present information to the user and do not care about how the data is managed.

The model-view-controller paradigm becomes very important when you start looking at the more advanced Cocoa features, like the document architecture (see Chapter 13) and bindings (see Chapter 11).

Delegation

Delegation is Cocoa's term for passing off some responsibilities of an object to another. An example of this in action is the UIApplication object, which represents an application on iOS. This application needs to know what should happen when the application moves to the background. Many other languages handle this problem by subclassing— for example, in C++, the UIApplication class would define an empty placeholder method for applicationDidEnterBackground, and then you as a developer would subclass UIApplication and override the applicationDidEnterBackground method.

However, this is a particularly heavy-handed solution and causes additional problems--it increases the complexity of your code, and also means that if you want to override the behavior of two classes, you need two separate subclasses for each one.[1] Swift's answer to this problem is built around the fact that an object can determine, at runtime, whether another object is capable of responding to a message.

An object that wants to let another object know that something is going to happen, or has happened, stores a reference to that object as an instance variable. This object is known as the delegate. When the event happens, it checks to see if the delegate object implements a method that suits the event—for delegates of the UIApplication class, for example, the application delegate is asked if it implements the applicationDidEnterBackground method. If it does, that method is called. An object can also be the delegate for multiple objects.

Because of this loose coupling, it's possible for an object to be the delegate for multiple objects. For example, an object could become the delegate of both an audio playback object and an image picker, and be notified both when audio playback completes and when an image has been captured by the camera.

Because the model-view-controller pattern is built around a very loose coupling of objects, it helps to have a more rigidly defined interface between objects so that your application can know with more certainty how one object expects others to behave.

The specific messages used by delegates are often listed in protocols. For example, if your object wants to be the delegate of an AVAudioPlayer object, it should conform to the AVAudioPlayerDelegate protocol.

Working with delegates in Swift is easy. Imagine you have two classes, and you want one of them to act as the delegate for another:

```
// Define a protocol that has a function called handleIntruder
protocol HouseSecurityDelegate {

    // We don't define the function here, but rather
    // indicate that any class that is a HouseSecurityDelegate
    // is required to have a handleIntruder() function
    func handleIntruder()
}

class House {
    // The delegate can be any object that conforms to the HouseSecurityDelegate
    // protocol
    var delegate : HouseSecurityDelegate?

    func burglarDetected() {
        // Check to see if the delegate is there, then call it
```

---

1. C++'s answer to this problem is multiple inheritance, which has its own problems.

```
        delegate?.handleIntruder()
    }
}

class GuardDog : HouseSecurityDelegate {
    func handleIntruder() {
        println("Releasing the hounds!")
    }
}


let myHouse = House()
myHouse.burglarDetected() // does nothing

let theHounds = GuardDog()
myHouse.delegate = theHounds
myHouse.burglarDetected() // prints "Releasing the hounds!"
```

In Swift, you can check to see if an optional variable is nil by using the ? operator. You can also check to see if an object contains a property or method using the same ? operator.

CHAPTER 3

Applications on OS X and iOS

As far as users are concerned, applications are the only thing on their computers besides their files. After all, a computer is defined by what it can do for the user, and what it can do is defined by the applications that are installed.

As a developer, it's easy to get drawn into the details of how an app is put together—the individual classes, methods, and structures. However, the application as a whole is what's sold to the user, and that's all users care about.

In this chapter, you'll learn how applications are structured on OS X and iOS, how they differ from other kinds of distributable code, what they can do on the system, and what they're prevented from doing by the built-in security measures provided by the OS.

What Is an Application?

Applications on iOS and OS X are packaged differently from applications on other platforms, most notably Windows. On other platforms, the end result of compiling your project is a binary file that contains the compiled code. It's then up to you as a developer to package that binary file up with the resources it needs. On Linux, you generate a package file (which can vary depending on the distribution you're using), and on Windows, it's traditional to create an "installer," which is an *additional* application that unpacks the binary and resources.

OS X and iOS take a different approach to applications. This approach stems from the concept of a "package"—a folder that contains a number of items but is presented to the user as a single file. Many document formats use packages as a convenient way to store and organize their data, because storing different chunks of data as separate files means that the program doesn't have to implement logic that unpacks a single file.

If you're coming from a Linux background, note that "package," in this context, means something different. A package file is just a folder that's presented as a single file, while on Linux "package" means a redistributable file used to install software. OS X also uses the word "package" in this way—you can generate *.pkg* files that contain software, which when opened install the software onto your machine. When you upload an app to the Mac App Store, for example, you upload a package.

And just to add to the confusion, the Cocoa framework doesn't call folders that are presented as single files "packages," but rather calls them "bundles."

Applications, therefore, are actually folders that contain the compiled binary, plus any resources they may need. The structure of applications differs slightly between OS X and iOS, but the fundamental philosophy of how an application is packaged remains the same. You can take a look inside an application by right-clicking one in the Finder and choosing Show Package Contents.

When you compile a project in Xcode and generate an application, Xcode creates the application package, and copies in any necessary resources. If you're creating a Mac application, you can then just zip it up and send it to anyone for them to run it. On iOS, it's a little different, because apps must be code-signed and provisioned before being run on the device.

One advantage to this is that applications are entirely self-contained and can be moved anywhere on a Mac.

Because applications can be moved, it used to be commonplace to add code to an application that detected if the app was not in the Applications folder and offered to move itself there to keep the user's Downloads folder tidy.

This is less common in the days of the App Store, which installs all applications directly into the Applications folder. However, if your application is being distributed by means other than the Mac App Store, it's worthwhile to include this logic anyway.

Applications, Frameworks, Utilities, and More

Applications aren't the only products that you can produce from Xcode. You can also generate *frameworks*, which are loadable bundles of code and resources that other applications (including your own) can use. Frameworks are actually very similar to applications in structure—they contain a binary file and any resources—but they're not standalone and are designed to be used by other apps.

One prime example of a framework is `AppKit.framework`, which is used by every Mac application. On iOS, the equivalent framework is `UIKit.framework`.

 "Cocoa" is the term used by Apple to refer to the collection of libraries used by applications on OS X. On iOS, the equivalent term is "Cocoa Touch," as it's adapted for touchscreen devices.

What Are Apps Composed Of?

In order to function as an application on iOS or OS X, an application must have two things at a minimum:

- The compiled binary
- An information file describing the app to the system

The compiled binary is simply the end result of Xcode compiling all of your source code and linking it together.

Information describing the app to the system is saved in a file called *Info.plist*. Among other things, *Info.plist* contains:

- The name of the application's icon file
- What kinds of documents the application can open
- The name of the compiled binary
- The name of the interface file to load when the application starts up
- What languages the application supports (such as French, English, etc.)
- Whether the application supports multitasking (for iOS apps)
- The Mac App Store category the application is in (for OS X apps)

Info.plist is really important—in fact, if you remove it from the application bundle, the app can't launch.

Applications also contain every resource that was compiled in—all the images, files, sounds, and other items that were added to the project via Xcode. The application can refer to these resources at runtime.

You can take a look at the structure of an OS X application by following these steps:

1. Open Xcode, and create a new OS X application. Don't bother changing any settings when Xcode asks—just name the app whatever you like and save it somewhere.
2. Build the application. Press ⌘-B, or choose Product→Build.

3. Open the Products group in the project navigator. It will now contain the *.app*, which is the end result of the build process. Right-click it and choose Show in Finder. The Finder will open, revealing where Xcode put the app.

4. Right-click the application and choose Show Package Contents. The Finder will show the contents of the bundle.

The structures of OS X and iOS application bundles are different: on iOS, everything is contained at the root of the package's folder, but on OS X, the structure is more rigorous.

The structure of a *Mac* application named MyApp looks like this:

MyApp.app
> The top level of the package

Contents
> A folder that contains the application itself

Info.plist
> The file that describes the application to the system

MacOS
> A folder that contains the app's compiled binary

MyApp
> The app's compiled binary

PkgInfo
> A legacy file that describes the app's maker and what the app is

Resources
> A folder that contains all of the compiled-in resources

The structure of an *iOS* application named MyApp looks like this:

MyApp
> The app's compiled binary

Info.plist
> The file that describes the application to the system

Default.png
> The image that is shown while the app is launching

Default@2x.png
> The double-resolution version of *Default.png*, used on certain high-resolution devices (e.g., the iPhone 6 or the iPad Air)

Default@3x.png
> The triple-resolution version of *Default.png*, used on higher resolution devices (e.g., the iPhone 6 Plus)

Embedded.mobileprovision
> The provisioning profile that identifies the app as able to run on a device

Entitlements.plist
> A file that describes what the application may or may not do

Because your application could be anywhere on the system, your code can't use absolute paths to determine the location of resources. Thankfully, Cocoa already knows all about packages and how to work with them.

Using NSBundle to Find Resources in Applications

As far as your code goes, your application works the same regardless of which platform it's running on, thanks to a useful class called NSBundle. This class allows your code to know where it is on the disk and how to get at the compiled resources.

This is especially important for iOS applications, as these apps are placed in arbitrary folders by the OS when they're installed. This means that your code cannot depend upon being in a single place, and you can't hardcode paths. Of course, doing that is a bad idea anyway, but on iOS, it's guaranteed to cause failures.

You can use NSBundle to determine the location of the application's package on disk, but most of the time you only need to know about the location of the individual resources.

NSBundle allows you to determine both URLs and plain file paths for resources on the disk. All you need to know is the name and type of the resource.

For example, the following code returns an NSString that contains the absolute path for a resource called *SomeFile.txt*:

```
let resourcePath = NSBundle.mainBundle()
    .pathForResource("SomeFile", ofType: "txt")
// resourcePath is now a string containing the
// absolute path reference to SomeFile.txt, or nil
```

Note that this code snippet calls NSBundle.mainBundle()—it's possible to have more than one bundle around. Remember that Cocoa refers to packages (i.e., folders containing app resources) as *bundles*.

You can also get URLs to resources as well:

```
let resourceURL = NSBundle.mainBundle()
    .URLForResource("SomeFile", withExtension: "txt")
// resourceURL is now an NSURL, or nil
```

This method looks inside the *Resources* folder in the application bundle for the named file. (On iOS, it looks inside the root folder of the application bundle.)

Absolute paths and URLs are functionally the same when referring to files stored on disk, but using URLs is preferred—a string could theoretically contain anything, whereas a URL always points to a location. This includes file URLs, which look like this: *file:/// Applications/Xcode.app/*. You can therefore use URLs in any case where you'd normally use a file path.

If you add an image or other resource to your project, it is copied into the application bundle when the project is built. For Mac apps, the resources are copied into the *Resources* folder, and for iOS apps, the resources are copied into the root folder of the application.

The Application Life Cycle

Every program starts, runs, and quits. What's interesting is what it does in between. For the most part, applications on OS X and iOS behave similarly, with the exception that iOS handles multitasking in a different way from standard desktop applications.

In this section, we'll walk through the life cycle of both kinds of applications, and discuss what happens at various stages of an app's life.

OS X Applications

When an application is launched, the first thing the system does is open the application's *Info.plist*. From this file, the system determines where the compiled binary is located, and launches it. From this point on, the code that you write is in control.

In addition to the compiled code, applications almost always have a collection of objects that were prepared at design time and bundled with the application. These are usually interface objects—pre-prepared windows, controls, and screens—which are stored inside a *nib file* when the application is built. When the application runs, these nib files are opened, and the premade objects are loaded into memory.

 For more information on nib files, as well as the related storyboards and how they're built, see Chapter 4.

The first thing an application does is open the nib file and deserialize its contents. This means that the application unpacks the windows, controls, and anything else stored in it and links them together. The main nib also contains the application delegate object, which is unpacked with all the rest.

When an object is unpacked from a nib, it is sent the `awakeFromNib` message. This is the moment at which that object can begin to run code.

Objects that are unpacked from a nib are *not* sent an `init` message because they were already initialized when the developer dragged and dropped them into the interface. This is different from objects that are created by calling their constructor in code.

When working with nib files, it's important to understand that when you add an object to a nib file, that object is created at that moment, and "freeze-dried" when the nib file is saved. When the nib file is opened, the object is "rehydrated" and gets back to work. After the object is rehydrated, it is sent the `awakeFromNib` message to let it know that it's awake.

To summarize: objects that are loaded from a nib receive the `awakeFromNib` message. Objects that are created by your code receive the `init` method.

At this point, the application is ready to start running properly. The first thing it does is to send the application delegate the `applicationDidFinishLaunching` method. After that method completes, the application enters the run loop.

The *run loop* continues looping until the application quits. The purpose of the run loop is to listen for events—keyboard input, mouse movement and clicks, timers going off, etc.—and send those events to the relevant destinations. For example, say you have a button hooked up to a method that should be run when the button is clicked. When the user clicks the button, the mouse-click event is sent to the button, which then causes its target method to get run.

On OS X, applications continue to run when the user selects another app. When the user changes applications, the application delegate receives the `applicationWillResignActive` message, indicating that the application is about to stop being the active one. Soon after, the app delegate receives the `applicationDidResignActive` method.

The reason these two methods are separate is to let your code manage what happens to the screen's contents when the home button is tapped on iOS, or when the user switches to another app on OS X. When `applicationWillResignActive` is called, your application is still present on the screen. When the application is no longer visible, the application delegate receives `applicationDidResignActive`.

When the user comes back to the app, the application delegate receives a pair of similar methods: `applicationWillBecomeActive` and `applicationDidBecomeActive`. These are sent immediately before and after the application returns to being the active one.

The event loop is terminated when the application quits. When this happens, the application delegate receives the `applicationWillTerminate` message, which is sent immediately before the app quits. This is the last opportunity an app has to save files before quitting.

iOS Applications

iOS applications behave in a broadly similar manner to OS X applications, with a few differences. The main one is that iOS applications are presented differently from desktop apps, and the tighter memory constraints on an iOS device mean that there are more stringent rules about multitasking.

On iOS, only one application is on the screen at a time—any other applications are completely hidden. The visible application is known as the *foreground application*, and any apps also running are *background applications*. There are strict limits on how long an application may run in the background, which we'll discuss shortly.

When using an application on iOS, a user may be interrupted by something else—an incoming phone call, for example—which replaces the app with which the user was interacting. The application is still technically considered to be in the foreground, but it is now *inactive*. If the user accepts the phone call, the phone application becomes the foreground application, and the previous app moves to the background.

There are other methods by which an application can become inactive, such as when the user pulls down the notifications tray (by swiping down from the top of the screen), or opens the task switcher (by double-tapping on the home button). When an application becomes inactive, it's a signal that it may be exited, so your app should make sure to save any work.

The iOS application life cycle is almost identical to that of an OS X application. When the app is launched, the *Info.plist* file is checked, the compiled binary is found and loaded, and the application begins running code, starting by unpacking the contents of the main storyboard.

When the application completes loading, the application delegate receives the `applicationDidFinishLaunching(_, withOptions:)` method. This is similar to the OS X counterpart, but adds an additional parameter—a dictionary, which contains information about why and how the application was launched.

Applications are most commonly launched directly by the user tapping on the icon. They can also be launched by other applications, such as when an app passes a file to another or is opened through a custom URL. The `options` dictionary contains information that describes the circumstances under which the application launched.

Just as with OS X applications, iOS applications also receive `applicationWillResignActive` and `applicationDidBecomeActive` messages (with one difference—on OS X, the parameter to these methods is an `NSNotification` object, whereas on iOS the parameter is a `UIApplication`).

When an application is quit by the user on OS X, we have seen that the application delegate receives the `applicationWillTerminate` method. This was also the case for iOS applications, until iOS 4. At this point, multitasking was introduced, and the life cycle of iOS applications changed.

Multitasking on iOS

Applications on iOS are permitted to run in the background, but only under certain very limited conditions. That's because iOS devices are much more constrained than OS X devices in the areas of CPU power, memory space, and battery capacity. A MacBook Pro is expected to run for around 7 hours on battery, with a full set of applications (e.g., a word processor, web browser, etc.) loaded and running. An iPhone 6 Plus, by contrast, is expected to last for greater than 8 hours on WiFi while browsing the Internet —on a battery with a fraction of the capacity of a full-size laptop battery. Additionally, a MacBook Pro (at the time of writing) ships with 8 GB of memory, while an iPhone 6 Plus has only 1 GB, and an iPad Air 2 has only 2 GB.

There's simply no room to fit all the applications at once, so iOS is forced to make some decisions about what applications can run in the background and for how long.

When an application exits (e.g., when the user hits the home button or another application launches), the application is *suspended*—it hasn't quit, but it stops executing code and its memory is locked. When the application resumes, it simply picks up where it left off.

This means that the application remains in memory, but stops consuming the system's power-draining resources such as the CPU and location hardware. However, memory is still tight on the iPhone, so if another app needs more memory, the application is simply terminated without notice.

Note that an application that is suspended doesn't get to run any code, and therefore can't get notified that it's being terminated while suspended. This means that any critical data must be saved when the application delegate is told that the application is being moved to the background.

Applications are not told when they are suspended or when they are woken up. They *are* told when they move into and out of the background, however, through the following delegate methods:

```
func applicationDidEnterBackground(_ application: UIApplication)
```

and

```
func applicationWillEnterForeground(_ application: UIApplication)
```

`applicationDidEnterBackground` is called immediately after the application has moved to the background state. The application will be suspended after the method has run, which means that the app needs to save any data it's working on because it may be terminated while suspended.

`applicationWillEnterForeground` is called just before the application comes back on screen, and is your application's opportunity to get set up to work again.

As mentioned earlier, applications that are suspended are candidates for termination if the new foreground app needs more memory. As an application developer, you can reduce the chances of this happening by reducing the amount of memory your application is using—by freeing large objects, unloading images, and so on.

 If possible, try to reduce the amount of memory being used to under 16 MB. When the application is suspended and the memory usage is under 16 MB, the system will store the application's memory on the flash chips and remove it from memory entirely. When the application is resumed, the application's memory state is reloaded from the stored memory on the flash chips—meaning that the application won't be evicted from memory due to another application's memory demands. We'll look at how to measure memory usage in "Fixing Problems Using Instruments" on page 370.

An application can request to run in the background for a short period of time. This background period can be no longer than 10 minutes, and it exists to allow your application to complete a long-running process—writing large files to disk, completing a download, or some other lengthy process. At the end of the 10 minutes, your application must indicate to the OS that it is done or it will be terminated (not suspended, but terminated—gone from memory completely).

To run tasks in the background, you need to add code that looks like this to your application delegate:

```
func applicationDidEnterBackground(application : UIApplication) {

    var backgroundTask : UIBackgroundTaskIdentifier! = nil

    // Register a background task, and provide a block to run when
    // time runs out
    backgroundTask = application
        .beginBackgroundTaskWithExpirationHandler() {

            // This block is called when we're out of time; if we haven't
            // called endBackgroundTask before this block returns,
            // the application is terminated

            application.endBackgroundTask(backgroundTask)
            backgroundTask = UIBackgroundTaskInvalid
    }
```

```
    let backgroundQueue = NSOperationQueue()

    backgroundQueue.addOperationWithBlock() {

        // Do some work. You have a few minutes to complete it; by the end,
        // you must call endBackgroundTask.

        NSLog("Doing some background work!")

        application.endBackgroundTask(backgroundTask)
        backgroundTask = UIBackgroundTaskInvalid
    }

}
```

There is no guarantee that the extra time to perform background tasks will be in one contiguous chunk; the time may be broken up into multiple chunks to improve battery life. Introduced with iOS 7 were two means of running tasks in the background: background fetching and background notifications.

Background fetching is designed for applications that require periodic updates, such as weather applications or social networking applications like Twitter. With background fetching enabled, an application can be woken up in the background to retrieve up-to-date information in the background to have ready to immediately display when the user brings the application to the foreground.

To use background fetching, there are a few things you need to do:

- Select the project in the project navigator, open the Capabilities tab, and enable Background Fetch from the Background Modes section.

- In your code, you need to call the setMinimumBackgroundFetchInterval function to let iOS know approximately how often to wake your application so it can fetch updates. If you do not set a minimum interval, iOS will default to never waking your application for performing fetches.

To actually perform the fetching when iOS wakes your application, you will have to add code to your application delegate that looks like this:

```
func application(application: UIApplication,
    performFetchWithCompletionHandler completionHandler:
    (UIBackgroundFetchResult) -> Void) {

        // We have 30 seconds to download some data and process it

        var error : NSError? = nil
        let data = downloadSomeData(&error)

        // Once done, let the OS know whether or not new data was
        // retrieved or not, or if there was an error
```

```
        if error != nil {
            completionHandler(UIBackgroundFetchResult.Failed)
            return
        }

        // This is a very simple check—your application would
        // do something more involved, like compare this data against
        // the most recently downloaded data to determine if it's 'new'
        if data?.length > 0 {
            completionHandler(UIBackgroundFetchResult.NewData)
            return
        } else {
            completionHandler(UIBackgroundFetchResult.NoData)
            return
        }


    }
```

Background notifications allow your application to receive notifications and process them in the background. Background notifications could be used in an instant messaging application to automatically update the conversation while the application is in the background or to alert your application when new content is available to be fetched.

Background notifications operate in a manner very similar to background fetching, and require a similar setup before being available for use in your application. Your application will need to be able to handle notifications, which are discussed in "Notifications" on page 395, and you'll need to enable remote notifications in your project.

To enable remote notifications, select the project in the project navigator, open the Capabilities tab, and enable "Remote notifications" from the Background Modes section.

Much like background fetch, an application method that handles the notifications is called whenever your application receives a notification. The code to receive this notifications looks like this:

```
func application(application: UIApplication,
    didReceiveRemoteNotification userInfo: [NSObject : AnyObject])
```

This method functions in a manner very similar to the method for handling background fetching and even requires the same results to be passed into the callback handler when completed. The main difference is the userInfo parameter, which is a dictionary containing the data that the remote notification contained.

Keep in mind that despite letting you set a minimum interval for fetching in the background, iOS will wake your application at what it determines is the best time without causing unnecessary drain on the device's battery. In a similar manner, Apple will limit how many remote notifications are sent to the device for the same reasons. If your application isn't behaving exactly as you set it, this might be the cause.

There are other cases in which an application can run in the background for longer periods of time, all of which are geared toward more specialized applications:

- Applications that play audio in the background can remain active for as long as they like, until the user starts playing audio from another app. For example, the Pandora Internet radio app can run in the background until the user starts playing music from the Music application.

- Applications that track the user's location in the background can run for as long as they like.

- Voice over IP (VoIP) applications like Skype are allowed to run periodically to check in with their server, but aren't allowed to run indefinitely except when a call is active.

In summary, if you're writing an application for iOS, you can only expect to be running on the device when the user is directly accessing your app. When the user can't see your application, it quite literally becomes a case of "out of sight, out of mind."

The Application Sandbox

OS X and iOS implement a number of features to improve the overall level of security for the user. One of these features is the *application sandbox*, a tool that restricts what an application is allowed to do. The application exists inside the sandbox, and may not try to access any system resources (hardware, user data, etc.) that is outside the sandbox. Sandboxes are somewhat optional for Mac applications, and mandatory for iOS applications.

A sandbox improves the security of the system by preventing an app from doing something that either Apple or the user does not want it to do. This is specifically useful for improving the security of apps, because the majority of hacks take the form of exploiting a bug in an existing application. Adobe's Acrobat Reader and Microsoft's Internet Explorer 6 are two applications through which malicious people have been able to compromise other users' systems (install extra software, retrieve private data, etc.). These exploits take the form of modifying the compromised application to make it perform the intruder's bidding.

Sandboxes solve this problem by preventing (at a kernel level) an application from accessing user data, communicating with the network, accessing hardware like the camera and microphone, and so on. Even if the software has an exploitable bug, the intruder cannot access user data because the application is not permitted to reach outside of its sandbox.

Applications that are downloaded from the iOS App Store are automatically placed in a sandbox; we will discuss this in more detail in "Working with the Sandbox" on page 219. Applications that are distributed via the Mac App Store require being sandboxed as well; however, apps that you distribute yourself do not.

Application Restrictions

As mentioned earlier, a sandbox restricts what an application can do. The restrictions vary significantly between iOS and OS X, because applications on OS X have traditionally been less restricted in terms of what they're allowed to do.

For example, a Mac application can request read/write access to any of the user's files. An iOS application can only work with its own documents, and can't open any files outside of its sandbox.

iOS application restrictions

When an iOS app is installed on the device, it's given a *container* to store its information in. This folder contains the following items:

Documents
　　Stores all documents belonging to the application

Library
　　Stores all settings and configuration info

Caches
　　Contains data that is useful to have on disk, but could be regenerated; items in this folder are deleted by the system if it needs to free some space

Preferences
　　Stores settings and preferences

tmp
　　Stores files temporarily; items in this folder are periodically deleted by the system

An iOS application is not allowed to work with any file outside of its folder. This prevents the bundle from reading private information (like phone call logs) or modifying any system files.

Mac application restrictions

The idea of putting restrictions on what Mac apps can do only arrived with the release of the Mac App Store in 2011, which means that Apple had quite a bit of time to figure out how to implement it.

When you decide to make your application sandboxed, Xcode presents you with a number of options that determine what your application is allowed to do. These options are called *entitlements*.

The available entitlements that your Mac application can request are:

Filesystem
> You can determine whether the application has read/write, read-only, or no access to the filesystem. You can also control whether the application can work with certain folders, such as the Downloads folder.

Network
> You can determine whether the application is allowed to make outgoing connections and accept incoming connections.

Hardware
> You can determine whether the application is allowed to access the built-in camera and microphone, communicate with devices via USB, and print.

App communication
> You can determine whether the application is allowed to work with the data managed by the Address Book or Calendar, and whether it is allowed to work with the user's location information.

Music, movies, and pictures folder access
> You can determine whether the application can work with the user's music, photos, and movies by controlling whether the app has read/write, read-only, or no access to these folders. You can set each folder's access permissions separately.

Private APIs

One of the rules that Apple imposes on applications that are sold via the iTunes App Store or the Mac App Store is that apps are only allowed to communicate with the system via the classes and methods that Apple has documented and indicated as being for developer use.

There are many "private" classes and methods that Apple uses behind the scenes. For example, the code that determines whether an iOS device is locked with a passcode is undocumented; Apple uses it (such as in the Find My Friends app), but developers like us may not.

Apple scans all submitted applications as part of the App Store review process. This happens automatically, before a human being sits down to review your application. If your application is rejected for using a private API, you must remove the private API usage and resubmit. If Apple notices that your app uses private APIs *after* the app has gone live in the App Store, they'll simply take down the app.

The point is clear: Apple does *not* like developers using undocumented APIs. This is because documented APIs are known by Apple to be safe and (mostly) bug-free. Documented APIs are also features that Apple has committed to, and won't change underneath you. Undocumented APIs, on the other hand, are often still under active development, or may provide access to parts of the OS that Apple considers out of bounds for app developers.

Notifications with NSNotification

It's often useful to broadcast notifications to any interested application when something of relevance happens. For example, when the user presses the home button on an iOS device, the only object that receives a notification by default is the application delegate, which receives the `applicationDidEnterBackground` message. However, objects in the application may wish to be notified of events like this, and while it's possible for the application delegate to do something like maintain an array of objects to send messages to when an app-wide event takes place, it can be cumbersome.

Enter the `NSNotification` class. `NSNotification` objects, or *notifications* for short, are broadcast messages sent by an object to any other object that has registered to be notified of such notifications. Notifications are managed by the `NSNotificationCenter`, which is a singleton object that manages the delivery of notifications.

Notifications are created by the object that wants to broadcast, or *post*, the notification. The `NSNotification` object is given to the notification center, which then delivers the notification to all objects that have registered for that notification type.

When an object wants to start receiving notifications, it first needs to know the name of the notification it wants to be told about. There are hundreds of different notification types; to continue with our earlier example, the specific notification posted when the application enters the background is `UIApplicationDidEnterBackgroundNotification`.

Notification types are actually just strings, so you can also define your own notification types.

Therefore, to register for this notification, all an object needs to do is this:

```
// Get the notification center to use (in this and almost all
// cases, use the default center)
let notificationCenter = NSNotificationCenter.defaultCenter()

// Get the operation queue to run the notification handler on
// (in this case, the main operation queue)
let operationQueue = NSOperationQueue.mainQueue()

// Register for the notification UIApplicationDidEnterBackgroundNotification
let applicationDidEnterBackgroundObserver =
    notificationCenter.addObserverForName(
        UIApplicationDidEnterBackgroundNotification,
        object: nil, queue: operationQueue) {

    (notification: NSNotification!) in

    println("Hello!")
}
```

The addObserverForName method returns an object, called the *observer*, which you need to keep around. You use this object when unregistering for notifications, like this:

```
notificationCenter.removeObserver(applicationDidEnterBackgroundObserver)
```

 If you don't unregister for notifications, you'll leave behind dangling notification handlers, which can cause wasted memory and crashes. Always unregister your notification handlers!

Once you've registered for a notification, your notification handler block will run every time the notification is fired.

You'll notice that the handler block receives one parameter: an NSNotification object. This object contains information about the notification itself, which varies between different notification types.

You can also post your own notifications, if you've defined a notification type:

```
let MyNotificationType = "MyNotificationType"

// the 'object' parameter is the object responsible for sending the
// notification, and can be nil
notificationCenter.postNotificationName(MyNotificationType, object: nil)
```

CHAPTER 4

Graphical User Interfaces

The graphical user interface (GUI) is one of the defining features of modern computers. No personal computer sold to consumers these days lacks a GUI, and the only time people work with a machine that doesn't present information graphically is when they're working with a server, supercomputer, or other specialized tool. Displaying a graphical interface to your user is fundamental to developing with Cocoa, and understanding both how to design an appealing and usable GUI and how to implement that GUI are critical skills for Cocoa developers.

This chapter covers the user interface system available in Cocoa and Cocoa Touch, in addition to implementing a UI. You'll also learn about Core Animation, the animation system on both OS X and iOS. Designing a usable and pleasant UI is a huge topic that wouldn't fit in this chapter (let alone in this book!), so if you're interested in learning how to make a great user interface, take a look at *Tapworthy* by Josh Clark (O'Reilly).

Interfaces in OS X and iOS

While both iOS and OS X devices use a screen to present their interfaces, there are distinct differences in how they accept user input and in how they display output back to the user.

On OS X, the top-level object is the *window*. Windows contain controls, such as buttons, labels, and text fields, and can be moved around the screen to suit the user. More than one window is displayed on the screen at a time. Some windows can be resized, which means that windows need to know how to present their layout when the window grows larger or smaller. Finally, some windows can take up the entire screen; this feature has become increasingly common in OS X since the introduction of OS X 10.7 (Lion), which added a standard way for windows to become fullscreen and for more than one window to be fullscreen at once.

iOS also deals with windows, but presents them in a different way. In iOS, the user only deals with one screenful of content at a time. Each screen is managed by an object called a *view controller*, which manages the presentation of screen-sized views. View controllers are embedded into the application's window, and there is only one window displayed on the screen at any one time. Almost every application on iOS only ever has one window. Some exceptions include applications that display content on multiple screens (such as when the device is connected to a television); in these cases, each screen has a window.

As mentioned in "OS X Applications" on page 68, applications load their user interfaces from files called *nib files*. Nib files take their name from an acronym that dates back to the days when Cocoa was being designed by NeXT, the company that Steve Jobs founded after leaving Apple in the late 1980s. NIB stands for "NeXT Interface Builder," the name of the program that designed the interfaces.

Interface Builder continued to be distributed as a separate application as part of the developer tools until the release of Xcode 4, at which point it was embedded in Xcode.

MVC and Application Design

In Chapter 3, we discussed how the model-view-controller paradigm shapes a lot of the design decisions in Cocoa. To recap, the MVC design pattern divides the responsibilities of an app into three categories: the model, which handles data storage; the view, which presents the user interface and accepts input such as mouse movement or touches on the screen; and the controller, which mediates between the view and the model and provides the main operating logic for the application.

The Interface Builder in Xcode deals exclusively with views. The rest of Xcode handles the model and controller parts of your application, allowing you to concentrate on building the interface in relative isolation.

Nib Files and Storyboards

At the broadest level, nib files contain objects, and a storyboard is an organized grouping of interlinked nib files. In almost all cases, nib files and storyboards contain only interfaces, but it's possible to (mis)use nib files as a generic container for objects.

 Nib files have the extension *.nib* or *.xib*. An *.xib* file is a nib file that's stored in an XML-based format. Unless you are working with legacy code, you will rarely see *.nib* files anymore. Regardless of the file extension, they're referred to as "nibs."

Nib files work by "freeze-drying" (Apple's terminology) objects and storing them in a serialized form inside the file. All of the properties of the objects (e.g., in the case of a button, its position, label text, and other information) are stored in the nib file. When an application needs to display a window, it loads the nib file, "rehydrates" the stored objects, and presents them to the user.

Effectively, views and screens assembled in Interface Builder are the exact same objects that appear on screen in your software.

Because nib files simply contain objects, they can also contain objects that are instances of your own class. You can therefore create an instance of a class that is created when a nib is loaded, and connect it to your views.

On their own, views aren't terribly useful unless you want to create an application that does nothing more than present some buttons that can be clicked on or a text field that does nothing with the text that is entered. If you want to create an application that actually responds to user input, you must connect the views to your controllers (i.e., your application code).

The Interface Builder provides two ways to connect views to code: *outlets* and *actions*. We will discuss both in more detail later in this chapter.

Structure of a Nib File

Nib files contain a tree structure of objects. This tree can have many roots—for example, a nib file could contain two windows, each with its own collection of buttons and controls. These objects at the top level of the tree are known as "top-level objects."

Top-level objects are usually the visible things that are presented to users—windows on OS X and view controllers on iOS. However, any object can be a top-level object in a nib.

On OS X, anything that's shown on screen is placed in a window. There are many different kinds of windows available in the Interface Builder:

Standard windows
> The common, garden-variety windows shown on the screen. They have a full-size title bar, and are usually the primary window for an application.

Panel windows
> These have a reduced-height title bar and are usually hidden when the application is not active. "Inspector" windows and other accessory windows usually use panels.

Textured windows
> Identical to standard windows, but have a different background color. These have changed quite a bit over the years; they've been pin-striped, brushed-metal, a plain gradient, and now a simple, dark gray background (as of OS X 10.10).

HUD (heads-up display)
> These windows are dark gray, translucent, and designed to show information about something that's currently selected or to contain auxiliary controls for your applications. These are most often seen in media applications like QuickTime, Logic, and Final Cut.

Windows can contain any view at all. For more information on views, see Chapter 6.

On iOS, as previously mentioned, there is only one window on the screen at any one time. In contrast to OS X, this window stays on the screen for as long as the app is in the foreground, and replaces its contents when the user moves from one screen of content to the next.

In order to manage the various screens of content, iOS uses a category of object called a *view controller*. View controllers are classes that manage a single view as well as its subviews. We'll discuss them in more detail later in this chapter, but for practical purposes, you can think of view controllers as a screen's worth of content.

 View controllers also exist on OS X, but their role is less important, as multiple windows can be shown on the screen at once.

Much like OS X's windows, view controllers on iOS come in a variety of different flavors. These variations are more functionally different than the styles of windows on OS X, which are primarily cosmetic. On iOS, the different categories of view controllers define the structure and behavior of the application and each kind of view controller is designed for a different style of presenting information to the user:

Standard view controllers
> These present a view, and nothing more. It is most often subclassed to add logic to the screen—in fact, being subclassed is the primary purpose of this view controller.

Navigation controllers
> These present a stack of view controllers, onto which the application can push additional view controllers. When a new view controller is pushed onto the stack, the navigation controller animates the view controller's view into being visible with a sideways scrolling motion. When the navigation controller is instructed to pop a view controller from the stack, the view animates off with a reverse sliding motion. A good example of this type of view controller is the Settings application.

Table view controllers
> These present a list of cells that can be individually configured, stylized, ordered, and grouped. Despite being named a *table* view controller, it only shows a single column of cells. Table view controllers are used to display a list of items, and are

often used in conjunction with a navigation controller to list the available views to the user (an example of this is in the Settings app on the iPhone). They're also seen in the Phone app, where the screens with Favorites, Recents, Contacts, and Voicemail all use table view controllers.

Tab bar controllers

These present a set of view controllers, selectable through a tab bar at the bottom of the screen. When a button on the tab bar is tapped by the user, the tab bar controller hides the currently shown view controller and displays another. An example of this style of interface is the Music application. Tab bar controllers are best for presenting multiple ways of viewing the application interface. For example, the App Store is all about finding and purchasing applications, and the tabs presented to the user are simply different views of the same information. Other applications may have more specific angles of presenting the key info that the app is designed around. For example, a chat application could use a tab bar that shows three different tabs: one that shows the list of contacts, one that shows the list of active chats, and one that shows information about the user's profile.

Split view controllers

These present a side-by-side parent and child view structure, allowing you to see an overview in the parent view and detailed information in the child view. Prior to iOS 8, split view controllers were only available on iPads, as the side-by-side nature generally does not work particularly well on iPhones. Now in iOS 8, when you use a split view controller, the system determines what appearance the controller will take; based on the available space, it will either show the views side by side, hide the parent view when viewing the child, or present the parent as an overlay. An example of the split view controller is in the Settings app on an iPad.

Page controllers

These present view controllers in a "page-turning" interface, similar to the iBooks application on the iPad and iPhone. Each "page" in the book is a view controller, and the user can drag a finger across the screen to turn the page. These are best used when creating a book or magazine-style application where there is a need to present sequential information.

GLKit controllers

These allow you to present 3D graphics to the user using OpenGL. These are a particularly specialized kind of view controller and we won't be discussing them here—the topic of OpenGL graphics is *way* outside the scope of a book about Cocoa.

Collection view controllers

These present a customizable and configurable grid of views in a manner similar to a table view controller but with flexible items instead of individual cells. An example of this is the Photos app on the iPhone.

AVKit player view controllers
These present a full screen video player and are designed, obviously, for playing video content. For more on how to play video and audio, see "AVKit" on page 197.

Windows and view controllers are simply containers that present controls to the user. Controls are the visible items on the screen that the user interacts with: buttons, text fields, sliders, and so forth. To build an interface in Xcode, you drag and drop the controls you want from the object library in the Utilities pane onto the window or view controller. You can then reposition or resize the control.

 View controllers can contain other view controllers on iOS. For example, a navigation controller is a view controller that manages the appearance of the navigation bar at the top of the screen, as well as one or more additional view controllers.

View controller containment can be a complex topic. For more information, see "View Controller Basics" (*https://developer.apple.com/ library/ios/featuredarticles/ViewControllerPGforiPhoneOS/About ViewControllers/AboutViewControllers.html*) in the *View Controller Programming Guide for iOS* in the Xcode developer documentation.

Storyboards

Originally introduced in iOS 5, storyboards are now the default way of creating your iOS UI in Interface Builder. When you create a new iOS application in Xcode, there will be a *Main.storyboard* created automatically for you to use in place of a nib. Starting with OS X 10.10, you can now use storyboards for your Mac apps as well. Nibs are still common for OS X apps, because you often don't need to manage and chain together multiple windows in a Mac app.

In a nutshell, a storyboard is a collection of view controllers all linked together via *segues*. It is easy enough to think of a storyboard as a collection of nibs inside a single file. They are composed of the same elements and are interpreted by the system and Xcode in the same way. The only significant difference is that a nib generally contains a single view controller whereas a storyboard contains multiple view controllers (although it can only contain one if you want).

One of the nicest features of storyboards are segues, which can be thought of as a link between two view controllers that allows you to transition, or segue, between view controllers without any code. Creating a segue is straightforward. Any element inside a view controller that can perform an action (see "Outlets and Actions" on page 87) can have its action turned into a segue. Simply Control-drag from the element inside the first view controller onto the second view controller and an appropriate segue will be created.

Once a segue has been created in the Interface Builder, it can also be triggered programatically through its *identifier*. If you select a segue and select the attribute inspector, you can set an identifier for that segue. Your view controller can then use the `performSegueWithIdentifier(_, sender:)` method to force that segue to run. Shortly before the segue occurs, your view controller's `prepareForSegue(_, sender:)` method will be called giving you a chance for final preparations before you transition into the next view controller.

Outlets and Actions

Objects can exist in isolation, but this means that they don't participate in the application as a whole. A button can look very pretty, but unless it triggers some kind of action when clicked, it won't do anything *but* look pretty.

In most cases, an object in an application needs to work with other objects in order to do something useful. For example, a table view, which displays information in a list or grid, needs to be able to contact another object in order to ask it what information should be displayed. The table view does not store the information itself—to do so would violate the model-view-controller pattern. Views should not know anything about the data they are presenting; they should ask their controller about it.

Another kind of relationship is the one between a button and the application—when a button is pressed or tapped, the application should be informed of it and then run code as a response. If there are multiple buttons on the screen, which is common, the application should know which code to run when a particular button is tapped.

In Cocoa, this kind of relationship is known as a *target–action* relationship. When you add a button to a window or view controller, you can specify two things: what object should be contacted when the button is clicked or tapped, and what message the object should receive when this happens. The object that is contacted is known as the *target*, and the message that is sent is called the *action*. This is shown in Figure 4-1.

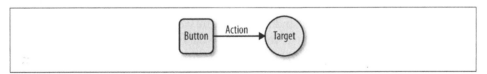

Figure 4-1. The target–action pattern

To allow these relationships between objects to be set up, Xcode allows you to make *connections* between objects in the interface. There are two kinds of connections:

- *Outlets* are relationships in which one object "plugs in" to another to communicate. An example is the table view that needs to contact another object to know what data to display.

- *Actions* are relationships that describe what method another object should run when an event occurs.

These connections are defined in the nib file, and are used when reconstructing the objects as the nib file loads.

How Nib Files and Storyboards Are Loaded

When a nib file is loaded, usually as part of application startup, every object it contains is re-created based on information stored in the nib: its class, position, label, size, and all its other relevant properties.

Once all objects exist in memory, every outlet defined in the nib file is connected. A nib file effectively describes a source object, a destination object, and the name of a property on the destination object. To connect the objects together, then, the nib file loading process sets the value of the destination object's property to the source object.

After all outlets are connected, every single object that was loaded receives the awake FromNib() message. By the time this method is called, every outlet has been connected, and all relationships between the objects have been reestablished.

Actions are a slightly different matter. An action is represented as a *target* object and an *action* message that is sent to that object. When a button is clicked, for example, it sends the action message to the target object.

Outlets and actions are independent of each other. Having an outlet connection doesn't imply that an action is sent, and vice versa. If you want to receive a message from a button *and* also have a variable that points to that button, you'll need both an outlet and an action.

The process for creating actions and outlets is the same for both: you make sure that you have the code for your view controller open in the assistant, and then hold down the Control key on your keyboard and drag from the view into your code. Once you do that, a dialog box will appear that lets you choose what the connection should be called, and whether the connection should be an outlet or an action. The dialog box is shown in Figure 4-2.

Figure 4-2. The connection creation box

It's very easy to accidentally create an outlet when you meant to create an action, and vice versa. If you do this, you need to both remove the line of code that the connection creation box inserts, and remove the connection itself from your interface. If you delete just the code, the connection itself remains—and your app may crash on launch, because the relevant property no longer exists.

Deleting the code is straightforward: simply remove it from your source code.

Removing the offending connection is slightly more complex. First, you need to go into your interface file and select the view that you accidentally added the connection for. Then go to the Connections Inspector, which is at the far right, and locate the connection you want to remove. Click the *x* that appears next to it, and you're done.

If your app is crashing on launch, and the console mentions something about not being *key-value coding compliant*, you probably have this issue. Check to make sure that all of your connections are valid!

Constructing an Interface

All interfaces in the Interface Builder are built by dragging components out of the object library and into a container. For windows, and view controllers that have no container, you just drag them out into the canvas.

The objects library, shown in Figure 4-3, is in the lower-right corner of the Xcode window. It lists every single object that can be dragged into an interface file—windows, controls, and hidden objects like view controllers are all available. If you are building an OS X interface, Mac controls appear; if you are building an iOS interface, iOS controls appear.

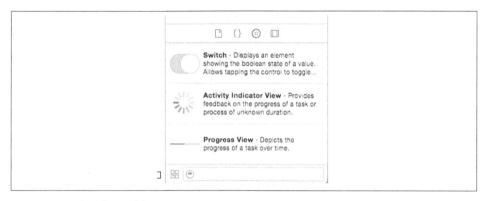

Figure 4-3. The objects library

You can filter the list by typing in the text field at the bottom of the list. This filter searches for the name of the object as well as its class name, so you can search for "NSButton" as well as just "button." If you know exactly what you're searching for, searching by class name is often faster—over time, you'll come to recognize objects by class name and start thinking in those terms.

Guidelines and Constraints

Cocoa tries to keep your views and windows laid out nicely. When you drag a button into a view, for example, Cocoa will offer guides as to where the button can be placed based on Apple's UI recommendations. If you drag in a button and place it next to another button, Cocoa will help you line them up and place the right amount of space between them. The same applies to resizing views—the Interface Builder will try to dissuade you from creating a layout that doesn't match up to Cocoa's standard sizes and margins.

The relationships between a view, its container view, and the other views around it are preserved in the form of *constraints*. You can view the constraints on an object by clicking on it and noting the blue lines that extend from it to other views or to the container view's edges.

Prior to the release of Xcode 5, constraints were quite tricky to get correct, and *very* easy to do incorrectly, leading to a variety of bizarre appearances and layouts in your application. With the introduction of Xcode 5, however, constraints have changed. Now when an object is added to a view, it has no visible constraints and Xcode will invisibly create constraints to glue that object at the exact position and size you placed it, because most objects won't need to move or resize. This lets you ignore most objects and focus on adding constraints only for the ones that actually need them.

Constraints are a new system of laying out a user interface, available from OS X 10.7 Lion and iOS 6 onwards. They replace an earlier model called *springs and struts*, sometimes referred to as *autosizing masks*. For more information on this older system, see "Repositioning and Resizing Views" in the *View Programming Guide* (*http://bit.ly/view_programming_guide*), included in the Xcode developer documentation.

A constraint defines a relationship between a *property* of a view, like its height or the position of its left edge, and a property of another view. This means that you can define constraints like this:

The left position of the Add button is equal to the left position of the table view above it.

You can also create constraints that are based on constant values:

The width of the Delete button is equal to 50 screen points.

Constraints can work together. If you have multiple constraints on a view, or constraints that affect multiple views, the layout system will attempt to resolve them simultaneously:

The width of the Delete button is equal to 50 screen points, *and* its left edge is equal to 10 screen points from the right edge of the Add button.

Constraints allow you to create simple rules that define the position and size of all the views on your screen. When the window that contains those views resizes, the layout system will update to satisfy all of the constraints.

You can add your own constraints, called *user constraints*, via the *constraints menu* in the lower right of the Interface Builder (Figure 4-4) or through the Editor menu.

Figure 4-4. The constraints menu

The constraints menu has four parts:

- *Align* defines how different views should line up relative to one another.
- *Pin* defines width, height, and spacing.
- *Resolve Auto Layout Issues* provides some solutions to common constraint issues.
- *Resizing Behavior* defines how constraints should be applied when resizing views.

Building an App with Nibs and Constraints

To demonstrate how to work with nibs and constraints, let's build a simple interface that makes use of different kinds of constraints. This application won't have any code—we'll only be looking at the constraint system. In this example we will be making an OS X application, but constraints work *exactly* the same way in iOS.

This interface will be for an application that lists a bunch of text documents and provides a text field for editing that text. We'll also include some buttons to add, remove, and publish these documents. Let's jump right in:

1. Create a new Cocoa application and name it `Constraints`.

2. Open the interface file (i.e., *MainMenu.xib*) and select the window in the Outline pane to make it appear.

3. Add the UI elements. Start by dragging an `NSTextView` into the window and placing it to take up most of the space in the window.

   Drag in three gradient buttons: place two beneath the lefthand side of the table side by side, and the other on the bottom lefthand side.

4. Customize the UI elements. Select the button at the bottom left, and open the Attributes Inspector. Set the button's Title to nothing (i.e., select all the text and delete it). Then change the Image of the button to `NSAddTemplate`, which will make the button contain a plus image.

   Do the same for the button immediately to the right, but set the image to `NSRemoveTemplate`.

   Finally, select the button in the lower right of the window, and set its Title to Publish.

When you're done, the window should look like Figure 4-5.

If you resize the window, the screen's carefully constructed layout breaks, and it looks ugly. So we're going to add constraints that make the layout look good at any size:

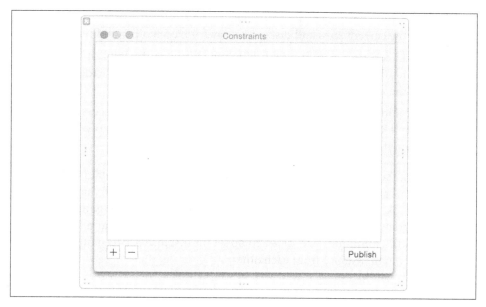

Figure 4-5. Our unconstrained interface

1. First, we'll add constraints to the text view. We want the text view to resize properly when the window is resized. For now, we want the view to resize to however large or small we make the window.

   Select the text view and click the Pin button, which is the second button inside the constraints menu. A small window will pop up with a bunch of different controls and options. To pin the position, select the small dotted red spacers for the Top, Right, and Left distance positions and leave the default values.

   Now when you select the text view, you will see small blue lines jutting out from it to the borders of the window (these are the constraints we just added). You can select them like any other element in Interface Builder.

2. Next, we'll add constraints to the + and - button.

   We want the + and - buttons to remain pinned to the bottom left of the screen and to keep their distance from the table view. Select the + button and click the Pin button. Select the spacers for the Left, Right, Top, and Bottom distance positions, with the default values. Also check the Width and Height boxes to force the button to remain its current size.

   Select the - button and click the Pin button. Select the spacers for the Left and Bottom distance positions, again leaving the default values.

   Now select both the + and - buttons and click on the Pin button. Select Equal Widths and Equal Heights.

Now both the + and - button are pinned to the lower-left corner, and they also maintain the current sizes and distances away from each other and the table view.

3. Finally, add constraints to the Publish button. We want the Publish button to be aligned with the right edge of the window and to maintain its spacing to the table view and the window edge.

   Select the Publish button and click the Pin button. Select the spacers for the Top, Bottom, and Right distance positions and also check the Height and Width to force it to remain its current size.

Now if you run the app, the table will resize and all elements will maintain their correct spacing. However, the app will also let you make the window so small that our careful layout won't look all that nice, so we need to stop the window from going too small. There are a variety of ways we could do this; we could set the width and height of the text view to have a minimum size, or we could set the distance between other elements to have a mimimum distance from each other:

1. Add a new button into the window, center it horizontally, and position it vertically in line with the other three buttons. Finally, set the button's title to Save.

2. Now we want this button to *always* be horizontally centered, which means that we need to add a constraint for it. Select the new button and open the Align constraints menu, using the first button in the constraints list, and select Horizontal Center in Container.

3. Select the Save button, open the Pin menu, and set the Width and Height to be the default values. Now our button has a size and a horizontal position.

4. Select the Save button, open the Pin menu, and set the Top distance position.

5. Now we can use this new button to restrict the size of the window. Select the button, click the Pin button, and select the spacers for the Left and Right positions, with the default values.

6. Select the Right distance spacer, and open the Attributes Inspector. Set the Relation of the spacer to be Greater Than or Equal.

Now we have a resizable window that has an effective minimum width, but not height. To do this, select the text view, open the Pin menu, and select Height, with the default values. Again, like with the distance spacers, select the Height constraint, open the Attributes Inspector and set the Relation to be Greater Than or Equal.

The window will now resize correctly while preserving the layout and correct dimensions: the + and = buttons pinned to the left, the Publish button to the right, and the Save button always dead center (see Figure 4-6).

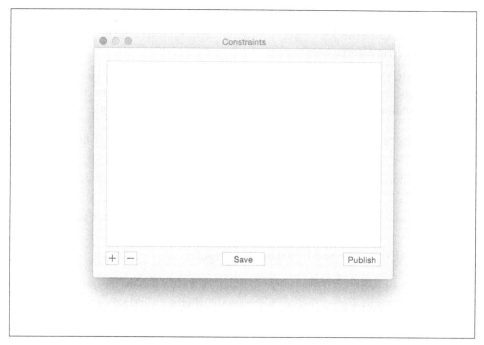

Figure 4-6. Our completed interface

You can also add constraints to UI elements in other ways. In the Xcode menu bar, under the Editor menu, there are options to add and remove constraints. You can also add constraints by selecting a UI element, holding down the Control key, and dragging to another UI element you want the constraint to be relative to. So to get our + and - buttons to have equal width and height, we could have instead selected the - button and Control-dragged onto the + button. A small constraints menu will pop up allowing us to select Equal Width and Equal Height from there. This menu is context sensitive and will change depending on what elements you select and in which direction you drag.

Interfaces on iOS

When you design interfaces on iOS, you use the exact same interface building tools as you do on OS X: you drag and drop items into a canvas, add constraints to define their size and position, and connect them to your code.

In iOS, however, you need to take into account the fact that there are several different kinds of iOS device. The various iPhones and iPads are all different shapes and sizes, and it's often not feasible to create a whole new interface for each different one. This is made even more complex when you consider that iOS devices can be held in both portrait and landscape modes. Taking all this into account, you could be looking at close to a dozen different interfaces to design.

To address this, the interface builder in Xcode has a concept called *size classes*. Size classes describe, in very general terms, whether the width and height of the current device's orientation is either *regular* sized or *compact* sized. For example:

- On an iPhone 5S and 6 in portrait orientation, the height is regular, and the width is compact.
- On an iPhone 5S and 6 in landscape orientation, both the height and width are compact.
- On an iPhone 6 Plus in landscape orientation, the height is compact, and the width is regular.
- On an iPad, the width and height are both regular.

When you design your interfaces, you can specify whether a view should appear in all size classes, or in only some. You can also specify whether a certain constraint should only appear when running under certain size classes.

If a view controller is entirely filling the screen, it uses the screen's size classes. For example, a view controller that fills an entire iPad screen has regular width and regular height.

However, a view controller might be presented in *another* view controller, which might alter its size class. For example, the split view controller presents two view controllers, side by side—one narrow and one wide. You can see an example in Figure 4-7. In a split view controller on an iPad, the view controller on the left uses a compact width and regular height, while the view controller on the right uses a regular width and regular height.

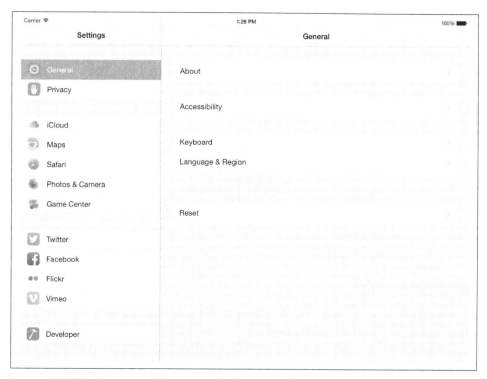

Figure 4-7. The Settings application, which uses a split view controller

Designing with size classes is surprisingly straightforward. At the bottom of the screen, you select which size class you want to view the interface in (Figure 4-8). By default, this is set to "Any" for both width and height, which means that views and constraints that you add will appear in any width and height configuration. In practical terms, this means that they'll appear on both the iPhone and the iPad, and in both orientations.

If you change this setting, however, any views and constraints that you add will only apply in the size class that you've selected. If you change the size class to "compact" for the height, for example, views and constraints that you add will only appear when the height of the size class is compact.

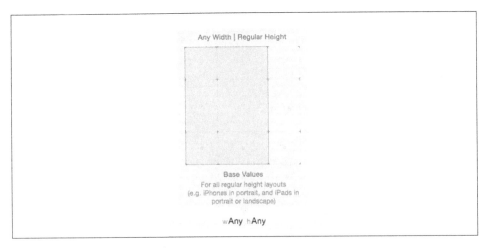

Figure 4-8. The size class picker

Launch Screen Files

When an application starts up, the first thing that iOS does is display a *launch image*. This image is the thing that you see as you transition from the home screen into an app. While you look at the launch image, the application is busily starting itself up, and getting ready to present itself to the user; once it's loaded, the launch image goes away, and you start looking at the application itself.

The purpose of the launch image is to create an impression that the app is launching faster than it actually is. Launch images aren't meant to be "splash images" (i.e., images that contain a big logo and company name, as is the case in some desktop apps like Photoshop). Instead, launch images should present a partial view of the loaded application—all of the toolbars and general shapes should be present, but nothing that looks like a button you can tap on. Once the app loads, the user sees the launch image replaced with buttons and controls that can actually be tapped.

Prior to iOS 8, you had to generate your own images for each of the possible resolutions that your app could be presented as, which could get laborious. Now, however, you use a *launch screen file*—a XIB file, instead of pictures.

When you create a new project, you get a launch screen file as part of the initial set of files that Xcode creates for you. It's named *LaunchScreen.xib*; if you open it, you can begin designing the view that appears on launch.

UI Dynamics

UI Dynamics are a new part of UIKit that provides physics-related capabilities and animations to views in iOS, which lets you impart forces and physical properties to views, allowing you to make your views bounce, swing, be affected by gravity, and more. This might seem a little silly and gimmicky at first glance, but creating interfaces with natural feeling elements and movements makes your users more willing to use your app long term. The workhorse of UI Dynamics is the UIDynamicAnimator class, which is responsible for actually animating the dynamic behavior. You pass multiple UIDynamic Behavior objects to the animator that describe how you want the animation to play out. You can create your own custom behaviors, but luckily for us, Apple has included some useful prebuilt ones you can use.

UI and Gravity

To demonstrate some of the capabilities of UI Dynamics, let's build a simple app with some gravity applied to the views:

1. Create a new single view iPhone application and call it DynamicGravity.

2. Next, create the interface. Open *Main.storyboard* and add an image view to the interface. Insert an image.

   When you are done, the interface should look like Figure 4-9.

3. Then create the image views outlet. Open *ViewController.swift* in the assistant. Control-drag from the image view to the view controller, and name the outlet imageView.

4. Finally, implement the dynamic behavior. Replace *ViewController.swift* with the following:

```
import UIKit

class ViewController: UIViewController {

    @IBOutlet weak var imageView: UIImageView!
    var dynamicAnimator = UIDynamicAnimator()

    override func viewDidAppear(animated: Bool) {
        super.viewDidAppear(animated)

        dynamicAnimator =
                UIDynamicAnimator(referenceView: self.view)
        // creating and adding a gravity behavior
        let gravityBehavior = UIGravityBehavior(items: [self.imageView])
        dynamicAnimator.addBehavior(gravityBehavior)

        // creating and adding a collision behavior
        let collisionBehavior =
            UICollisionBehavior(items: [self.imageView])
        collisionBehavior.translatesReferenceBoundsIntoBoundary = true
        dynamicAnimator.addBehavior(collisionBehavior)
```

```
    }
  }
```

If you run the app, you should see the image drop down and hit the bounds of the screen.

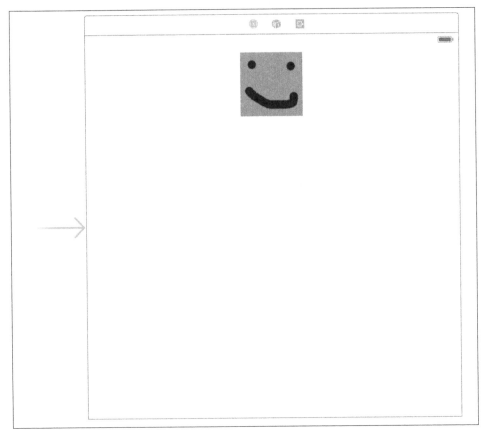

Figure 4-9. The completed interface for the UI Dynamics app

Snapping UI

Gravity is pretty awesome, but it isn't that often that we want our views to fall from the virtual sky. However, there are many situations where we want UI elements to move around with a bit of physical momentum without having to manually animate that movement. To quickly show this off, let's create another iPhone app to demonstrate:

1. Create a new single view iPhone application, and call it DynamicSnap.

2. Next, create the interface. Open *Main.storyboard* and add an image view into the interface. Then add an image to that view.

When you are done, the interface should look similar to Figure 4-9.

3. Then create the image views outlet. Open *ViewController.swift* in the assistant. Control-drag from the image view to the view controller, and name the outlet imageView.

4. At this point, create a tap recognizer. Open *Main.storyboard* and drag in a Tap Gesture Recognizer. Open *ViewController.swift* in the assistant, Control-drag from the tap recognizer to the view controller, select Action from the menu, and name the action tapped.

5. Finally, implement the snapping dynamic. Replace *ViewController.swift* with the following:

```
import UIKit

class ViewController: UIViewController {

    @IBOutlet weak var imageView: UIImageView!

    var dynamicAnimator:UIDynamicAnimator?
    var snap:UISnapBehavior?

    override func viewDidLoad() {
        super.viewDidLoad()

        self.dynamicAnimator = UIDynamicAnimator(referenceView: self.view)
    }

    @IBAction func tapped(sender: AnyObject) {
        // getting the tap location
        let tap = sender as UITapGestureRecognizer
        let point = tap.locationInView(self.view)

        // removing the previous snapping and adding the new one
        self.dynamicAnimator?.removeBehavior(self.snap)
        self.snap = UISnapBehavior(item: self.imageView, snapToPoint: point)
        self.dynamicAnimator?.addBehavior(self.snap)
    }
}
```

Run the app and the little image will dynamically move around to wherever you tap.

Core Animation

At its most basic Core Animation level, a view is a picture drawn in a rectangle, which is then displayed to the user alongside other views. Prior to modern computing hardware's ubiquitous graphics acceleration hardware, this involved carefully calculating how views overlapped and making sure that they didn't overlap or intersect other views. This made it challenging to create smooth animations for interfaces.

To address this, Apple developed Core Animation, which is a compositing and animation system for interfaces. Originally devised for iOS, it was ported to OS X in version 10.5.

Core Animation, like many frameworks developed on iOS and later brought to OS X, has an almost identical API on both platforms. This makes it straightforward to port interface code that uses Core Animation between the platforms.

Despite its name, Core Animation is not simply an animation tool, though it is tremendously good at that. Core Animation also provides the rendering architecture for displaying views, which allows for very fast transparency and effects.

Core Animation and UI Dynamics are not mutually exclusive; you can, and will, use both in your applications. When you are after natural feeling motions and behaviors, UI Dyamics is the way to go. When you want precise control over exactly what and how your elements animate, Core Animation will be a better fit. Core Animation also allows you to animate nongeometric properties of your elements, such as color or opacity.

Core Animation is optional, though recommended, on OS X. On iOS, it's integral, and therefore required—but you rarely need to deal with it directly unless you want to.

Layers

Core Animation works with *layers*, which are rectangular regions of space rendered by the graphics card. Layers are what the user actually sees; when a view needs to show something, it renders it onto a layer.

Core Animation layers are instances of the `CALayer` class, and work like `NSView` and `UIView` in that you can add a layer as a sublayer of another layer. Unlike the view classes, however, a layer object does nothing more than display content.

Working with any of the CA classes and methods requires that you import the `QuartzCore` framework at the top of your files, like this:

```
import QuartzCore
```

View objects handle layers differently on OS X and iOS:

- On OS X, `NSView` objects *manage* a `CALayer`, which they keep separate from themselves. This is because on OS X, views are optionally allowed to have layers.

- On iOS, `UIView` objects are actually just thin wrappers around `CALayer`. When you set the position of a view on the screen, you're actually moving its `CALayer`.

In the background, `CALayer`s are actually just graphics quadrangles and textures. The reason for Core Animation's performance improvements is that graphics hardware is very good at quickly drawing such quadrangles.

To access a view's layer, use the `layer` property (on both `UIView` and `NSView`):

```
// aView is an NSView or UIView
var layer = aView.layer
```

Animations

As its name suggests, Core Animation is useful for animating visual content. For the most part, your animations will involve moving views around, or animating changes in parameters like background color or opacity.

Unfortunately, animations work differently on iOS and OS X.

Animations on OS X

On OS X, if you want to animate a view, you need to create a `CAPropertyAnimation` (a subclass of the general `CAAnimation` class) that describes what exactly you want the animation to do. This is done by setting the `keyPath` property of the animation. This `keyPath` corresponds to a property on the layer, such as `opacity`, `cornerRadius`, or `bounds`.

There are a great deal of different layer properties you can animate through Core Animation. For a full list, see Apple's *Core Animation Programming Guide* (*http://bit.ly/abt_core_animation*).

After deciding what property to change, you need to set the `toValue` property to whatever value you need to animate; it is also a good idea to set the `fromValue` property as well.

Finally, you set the `duration` of the animation, in seconds, to represent how long you want the animation to last. Once the animation is fully configured, you call `addAnima tion(_:, keyPath:)` on the layer you want to animate. After creating and adding the animation to the layer, it is good practice to set the layer's properties to match the toValue set in the animation.

 If you don't set the properties of your layer to match the values set in the animation, the final state of the layer might not be what you think it is!

The following code demonstrates how to create a CABasicAnimation that animates the background color of a layer over 1.5 seconds:

```
// creating the animation
var colorAnim = CABasicAnimation(keyPath: "backgroundColor")
colorAnim.fromValue = NSColor.redColor().CGColor
colorAnim.toValue = NSColor.greenColor().CGColor
colorAnim.duration = 1.5

// getting the views layer
var layer = myView.layer!
layer.addAnimation(colorAnim, forKey: "backgroundColor")

// setting the final value after the animation
layer.backgroundColor = NSColor.greenColor().CGColor
```

This is a simple example, and while CABasicAnimation is obviously designed for simple animations, the principles are the same for building up more complex animations using CAKeyframeAnimation.

 In OS X, it is generally bad practice to move a view by changing its CALayer, and it very likely won't do what you expect. If you want to move an NSView, it is worth looking at the NSViewAnimation class.

Animations on iOS

The animation API on iOS is much more straightforward, and is based on closures, which are discussed in more detail in "Functions and Closures" on page 35. To animate a view, call UIView.animateWithDuration(_, animations:), and provide the duration of the animation and a closure that contains the actual state changes you want to have animated.

For example, to animate a change in position that lasts 0.25 seconds, you do this:

```
UIView.animateWithDuration(0.25) { () -> Void in
    myView.center = CGPointMake(200, 200)
    }
}
```

When you call this code, an animation will be created for you that transitions from the view's current state to the state you specified.

If you want to chain up a number of different animations to all occur within a certain sequence and with specific timing, such as move a view's position multiple times over 1 second, you do this:

```
// an example of a keyframe animation
        UIView.animateKeyframesWithDuration(2.0, delay: 0.0,
            options: UIViewKeyframeAnimationOptions.LayoutSubviews,
            animations: { () -> Void in
            UIView.addKeyframeWithRelativeStartTime(0.0, relativeDuration: 1,
                animations: { () -> Void in
                myView.center = CGPointMake(100, 100)
            })
            UIView.addKeyframeWithRelativeStartTime(0.0, relativeDuration: 0.5,
                animations:
            { () -> Void in
                var rotation:CGFloat = CGFloat(45 * M_PI / 180.0)
                myView.transform = CGAffineTransformMakeRotation(rotation)
            })
            UIView.addKeyframeWithRelativeStartTime(0.0, relativeDuration: 0.5,
                animations:
            { () -> Void in
                myView.backgroundColor = UIColor.greenColor()
            })
            }, completion:
            { (finished:Bool) -> Void in
                // completion handler, in this case we are doing nothing
                println("Animation completed:\(finished)")
            })
```

As with OS X, when animating changes in iOS, you can change many of the properties, including the color, the shadow, the corner radii, and the position (*and* you can change any number of these in a single animation).

However, just because you *can* do all this does not mean that you *should*. A little animation goes a long way; too much, and you can give the users of your app motion sickness.

Core Animation is hugely powerful, giving you amazing control over how your apps will move and look. However, it is another of those topics that's large and complex, and, as always, the Apple documentation on the subject is vast and comprehensive. To learn more about using Core Animation, a great place to start is Apple's *Core Animation Programming Guide* (*http://bit.ly/abt_core_animation*), which is included in the Xcode documentation.

CHAPTER 5

Closures and Operation Queues

The Swift language allows you to store code in variables. When you do this, the code is known as a *closure*, and Cocoa provides a number of tools that allow you to work with closures. One of the most important tools is called an *operation queue*, which lets you schedule closures to run in the future.

Closures allow code to do some very interesting things, including the following:

- Provide code to a function that should be run when that function is complete, such as a download or a long-running computation
- Enumerate over a collection of objects, and run some code on each one
- Provide code for objects to call when they feel it's necessary (e.g., event handlers)

Closures are discussed in detail in "Functions and Closures" on page 35. From a language perspective, they're identical to functions—they take parameters and return values. From a code-writing perspective, the only real difference between functions and closures is that closures don't have parameter names, while functions do.

To quickly refresh your memory, this is what closures look like:

```
let aClosure : Void -> Int = { return 1 }

aClosure() // returns 1
```

Because code can be divided up into chunks using closures, you can also give closures to the system for it to run. The mechanism that you use to do this is called *operation queues*, and they're tremendously powerful tools for managing how the system does the work that you need to do.

In Objective-C, closures are known as *blocks*. For this reason, several methods that belong to Cocoa and Cocoa Touch contain the word *block*, where you should provide a closure.

For example, the NSOperationQueue class has a method called addOperationWithBlock, which takes a single closure parameter. Just remember to keep in mind that the terms *block* and *closure* are effectively identical.

In this chapter, you'll learn how to use closures effectively in your apps, what they're good for, and how to use them in conjunction with operation queues, a powerful tool for performing tasks in the background.

Closures in Cocoa

Many classes in Cocoa have methods that make use of closures. These are typically methods that use a closure as a *completion handler*—that is, the method will perform some action that might take a moment (e.g., an animation), and once that action is complete, the completion handler closure is called:

```
// In this code, aViewController and anotherViewController
// are both UIViewControllers.

// Slide up a view controller, and then when the slide animation is
// finished, change its view's background color to yellow.

aViewController.presentViewController(anotherViewController, animated: true) {
    // This closure is run after the animation is finished
    anotherViewController.view.backgroundColor = UIColor.yellowColor()
}
```

Closures allow you to defer the execution of something until you need it to actually happen. This makes them very useful in the context of animations ("when the animation's done, do this thing"), for networking ("when the download's done, do something else"), or in general user interface manipulation ("when I return from this new screen, do some work").

They also allow you to keep related pieces of code close together. For example, before the introduction of closures, the only way that it was possible to filter an array was to create a function elsewhere in your code that was called for each element in the array. This made for a lot of scrolling around your source code. Now you can do this:

```
// Filter an array of strings down to only strings that begin with the word
// "Apple"
let array = ["Orange", "Apple", "Apple Juice"]
let filteredArray = array.filter() {
    return $0.hasPrefix("Apple")
```

```
    }
// filteredArray now contains "Apple", "Apple Juice"
```

In this case, the code that actually performs the processing of the objects is very close to the line that instructs the array to be filtered. This means that your code isn't scattered in as many places, which makes it clearer and less confusing. The less confusing your code is, the less likely it is that bugs will be introduced.

Concurrency with Operation Queues

In many cases, your application will need to do more than one thing at the same time. At least one of those things is responding to the user and ensuring that the user interface is responsive; other things could include talking to the network, reading and writing large amounts of data, or processing a chunk of data.

The highest priority of your application is to be responsive at all times. Users are willing to wait a few seconds for a task to complete, as long as they get feedback that work is happening. When the application stops responding to input, users perceive that the application, and by extension the device it's running on, is slow.

The second priority of your application is to make sure that all of the resources available are being used, so that the task completes quickly.

Operation queues allow you to achieve both goals. Operation queues are instances of the NSOperationQueue class. They manage a list, or queue, of operations, which are closures containing code to perform a chunk of work.

More than one operation queue can exist at the same time, and there is always at least one operation queue, known as the *main queue*. So far, all the code in this book has been run on the main queue. All work that is done with the GUI is done on the main queue, and if your code takes up too much time in processing something, the main queue slows down and your GUI starts to lag or freeze up.

Operation queues are not quite the same thing as *threads*, but they share some similarities. The operation queue system manages a pool of threads, which are activated whenever work needs to be done. Because threads are a rather resource-intensive way of doing work concurrently (to say nothing of the development complexity involved in managing them properly), operation queues provide a much simpler and more efficient way of dealing with them.

Operation queues are also aware of the computing resources available on whatever hardware your application is running on. If you create an operation queue and add operations to it, the operation queue will attempt to balance those operations across as many CPU cores as are available on your computer. Every single device that Apple ships now has two or more CPU cores, which means that code that uses operation queues automatically gains an increase in speed when performing concurrent work.

Operation Queues and NSOperation

At its simplest, an operation queue runs operations in a first-in-first-out order. Operations are instances of the NSOperation class, which define exactly how the work will be done. NSOperations can be added to an NSOperationQueue; once they are added, they will perform whatever task they have been designed to do.

The simplest way to add an operation to an operation queue is to provide a closure to the queue by sending the addOperationWithBlock message to an NSOperationQueue object:

```
var mainQueue = NSOperationQueue.mainQueue()

mainQueue.addOperationWithBlock() {
    // Add code here
}
```

There are other kinds of operations, including *invocation operations* and concrete subclasses of the NSOperation base class, but they're very similar to closure operations—they offer more flexibility and features at the cost of having to write more setup code.

If you don't deliberately choose to run code on another queue, it will run on the main queue. You can also explicitly instruct the main queue to perform an operation; when you do this, the work for this operation is scheduled to take place at some point in the future.

Performing Work on Operation Queues

To add things to an operation queue, you need an NSOperationQueue instance. You can either ask the system for the main queue, or you can create your own. If you create your own queue, it will run asynchronously. If you add multiple operations to a background queue, the operation queue will run as many as possible at the same time, depending on the available computing hardware:

```
// Getting the main queue (will run on the main thread)
var mainQueue = NSOperationQueue.mainQueue()

// Creating a new queue (will run on a background thread, probably)
var backgroundQueue = NSOperationQueue()
```

 Queues aren't the same as threads, and creating a new queue doesn't guarantee that you'll create a new thread—the operating system will reuse an existing thread if it can, because creating threads is expensive. The only thing using multiple queues guarantees is that the operations running on them won't block each other from running at the same time.

Once you have a queue, you can put an operation on it:

```
mainQueue.addOperationWithBlock() {
    println("This operation ran on the main queue!")
}

backgroundQueue.addOperationWithBlock() {
    println("This operation ran on another queue!")
}
```

If your code is running on a background queue and you want to update the GUI, you need to run the GUI updating code on the main queue. One way to do this is to add a closure to the main queue:

```
backgroundQueue.addOperationWithBlock() {
    // Do some work in the background
    println("I'm on the background queue")

    // Schedule a block on the main queue
    mainQueue.addOperationWithBlock() {
        println("I'm on the main queue")
        // GUI work can safely be done here.
    }
}
```

 Any work involving the GUI can only be done from the main queue. If you access it from any other queue, your application will crash.

Putting It All Together

We'll now write an application that downloads the favicons from a number of websites asynchronously. To do this, it will create a table view that has a list of websites, and each cell in the table view will show both the website's name as well as download its favicon. It will also contact a server when the application exits.

We'll need to create a subclass of UITableViewCell that has a NSURL property, and uses operation queues to download the favicon whenever that property changes.

The steps to create the new app are as follows:

1. Create a new, single view iOS application and call it OperationQueues.
2. Create a new Cocoa Touch subclass:

   • Set the "Subclass Of" to UITableViewCell.
   • Set the name of the class to FaviconTableViewCell.

3. Because this table view cell downloads in the background, we should give it an NSOperationQueue that it should use to manage the download. This means that we need to give it a property to store it in.

Add the following code to *FaviconTableViewCell.swift*:

```
// The operation queue to run the download's completion handler
var operationQueue : NSOperationQueue?
```

4. The next step is to implement the property that stores the URL that the cell is showing. When this property is changed, we want the cell to download the appropriate favicon, and then display the image. To do this, we'll use the NSURLConnection class's sendAsynchronousRequest method, which takes an NSURLRequest, an NSOperationQueue, and a closure; it then performs the download specified in the NSURLRequest, and runs the provided closure on the specified NSOperationQueue.

The closure itself takes three parameters: an NSURLResponse, which describes the response that the server sent back; an NSData, which contains the data that was delivered (if any); and an NSError, which contains information about any problem that the download might have encountered. Potential problems include issues with reaching the server (such as the user being in airplane mode), as well as problems on the server's end (such as the file not being found).

Add the following code to FaviconTableViewCell:

```
// The URL that this cell shows.
var url : NSURL? {

// When the URL changes, run this code.
didSet {

    // We've just been given a URL, so create a request
    var request = NSURLRequest(URL: self.url!)

    // Display this text
    self.textLabel.text = self.url?.host

    // Fire off the request, and give it a completion handler
    // plus a queue to run on
    NSURLConnection.sendAsynchronousRequest(request,
        queue: self.operationQueue!,
        completionHandler: {
            (response: NSURLResponse!, data: NSData!, error: NSError!) in

            // The 'data' variable now contains the loaded data;
            // turn it into an image
            var image = UIImage(data: data)

            // Updates to the UI have to be done on the main queue.
            NSOperationQueue.mainQueue().addOperationWithBlock() {
```

```
                    // Give the image view the loaded image
                    self.imageView.image = image

                    // The image view has probably changed size because of
                    // the new image, so we need to re-layout the cell.
                    self.setNeedsLayout()
                }

            })

        }
    }
```

We're now done setting up the table view cell. It's time to make a table view that uses this cell! Here are the steps to accomplish this:

1. Add a table view to the view controller.

2. Add a prototype cell to the table view by selecting it and changing the Prototype Cells number from 0 to 1.

3. Change the table view's new prototype cell style to Basic.

4. Select the prototype cell and change its identifier to `FaviconCell`.

5. Switch to the Identity Inspector for the table view cell, and change its class to `FaviconTableViewCell`.

6. Change the table's Selection style to No Selection.

7. Make the view controller the table view's data source and delegate by holding the Control key, dragging from the table view to the View Controller, and choosing `dataSource`.

8. Repeat the process and choose `delegate`.

9. Open *ViewController.swift* in the assistant.

10. The first thing to do is to define the list of websites that the app should show. We'll store this an an array of strings.

    Create the `hosts` property, by adding the following code:

    ```
    let hosts = ["google.com", "apple.com", "secretlab.com.au",
        "oreilly.com", "yahoo.com", "twitter.com", "facebook.com"]
    ```

11. Next, we need an NSOperationQueue to give to the FaviconTableViewCell instances that this class will be displaying.

    Create the queue property, by adding the following code:

    ```
    let queue = NSOperationQueue()
    ```

12. As with all table views, we need to provide information about how many sections it has, and how many rows are in each section. In this application, there is only one section, and the number of rows in that section is equal to the number of websites in the hosts array.

    Implement the numberOfSectionsInTableView and tableView(tableView: numberOfRowsInSection) methods:

    ```
    func numberOfSectionsInTableView(tableView: UITableView!) -> Int  {
        return 1
    }

    func tableView(tableView: UITableView,
        numberOfRowsInSection section: Int) -> Int  {
        return hosts.count
    }
    ```

13. The last thing to do is to make the table view use the FaviconTableViewCell class for its table view cells, and for each cell to use the right website. It does this by using the table view's dequeueReusableCellWithIdentifier method to retrieve the cell, and then uses the hosts array to create an NSURL to give it.

    Implement the tableView(tableView: cellForRowAtIndexPath:) method:

    ```
    func tableView(tableView: UITableView,
        cellForRowAtIndexPath indexPath: NSIndexPath) -> UITableViewCell  {

        var cell = tableView.dequeueReusableCellWithIdentifier("FaviconCell")
                                                as FaviconTableViewCell

        var host = hosts[indexPath.row]
        var url = NSURL(string: "http://\(host)/favicon.ico")

        cell.operationQueue = queue
        cell.url = url

        return cell

    }
    ```

14. Run the application.

The app will start up, and you'll see the list of websites; after a moment, website icons will start appearing next to them.

Finally, we'll make the application run some code in the background when the application quits.

15. Open *AppDelegate.swift*.

16. Replace `applicationWillEnterBackground:` with the following method:

```
var backgroundTask : UIBackgroundTaskIdentifier?

func applicationDidEnterBackground(application: UIApplication) {

    // Register a background task. This keeps the app from being
    // terminated until we tell the system that the task is complete.

    self.backgroundTask =
            application.beginBackgroundTaskWithExpirationHandler {
                () -> Void in

                // When this method is run, we're out of time.
                // Clean up, and then run endBackgroundTask.

                application.endBackgroundTask(self.backgroundTask!)

    }

    // Make a new background queue to run our background code on.
    var backgroundQueue = NSOperationQueue()

    backgroundQueue.addOperationWithBlock() {
        // Send a request to the server.

        // Prepare the URL
        var notificationURL = NSURL(string: "http://www.oreilly.com/")

        // Prepare the URL request
        var notificationURLRequest = NSURLRequest(URL: notificationURL!)

        // Send the request, and log the reply
        var loadedData =
            NSURLConnection.sendSynchronousRequest(
                            notificationURLRequest,
                            returningResponse: nil,
                            error: nil)

        if let theData = loadedData {
            // Convert the data to a string
            var loadedString = NSString(data: theData,
```

```
                                    encoding: NSUTF8StringEncoding)

                println("Loaded: \(loadedString)")

            }


            // Signal that we're done working in the background
            application.endBackgroundTask(self.backgroundTask!)
        }

    }
```

17. Run the application.

The application will now perform tasks when it quits.

CHAPTER 6

Drawing Graphics in Views

The fundamental class for showing any kind of graphical image to the user is the view. Graphical images are things like buttons, photos, and text—anything that the user can see.

Cocoa and UIKit provide a wide variety of controls that suit almost all needs—you can display text, images, buttons, and more. However, some data needs to be drawn in a specific way: you might want to draw a chart for data, or create a custom button class that displays exactly the way you want it to. If you're making a graphics app, you'll need to be able to display any kind of graphical content, which means that your code will need to know how to draw it.

In this chapter, you'll learn how to create custom view objects that display any kind of image to the user. You'll learn how to use the high-level APIs for drawing, and create a custom view class that will scale up to any size at all without losing quality. Finally, you'll learn how to design your graphics to take advantage of the Retina display on iOS and OS X hardware.

How Drawing Works

Before we start writing code that draws content for the user to see, it's helpful to review how graphics work in OS X and iOS. Note that the same terminology and techniques apply for both OS X and iOS, but the specific API is different.

When an application draws graphics, it does so by first creating a canvas for drawing in. Cocoa calls this the graphics *context*. The context defines, among other things, the size of the canvas and how color information is used (e.g., you can have a black-and-white canvas, a grayscale canvas, a 16-bit color canvas, etc.).

Once you have a graphics context to draw in, you start asking Cocoa to begin drawing content.

The fundamental drawing unit is the *path*. A path is just the name for any kind of shape: circles, squares, polygons, curves, and anything else you can imagine.

Paths can be stroked or filled. *Stroking* a path means drawing a line around its edge (Figure 6-1). *Filling* a path means filling it with a color (Figure 6-2).

Figure 6-1. A stroked path

Figure 6-2. A filled path

When you stroke or fill a path, you tell the drawing system which color you want to use. You can also use gradients to stroke and fill paths. The color that you use to stroke and fill can be partially transparent, which means that you can build up a complex graphic by combining different paths and colors (Figure 6-3).

Figure 6-3. A stroked and filled path

The Pixel Grid

Every display system in iOS and OS X is based on the idea of a grid of pixels. The specific number of pixels on the display varies from device to device, as does the physical size of each pixel. The trend is toward larger numbers of smaller pixels, because the smaller the pixels get, the smoother the image looks.

When you create a graphics context, you indicate what size that context should be. So, for example, if you create a context that is 300 pixels wide by 400 pixels high, the canvas is set to that size. Any drawing that takes place outside the canvas is ignored, and doesn't appear on the canvas (Figure 6-4).

Creating a context defines a *coordinate space* where the drawing happens. This coordinate space puts the coordinate (0,0) in either the upper-left corner (on iOS) or the lower-left corner (on OS X). When you build a path, you specify the points that define it. So, for example, a line that goes from the upper-left corner (on iOS) to 10 pixels below and to the right looks like Figure 6-5.

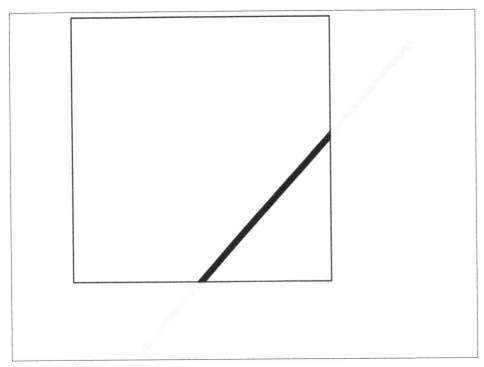

Figure 6-4. Content that is drawn outside of the context's canvas doesn't appear

Retina Displays

The newest devices sold by Apple feature a *Retina display*. A Retina display, according to Apple, is a screen where the pixels are so small that you can't make out the individual dots. This means that curves and text appear much smoother, and the end result is a better visual experience for the user.

Retina displays are available on the MacBook Pro with Retina display, iPod touch 4th generation and later, iPhone 4 and later, Retina iPad Mini and later, and iPad third-generation and later.

Retina displays are so named because, according to Apple, a 300 dpi (dots per inch) display held at a distance of about 12 inches from the eye is the maximum amount of detail that the human retina can perceive.

Apple achieves this resolution by using displays that are the same physical size as more common displays, but double or triple the resolution. For example, the screen on the iPhone 3GS (and all previous iPhone and iPod touch models) measures 3.5 inches diagonally and features a resolution of 320 pixels wide by 480 pixels high. When this resolution is doubled in the iPhone 4's Retina display, the resolution is 640 by 960.

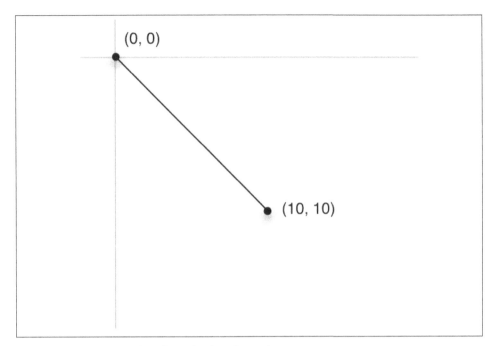

Figure 6-5. Drawing a line from (0,0) to (10,10) on iOS

This increase in resolution can potentially lead to additional complexities for application developers. In all other cases where the resolution of a display has increased, everything on the screen appears smaller (because the drawing code only cares about pixel distances, not physical display size). However, on a double-resolution Retina display, everything remains the same size, because even though the pixels are twice as small, everything on the screen is drawn *twice as large*. The net result is that the graphics on the screen look the same size, but much smoother.

Pixels and Screen Points

Of course, we application developers don't want to write code for both Retina and non-Retina displays. Writing a chunk of code twice for the two resolutions would lead to twice the potential bugs!

To solve this problem, don't think about pixels when you're writing your graphics code and thinking about the positions of the points your paths are constructed with. Instead, think in terms of *screen points*.

A pixel is likely to change between different devices, but a screen point does not. When you construct a path, you specify the position of each screen point that defines the path. On a non-Retina display, one screen point is equal to one pixel. On a double-resolution Retina display, one screen point is equal to four pixels—a square, two pixels wide and two high. On a triple-resolution Retina display, one screen point is nine pixels—a three-by-three box. This scaling is done for you automatically by the operating system.

The end result is that you end up with drawing code that doesn't need to be changed for different resolutions.

Drawing in Views

As discussed earlier, objects that display graphics to the user are called *views*. Before we talk about how to make your own view objects that display your pixels before the user's very eyes, let's take a closer look at how views work.

A view is defined by a rectangle inside its content window. If a view isn't inside a window, the user can't see it.

 Even though only one app is displayed at a time on iOS, all views shown on the screen are technically inside a window. The difference is that only one window is shown on the screen at a time, and it fills the screen.

Frame Rectangles

The rectangle that defines the view's size and position is called its *frame rectangle*.

Views can contain multiple *subviews*. When a view is inside another view (its *superview*), it moves when the superview moves. Its frame rectangle is defined relative to its superview (Figure 6-6).

On OS X, all views are instances of NSView (or one of NSView 's subclasses). On iOS, they're instances of UIView. There are some minor differences in how they work, but nothing that affects what we're talking about here. For now, we'll talk about NSView, but everything applies equally to UIView.

When the system needs to display a view, it sends the drawRect(rect:) message to the view. The drawRect method looks like the following:

```
override func drawRect(rect: NSRect)  {

}
```

(This method is the same on iOS, but CGRect is used instead of NSRect.)

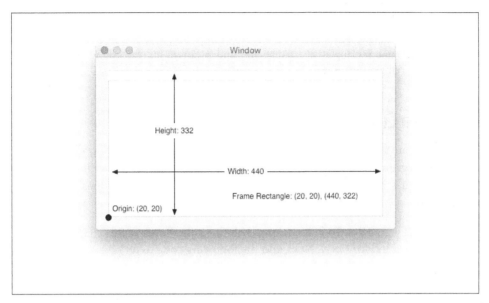

Figure 6-6. The frame rectangle for the view defines its position and size relative to its superview

When this method is called, a graphics context has already been prepared by the OS, leaving the method ready to start drawing. When the method returns, the OS takes the contents of the graphics context and shows it in the view.

The single parameter that drawRect receives is the *dirty rectangle*. This eyebrow-raising term is actually a lot more tame than it sounds—"dirty" is simply the term for "something that needs updating." The dirty rectangle is the region of the view that actually needs updating. This concept becomes useful in cases where you have a view that was previously covered up by another view—there's no need to redraw content that was previously visible, and so the dirty rectangle that's passed to drawRect will be a reduced size.

Bounds Rectangles

The frame rectangle defines the size and position of its view, but it's also helpful for a view to know about its size and position relative to itself. To support this, view objects also provide a *bounds rectangle*. While the frame rectangle is the view's size and position relative to its superview's coordinate space, the bounds rectangle is the view's position and size relative to its own coordinate space. This means that the (0,0) coordinate always refers to the upper-left corner on iOS (the lower-left on OS X).

While the bounds rectangle is usually the same size as the frame rectangle, it doesn't have to be. For example, if the view is rotated, the frame rectangle will change size and position, but the bounds will remain the same.

Building a Custom View

We'll now create a custom view that displays a solid color inside its bounds. This will be a Mac playground, so we'll be using NSView. Later in the chapter, we'll see how the same techniques apply to iOS and the UIView class. Here are the steps you'll need to take:

1. Create the view class. To follow along with the code shown in this chapter, create a new playground for OS X. Next, add the following code to it:

   ```
   class MyView : NSView {
       override func drawRect(rect: NSRect)  {

       }
   }
   ```

2. Once you've defined the class, create an instance of it:

   ```
   let viewRect = NSRect(x: 0, y: 0, width: 100, height: 100)
   let myEmptyView = MyView(frame: viewRect)
   ```

3. Create an instance of the class. At this point, you can preview the view. In the righthand pane of the playground, you'll see the result of creating that instance (it will appear as the text "MyView").

   To the right of that, you'll see a circle. Click on that, and a new pane will open on the right, showing a preview (Figure 6-7). Now, when you make changes to your class, you'll see the view update live. It's blank for now, but you'll be changing that very shortly.

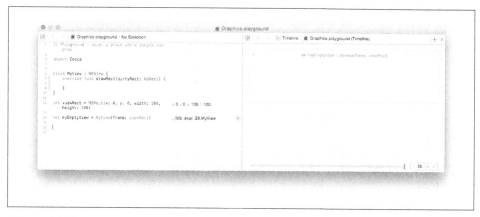

Figure 6-7. Previewing a view

Filling with a Solid Color

Let's start by making the view fill itself with the color green. Afterward, we'll start making the view show more complex stuff.

Replace the `drawRect` method of `MyClass` with the following code:

```
override func drawRect(rect: NSRect) {
    NSColor.greenColor().setFill()

    let path = NSBezierPath(rect: self.bounds)

    path.fill()
}
```

This view code creates an `NSBezierPath` object, which represents the path that you'll be drawing. In this code, we create the Bézier path with the `bezierPath(rect:)` method, which creates a rectangular path. We use the view's bounds to create a rectangle that fills the entire view.

Once the path is created, we can fill it. Before we do that, however, we tell the graphics system to use green as the fill color. Colors in Cocoa are represented by the `NSColor` class, which is capable of representing almost any color you can think of.[1] `NSColor` provides a number of convenience methods that return simple colors, like green, red, and blue, which we use here.

So, we create the path, set the color, and then fill the path. The end result is a giant green rectangle.

---

1. Almost any color, that is. All displays have physical limits that restrict their range of colors, and no displays currently on the market are capable of displaying impossible colors (*http://en.wikipedia.org/wiki/Impossible_colors*).

The exact same code works on iOS, with two changes: NSBezier
Path becomes UIBezierPath, and NSColor becomes UIColor:

```
override func drawRect(rect: CGRect) {
    UIColor.greenColor().setFill()

    let path = UIBezierPath(rect: self.bounds)

    path.fill()
}
```

Now run the application. The view you added will display as green, as shown in
Figure 6-8.

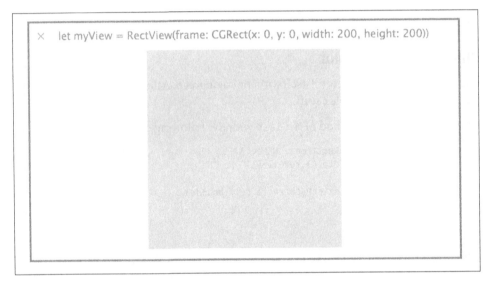

```
× let myView = RectView(frame: CGRect(x: 0, y: 0, width: 200, height: 200))
```

Figure 6-8. A green view

Working with Paths

Let's now update this code and create a slightly more complex path: a rounded rectangle.
We'll also stroke the path, drawing an outline around it.

Replace the drawRect method with the following code:

```
override func drawRect(rect: NSRect) {
    var pathRect = NSInsetRect(self.bounds, 1, 1);

    var path = NSBezierPath(roundedRect:pathRect, xRadius:10, yRadius:10);

    path.lineWidth = 4

    NSColor.greenColor().setFill();
```

```
        NSColor.blackColor().setStroke();
        path.fill()
        path.stroke()
    }
```

The first change you'll notice is a call to the `NSInsetRect` function. This function takes an `NSRect` and shrinks it while preserving its center point. In this case, we're insetting the rectangle by one point on the x-axis and one point on the y-axis. This causes the rectangle to be pushed in by one point from the left and one point from the right, as well as one pixel from the top and bottom.

We do this because when a path is stroked, the line is drawn around the outside—and because the bounds are the size of the view, some parts of the line are trimmed away. This can look ugly, so we shrink the rectangle a bit to prevent the problem.

We then create another `NSBezierPath`, this time using the newly shrunk rectangle. This path is created by calling the `bezierPath(roundedRect:xRadius:yRadius:)` method, which lets you specify how the corners of the rounded rectangle are shaped.

The final change to the code is setting black as the stroke color, and then stroking the path after it's been filled.

Now run the application. You'll see a green rounded rectangle with a black line around it (Figure 6-9).

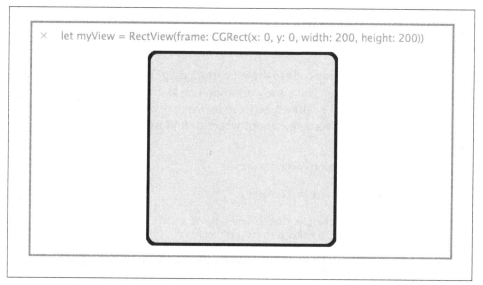

Figure 6-9. A stroked rounded rectangle

All drawing operations take place in the order in which you call them. In this code, we stroke the rectangle after filling it. If we instead swapped the order of the calls to `path.fill()` and `path.stroke()`, we'd get a slightly different effect, with the green fill overlapping the black stroke slightly.

Creating Custom Paths

Creating paths using rectangles or rounded rectangles is useful, but you often want to create a shape that's entirely your own—a polygon, perhaps, or an outline of a character.

The `NSBezierPath` class is capable of representing any shape that can be defined using Bézier curves. You can create your own custom curves by creating a blank curve and then adding the control points that define the curve. Once you're done, you can use the finished `NSBezierPath` object to fill and stroke, just like any other path.

To create a custom path, you first create an empty path, and then start issuing commands to build it. As you build the path, you can imagine a virtual pen that you move around the canvas. You can:

- Move the pen to a point
- Draw a line from where the pen currently is to another point
- Draw a curve from where the pen currently is to another point, using two additional control points that define how the curve bends
- Close the path by drawing a line from where the pen currently is to the first point

We'll now update our drawing code to draw a custom shape by replacing the `drawRect` method with the code below. This code works out how to draw the path by calculating the points that lines should be drawn between by first calculating a rectangle to draw with, and then asking that rectangle about where to find its leftmost edge, rightmost edge, and so on:

```
override func drawRect(rect: NSRect) {

    var bezierPath = NSBezierPath()

    // Create a rectangle that's inset by 5% on all sides
    var drawingRect = CGRectInset(self.bounds,
                                  self.bounds.size.width * 0.05,
                                  self.bounds.size.height * 0.05);

    // Define the points that make up the drawing
    var topLeft = CGPointMake(CGRectGetMinX(drawingRect),
                              CGRectGetMaxY(drawingRect));

    var topRight = CGPointMake(CGRectGetMaxX(drawingRect),
```

```
                              CGRectGetMaxY(drawingRect));

      var bottomRight = CGPointMake(CGRectGetMaxX(drawingRect),
                                    CGRectGetMinY(drawingRect));

      var bottomLeft = CGPointMake(CGRectGetMinX(drawingRect),
                                   CGRectGetMinY(drawingRect));

      var center = CGPointMake(CGRectGetMidX(drawingRect),
                               CGRectGetMidY(drawingRect))

      // Start drawing
      bezierPath.moveToPoint(topLeft)
      bezierPath.lineToPoint(topRight)
      bezierPath.lineToPoint(bottomLeft)
      bezierPath.curveToPoint(bottomRight,
                              controlPoint1: center,
                              controlPoint2: center)

      // Finish drawing by closing the path
      bezierPath.closePath()

      // Set the colors and draw them
      NSColor.redColor().setFill()
      NSColor.blackColor().setStroke()

      bezierPath.fill()
      bezierPath.stroke()

  }
```

Now run the application. The window will show a red shape (Figure 6-10).

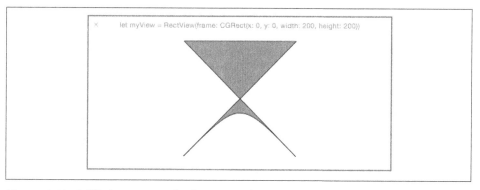

Figure 6-10. A filled custom path, showing a shape

Multiple Subpaths

So far, the paths that we've been drawing have contained only one *subpath*. A subpath is a connected series of points in a Bézier path. This means that you can have a path that contains two circles—every time you issued a stroke or fill command, you would be drawing those two circles.

Using subpaths is also a great way to create complex shapes. In this next example, we'll create a circle that combines a rounded rectangle with a circle. We'll do this by first creating a rounded rectangle path, and then adding a circular path to it. Replace the drawRect method with the following code:

```
override func drawRect(rect: NSRect)  {

    // Create an empty Bézier path
    let bezierPath = NSBezierPath()

    // Define the rectangles for the two components
    let squareRect = CGRectInset(rect,
        rect.size.width * 0.45,
        rect.size.height * 0.05)

    let circleRect = CGRectInset(rect,
        rect.size.width * 0.3,
        rect.size.height * 0.3)

    let cornerRadius : CGFloat = 20

    // Create the paths
    var circlePath = NSBezierPath(ovalInRect: circleRect);
    var squarePath = NSBezierPath(roundedRect: squareRect,
                                        xRadius: cornerRadius,
                                        yRadius: cornerRadius)

    // Add them to the main path
    squarePath.appendBezierPath(circlePath)
    bezierPath.appendBezierPath(squarePath)

    // Set the color and draw them
    NSColor.redColor().setFill()

    // Draw the path
    bezierPath.fill()

}
```

In this code, we're creating a new empty Bézier path. We then create an additional Bézier path that defines a circle, and append it to the first path. Next, we create a rounded rectangle path, and append it as well. This combined path is then drawn, as shown in Figure 6-11.

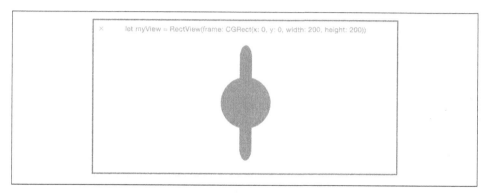

Figure 6-11. Multiple subpaths

Shadows

Shadows are a great way to imply depth in your graphics. If a shape casts a shadow, it appears "closer" than one that does not.

On OS X, shadows are drawn using the NSShadow class (on iOS, the technique is similar but not identical; see "Drawing shadows on iOS" on page 133). An NSShadow object stores all of the information needed to draw a shadow. Three pieces of information are needed:

- The color to use for the shadow (an NSColor)
- How many points the shadow should be offset by (an NSSize struct)
- How blurry the shadow should be (a CGFloat)

To draw a shadow, you create an NSShadow object, provide it with the drawing settings you want to use, and then send it the set message:

```
let shadow = NSShadow()  ❶
shadow.shadowColor = NSColor.blackColor()  ❷
shadow.shadowOffset = NSSize(width: 3, height: -3)  ❸
shadow.shadowBlurRadius = 10  ❹
shadow.set()  ❺
```

This code does the following things:

❶　Creates the shadow object.

❷　Sets the color to black.

❸　Sets the shadow offset to be drawn three pixels to the right, and three pixels down from what's drawn.

❹　Sets the blur radius to be 10 points.

❺　Sets the shadow. Anything drawn after this call will cast a shadow.

Saving and restoring graphics contexts

The set method causes the shadow to be applied to anything that you ask Cocoa to draw. This lasts until another shadow is set or the context is closed by the graphics system (which is what happens after the drawRect call returns). This means that once you set a shadow, it could stay around forever.

However, you might want to draw an object with a shadow followed by an object that doesn't have one. To support this, and to help deal with similar cases where the graphics context itself is changed (such as when you set the stroke and fill color, or change the current transformation matrix or CTM—more on that in the section "Transforms" on page 137), the drawing system allows you to save the state of the context and restore it later.

In order to save the graphics context, you send the saveGraphicsState message to the NSGraphicsContext class. This saves all of your drawing settings and pushes the context state onto a stack for you to retrieve later. It doesn't affect the pixels you've drawn, though:

```
NSGraphicsContext.saveGraphicsState()
```

When you're done, you can retrieve the saved context state by sending the NSGraphics Context class the restoreGraphicsState message. This pops the most recently saved state from the stack, and restores its settings (such as the shadow and colors):

```
NSGraphicsContext.restoreGraphicsState()
```

Always make sure to balance every call to saveGraphicsState with a call to restoreGraphicsState, or unusual behavior such as crashes may occur.

Drawing a shadow

We'll now update the drawing code to draw a rectangle with a shadow. Replace the drawRect(rect:) method with the following code:

```
override func drawRect(rect: NSRect)  {

    let drawingRect = CGRectInset(rect,
        rect.size.width * 0.1,
        rect.size.height * 0.1);

    let cornerRadius : CGFloat = 20

    let bezierPath = NSBezierPath(roundedRect: drawingRect,
        xRadius: cornerRadius,
        yRadius: cornerRadius)

    NSGraphicsContext.saveGraphicsState()
```

```
let shadow = NSShadow()
shadow.shadowColor = NSColor.blackColor()
shadow.shadowOffset = NSSize(width: 3, height: -3)
shadow.shadowBlurRadius = 10
shadow.set()

NSColor.redColor().setFill()
bezierPath.fill()

NSGraphicsContext.restoreGraphicsState()

    }
```

This code starts by creating the NSShadow object and prepares it much like we saw previously. A rounded rectangle NSBezierPath object is also created. The code then saves the graphics state, sets the shadow, and fills the rectangle path. Once the drawing is done, the graphics state is restored. Any further drawing that's done won't include a shadow.

Now run the application. You'll see a box with a shadow (Figure 6-12).

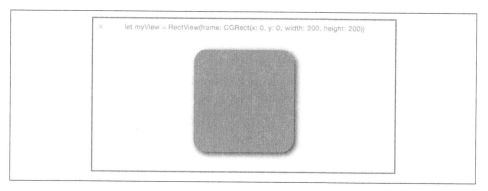

Figure 6-12. Drawing a shadow

Drawing shadows on iOS

The NSShadow class exists only in OS X. The techniques for drawing shadows on iOS are similar, but instead of using Objective-C classes to draw the shadows, you use some C functions that belong to Core Graphics, the C-based drawing API that Cocoa wraps.

Here's the equivalent drawing code for drawing a shadow on iOS:

```
// Get the drawing context
var context = UIGraphicsGetCurrentContext()

// Work out a rectangle to draw in
var pathRect = CGRectInset(self.bounds,
```

```
                    self.bounds.size.width * 0.1,
                    self.bounds.size.height * 0.1)

        // Create a rounded rect path
        var rectanglePath = UIBezierPath(roundedRect: pathRect, cornerRadius: 20)

        // Equivalent to NSGraphicsContext.saveGraphicsState()
        CGContextSaveGState(context)

        // Prepare the shadow
        var shadow = UIColor.blackColor().CGColor
        var shadowOffset = CGSize(width: 3, height: 3)
        var shadowBlurRadius : CGFloat = 5.0

        // This function creates and applies the shadow
        CGContextSetShadowWithColor(context,
                                    shadowOffset,
                                    shadowBlurRadius,
                                    shadow)

        // Draw the path; it will have a shadow
        UIColor.redColor().setFill()
        rectanglePath.fill()

        // Equivalent to NSGraphicsContext.restoreGraphicsState()
        CGContextRestoreGState(context)
```

You'll note that instead of creating an Objective-C object, we instead store the settings in separate variables and then call the CGContextSetShadowWithColor function. Also, instead of calling saveGraphicsState and restoreGraphicsState like we do on OS X, we call CGContextSaveGState and CGContextRestoreGState. Otherwise, it's almost exactly the same.

 The shadow offset used on iOS is (3, 3) while on OS X it's (3, -3). That's because the coordinate system on iOS is flipped from that of OS X: on iOS, (0, 0) is the upper-left corner and positive y-values advance down the screen, while on OS X, (0, 0) is the lower-left corner and positive y-values advance up the screen.

Gradients

So far, we've worked entirely with solid colors when filling our shapes. However, the human eye quickly tires of seeing large blocks of solid color, and adding a gradient between two colors is a great way to add visual interest.

Drawing a gradient on OS X is similar to drawing a shadow—that is, you create an NSGradient object, and then set it up. However, instead of setting the gradient as a color, you instruct the gradient object to fill itself into a path object you provide. This is necessary because the gradient needs to know precisely where to start blending.

A gradient has at least two colors; when the gradient is drawn into an area, the area is filled with a smooth shade that blends between the gradient's colors. Each color also has a location, which controls how the blending is performed.

When you draw the gradient, you also specify the angle at which you want the gradient to be drawn. If you provide an angle of zero, the gradient draws from left to right, using each color you provide in sequence. If you provide an angle of 90 degrees, the gradient draws from bottom to top.

Drawing gradients on iOS is different, because you use Core Graphics C functions instead of using the NSGradient class. See "Drawing gradients on iOS" on page 136.

When constructing the gradient, the only information you need to provide is the colors. You do this with the NSGradient(startingColor: endingColor:) method, which takes a pair of NSColor objects:

```
let startColor = NSColor.blackColor()
let endColor = NSColor.whiteColor()

let gradient = NSGradient(startingColor:startColor, endingColor:endColor)
```

 Do not actually use these colors in a real app. Black-to-white gradients look *terrible* on screens.

Then, when you want to draw the gradient, give it the shape you want it to fill (you can also stroke shapes with gradients):

```
gradient.drawInBezierPath(bezierPath, angle: 90)
```

We'll now update the code to draw a gradient inside the custom view. Replace the drawRect method with the following code:

```
override func drawRect(rect: NSRect)  {

    // Defining the shape
    let drawingRect = CGRectInset(rect,
        rect.size.width * 0.1,
        rect.size.height * 0.1);

    let cornerRadius : CGFloat = 20

    let bezierPath = NSBezierPath(roundedRect: drawingRect,
        xRadius: cornerRadius,
        yRadius: cornerRadius)
```

```
// Define the gradient
let startColor = NSColor.blackColor()
let endColor = NSColor.whiteColor()

let gradient = NSGradient(startingColor:startColor, endingColor:endColor)

// Draw the gradient in the path
gradient.drawInBezierPath(bezierPath, angle: 90)

}
```

Now run the application. You'll see a black-to-white gradient (Figure 6-13).

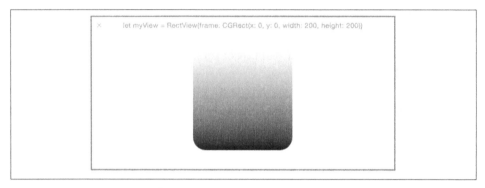

Figure 6-13. Drawing a gradient

Drawing gradients on iOS

On iOS, the process of drawing gradients is a little more verbose but conceptually the same. You still create an *object*, but it's done via the Core Graphics C function calls.

Instead of providing a path object to a gradient and asking the gradient to draw itself, you instead *clip* the current graphics context, and then draw the gradient from one point on the screen to another. Clipping means to restrict the drawing to a shape, which prevents the view from being completely filled with the gradient.

In addition, instead of providing an angle at which the gradient should be drawn, you pass in the coordinates converted into the coordinate space of the view that the gradient should be drawn from and to.

Here's the equivalent drawing code for iOS:

```
override func drawRect(rect: CGRect) {
    let colorSpace = CGColorSpaceCreateDeviceRGB()
    let context = UIGraphicsGetCurrentContext()

    let gradientStartColor = UIColor(red: 0.1, green: 0.1, blue: 0.8,
                                     alpha: 1)
```

```
let gradientEndColor = UIColor(red: 1, green: 0.6, blue: 0.8, alpha: 1)

let gradientColors : CFArray = [gradientStartColor.CGColor,
                                gradientEndColor.CGColor]
let gradientLocations : [CGFloat] = [0.0, 1.0]

let gradient = CGGradientCreateWithColors(colorSpace,
    gradientColors, gradientLocations)


let pathRect = CGRectInset(self.bounds, 20, 20)

let topPoint = CGPointMake(self.bounds.size.width / 2, 20)
let bottomPoint = CGPointMake(self.bounds.size.width / 2,
    self.bounds.size.height - 20)

let roundedRectanglePath = UIBezierPath(roundedRect: pathRect,
                                        cornerRadius: 4)

CGContextSaveGState(context)

roundedRectanglePath.addClip()
CGContextDrawLinearGradient(context, gradient, bottomPoint, topPoint, 0)

CGContextRestoreGState(context)

}
```

Transforms

Drawing shapes is fine, but sometimes you want to be able to handle something slightly more complex, like rotating or stretching a shape. It's certainly possible to simply create a new path by providing a different set of coordinates, but it's often better to just ask the OS to do the rotation for you.

To do this, you use *transforms*, which are representations of transformation matrices. We won't go into the math of them in this book, but they're tools that can be used to translate, rotate, scale, skew, and generally perform any kind of distortion or manipulation of content.

All drawing that's done by your code is affected by the *current transform matrix* (CTM), which transforms every path and drawing operation that's performed. By default, the transform matrix is the *identity matrix* —that is, it doesn't do anything at all. However, the CTM can be modified to affect your drawing.

To modify the CTM, you first need a reference to the low-level drawing context. This context, which is set up for you by Cocoa before your drawRect(rect:) method is called, is of type CGContextRef. On OS X, you get the context with the following code:

```
var context = NSGraphicsContext.currentContext()?.CGContext
```

On iOS, you get the context with this code:

```
var context = UIGraphicsGetCurrentContext()
```

Once you have the context, you can change the CTM. In the following example, we'll change the CTM so that everything that gets drawn is rotated around the origin (the lower-left corner on OS X) by a few degrees.

 If you change the CTM, that change will stick around until the context's state is restored. If you only want to rotate part of your drawing, save the context's state before changing the CTM, and restore the state when you're done. See "Saving and restoring graphics contexts" on page 132.

Replace the drawRect method with the following code:

```
override func drawRect(rect: NSRect) {
    var pathRect = CGRectInset(self.bounds,
        self.bounds.size.width * 0.1,
        self.bounds.size.height * 0.1)

    let cornerRadius : CGFloat = 20.0

    var rotationTransform =
        CGAffineTransformMakeRotation(CGFloat(M_PI) / 4.0)

    var rectanglePath = NSBezierPath(roundedRect:pathRect,
        xRadius:cornerRadius,
        yRadius:cornerRadius)

    var context = NSGraphicsContext.currentContext()!.CGContext

    CGContextSaveGState(context)

    CGContextConcatCTM(context, rotationTransform)

    NSColor.redColor().setFill()
    rectanglePath.fill()

    CGContextRestoreGState(context)

}
```

Now run the application. You'll see a rectangle that's been rotated slightly (Figure 6-14).

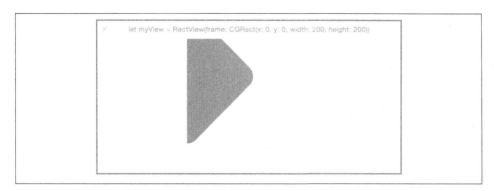

Figure 6-14. A rotated rounded rectangle

CHAPTER 7

SpriteKit

The SpriteKit framework was first introduced in iOS 7 and OS X 10.9, and because it is designed purposely for creating games, it is heavily optimized for rendering and animating 2D graphics.

At its core, SpriteKit is a simple, object-oriented toolkit for drawing sprites (i.e., images and text) that provides you with significantly more flexibility and performance than using UIKit for the same purposes, while at the same time not forcing you to go down to the level of writing OpenGL code.

In addition to its graphical features, SpriteKit also comes with a built-in 2D physics engine, which handles collision detection, collision resolution, and rigid-body simulation.

In this chapter, you'll learn how to create SpriteKit scenes, how to work with sprites and shape nodes, as well as how to take advantage of new features added in iOS 8.

SpriteKit's Architecture

At the high level, SpriteKit is all about *nodes*. There are three things to know about nodes:

- Nodes are contained within a SpriteKit *view*.
- Nodes can have other nodes as their children.
- Nodes render graphics into the view (depending on their type).

SpriteKit nodes are all instances of SKNode, or one of its subclasses. There are a *lot* of different subclasses: at its base, the empty SKNode class represents an empty, invisible node, while SKSpriteNode represents an image or colored rectangle, SKShapeNode draws a Bézier path, `SKEffectNode` applies image effects like blurs or tints on its children, and more.

When you want to make a game that uses SpriteKit, you assemble a scene full of these nodes, and add them to a *scene*. Scenes can be thought of as different *screens* in your game—you might have a main menu scene, a settings scene, and a scene for each of your game's different levels. Scenes are represented by the `SKScene` class.

Each scene is presented in a SpriteKit *view*. This view, which is an instance of `SKView`, is the context in which all of your game's graphics are presented. The SpriteKit view is a subclass of `UIView`, and is mananged in a view controller much like any other view in an app.

Making an App That Uses SpriteKit

Xcode comes with a template for SpriteKit games, but the framework is seriously simple to add. Additionally, it's easier to pick up the technology when you build it from scratch; with that in mind, we'll build a simple little app that uses SpriteKit. Once you've built it, you can use it as a playground for testing out different techniques and features in SpriteKit:

1. Create a new, single view application and name it SpriteKit.

2. Add the SpriteKit framework. Select the project at the top of the project navigator, and then scroll down in the main editor until you find the Linked Frameworks and Libraries section. Click the + button, and select "SpriteKit.framework" from the list that appears.

Once you've added the SpriteKit framework, you get access to all of its classes. One of those is the `SKView` class, which we need to make the app's main view controller use.

3. To make the main view controller use a SpriteKit view, open the main storyboard and go to the single view controller that comes as part of the template.

    Select the view by clicking on it, and go to the Identity inspector.

    Change the view's class from `UIView` to `SKView`.

We'll now add code that presents an empty SpriteKit scene in the view. To prove that what we're adding is actually new, custom content, we'll make the empty scene use a bright green background. (This means that if you're not seeing a bright green screen when you're done with this part of the exercise, something's gone wrong!)

4. At this point, open the *ViewController.swift* file and add the following code to the `viewDidLoad` method:

```
let scene = SKScene(size: self.view.bounds.size)

scene.backgroundColor = UIColor.greenColor()

let skView = self.view as SKView

skView.presentScene(scene)
```

5. Run the application. When it loads, you should see a green screen (Figure 7-1).

Figure 7-1. The empty scene

Working with SpriteKit Scenes

A SpriteKit game is composed of *scenes*. Each scene contains all of the graphical elements that make up a part of your game. For example, you could have a scene that contains your main menu, a scene that shows the high scores, and a scene for each of your game's levels.

 Depending on the type of your game, you could also have a single scene for *all* levels, and customize that based on the specifics of each level. Puzzle games tend to do this, as they have a number of common elements in each level (like the score display, a back button, etc.), and only change the contents of the puzzle itself.

In SpriteKit, you can think of scenes as being similar to view controllers in a regular application. Both scenes and view controllers are responsible for the visible parts of the app, and handle the behavior of these elements on the screen—a view controller is in charge of providing data to views and responding to user actions, and a scene is in charge of creating the appropriate sprites and responding to user input.

To make a SpriteKit scene, you create a subclass of the SKScene class, and then make your game's SKView *present* it. Presenting a scene can be done directly, or with a transition.

When you present a scene directly, the scene immediately appears in the view. Presenting a scene directly is done using the presentScene method:

```
skView.presentScene(scene)
```

You generally present the first scene of your game directly, without using a transition.

You can also present a screen using a *transition*, which is an animation that the SpriteKit view uses to indicate that the game is moving to a new scene. These include things like fading from one to the other, fading down to black and then back up to the new scene, or sliding the old scene off-screen and the new one on.

There's a wide variety of different transitions available. For the full list, check out the documentation for the SKTransition class in the Xcode documentation (*http://bit.ly/sktransition*).

To present a transition, you create an instance of the SKTransition class. The specific animation that the transition uses depends on the method you use to create the transition, as well as the parameters you provide to that method. For example, to create a transition that slides the new scene in from the right over half a second, you call the moveInWithDirection(_, duration:) method, which returns your SKTransition object.

Once you've created the transition, you then give it to the SKView along with the new scene, like so:

```
let transition = SKTransition.moveInWithDirection(
    SKTransitionDirection.Right, duration: 0.5)

self.view?.presentScene(game, transition: transition)
```

Once a scene is presented, or begins appearing through a transition, it receives the didMoveToView message. This is the scene's opportunity to prepare its content so that it's ready for the user to see it. This is your chance to add sprites, set the scene's background, and do other necessary setup tasks.

To demonstrate this, we're going to extend the SpriteKit example to use our own custom subclass of SKScene:

1. First, create the new SKScene subclass. Go to the File menu, and choose New → New File.

   Create a new Cocoa Touch class called GameScene. Make it a subclass of SKScene.

2. Add the didMoveToView method. Open *GameScene.swift*, and add the following method to the class:

   ```
   override func didMoveToView(view: SKView!) {
       self.scaleMode = .AspectFill

       let label = SKLabelNode(text: "Hello")
       label.position = CGPoint(x: size.width / 2.0, y: size.height / 2.0)

       self.addChild(label)

   }
   ```

3. Make the view controller present the new scene on startup. Open *ViewController.swift*, and replace the code for viewDidLoad with the following:

   ```
   let scene = GameScene(size: self.view.bounds.size)

   let skView = self.view as SKView

   scene.scaleMode = .AspectFill
   scene.backgroundColor = UIColor.blackColor()

   skView.presentScene(scene)
   ```

SpriteKit Nodes

SpriteKit scenes contain *nodes*. Nodes, on their own, don't do anything at all except exist; however, the base SKNode class has a number of important subclasses, each of which does something specific to the scene.

All nodes have the concept of *parenting*. When a node is in a scene, it's a *child* of another node. That other node may itself be a child of another, and so on, right up to the SKScene.

To add a node as a child of another node, you use the addChild method:

```
self.addChild(label)
```

A node can only have a single parent, though it can have any number of children. If you want to move a node from one parent to another (also known as *re-parenting*), you use the removeFromParent method on the node:

```
label.removeFromParent()
```

 If you try to add one node to another node, and the first node already has a parent, you'll throw an exception. Always call remove FromParent before moving a node from one parent to another.

It's OK for a node to have no parent. It just won't be visible to the user unless it's attached to a node in the scene.

Different nodes do different things. For example:

- SKSpriteNode shows an image, or a colored rectangle. It's the most common type of node.
- SKLabelNode shows text.
- SKShapeNode renders any UIBezierPath, such as rounded rectangles, circles, or any other kind of shape.
- SKEffectNode applies image effects, such as blurs or color shifts, to all of its child nodes.
- Empty SKNode objects, even though they don't actually display anything in the scene, are useful for grouping multiple nodes together.

Putting Sprites in Scenes

The SKSpriteNode class is the main workhorse of SpriteKit. Given that pretty much every game will be displaying graphics of some kind, even if it's just a button labeled "win the game,"[1] you need a way to put those graphics into the game.

Sprite nodes are designed for just this purpose, and are very simple to use. All you need is an image to show; once you've added that to your project, you create an SKSprite Node instance that uses it.

In this section, the name of the image that we're using will be called *BlockSquareBlue*, but you can use any image you want. The *BlockSquareBlue* image, along with some other images, are contained in the source code that accompanies this book.

Here are the steps you'll need to take:

1. First, add the image. To begin working with images, simply drag and drop the image into the project navigator. Xcode will ask you if you want to copy the image in; you generally want to do this.

2. Then create the sprite node and make it use the image. Open *GameScene.swift*, and add the following code to the didMoveToView method:

```
// Create the sprite
let spriteNode = SKSpriteNode(imageNamed: "BlockSquareBlue")

// Position the sprite right in the center of the scene
spriteNode.position = CGPoint(x: size.width / 2.0,
                             y: size.height / 2.0)

// Add the sprite
self.addChild(spriteNode)
```

Once you're done, the sprite will be visible in the scene, as seen in Figure 7-2.

---

1. Jon's getting pretty close to finally beating this game.

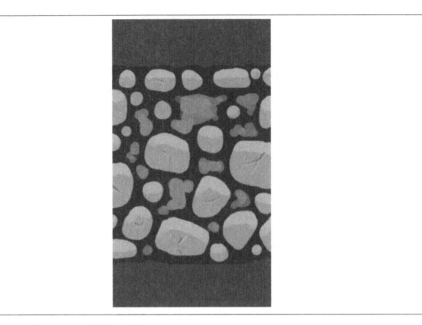

Figure 7-2. The sprite, added to the scene

Responding to Touches

Most games require input of some kind.[2] SpriteKit makes it very easy to add code that runs when something on the screen is touched.

Just like a UIView, SKNode objects can respond to touches. When this happens, they receive the touchesBegan(_, withEvent:) message, which indicates that a touch landed on the node.

Scenes are nodes, which means they also have the ability to detect when the user is touching them. Because scenes fill the entire screen, this means that a scene can detect a touch anywhere on the screen.

To demonstrate this, we're going to add an additional scene to the game, which will show a main menu (really, some text); when it's tapped, the game scene will appear:

1. First, create a new scene. Create a new SKScene subclass, and call it MenuScene.

2. Then add code that sets up the new scene. Add the didMoveToView method to the MenuScene class:

---

2. A notable exception is David O'Reilly's *Mountain* (*http://bit.ly/mtn_by_oreillly*), which is described by the author as a *relax-em-up*, in which the player is a mountain and therefore doesn't need to do anything at all.

```
override func didMoveToView(view: SKView) {

    let label = SKLabelNode(text: "Welcome to My Awesome Game")
    label.fontSize = 20

    label.position = CGPoint(x: self.size.width / 2.0,
                             y: self.size.height / 2.0)

    self.addChild(label)

}
```

3. Next, add code that responds to the user touching the screen. Add the touchesBe
gan(_, withEvent:) method:

```
override func touchesBegan(touches: NSSet, withEvent event: UIEvent) {
    let game = GameScene(size: self.size)

    let transition = SKTransition.moveInWithDirection(
        SKTransitionDirection.Right, duration: 0.5)

    self.view?.presentScene(game, transition: transition)
}
```

4. Finally, make the app start with this scene. Open *ViewController.swift*, and change
the code for the view controller so that it starts out with a MenuScene, like so:

```
let menuScene = MenuScene(size: self.view.bounds.size)

let skView = self.view as SKView

menuScene.scaleMode = .AspectFill
skView.presentScene(menuScene)
```

> A node won't respond to touches unless its userInteractionEnabled
> property is set to true. Only SKScene objects have this turned on by
> default; everything else, you'll need to manually enable.

Working with Textures

A *texture* is a chunk of image data that SpriteKit can use. If you've been following along
with the examples in this chapter, you've already used textures: the SKSpriteNode automatically converts images into textures as part of setting up.

Textures are generally the biggest consumers of memory that any game has, and SpriteKit automatically takes steps to minimize the memory usage of the textures in your

app. If you create two sprite notes that use the same image, SpriteKit will notice this and make them share the same image.

Most textures are loaded from images, with a few being generated at runtime by code. You can either do this automatically, such as when a sprite node is created, or you can directly create an SKTexture object to store and manage the texture memory.

You can also create *subtextures*—textures that use a subsection of another texture's image. This is useful for creating sprites in a game that need to be divided into smaller sections. For example:

```
let texture = SKTexture(imageNamed: "BlockSquareRed")
let rect = CGRect(x: 0.25, y: 0.25, width: 0.5, height: 0.5)
let subTexture = SKTexture(rect: rect, inTexture: texture)
```

Texture Atlases

Another way to save texture memory and improve performance is to bundle as many different pictures as possible into a single texture. This is more efficient for graphics cards, as each individual texture has its own overhead. It's better to have a hundred small pictures packed into a single texture than it is to have a hundred small pictures stored in individual textures.

One way you could do this in your game could be to load an SKTexture, and then manually create subtextures. However, this is a very tedious process, and would require massive amounts of work if the layout of the texture ever changed.

Instead, Xcode provides built-in support for generating *texture atlases*. All you need to do is create a folder whose name ends in *.atlas*, and put the individual images into it; at compile time, Xcode packs all of the images into one or more larger images and writes out a file indicating where each individual image can be found in the larger atlas image.

(((("SKTextureAtlas objectusing the SKTextureAtlas object. You create an SKTextur eAtlas by providing the name of the folder you added to your project. Once you have a texture atlas, you can ask it to provide you with specific named textures:

```
let atlas = SKTextureAtlas(named: "Sprites")

let textureInAtlas = atlas.textureNamed("BlockSquareBlue")
```

You can also ask a texture atlas to provide an array of all the texture names that it contains:

```
let textureNames = atlas.textureNames as [String]
```

If you have an image stored in a texture atlas, you don't *need* to use the SKTextureAtlas class to access it. The SKTexture(image Named:) method actually searches all texture atlases to find the image you specify. The SKTextureAtlas class is designed to make it easier to group different textures together.

Working with Text

Sprites aren't the only things that the player wants to see. Sometimes, you've just got to show them text.

The SKLabelNode class is designed to show text to the user. SKLabelNode works just like SKSpriteNode, only it uses text that you specify in conjunction with a font that you provide to render an image that contains the text that you want (Figure 7-3).

The fonts available to display your text in vary between versions of iOS. Certain fonts are only available in certain versions of iOS; to our knowledge, fonts have never been *removed* from iOS, only added, but it pays to check to see if the font you want to use is available.

To that end, a great resource for checking this is the website *http://iosfonts.com*, which lists all fonts currently available in iOS, along with when they were added.

If you'd prefer to go straight to the source to find out which fonts you can use, you can ask iOS directly, using the UIFont class. Fonts are grouped into *family names* (e.g., the Helvetica font family contains Helvetica Bold Oblique, Helvetica Light, etc.). Each of these individual fonts have their own name, which you use when preparing an SKLabelNode.

To find out which fonts are available to use, you can use the UIFont class's family Names method, like so:

```
for familyName in UIFont.familyNames() as [String] {
    for fontName in UIFont.fontNamesForFamilyName(familyName)
        as [String] {
        println(fontName)
    }
}
```

Once you have a font you want to use, you simply create the SKLabelNode instance with the text you want to use:

```
let textLabel = SKLabelNode(text: "This is some text")
```

Once you've created it, prepare it with the font, size, and color you want to use:

```
textLabel.fontName = "Zapfino"
textLabel.fontSize = 30
textLabel.fontColor = UIColor.blueColor()
```

Label nodes can be aligned in different ways. By default, the center point of the label (i.e., the node's position in the scene) is equal to the baseline and the horizontal center of the text. However, you can change this by changing the node's `verticalAlignmentMode` and `horizontalAlignmentMode` properties:

```
textLabel.verticalAlignmentMode = .Top
textLabel.horizontalAlignmentMode = .Left
```

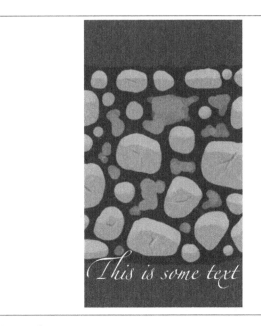

Figure 7-3. Text in the scene

Animating Content with Actions

The content of your game's scene is likely to need some animation. Animations in SpriteKit are done using the `SKAction` class, which represent changes in a node's state.

An `SKAction` represents a movement, rotation, change in color, or just about any other change that a node can have applied to it. Importantly, actions take place over time, and can be arranged into *sequences* and *groups*.

To use an `SKAction`, you first create one.

 There's a huge number of possible actions that you can use. For full details, see the class reference for `SKAction` in the Xcode documentation.

For example, to create an action that moves a node upwards by 50 pixels, you do this:

```
// Move upwards by 50 pixels
let moveAction = SKAction.moveBy(CGVector(dx: 0, dy:50), duration: 1.0)
```

Most actions can be *reversed* (i.e., they can be asked to generate an action that performs the opposite of what they do). Not all actions can be reversed, but all actions that have an obvious way of reversing themselves can. For example, to make an action that moves a node *down* by 50 pixels, you could simply reverse the action that was just demonstrated:

```
// Move down by 50 pixels
let moveBackAction = moveAction.reversedAction()
```

You can use actions to rotate a node, by creating a rotation action and giving it an angle. Note that this is measured in radians—while there are 360 degrees in a circle, there are 2π radians in a circle:

```
// Rotate by half a circle (n radians) over 1 second
let rotateAction = SKAction.rotateByAngle(CGFloat(M_PI), duration: 1.0)
```

You can also scale a node using actions:

```
// Scale to double normal size over half a second
let scaleAction = SKAction.scaleTo(2.0, duration: 0.5)
```

Actions can be grouped together, using the group method. This method takes an array of actions, and returns a single action; when this action is run, all of the actions in the array are started at the same time:

```
// Grouping actions means the actions run together
let rotateWhileScaling = SKAction.group([rotateAction, scaleAction])
```

If you want to run actions one after another, you use a *sequence*. These are created in a similar way to groups, in that you provide an array of actions; the resulting action, when started, kicks off each action one at a time, and waits for the current action to finish before starting the next:

```
// Sequences mean the actions run one after the other
let rotateThenScale = SKAction.sequence([rotateAction, scaleAction])
```

Finally, to actually run actions on a node, you use the node's runAction method:

```
// Run an action on a node using runAction
textLabel.runAction(repeatingMoveAction)
```

Using Shape Nodes

While sprite nodes show pictures and label nodes show text, you often want to quickly show some kind of generic shape (e.g., a rectangle, a circle, a triangle, etc.). This is where *shape nodes* come in (Figure 7-4).

To create a shape node that draws a rectangle, you can use the `ShapeNode(rectOf Size:)` method, like so:

```
let shapeNode = SKShapeNode(rectOfSize: CGSize(width: 50.0, height: 50.0))
```

Shape nodes can also use a `UIBezierPath` to draw a shape. The advantages of Beziér paths include the fact that they can describe almost any shape you want, which means you can display them using a shape node. Beziér paths are discussed in detail in "Creating Custom Paths" on page 128:

```
// Can also provide a custom path
let path = UIBezierPath(ovalInRect: CGRect(x: 0,
                                           y: 0,
                                           width: 50,
                                           height: 70))
let shapeNodeWithPath = SKShapeNode(path: path.CGPath,
                                    centered: true)
```

Once you've created a shape node, you configure its various properties. These include the colors used to both fill the shape as well as to draw its outline, how thick the lines should be, and whether or not the shape should have a glow:

```
shapeNode.lineWidth = 4.0
shapeNode.lineCap = kCGLineCapRound
shapeNode.strokeColor = UIColor.whiteColor()
shapeNode.fillColor = UIColor.redColor()
shapeNode.glowWidth = 4.0
```

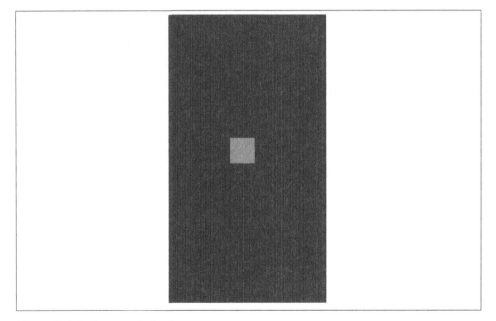

Figure 7-4. A shape node in the scene

Using Image Effect Nodes

Image effect nodes allow you to create sophisticated visual effects with SpriteKit—things like blurring, color shifting, and other nifty effects.

Image effect nodes, which are implemented using the SKEffectNode class, work in a different way to the other kinds of nodes previously discussed in this chapter. While the other nodes add something new to the scene, like images or text, image effect nodes instead change their *children*. This means that you could create, say, a blur effect, and then add nodes underneath it; all of its children would then be blurred (Figure 7-5).

Image effects get their power through the CIFilter API. CIFilter objects are *Core Image filters*, which have been a part of iOS and OS X for some time. They're best known for their use in Instagram, where they provide the color shifting and tinting effects; now, thanks to SpriteKit, you can use them to modify your game in real time.

To create an image effect node, we're going to use a Gaussian blur filter as an example. Before you can create an image effect node, you first have to create the image effect itself. In the case of a Gaussian blur, this means asking the CIFilter class to create a CIGaussianBlur filter, and then configuring that filter's blurring radius:

```
let blurFilter = CIFilter(name: "CIGaussianBlur")
blurFilter.setDefaults()
blurFilter.setValue(5.0, forKey: "inputRadius")
```

Once you've created your image effect, you then create the image effect node, and provide it with your effect:

```
let blurEffectNode = SKEffectNode()
blurEffectNode.filter = blurFilter
blurEffectNode.shouldEnableEffects = true
self.addChild(blurEffectNode)
```

 By default, an image effect node will not apply its CIFilter unless you set shouldEnableEffects to true.

Once you've added the image effect node to the scene, you then add nodes underneath it. Those nodes will then have the CIFilter applied to them.

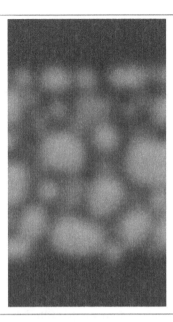

Figure 7-5. A blurred sprite, using an SKEffectNode

 It's worth pointing out that SKScenes are image effect nodes. This means that you can just give the scene a CIFilter, and the whole scene will be affected by it:

```
self.filter = blurFilter
```

Note that image effects might impact the performance of your game.

Adding Physics to SpriteKit Objects

SpriteKit comes bundled with a built-in 2D physics engine. This means that your sprites get physical interactions for free—they get affected by gravity, collide with each other, and can be attached to each other. This gives you a lot of power for very little development effort.

To enable physics in your game, all you need to do is create a SKPhysicsBody object and attach it to each node that you want to have physical properties. Once attached to a node, it will start being affected by gravity, and collide with other objects that have their own bodies.

When you create a body, you also specify its collision shape. This can be different to the overall shape of the sprite—for example, you could have a basketball sprite with a rectangular physics body, which wouldn't be able to roll:

```
let body = SKPhysicsBody(rectangleOfSize: shapeNode.frame.size)
shapeNode.physicsBody = body
```

Once you've got a physics body, you'll likely want to configure its mass. In SpriteKit, mass is measured in kilograms. So, to set a body's mass to 1 kilogram, you do this:

```
body.mass = 1.0
```

When working with physics in SpriteKit, it's *very* useful to see the behind-the-scenes outlines of where your physics bodies are. This allows you to work out if you've got a problem with objects appearing to bounce off things that don't appear to be there, and other annoying bugs. To enable physics debugging in SpriteKit, you simply turn on showsPhysics on your SKView:

```
self.view?.showsPhysics = true
```

Usually, physics bodies represent complete, enclosed shapes—rectangles, polygons, circles, and the like. However, you can also create physics bodies that are composed entirely of disconnected edges. These are useful for, among other things, creating boundary walls for your game.

To create a physics body that represents a connected loop of edges, you use the SKPhysicsBody(edgeLoopFromRect:) method. Bodies made up of edges are never affected by gravity:

```
let wallsBody = SKPhysicsBody(edgeLoopFromRect: self.frame)
```

Because the scene is a node, you can attach physics bodies to the scene itself. So, to attach this edge loop to the scene, you simply do this:

```
self.physicsBody = wallsBody
```

Adding Joints to SpriteKit Objects

When nodes have physics bodies, they can be attached to each other. This is accomplished using *joints*, which describe a relationship between two physics bodies.

Joints in SpriteKit are represented by subclasses of the SKPhysicsJoint class. There are several different kinds of joints built into SpriteKit. For example:

SKPhysicsJointFixed
> The two bodies are fixed, and cannot move relative to each other. They're still allowed to move around, but they're tied together.

SKPhysicsJointSpring
> The two bodies are allowed to move relative to each other, but if they get too far apart, a force will be applied to push them back together.

SKPhysicsJointSliding

The two bodies are allowed to move relative to each other, but only along a single axis.

SKPhysicsJointPin

One object is *pinned* to another—it can rotate, but can't move.

To create a joint, you simply create an instance of the type of joint you want to create, and then add it to your scene's `physicsWorld`. When you create a joint, you specify the two `SKPhysicsBody` objects that the joint should constrain:

```
let pinJoint = SKPhysicsJointPin.jointWithBodyA(hingeNode.physicsBody,
                                    bodyB: shapeNode.physicsBody,
                                    anchor: hingeNode.position)

self.physicsWorld.addJoint(pinJoint)
```

Lighting SpriteKit Scenes

Lighting a scene can bring a game to life. SpriteKit has built-in support for lights and shadowing, and you don't have to do much work to get great results.

Lights in SpriteKit are represented by the `SKLightNode` class. This node is invisible on its own, but causes lighting effects to get applied to nearby sprite nodes.

 Lights are *only* applied to sprite nodes. They won't apply to label nodes, for example.

To create a light node, you create it and configure it with a color:

```
let light = SKLightNode()
light.enabled = true
light.lightColor = UIColor.yellowColor()
```

The position of the light node determines where the light is shining from. Once you've got it set up, you simply add it to your scene.

Lighting a sprite is expensive, which means you need to specify what nodes should get lit up by your lights. This is done through *bitmasks*: if the result of a logical AND between the bitmask of a light and a sprite node results in a `true` value, the sprite is lit up.

This means that you need to specify both a category bitmask for the light, as well as a lighting bitmask for the node that you want to be lit:

```
// Light all nodes
light.categoryBitMask = 0xFFFFFFFF
```

```
// This node will be lit, because 0xFFFFFFFF AND 0x1 = true
spriteNode.lightingBitMask = 0x1
```

Constraints

Nodes can be *constrained* to each other: you can tell SpriteKit to ensure that one node is always at the same position as another, or that it should always be pointing at a node. Constraints are significantly cheaper than full-on physics, and are easier to set up. They're also a lot less prone to annoying problems; however, they're nowhere near as powerful.

To create a constraint, you create an instance of the SKConstraint class, and provide information on how the constraint should work. Once you have that, you apply it to the node that you want to constrain.

For example, to make one node point at another, you create an SKConstraint using the orientToNode(_, offset:) method:

```
let pointAtConstraint = SKConstraint.orientToNode(
    shapeNode, offset: SKRange(constantValue: 0.0))

pointingNode.constraints = [pointAtConstraint]
```

Using Shaders in SpriteKit

A *shader* is a custom program that lets you completely customize how SpriteKit should draw a node's contents. By default, SpriteKit handles everything in a fairly sane way: a texture is loaded and displayed, taking into account lighting where applicable.

However, custom shaders let you take things far beyond this. Using a custom shader, you have total control over the final color result of every pixel in a node. This means you can create refraction effects, reflection, generative textures, and more.

When you write shaders, you write a program in a language called *GLSL*, which is the OpenGL Shading Language. In addition to this written program, you provide data to it through special variables called *uniforms*.

To demonstrate this, we'll create a custom shader that renders the contents of a sprite as red. We'll then customize it to make chunks of the sprite transparent:

1. First, create the shader. Create a new empty file called *CustomShader.fsh*, and add it to your project.

2. Then add the shader code. Put the following code in the *CustomShader.fsh* file:

```
void main()
{
    // Get the original color
```

```
vec4 color = SKDefaultShading();

// Set the color to red
color = vec4(1.0, 0.0, 0.0, color.a);

// Multiply this by alpha to preserve transparency
color.rgb *= color.a;

// Return the finished color
gl_FragColor = color;
}
```

 .fsh stands for Fragment SHader. In computer graphics, a *fragment* is effectively another term for a pixel. The purpose of a fragment shader is to *shade* (i.e., determine the color of) each fragment that makes up the content of a sprite.

3. Next, create the `SKShader` object. Open *GameScene.swift*, and add the following code to the end of the `didMoveToView` method:

```
let shader = SKShader(fileNamed: "CustomShader")
spriteNode.shader = shader
```

When you run the application, the entire sprite will be bright red.

 The main() function of your shader needs to return a color that's premultiplied against the alpha channel. This means that if you're providing your own colors, you'll need to multiply them against the alpha channel that SpriteKit's already calculated.

This shader is very simple, and doesn't do much—it's hardcoded to use a red color. It would be significantly nicer if our code could configure the shader, so we'll add support for this now.

You provide data to your shaders through *uniforms*, which are represented by instances of the `SKUniform` class. Uniforms can be textures, floats, or arrays of floats (also known as *vectors*).

To provide a texture to your shader, you first acquire a texture from somewhere, and then put that in an `SKUniform`. You then provide that `SKUniform` to the `SKShader`. Once you've done that, you can modify your shader code to make use of the new uniform:

1. First, add the uniforms. Add the following code to the end of the `didMoveToView` method:

```
let noiseTexture = SKTexture(noiseWithSmoothness: 0.5,
                             size: CGSize(width: 256, height: 256),
                             grayscale: true)
let textureUniform = SKUniform(name: "noiseTexture",
                               texture: noiseTexture)
let thresholdUniform = SKUniform(name: "threshold", float: 0.5);

shader.addUniform(textureUniform)
shader.addUniform(thresholdUniform)
```

2. Then update the shader code. Replace the contents of *CustomShader.fsh* with the following code:

```
void main()
{
    // Get the original color for this pixel
    vec4 color = SKDefaultShading();

    // Get the corresponding point in the noise shader
    vec4 noiseSample = texture2D(noiseTexture, v_tex_coord);

    // If the noise value is below the threshold,
    // then set the alpha value to 0
    if (noiseSample.a < threshold) {
        color.a = 0.0;
    }

    // Premultiply the color channels (red, green, and blue)
    // with the alpha channel
    color.rgb *= color.a;

    // Return the finished color
    gl_FragColor = color;
}
```

When you run the application, the sprite will have holes in it (Figure 7-6). Try playing with the threshold uniform to vary the size of the holes.

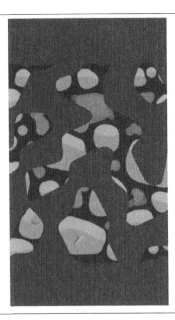

Figure 7-6. Using a custom shader

Using SpriteKit Editor

The SpriteKit editor is a feature built into Xcode that lets you visually compose a SpriteKit scene. This means that you don't have to manually type in the position and image name of each of your sprites—all you have to do is drag and drop them into place, just like you do with the Interface Builder.

The files that the SpriteKit editor creates can be loaded using the `SKScene` class's `SKScene(fileName:)` constructor. This loads the file, unpacks all of the nodes, and prepares the scene for launch. You still get to run your own setup code after this happens, using the `didMoveToView` method. Here's how it's done:

1. First, create a new SpriteKit scene file. Go to the File menu, and choose New → New File. Select the Resource section, and create a new SpriteKit scene. Name it `GameScene`.

   The file will be created, and when you select it in the project navigator, you'll be treated to a delightfully boring and empty scene.

2. Then drag in a Color Sprite. Find the Color Sprite, and drag it into the scene. A red box will appear.

3. Finally, make the game load the scene from the file. Open *ViewController.swift*, and replace the `viewDidLoad` method with the following code:

```
let scene = GameScene(fileNamed: "GameScene")

let skView = self.view as SKView

skView.presentScene(scene)
```

Run the app again. It'll look the same, but with the addition of the red box—this is because the scene first starts up with the red box, and then the code in didMoveTo View sets the background color, and adds the label.

CHAPTER 8

SceneKit

The SceneKit framework is a collection of classes that let you compose and present a 3D scene in your app. It works on both iOS and OS X, and is an incredibly simple way of drawing 3D graphics.

SceneKit is great for both games and apps that need to show some kind of 3D content. It also interacts seamlessly with Core Animation and SpriteKit, which means that you can use SceneKit in a variety of different contexts.

For example:

- You can make your entire app centered around SceneKit, and have all of your user interactions take place using a 3D view. Most games are likely to do this, to some extent.

- You can embed a 3D view as part of a larger document. The 3D graphs in Numbers, Apple's spreadsheet app, are an example of this kind of usage.

- You can render a SpriteKit scene on top of 3D graphics in a SceneKit scene, as an overlay.

- You can render SpriteKit scenes as textures *inside* a SceneKit scene. This means you can do things like render a 2D GUI in SpriteKit, and display them on a computer monitor in a 3D game.

SceneKit is also capable of loading 3D content from COLLADA, an industry-standard format for exchanging 3D graphics information. If you have any kind of 3D modeling program, it probably supports exporting 3D content in the COLLADA format, which you can import into your SceneKit scenes. If you don't have any 3D models to use, you can also use SceneKit to generate basic 3D objects, like cubes, spheres, and capsules.

SceneKit Structure

SceneKit presents everything through an SCNView, which is a subclass of either UI View or NSView, depending on your platform. Inside your SCNView, you create and prepare a *scene*, which is represented by the SCNScene class. Scenes contain *nodes*, which are composed into a *scene graph*: a node has zero or more children, and has a single parent.

On their own, nodes are invisible—all they do is exist in a scene. To make things visible to the user, you attach items to nodes. The items you can attach include:

Geometry
These are 3D objects, such as cubes, text, or models loaded from disk.

Cameras
These determine the position and the angle from which the user can view the scene.

Lights
These cast light into the scene, and illuminate objects.

Physics bodies
These cause physical effects to be applied to the objects in your scene, such as collisions and gravity.

A scene, therefore, is composed of a collection of these nodes, with multiple different items attached to them.

In addition to these attached items, geometry objects have *materials* attached to them. Materials define how the geometry is rendered—what color to use, what textures to apply, and how the surface should react to light. You define these materials either through code or by loading them from a COLLADA file; SceneKit then takes your settings, and turns them into the appropriate GLSL shader.

This chapter discusses using SceneKit inside an SCNView, but this isn't the only way you can use SceneKit in your apps. If you have a Core Animation layer hierarchy, you can create and use an SCNLayer; additionally, if you've written your own OpenGL renderer, you can take advantage of SceneKit's functionality through the SCNRenderer class, which emits OpenGL commands at a time that you control. This is a bit outside of the scope of this chapter, but it's worth knowing that it's there; check the class documentation for SCNLayer and SCNRender er in the Xcode documentation for more details.

Working with SceneKit

To demonstrate how SceneKit works, this chapter will walk through a simple tutorial app that shows how the different parts of SceneKit fit together.

To get started, we'll create a simple iOS app, and configure a SceneKit view. We'll then start adding more and more stuff to it.

 SceneKit works on OS X as well as iOS. If you'd prefer to do this on the Mac, just make a Cocoa application, add a SceneKit view to your window, connect it to your App Delegate, and continue from there.

Adding a SceneKit View

The first thing to do will be to create the app and make it use an `SCNView`:

1. Create a new, single view iOS application, and call it `SceneKit`.
2. Next, add the SceneKit framework. Select the project at the top of the project navigator, and the project settings will appear. Scroll down to the Linked Frameworks and Libraries section, and click the + button below the list.

   Select "SceneKit.framework" from the list that appears.
3. The next step is to make the application create a SceneKit scene when the app starts up.

   We want to make the storyboard use an `SCNView`. Open the application's storyboard file, and select the view inside the main view controller.

   Open the Identity Inspector, and change the view's class from `UIView` to `SCNView`.

   The storyboard will now use a SceneKit view as its main view.

Once you've got a SceneKit view, you can begin configuring it. The first thing we'll do in this example is set its background color; later, we'll add 3D graphics to it. To set the background color of the scene view, open *ViewController.swift* and add the following code to the `viewDidLoad` method:

```
let sceneView = self.view as SCNView
sceneView.backgroundColor = UIColor.grayColor()
```

The first step in working with the SceneKit view is to cast it to the apporiate type, using the `as` operator. Once you've done that, changing the background ensures that you've got a visible result. You can see the result in Figure 8-1.

Figure 8-1. An empty SceneKit view

Adding a Scene

The next step is to add a *scene* to the SceneKit view. To create the scene, add the following code to the end of viewDidLoad:

```
let scene = SCNScene()
sceneView.scene = scene
```

An SCNScene object is the container for all of your SceneKit objects. Anything that you want to show to the user will be placed inside the scene. Note that while you can have multiple scenes, only one is visible in the view at a time.

On its own, an empty scene is kind of boring. To improve this, we're going to add two things: a 3D capsule shape, and a camera to view it with.

Adding a Camera

Cameras in SceneKit are your portals into the 3D scene. They're your virtual eyes into the 3D world; what you see depends on their position, their angle, and a few other parameters that you've configured, such as their field of view or whether they're a perspective or orthographic camera.

We'll start by adding a camera first, and then add the capsule shape. To add the camera, include the following code at the end of the `viewDidLoad` method:

```
let camera = SCNCamera()
camera.xFov = 45
camera.yFov = 45
```

This code creates an `SCNCamera` object, and indicates to it that its field of view is 45 degrees both horizontally and vertically.

 The human eye has a field of vision that's roughly 180 degrees horizontally and 90 degrees vertically. However, because an iPhone or iPad takes up only a part of the user's field of vision, your 3D scene won't look correct if you use too wide an angle. Play around with different numbers and see what works best for your app or game.

On its own, however, an `SCNCamera` does nothing—it isn't in the scene, and it has no position from which the player can see the 3D scene. It needs to be added to an `SCNNode` first, because nodes are the objects that have positions and attachments to the scene.

To that end, the next step is to attach the camera to a node. To do that, add the following code to the end of the `viewDidLoad` method:

```
let cameraNode = SCNNode()
cameraNode.camera = camera

cameraNode.position = SCNVector3(x: 0, y: 0, z: 20)

scene.rootNode.addChildNode(cameraNode)
```

An `SCNNode` is empty on its own. You need to add items to it, such as the camera, in order to make it do useful work.

Once you create the node, it's given a position in 3D space. In this example, we're setting it to the location (0, 0, 20), which means that it's centered on the x- and y-axes, but moved back by about 20 meters.

The final step with any node is to add it to the scene. You do this by adding it as a *child node* of any other node that's also in the scene. If there aren't any nodes in the scene yet, you can add it to the scene's *root node*, which is the top level of the scene.

If you run the application, you'll see no difference from before, because the camera has nothing to look at—there's just the featureless gray void. To address this stark nihilistic horror, we'll add an object.

Adding a 3D Object

The object that we're adding to the scene will be a capsule. There are two stages to this: first, we create the capsule's *geometry*, which defines the shape. Next, we attach that geometry to an SCNNode, so that it's located somewhere in the scene:

1. To create the capsule's geometry, add the following code to the end of viewDidLoad:

   ```
   let capsule = SCNCapsule(capRadius: 2.5, height: 10)
   ```

   The SCNCapsule class is a subclass of the more generic . There are a wide va riety of other types of geometries you can use, including boxes (`SCNBox), pyramids (SCNPyramid), toruses (SCNTorus), as well as text (SCNText), which we'll be spending some more time talking about later in this chapter.

   Once you've created some geometry, you attach it to a node and place that node in the scene somewhere.

2. Then add the geometry to a node. To do so, include the following code at the end of the viewDidLoad method:

   ```
   let capsuleNode = SCNNode(geometry: capsule)
   capsuleNode.position = SCNVector3(x: 0, y: 0, z: 0)
   scene.rootNode.addChildNode(capsuleNode)
   ```

> Setting the node's position to (0,0,0) doesn't actually change anything, as that's the default position of all nodes. It's included here just for clarity.

Now, when you run the application, you'll see a capsule shape, as seen in Figure 8-2. However, the first thing you'll notice about it is that it's entirely white—there's no lights in the scene, so SceneKit is simply displaying every part of the object as full-brightness white.

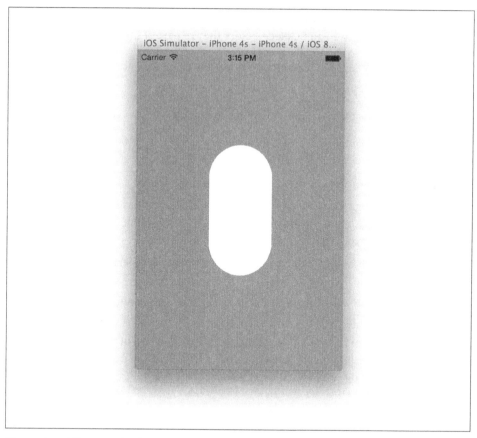

Figure 8-2. The capsule shape

Adding Lights

To improve the picture, we're going to add some lights. In 3D graphics, there are a number of different types of lights that can be used:

- *Ambient lights*, which cast an even light across the entire scene
- *Omni lights*, also known as *point lights*, which radiate light in all directions from a single point
- *Directional lights*, which cast light in a single direction
- *Spotlights*, which cast light from a single position in a given direction

We're going to add two lights to the scene: an omni light, which will provide the main light of the scene, as well as an ambient light, which will fill in the rest of the scene:

Lights in SceneKit are represented by the SCNLight class. Just like SCNCamera objects, lights need to be attached to an SCNNode before they're part of the scene.

1. To create the ambient light, add the following code to the end of viewDidLoad:

```
let ambientLight = SCNLight()
ambientLight.type = SCNLightTypeAmbient
ambientLight.color = UIColor(white: 0.25, alpha: 1.0)

let ambientLightNode = SCNNode()
ambientLightNode.light = ambientLight

scene.rootNode.addChildNode(ambientLightNode)
```

The light is configured with two main properties. The first is its type, which we're setting to SCNLightTypeAmbient to make it an ambient light. The next is its color; we're setting that to be a 25% brightness white light.

When you attach an SCNLight to an SCNNode's light property, that node begins emitting light.

2. The next step is to add the omni light, which is a very similar process to that of adding the omni light.

To create the omni light, add the following code to the end of viewDidLoad:

```
let omniLight = SCNLight()
omniLight.type = SCNLightTypeOmni
omniLight.color = UIColor(white: 1.0, alpha: 1.0)

let omniLightNode = SCNNode()
omniLightNode.light = omniLight
omniLightNode.position = SCNVector3(x: -5, y: 8, z: 5)

scene.rootNode.addChildNode(omniLightNode)
```

This creates an omni light, attaches it to a node, and positions it up and to the left a little. The result is shown in Figure 8-3.

Animating Content in the Scene

Content in an SCNScene can be animated: you can move it around, fade colors up and down, rotate, and more. Importantly, you can also combine animations, and take advantage of node parenting: if you apply a movement animation to a node, it will move all of its child nodes along with it.

In SceneKit, animations are represented using the CAAnimation class. This means that if you're familiar with using Core Animation to animate content in your apps, you already know how to animate your 3D scenes.

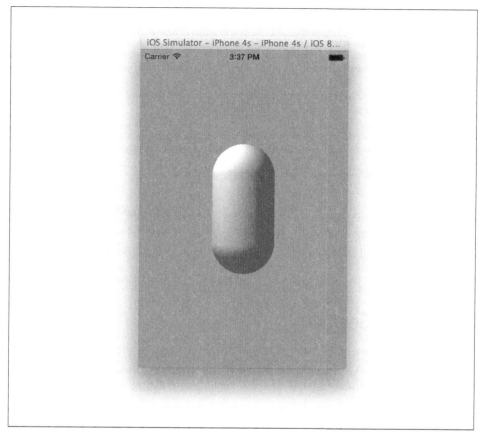

Figure 8-3. The lit capsule

 Each thing in your scene has different properties that can be animated. Most of the obviously animatable properties can be animated, such as position and orientation; to see if a specific property can be animated, check out the class documentation for the item you want to animate. Anything that can be animated in SceneKit is marked with a little "Animatable" comment.

We're going to add an animation that makes the capsule smoothly move up and down:

1. To create the animation object, add the following code to the end of `viewDidLoad`:

```
// This animation changes the 'position' property
let moveUpDownAnimation = CABasicAnimation(keyPath: "position")

// Move 5 units on the y-axis (i.e., up)
```

```
moveUpDownAnimation.byValue =
    NSValue(SCNVector3: SCNVector3(x: 0, y: 5, z: 0))
// Accelerate and decelerate at the ends, instead of
// mechanically bouncing
moveUpDownAnimation.timingFunction =
    CAMediaTimingFunction(name: kCAMediaTimingFunctionEaseInEaseOut)

// Animation automatically moves back at the end
moveUpDownAnimation.autoreverses = true

// Animation repeats an infinite number of times (i.e., loops forever)
moveUpDownAnimation.repeatCount = Float.infinity

// The animation takes 2 seconds to run
moveUpDownAnimation.duration = 2.0
```

2. Once an animation object has been created, you add it to a node, using the addAni
   mation(_, forKey:) method. Add the following code to the end of viewDidLoad:

```
capsuleNode.addAnimation(moveUpDownAnimation, forKey: "updown")
```

When you run the application, the capsule will be slowly moving up and down.

Creating Text Geometry

When we created the capsule, we created an instance of the SCNCapsule class, which
represents the geometry of a capsule. There are many other types of geometry classes
available, and one of them in particular is especially interesting to graphics programmers: SCNText.

The SCNText class is a subclass of the SCNGeometry class that generates geometry that
represents text. All you need to do is to give it your text and a font to use, and it creates
geometry that you can attach to a node. Once you've done that, you've got 3D text.

When configuring your SCNText object on iOS, you provide a UIFont.
On OS X, you provide an NSFont.

We'll now add some text to the scene. This will be added as a child node of the capsule,
which means that it will move with the capsule without us having to add any new logic
to support it. To create the text geometry, add the following code to the end of
viewDidLoad:

```
let text = SCNText(string: "SceneKit!", extrusionDepth: 0.2)

// text will be 2 units (meters) high
```

```
text.font = UIFont.systemFontOfSize(2)
let textNode = SCNNode(geometry: text)
// Positioned slightly to the left, and above the
// capsule (which is 10 units high)
textNode.position = SCNVector3(x: -2, y: 6, z: 0)

// Add the text node to the capsule node (not the scene's root node!)
capsuleNode.addChildNode(textNode)
```

When you run the app, you'll see text hovering above the capsule, and moving with it (see Figure 8-4).

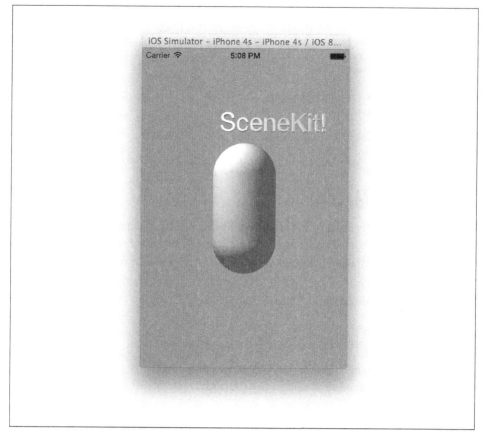

Figure 8-4. The text hovers above the capsule

Combining Animations

When a node is a child of another node, it inherits all animations of the parent. This is why the text moves with the capsule—the animation is changing the position of the capsule, and the text's position is defined relative to the capsule's position.

You can add animations to child nodes, and they won't affect the parent node. Instead, the animations will be combined together. For example, if you add a rotation animation to the text node (which is, as you'll remember, a child of the capsule), the text node will rotate *and* move up and down.

You can see this in action by creating an animation of your own. To add the rotation animation, include the following code at the end of `viewDidLoad`:

```
// Rotate one full circle (2π) around the Y (up) axis
let rotate = CABasicAnimation(keyPath: "eulerAngles")
rotate.byValue =
    NSValue(SCNVector3: SCNVector3(x: Float(0.0),
                                   y: Float(M_PI * 2.0),
                                   z: Float(0.0)))

// Do it forever
rotate.repeatCount = Float.infinity

// Take 4 seconds doing it
rotate.duration = 4.0

textNode.addAnimation(rotate, forKey: "rotation")
```

When you run the animation, you'll see the text spinning and moving at the same time.

Working with Materials

A *material* defines how an object is rendered. By default, all objects are made of a plain, white, nonshiny material. However, you can change pretty much every aspect of this. Among other things, you can change:

The diffuse component
    The material's base color, its texture, and so on

The specular component
    How shiny the material is, and how light should reflect off it

The emissive component
    Whether the material should appear to be emitting light[1]

The normal component
    Whether the surface of the material should have additional detail for light to bounce off

---

1. This is a different concept from `SCNLight` objects. When an object has an emissive material, it doesn't cast light onto other nearby objects, but rather it looks to the camera like the surface is glowing.

A material in SceneKit is represented by the SCNMaterial class. Each material object has a variety of *material properties*, which map to the items in the preceding list.

Material properties are represented by the SCNMaterialProperty class, which each have a contents property. You can assign a variety of different things to this property:

- Colors
- Images (either NSImage, UIImage, or CGImageRef objects)
- SpriteKit textures (SKTexture)
- SpriteKit scenes (SKScene)

To demonstrate, we're going to apply a texture to the text node, and a shiny metallic surface to the capsule. To create the capsule's red surface, add the following code to the end of viewDidLoad:

```
let redMetallicMaterial = SCNMaterial()
redMetallicMaterial.diffuse.contents = UIColor.redColor()
redMetallicMaterial.specular.contents = UIColor.whiteColor()
redMetallicMaterial.shininess = 1.0
capsule.materials = [redMetallicMaterial]
```

When you want to apply a material to an object, you apply it to its geometry. Geometries can have multiple materials—for example, a car might be composed of its main chassis, which should be opaque and metallic, and its windows, which should be semi-transparent. For this reason, when you apply materials to geometry, you actually provide an *array* of materials.

In the preceding example, the contents property of both the diffuse and specular material properties were set to a UIColor. This has the effect of using a uniform color over the entire surface. However, if you provide an image to the contents property, the color that's used on the surface will be taken from the image.

You can provide any image you like. However, one useful thing in SceneKit is the ability to use SpriteKit textures (i.e., SKTexture objects) as contents for material properties. This means that you can use SpriteKit's SKTexture(noiseWithSmoothness:, size:, grayscale:) method to generate a texture filled with random noise, and then use that in your scene. In this next example, we'll do just that:

1. To generate the texture, add the following code to the viewDidLoad method:

```
let noiseTexture = SKTexture(noiseWithSmoothness: 0.25,
    size: CGSize(width: 512, height: 512), grayscale: true)
```

Once the texture is generated, it can then be used in a material.

2. Then create a material for the text node. You'll need to add the following code to the end of the viewDidLoadMethod:

```
let noiseMaterial = SCNMaterial()
noiseMaterial.diffuse.contents = noiseTexture

text.materials = [noiseMaterial]
```

When you run the application, the capsule should be bright red, and the text should have a noise pattern applied over it, as seen in Figure 8-5.

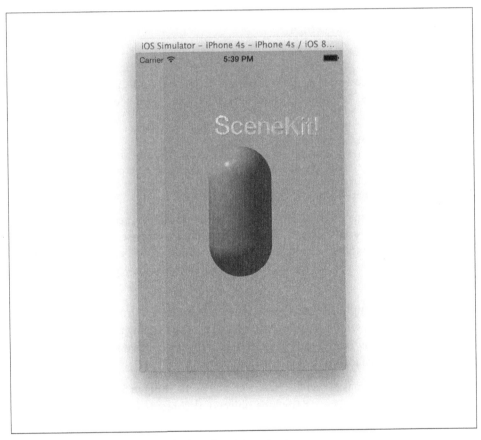

Figure 8-5. The materials, applied to the objects in the scene

Normal Mapping

When a light hits a surface, the light waves bounce off the surface and and enter the camera. The amount of light that's reflected back at the camera depends on the angle at which the light hit the surface. This is described by *Lambert's cosine law*, which states that the apparent brightness of a surface depends on the cosine of the angle between the light's direction and the *normal* of the surface.

The normal of a surface is the direction that's perpendicular to the surface. For example, if you closed this book and put it down on the table, the normal of the book's front cover would point straight up.

For each polygon that you want to light in a SceneKit scene, the normal of that polygon needs to be calculated. SceneKit does this behind the scenes for you, and it does a decent job of it. However, if you want more detail in your lighting, you'd need to have more polygons. This can lead to performance problems, as it's more effort for a graphics chip to process a large number of polygons.

Instead, 3D graphics use a technique called *normal mapping*. Normal mapping involves taking a texture, and using it to work out how light should bounce off the surface at any given point.

Normal mapping means that you get to fake having a higher detail model than you actually do. It's also very easy to implement: all you need to do is to get a normal map, which is just an image, and apply that to the `normal` property of your material.

 Normal maps are usually generated by other software, such as 3D modeling tools. However, SpriteKit has support for generating an approximate normal map from any given texture.

To implement a rough normal map that makes the capsule look very slightly beaten up, we're going to first create a normal map from the noise texture, and then apply that to the capsule's material:

1. To create the normal map texture, the noise texture needs to generate a normal-mapped version of itself. Add the following code to the end of the `viewDidLoad` method:

   ```
   let noiseNormalMapTexture =
       noiseTexture.textureByGeneratingNormalMapWithSmoothness(0.1,
           contrast: 1.0)
   ```

2. Apply the normal map to the capsule's material:

   ```
   redMetallicMaterial.normal.contents = noiseNormalMapTexture
   ```

When you run the app, the capsule will appear very slightly deformed. You can see the result in Figure 8-6.

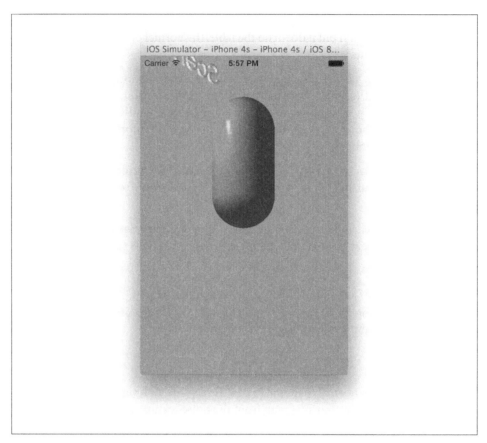

Figure 8-6. The normal-mapped capsule

Hit Testing

Hit testing is the process of taking a position in the view and working out which objects in the 3D are underneath that point in the view. In practical terms, it's an answer to the question, "What objects am I clicking on or touching?"

When you hit test a SceneKit view, you get back an array of SCNHitTestResult objects, which describe the objects that were found, as well as information like the exact point in 3D space at which the touch or click was, relative to the object.

Hit testing is one of the primary ways in which you interact with a 3D scene, and it allows you to implement things like buttons, object selection, and more. To demonstrate this, we're going to extend the application to make any object that's tapped on briefly glow.

The glow effect will be achieved by animating the emission property of the object from black (invisible) to yellow. To detect the taps themselves, we're going to use a UITap GestureRecognizer:

1. To create and add the tap gesture recognizer, add the following code to the view DidLoad method:

```
let tapRecognizer
    = UITapGestureRecognizer(target: self, action: "tapped:")
sceneView.addGestureRecognizer(tapRecognizer)
sceneView.userInteractionEnabled = true
```

 By default, SceneKit views don't have user interaction enabled. You need to manually turn on the userInteractionEnabled property for gesture recognizers to work.

2. Next, you need to add the method that responds to the user tapping the view. To implement the tap handler method, add the following method to the View Controller class:

```
func tapped(tapRecognizer: UITapGestureRecognizer) {
    // If a tap has happened:
    if tapRecognizer.state == UIGestureRecognizerState.Ended {

        // Find the object that was tapped
        let sceneView = self.view as SCNView
        let hits = sceneView.hitTest(tapRecognizer.locationInView(
                            tapRecognizer.view),
                            options: nil) as [SCNHitTestResult]

        // Make all selected items highlight
        for hit in hits {

            // Get the first material, if one exists
            if let theMaterial =
                hit.node.geometry?.materials?[0] as? SCNMaterial {
                // Animate from black to yellow
                let highlightAnimation =
                    CABasicAnimation(keyPath: "contents")
                highlightAnimation.fromValue = UIColor.blackColor()
                highlightAnimation.toValue = UIColor.yellowColor()
                highlightAnimation.autoreverses = true
                highlightAnimation.repeatCount = 0
                highlightAnimation.duration = 0.3

                // Apply this animation to the material's
```

```
            // emission property
            theMaterial.emission.addAnimation(
                highlightAnimation, forKey: "highlight")
        }

    }
}
}
```

Run the application. Tap on the capsule, and marvel at the wonder of it briefly highlighting, as seen in Figure 8-7.

Figure 8-7. The capsule, highlighting yellow

Constraints

You can add *constraints* to nodes. Constraints are rules that affect a node's position and orientation; for example, you can add a rule that says, in effect, "your orientation should always be pointing toward another node." Constraints, in conjunction with animations, physics, or user input, allow you to quickly set up complex scenes and relationships between nodes. Constraints are implemented using the SCNConstraint class, and there are a variety of different subclasses available for you to use.

To demonstrate constraints, we're going to add a little pyramid, and make it rotate to *watch* the capsule going up and down:

1. Adding the pyramid is simple: it involves creating some pyramid geometry, attaching it to a node, and then attaching the node to the scene. Add the following code to the end of the viewDidLoad method:

    ```
    let pointer = SCNPyramid(width: 0.5, height: 0.9, length: 4.0)
    let pointerNode = SCNNode(geometry: pointer)
    pointerNode.position = SCNVector3(x: -5, y: 0, z: 0)

    scene.rootNode.addChildNode(pointerNode)
    ```

2. To implement the constraint, add the following code:

    ```
    let lookAtConstraint = SCNLookAtConstraint(target: capsuleNode)

    // When enabled, the constraint will try to rotate
    // around only a single axis
    lookAtConstraint.gimbalLockEnabled = true
    pointerNode.constraints = [lookAtConstraint]
    ```

Run the application. You'll see something similar to Figure 8-8—a pyramid will be visible to the left of the capsule, and rotates to *look* at the capsule as it moves.

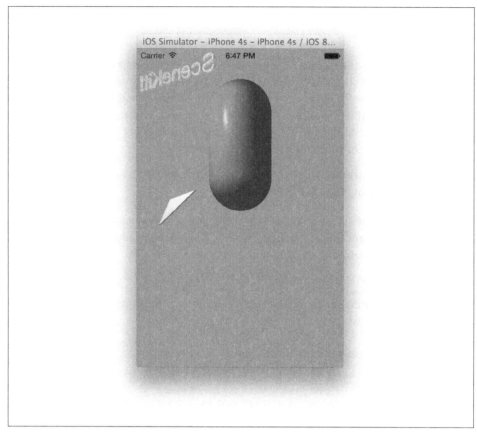

Figure 8-8. The pyramid, constrained to look toward the capsule

Loading Data from COLLADA Files

The COLLADA file format is an industry-standard XML format for exchanging 3D graphics information. COLLADA files can contain a wide variety of useful things, including geometry info (i.e., meshes), materials, textures, and even complete scenes with a node hierarchy.

It's not fun having to build your scenes entirely in code, and SceneKit is able to make use of COLLADA files to simplify the process.

Pretty much any modern 3D modeling tool out there can export to the COLLADA file format. If you don't have one, or don't want to get one, you'll find a simple COLLADA file that contains a squid… *thing* that Jon made in the sample code provided with this book. Jon is very proud of his squid thing.

COLLADA files are similar to *libraries*—you can reach into them and pull out only the items that you want, such as materials, or specific models. Alternatively, you can treat them as entire scenes, and give them to SceneKit to render. In this example, we're going to take the example *Critter* COLLADA file and pull a node out of it, and then display it in the scene.

The first step when working with any file in your project is adding it. Find your COLLADA file (it has the extension *.dae*) and drag and drop it into the project navigator. In the pop-up box that appears, ensure that the "Copy items if needed" checkbox is selected.

Xcode has built-in support for viewing and modifying COLLADA files. If you select the file *Critter.dae* in the project navigator, the COLLADA editor will open, and you can view the contents of the file, as shown in Figure 8-9.

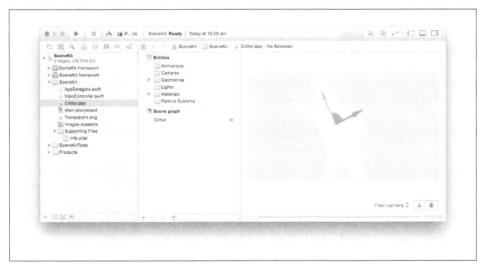

Figure 8-9. The SceneKit COLLADA editor

COLLADA files are arranged in a tree-like structure, much like your SceneKit scenes. If you look at the Outline view at the left of the editor, you'll notice that the scene graph contains a single node, called *Critter* (see Figure 8-10). This node can be loaded by your code and inserted into your scene.

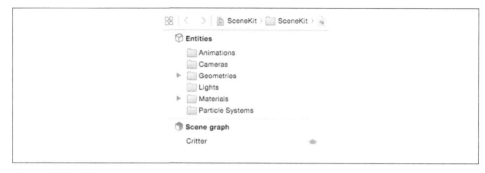

Figure 8-10. The scene graph

You can ask Cocoa to give you an NSURL that refers to the location of this file. Once you have *that*, you can construct a COLLADA file loader.

The file loader is represented by the SCNSceneSource class; all you need to do is to give it a URL to load from:

1. First, load the data into an SCNSceneSource object. Add the following code to the end of the viewDidLoad method.

```
let critterDataURL =
    NSBundle.mainBundle().URLForResource("Critter",
        withExtension: "dae")
let critterData = SCNSceneSource(URL: critterDataURL!, options: nil)
```

2. COLLADA files contain named objects. As we saw earlier, there's a node called *Critter* in the scene graph; this can be accessed and inserted into the SKScene. To include the Critter node in the scene, add the following code to the end of the viewDidLoad method:

```
// Find the node called 'Critter'; if it exists, add it
let critterNode = critterData?.entryWithIdentifier("Critter",
    withClass: SCNNode.self) as? SCNNode
if critterNode != nil {
    critterNode?.position = SCNVector3(x: 5, y: 0, z: 0)
    scene.rootNode.addChildNode(critterNode!)
}
```

Run the game. The critter will be visible to the right of the capsule, as seen in Figure 8-11.

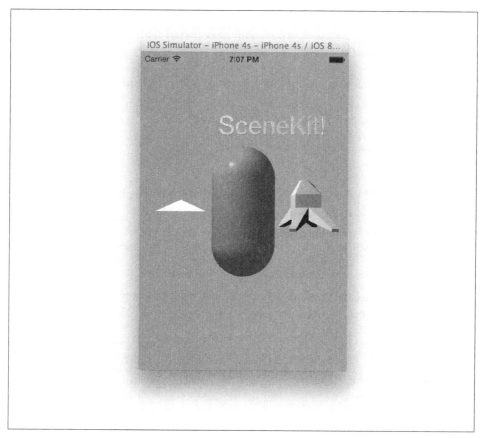

Figure 8-11. The critter, visible in the scene

Adding Physics to the Scene

SceneKit comes equipped with a 3D physics engine. Physics engines add physical simulation to your scene (i.e., they apply gravitational forces, detect and handle collisions, and generally add realism to the scene).

To add physics to a node in SceneKit, you create an instance of SCNPhysicsBody, and attach it to the node. Once the object has a physics body, it begins being affected by physics.

Physics bodies have their own requirements. In order to know how objects should collide with each other, the physics system needs to know about the object's physical shape. This is kept deliberately separate from the node's visible geometry, as you'll often have cases where you have a very high-detail object (like a super-sci-fi crate), but only need to represent that as a simple six-sided box. If you need to, though, you can create a physics shape with arbitrary geometry.

We'll start by creating the shape, and then use that to create the physics body. We can then add that to the critter mesh, which will make it start falling due to gravity. Here are the steps you'll need to follow:

1. To create the physics shape, add the following code to the end of `viewDidLoad`:

    ```
    var critterPhysicsShape : SCNPhysicsShape?
    if let geometry = critterNode?.geometry {
        critterPhysicsShape =
            SCNPhysicsShape(geometry: geometry,
                options: nil)
    }
    ```

2. Then, once the physics shape is ready, you can construct the physics body, and give it to the node. Add the following code:

    ```
    let critterPhysicsBody =
        SCNPhysicsBody(type: SCNPhysicsBodyType.Dynamic,
            shape: critterPhysicsShape)
    critterNode?.physicsBody = critterPhysicsBody
    ```

3. At this point, you can run the application. The critter object will begin falling, and will move off-screen.

 When you create a physics body, you provide a *type*. There are three different possible types:

- *Static* bodies never move. They're not affected by gravity, but objects collide with them. They're perfect for terrain and other fixed items in your scene.

- *Kinematic* bodies aren't affected by physical forces, but if an animation is running on them, they'll push other physics bodies out of the way. This means that they can be used, for example, as elevators.

- *Dynamic* bodies are affected by gravity and by other objects. If another object collides, they'll move.

There's one last thing to add: a floor for things to land on. The `SCNFloor` class, which defines the geometry of a floor, is perfect for this. We'll also create a physics body for this floor, and make it static, so that it stays locked in place and lets the critter land on it. To include a floor, add the following code to the end of the `viewDidLoad` method:

```
let floor = SCNFloor()
let floorNode = SCNNode(geometry: floor)
floorNode.position = SCNVector3(x: 0, y: -5, z: 0)
scene.rootNode.addChildNode(floorNode)
```

```
let floorPhysicsBody =
    SCNPhysicsBody(type: SCNPhysicsBodyType.Static,
        shape: SCNPhysicsShape(geometry: floor, options: nil))
floorNode.physicsBody = floorPhysicsBody
```

Run the application. You'll see a nice, shiny, reflective floor, like the one you see in Figure 8-12.

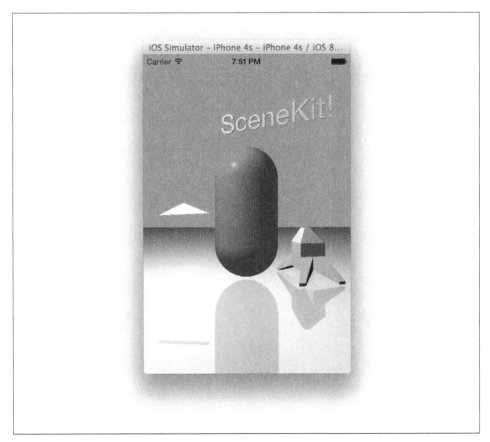

Figure 8-12. The final SceneKit scene

CHAPTER 9

Audio and Video

As we've seen, Cocoa and Cocoa Touch have a lot of support for displaying still images and text. The APIs also have great support for displaying video and audio—either separately or at the same time.

OS X and iOS have historically had APIs for displaying audiovisual (AV) content, but only recently did Apple introduce a comprehensive API for loading, playing, and otherwise working with AV content. This API, *AV Foundation*, is identical on both OS X and iOS, and is the one-stop shop for both AV playback and editing.

In this chapter, you'll learn how to use AV Foundation to display video and audio. We'll demonstrate how to use the framework in OS X, but the same API also applies to iOS.

You'll also learn how to access the user's photo library on iOS, as well as how to capture photos and videos using the built-in camera available on iOS and OS X.

 AV Foundation is a large and powerful framework, capable of performing very complex operations with audio and video. Final Cut Pro, Apple's professional-level video editing tool, uses AV Foundation for all of the actual work involved in editing video. Covering all the features of this framework is beyond the scope of this book, so we address only audio and video playback in this chapter. If you want to learn about the more advanced features in AV Foundation, check out the *AV Foundation Programming Guide* in the Xcode documentation (*http://bit.ly/abt_av_foundation*).

AV Foundation

AV Foundation is designed to load and play back a large number of popular audiovisual formats. The formats supported by AV Foundation are:

- QuickTime (*.mov* files)
- MPEG4 audio (including *.mp4*, *.m4a*, and *.m4v*)
- Wave, AIFF, and CAF audio
- Apple Lossless audio
- MP3 and AAC audio

From a coding perspective, there's no distinction between these formats—you simply tell AV Foundation to load the resource and start playing.

AV Foundation refers to media that can be played as an *asset*. Assets can be loaded from URLs (which can point to a resource on the Internet or a file stored locally), or they can be created from other assets (content creation apps, like iMovie, do this). In this chapter, we'll be looking at media loaded from URLs.

When you have a file you want to play—such as an H.264 movie or an MP3 file—you can create an AVPlayer to coordinate playback.

Playing Video with AVPlayer

The AVPlayer class is a high-level object that can play back any media that AV Foundation supports. AVPlayer is capable of playing both audio and video content, though if you only want to play back audio, AV Foundation provides an object dedicated to sound playback (AVAudioPlayer, discussed later). In this section, we talk about playing videos.

When you want to play back media, you create an AVPlayer and provide it with the URL of the video you want to play back:

```
let contentURL = NSURL(fileURLWithPath:"/Users/jon/Desktop/AVFile.m4v")
let player = AVPlayer(URL: contentURL)
```

When you set up a player with a content URL, the player will take a moment to get ready to play back the content. The amount of time needed depends on the content and where it's being kept. If it's a video file, the decoder will take longer to get ready than for an audio file, and if the file is hosted on the Internet, it will take longer to transfer enough data to start playing.

AVPlayer acts as the controller for your media playback. At its simplest, you can tell the player to just start playing:

```
player.play()
```

In the background, the `play` method actually just sets the playback rate to 1.0, which means that it should play back at normal speed. You could also start playback at half-speed by saying `player.rate = 0.5`. In the same vein, setting the rate to 0 pauses playback—which is exactly what the `pause` method does.

AVPlayerLayer

`AVPlayer` is only responsible for coordinating playback, not for displaying the video content to the user. If you want video playback to be visible, you need a Core Animation layer to display the content on.

AV Foundation provides a Core Animation layer called `AVPlayerLayer` that presents video content from the `AVPlayer`. Because it's a `CALayer`, you need to add it to an existing layer tree in order for it to be visible. We'll recap how to work with layers later in this chapter.

You create an `AVPlayerLayer` with the `AVPlayerLayer(player:)` method:

```
var playerLayer = AVPlayerLayer(player: player)
```

(Yes, we are now in tongue-twister territory.)

Once created, the player layer will display whatever image the `AVPlayer` you provided tells it to. It's up to you to actually size the layer appropriately and add it to the layer tree:

```
var view = UIView(frame: CGRectMake(0, 0, 640, 360))
playerLayer.frame = view.bounds
view.layer.addSublayer(playerLayer)
```

Once the player layer is visible, you can forget about it—all of the actual work involved in controlling video playback is handled by the `AVPlayer`.

Putting It Together

To demonstrate how to use `AVPlayer` and `AVPlayerLayer`, we'll build a simple video player application for OS X.

The same API applies to iOS and OS X.

Before you start building this project, download the sample video from the book's examples (*http://bit.ly/swift_dev_w_cocoa_ex*). Here are the steps you'll need to take to build the video player application:

1. First, create a new Cocoa application named VideoPlayer, and drag the sample video into the project navigator.

    The interface for this project will consist of an NSView, which will play host to the AVPlayerLayer, as well as buttons that make the video play back at normal speed, play back at one-quarter speed, and rewind.

    In order to add the AVPlayerLayer into the view, that view must be backed by a CALayer. This requires checking a checkbox in the Interface Builder—once that's done, the view will have a layer to which we can add the AVPlayerLayer as a sublayer.

On OS X, NSViews do not use a CALayer by default. This is not the case in iOS, where all UIViews have a CALayer.

2. Next, create the interface. Open *MainMenu.xib* and drag a custom view into the main window. Make it fill the window, but leave some space at the bottom. This view will contain the video playback layer.

    Drag in three buttons and place them underneath the video playback view. Label them Play, Play Slow Motion, and Rewind.

To add an AVPlayerLayer to the window, the view that it's being inserted into must have its own CALayer. To make this happen, you tell either the video playback view or any of its superviews that it should use a CALayer. Once a view has a CALayer, it and all of its subviews each use a CALayer to display their content.

3. Make the window use a CALayer. Click inside the window and open the View Effects Inspector, which is the last button at the top of the inspector.

    The Core Animation Layer section of the inspector will list the selected view. Check the checkbox to give it a layer; once this is done you should have an interface looking like Figure 9-1.

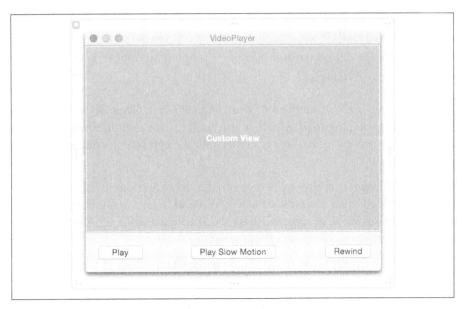

Figure 9-1. The interface layout for the VideoPlayer app

4. Finally, connect the code to the interface. Now that the interface is laid out correctly, we'll make the code aware of the view that the video should be displayed in, and create the actions that control playback.

   Open *AppDelegate.swift* in the assistant.

   Control-drag from the video container view into `AppDelegate`. Create an outlet called `playerView`.

   Control-drag from each of the buttons under the video container view into `App Delegate`, and create actions for each of them. Name these actions `play`, `playSlow Motion`, and `rewind`.

Now we'll write the code that loads and prepares the `AVPlayer` and `AVPlayerLayer`. Because we want to control the player, we'll keep a reference to it around by adding a class extension that contains an instance variable to store the `AVPlayer`. We don't need to keep the `AVPlayerLayer` around in the same way, because once we add it to the layer tree, we can forget about it—it will just display whatever the `AVPlayer` needs to show.

We'll also need to import the AV Foundation and Quartz Core framework headers in order to work with the necessary classes:

1. To import the headers, add the following code to the import statements at the top of *AppDelegate.swift*:

```
import AVFoundation
import QuartzCore
```

2. To include the class extension, add a new property to *AppDelegate.swift*:

```
var player: AVPlayer?
```

Next, we'll create and set up the AVPlayer and AVPlayerLayer. To set up the AVPlayer, you need something to play. In this case, we'll make the application determine the location of the test video that was compiled into the application's folder, and give that to the AVPlayer.

Once the AVPlayer is ready, we can create the AVPlayerLayer. The AVPlayerLayer needs to be added to the video player view's layer and resized to fill the layer. Setting the frame property of the layer accomplishes this. As a final touch, we'll also make the layer automatically resize when its superlayer resizes.

Finally, we'll tell the AVPlayer that it should pause when it reaches the end of playback:

1. To set up the AVPlayer, replace the applicationDidFinishLaunching() method in *AppDelegate.swift* with the following code:

```
func applicationDidFinishLaunching(aNotification: NSNotification?) {
    let contentURL = NSBundle.mainBundle().URLForResource("TestVideo",
        withExtension: "m4v")
    player = AVPlayer(URL: contentURL)

    var playerLayer = AVPlayerLayer(player: player)
    self.playerView.layer?.addSublayer(playerLayer)
    playerLayer.frame = self.playerView.bounds
    playerLayer.autoresizingMask =
        CAAutoresizingMask.LayerHeightSizable |
        CAAutoresizingMask.LayerWidthSizable

    self.player!.actionAtItemEnd = AVPlayerActionAtItemEnd.None
```

2. The last step in coding the application is to create the control methods, which are run when the buttons are clicked. These controls—Play, Play Slow Motion, and Rewind—simply tell the AVPlayer to set the rate of playback. In the case of rewinding, it's a matter of telling the player to seek to the start.

To add the control methods, replace the play(), playSlowMotion(), and rewind() methods in *AppDelegate.swift* with the following code:

```
@IBAction func play(sender: AnyObject) {
    self.player!.play()
}
@IBAction func playSlowMotion(sender: AnyObject) {
    self.player!.rate = 0.25
}
@IBAction func rewind(sender: AnyObject) {
```

```
        self.player!.seekToTime(kCMTimeZero)
    }
```

It's time to test the app, so go ahead and launch it. Play around with the buttons and resize the window. Video should be visible in the window, as seen in Figure 9-2.

Figure 9-2. The completed interface for our VideoPlayer app

AVKit

The preceding example is a good way of loading media into a layer, but it is also a little clunky. Your users are already used to a particular way of how videos and audio and their controls should be displayed. Luckily, new in OS X 10.9, there is a dedicated sub-class of NSView called AVPlayerView specifically designed for playing audio and video. AVPlayerView is the same view that QuickTime Player uses when it wants to play audio or video and is part of the AVKit framework. It is designed to work with an AVPlayer and allows your code to pass any messages to the AVPlayer it is displaying. Starting with iOS 8, AVKit is also available for iOS; instead of an AVPlayerView it uses an AVPlayer ViewController, but it works in a very similar manner to its OS X cousin.

The desktop version of AVKit is only available on OS X 10.9 and later, and the mobile version is only for iOS 8 and later. Sorry iOS 7 and Mountain Lion users!

Hooking an `AVPlayerView` up to an existing `AVPlayer` is straightforward. To demonstrate, let's make a few changes to our VideoPlayer app:

1. First, to modify the interface, open *MainMenu.xib* and delete the custom view and all buttons.

   Drag an `AVPlayerView` onto the main window, and resize it to be the full size of the window.

   At this stage, your interface should look similar to Figure 9-3.

Figure 9-3. The updated interface for our app

2. Then, to connect the code, open *AppDelegate.swift* in the assistant.

   Control-drag from the `AVPlayerView` into the `AppDelegate`, and create an outlet called `playerView`.

   Delete or comment out the previous `playerView` outlet.

3. Next, to import the headers, add the following code to the top of *AppDelegate.swift*:

   ```
   import AVKit
   ```

4. Finally, we need to set up the `AVPlayerView`. Replace the `applicationDidFinish Launching()` method in *AppDelegate.swift* with the following code:

```
func applicationDidFinishLaunching(aNotification: NSNotification?) {
    let contentURL = NSBundle.mainBundle().URLForResource("TestVideo",
        withExtension: "m4v")

    self.playerView.player = AVPlayer(URL: contentURL)
}
```

Now when you run the application, you should see an app which is very similar to the QuickTime Player.

Finally, it is good practice to delete the methods for handling the play, slow motion, and rewind options, and remove the Quartz Core framework as it is no longer needed.

AVKit on iOS

AVKit behaves a little bit differently on iOS than it does on OS X. In OS X, you use an `NSView` subclass to present the player, its content, and its controls. In iOS, you instead use an `AVPlayerViewController`, a subclass of `UIViewController`, which despite being an entire view controller works in a very similar fashion. Just like AVKit in OS X, it is very simple to start using an `AVPlayerViewController` in your code. To demonstrate this, lets create a simple iOS video app:

1. Create a new, single view iOS application, and call it AVKit-iOS.

   Drag a video into the project navigator to add it to the project.

2. Then create the interface, which for this application will use an `AVPlayerViewCon troller` and a container view. A container view is a specialized `UIView` subclass that can embed an entire view controller within it and will let us display the `AVPlayerViewController` and its content.

   Open *Main.storyboard*. In the object library search for a container view, and drag it into the view controller. Resize the container view to be as large or as small as you want; in our app we made it take up about a third of the screen but you can make it as big or small as you want.

   Delete the additional view controller. By default, adding a container view to an app will also include an additional view controller that will be the contents for the container view to show; we don't want this.

   Add an `AVPlayerViewController` to the interface. Place the new view controller off to the side of the main view controller.

   Connect the `AVPlayerViewController` to the container view. Control-drag from the container view to the `AVPlayerViewController` and select the *embed* segue option from the list of segues that appears. This will embed the `AVPlayerViewCon troller` and its content into the container view.

The final step is to give this new segue an identifier. Select the segue in the Interface Builder and open the Attributes Inspector in the Utilities tab on the right of Xcode. Change the identifier of the segue to `videoSegue`; we will be using this identifier later to configure the video content.

Once complete the interface should look similar to Figure 9-4.

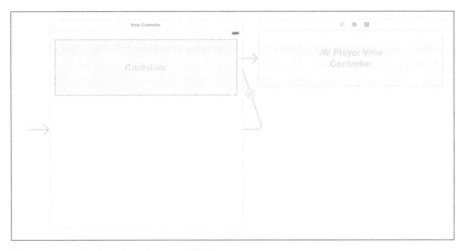

Figure 9-4. The interface for our AVKit app

3. To import the frameworks, open *ViewController.swift* and add the following to the top of the file:

```
import AVKit
import AVFoundation
```

 It is very important to remember to import the AV Foundation framework as well as AVKit, as AVKit only provides the `AVPlayerViewController` and does not come with any of the classes needed to actually configure the view controller.

4. The last thing we need to do is configure what content we want the `AVPlayerView Controller` to show.

Inside *ViewController.swift*, add the following function:

```
override func prepareForSegue(segue: UIStoryboardSegue, sender: AnyObject?)
{
    if segue.identifier == "videoSegue"
    {
```

```
    // set up the player
    let videoURL = NSBundle.mainBundle().URLForResource("TestVideo",
                                            withExtension: "m4v")
    let videoViewController =
            segue.destinationViewController as AVPlayerViewController
    videoViewController.player = AVPlayer(URL: videoURL)
    }
}
```

This code is waiting for the VideoSegue we named earlier to be called. Once this is called we are getting a reference to our sample video and configuring the player property of the AVPlayerViewController to play this video.

Now if you run the app you should see a small window in the app playing the video. It has the default iOS video controls and as an added bonus, the fullscreen button will also automagically expand the video to full size and will also support landscape!

Playing Sound with AVAudioPlayer

AVPlayer is designed for playing back any kind of audio or video. AV Foundation also provides a class specifically designed for playing back sounds, called AVAudioPlayer.

AVAudioPlayer is a simpler choice than AVPlayer for playing audio. It's useful for playing back sound effects and music in apps that don't use video, and has a couple of advantages over AVPlayer:

- AVAudioPlayer allows you to set volumes on a per-player basis (AVPlayer uses the system volume).

- AVAudioPlayer is easier to loop.

- You can query an AVAudioPlayer for its current output power, which you can use to show volume levels over time.

 AVAudioPlayer is the simplest way to play back audio files, but it's not the only option. If you need more control over how the audio is played back (e.g., you might want to generate audio yourself, or apply effects to the audio), then you should use the more powerful AVAudioEngine API. For more information on this, see the Xcode documentation for the AVAudioEngine class (*http://bit.ly/avaudioengine*).

AVAudioPlayer works in the same way as AVPlayer. Given an NSURL that points to a sound file that OS X or iOS supports, you create an AVAudioPlayer, set it up the way you want (by setting balance, volume, and looping), and then play it:

```
let soundFileURL = NSBundle.mainBundle().URLForResource("TestSound",
                                              withExtension: "wav")
var error: NSError?
audioPlayer = AVAudioPlayer(contentsOfURL: soundFileURL, error: &error)
```

You need to keep a reference to your AVAudioPlayer, or it will be removed from memory and stop playing. Therefore, you should keep an instance variable around that stores a reference to the player to keep it from being freed.

Telling an AVAudioPlayer to play is a simple matter:

```
audioPlayer.play()
```

You can also set the volume and indicate how many times the sound should loop. The volume is a number between 0 and 1. The number of loops defaults to 0 (play once); if you set it to 1, it will play twice. Set the number of loops to –1 to make the sound loop until stopped:

```
audioPlayer.volume = 0.5
audioPlayer.numberOfLoops = -1
```

To seek to a point in the sound, set the currentTime property. This property is measured in seconds, so to seek to the start of the sound, set currentTime to 0:

```
audioPlayer.currentTime = 0
```

Seeking to a point in the sound doesn't affect whether the sound is playing or not. If you seek while the sound is playing, the sound will jump.

In this chapter, we've focused on media playback. However, AV Foundation has full support for capturing media as well, including audio and video. For information on how this works, see the "Media Capture" section in the *AV Foundation Programming Guide* (*http://bit.ly/programming_guide_media_capture*), available in the Xcode documentation.

Speech Synthesis

A feature introduced in iOS 7 within AV Foundation is the ability to synthesize speech: you can now have your application say almost any text that you want. There are two main components to synthesizing speech. The first is an AVSpeechUtterance, which represents the text you want to have synthesized. This includes the rate at which you want it to be spoken, the volume, pitch, any delay, and the voice to use when synthesizing the text. The second component, an AVSpeechSynthesizer, is the object responsible for actually synthesizing, speaking, and controlling any utterances passed to it:

```
// creating a synthesizer
var synthesizer = AVSpeechSynthesizer()

// creating an utterance to synthesize
let utteranceString = "I am the very model of a modern major general"
var utterance = AVSpeechUtterance(string: utteranceString)
// setting a rate to speak at
utterance.rate = 0.175

// synthesizing and speaking the utterance
synthesizer.speakUtterance(utterance)
```

Should you want to pause the utterance, call `pauseSpeakingAtBoundary()` on your AVSpeechSynthesizer, which takes in a AVSpeechBoundary as a parameter for controlling when to pause the utterance. Passing in `AVSpeechBoundary.Immediate` will pause the utterance immediately, whereas `AVSpeechBoundary.Word` will pause the utterance at the completion of the current word. Call `continueSpeaking()` to continue the utterance. To fully stop a speech synthesizer and all utterances associated with it, call `stopSpeakingAtBoundary()`, which also takes in a speech boundary to inform the synthesizer when to stop.

Working with the Photo Library

In addition to playing back video and audio, iOS and OS X allow you to access the built-in camera system to capture video and audio. Similar hardware is available on both systems—in fact, Apple refers to the front-facing camera on the iPhone, iPad, and all Mac machines as the "FaceTime camera," suggesting that users are meant to treat the camera the same way across all devices. The camera can record still images as well as video.

The APIs for accessing the camera are different on OS X and iOS. The camera was introduced on the Mac well before iOS was released, and iOS's implementation is somewhat easier to use and cleaner, as the API benefited from several years of development experience.

 If you really need a consistent API for recording camera content across both iOS and OS X, AV Foundation provides a set of classes for capturing content—the key ones being AVCaptureSession, AVCaptureInput, and AVCaptureOutput. However, this system is designed for more finely grained control over data flows from the camera to consumers of that data, and isn't terribly convenient for simple uses like recording video and saving it to a file. In this chapter, therefore, we'll only be covering the iOS implementation. For OS X developers, please refer to the *QTKit Application Tutorial* (*http://bit.ly/qtkit_tutorial*) included in the Xcode documentation.

Capturing Photos and Video from the Camera

To capture video and photos from the camera on iOS, you use a view controller called `UIImagePickerController`.

At its simplest, `UIImagePickerController` allows you to present an interface almost identical to the built-in camera application on the iPhone and iPad. Using this interface, the user can take a photo that is delivered to your application as a `UIImage` object.

You can also configure the `UIImagePickerController` to capture video. In this case, the user can record up to 30 minutes of video and deliver it to your application as an `NSString` that contains the path to where the captured video file is kept.

`UIImagePickerController` can be set up to control which camera is used (front-side or back-side camera), whether the LED flashlight is available (on devices that have them), and whether the user is allowed to crop or adjust the photo he took or trim the video he recorded.

`UIImagePickerController` works like this:

1. You create an instance of the class.

2. You optionally configure the picker to use the settings that you want.

3. You provide the picker with a delegate object that conforms to the `UIImagePicker ControllerDelegate` protocol.

4. You present the view controller, usually modally, by having the current view controller call `presentViewController(animated:, completion:)`.

5. The user takes a photo or records a video. When they're done, the delegate object receives the `imagePickerController(didFinishPickingMediaWithInfo:)` message.

   This method receives a dictionary that contains information about the media that the user captured, which you can query to retrieve data like the original or edited photos, the location of the video file, and other useful information.

   In this method, your view controller must dismiss the image picker controller, by calling the `dismissViewControllerAnimated(:completion:)` method on the current view controller.

6. If the user chooses to cancel the image picker (by tapping the Cancel button that appears), the delegate object receives the `imagePickerControllerDidCancel()` message.

   In this method, your view controller must also dismiss the image picker by calling `dismissViewControllerAnimated(completion)`. If this method isn't called, the

Cancel button won't appear to do anything when tapped, and the user will think that your application is buggy.

When using UIImagePickerController, it's important to remember that the hardware on the device your app is running on may vary. Not all devices have a front-facing camera, which was only introduced in the iPhone 4 and the iPad 2; on earlier devices, you can only use the rear-facing camera. Some devices don't have a camera at all, such as the early iPod touch models and the first iPad. As time goes on, devices are getting more and more capable, but it is always good practice to make sure a camera is there before you use it.

You can use UIImagePickerController to determine which features are available and adjust your app's behavior accordingly. For example, to determine if any kind of camera is available, you use the isSourceTypeAvailable() class method:

```
let sourceType = UIImagePickerControllerSourceType.Camera
if (UIImagePickerController.isSourceTypeAvailable(sourceType))
{
    // we can use the camera
}
else
{
    // we can't use the camera
}
```

You can further specify if a front- or rear-facing camera is available by using the class method isCameraDeviceAvailable():

```
let frontCamera = UIImagePickerControllerCameraDevice.Front
let rearCamera = UIImagePickerControllerCameraDevice.Rear
if (UIImagePickerController.isCameraDeviceAvailable(frontCamera))
{
    // the front camera is available
}
if (UIImagePickerController.isCameraDeviceAvailable(rearCamera))
{
    // the rear camera is available
}
```

The iOS simulator does not have a camera, and UIImagePicker Controller reports this. If you want to test out using the camera, you must test your app on a device that actually has a built-in camera. This doesn't stop you from using UIImagePickerController itself, because you can still access the user's photo library. We'll be talking about this in more detail in the next section.

Building a Photo Application

To demonstrate how to use `UIImagePickerController`, we'll build a simple application that allows the user to take a photo, which is then displayed on the screen. The image picker will be configured to take only photos, and will use the front-facing camera if it's available and the rear-facing camera if it's not:

1. Create a single view iPhone application and name it Photos.

2. The interface for this application will be deliberately simple: a button that brings up the camera view, and an image view that displays the photo that the user took.

   To create the interface, open *Main.storyboard* and drag a `UIImageView` into the main screen. Resize it so that it takes up the top half of the screen.

   Drag a `UIButton` into the main screen and place it under the image view. Make the button's label read `Take Photo`.

   When you're done, the interface should look like Figure 9-5.

3. Next, connect the interface to the code. Open *ViewController.swift* in the assistant.

   Control-drag from the image view into `ViewController`. Create an outlet called `imageView`.

   Control-drag from the button into `ViewController`. Create an action called `takePhoto`.

4. Then make the view controller conform to the `UIImagePickerController Delegate` and `UINavigationControllerDelegate` protocols. Update *ViewController.swift* to look like the following code:

```
class ViewController: UIViewController,
                      UIImagePickerControllerDelegate,
                      UINavigationControllerDelegate {
```

Figure 9-5. The photo-picking app's interface

5. Then add the code that shows the image picker. When the button is tapped, we need to create, configure, and present the image picker view. Replace the `takePhoto()` method with the following code:

```
@IBAction func takePhoto(sender: AnyObject) {
    var picker = UIImagePickerController()

    let sourceType = UIImagePickerControllerSourceType.Camera
    if (UIImagePickerController.isSourceTypeAvailable(sourceType))
    {
        // we can use the camera
        picker.sourceType = UIImagePickerControllerSourceType.Camera

        let frontCamera = UIImagePickerControllerCameraDevice.Front
        let rearCamera = UIImagePickerControllerCameraDevice.Rear
```

```
    //use the front-facing camera if available
    if (UIImagePickerController.isCameraDeviceAvailable(frontCamera))
    {
        picker.cameraDevice = frontCamera
    }
    else
    {
        picker.cameraDevice = rearCamera
    }
    // make this object be the delegate for the picker
    picker.delegate = self

    self.presentViewController(picker, animated: true,
        completion: nil)
    }

}
```

6. We now need to add the UIImagePickerControllerDelegate methods—specifically, the one called when the user finishes taking a photo, and the one called when the user cancels taking a photo.

Add the following methods to *ViewController.swift*:

```
func imagePickerController(picker: UIImagePickerController!,
        didFinishPickingMediaWithInfo info: [NSObject : AnyObject]!)
{
    let image: UIImage =
            info[UIImagePickerControllerOriginalImage] as UIImage
    self.imageView.image = image
    picker.dismissViewControllerAnimated(true, completion: nil)
}
func imagePickerControllerDidCancel(picker: UIImagePickerController!) {
    picker.dismissViewControllerAnimated(true, completion: nil)
}
```

Now run the application and test it out on an iPhone or iPad. Take a photo of yourself, and see that it appears in the image view.

If you try to test out the application on the iOS Simulator, the button won't appear to do anything at all. That's because the if statement in the takePhoto() method keeps the image picker from trying to work with hardware that isn't there.

If you ask UIImagePickerController to work with a camera and there isn't one present on the device, an exception will be thrown and your application will crash. Always test to see if the camera device that you intend to use is actually available.

The Photo Library

Capturing a photo with the camera is useful, but the user will likely also want to work with photos that he's previously taken or downloaded from the Internet. For example, a social networking application should include some method of sharing photos from the user's photo collection.

To let the user access his photo library from within your app, you use `UIImagePicker Controller` again. If you want to present the photo library instead of the camera, set the `sourceType` property of the image picker to `UIImagePickerControllerSource Type.PhotoLibrary` or `UIImagePickerControllerSourceType.SavedPhotosAlbum`.

 `UIImagePickerControllerSourceType.PhotoLibrary` makes the `UIImagePickerController` display the entire photo library, while `UIImagePickerControllerSourceType.SavedPhotosAlbum` makes the `UIImagePickerController` display only the Camera Roll album on devices that have a camera, or the Saved Photos album on devices that don't.

When you present an image picker controller that has been set up to use a noncamera source, the photo library interface used in the built-in Photos application appears. The user then browses for and selects a photo, at which point the image picker's delegate receives the `imagePickerController(didFinishPickingMediaWithInfo:)` message, just like if the image picker had been set up to use the camera.

To demonstrate this, we'll update the application to include a button that displays the Saved Photos album:

1. To update the interface, add a new button to the application's main screen and make its label read `Photo Library`.

2. Then connect the interface to the code. Open *ViewController.swift* in the Assistant again. Control-drag from the new button into `ViewController`, and create a new action called `loadFromLibrary`.

3. Replace the `loadFromLibrary()` method in *ViewController.swift* with the following code:

```
@IBAction func loadFromLibrary(sender: AnyObject) {
    var picker = UIImagePickerController()
    picker.sourceType =
        UIImagePickerControllerSourceType.SavedPhotosAlbum
    picker.delegate = self
    self.presentViewController(picker, animated: true, completion: nil)
}
```

Test the application by running the app and tapping the Photo Library button. Select a photo to make it appear on the screen.

If you're testing this in the simulator, you won't have access to a large array of user-taken photos, but since Xcode 6, the iOS Simulator does come with a few photos in the library for testing purposes.

iCloud and Data Storage

Unless your application is a trivial one, it will need to work with data at some point. This data could be as simple as a list of high scores that the user has achieved, or as complex as a multimedia document like a presentation.

This information needs to be accessible to other parts of your application, such as the controller objects, so that work can be done on it. The information needs to be stored somewhere—either in memory, on disk, or on the network.

OS X and iOS provide tools for storing information on disk and on the network. One of the more recent additions to the APIs available to developers is *iCloud*, a network-based storage system that is designed to allow users to keep the same information on all their devices, without having to do any work to enable this.

In this chapter, you will learn how to work with the filesystem to store your information on disk, and how to store simple data in the built-in user preferences database. You'll also learn how to work with iCloud storage to store data and files in the cloud. Finally, you'll learn how the sandbox works on OS X, and how to use security-scoped bookmarks to allow your application to access data outside its sandbox across multiple launches.

While iCloud provides the means for storing files and folders in the cloud, you also need to know how to present documents to the user. This chapter only covers the mechanics of storing the data; to learn more about how to write a document-based application on OS X and iOS, head to Chapter 13.

Preferences

Most applications need to store some information about the user's preferences. For example, if you open the Safari web browser and go to its preferences (by pressing ⌘-, [comma] or choosing Safari→Preferences), you'll see a rather large collection of settings that the user can modify. Because these settings need to remain set when the application exits, they need to be stored somewhere.

The NSUserDefaults class allows you to store settings information in a key-value based way. You don't need to handle the process of loading and reading in a settings file, and preferences are automatically saved.

To access preferences stored in NSUserDefaults, you need an instance of the NSUser Defaults class. To get one, you must ask the NSUserDefaults class for the standardUserDefaults:

```
let defaults = NSUserDefaults.standardUserDefaults()
```

It's also possible to create a new NSUserDefaults object instead of using the standard user defaults. You only need to do this if you want more control over exactly whose preferences are being accessed. For example, if you are creating an application that manages multiple users on a Mac and accesses their preferences, you can create an NSUserDefaults object for each user's preferences.

Registering Default Preferences

When your application obtains a preferences object for the first time (i.e., on the first launch of your application), that preferences object is empty. In order to create default values, you need to provide a dictionary containing the defaults to the defaults object.

The word *default* gets tossed around quite a lot when talking about the defaults system. To clarify:

- A *defaults object* is an instance of the class NSUserDefaults.
- A *default* is a setting inside the defaults object.
- A *default value* is a setting used by the defaults object when no other value has been set. (This is the most common meaning of the word when talking about non-Cocoa environments.)

To register default values in the defaults object, you first need to create a dictionary. The keys of this dictionary are the same as the names of the preferences, and the values associated with these keys are the default values of these settings. Once you have the dictionary, you provide it to the defaults object with the registerDefaults method:

```
// Create the default values dictionary
let myDefaults = [
    "greeting": "hello",
    "numberOfItems": 1
]
```

```
// Provide this dictionary to the defaults object
defaults.registerDefaults(myDefaults)
```

Once this is done, you can ask the defaults object for values.

The defaults that you register with the `registerDefaults` method are not saved on disk, which means that you need to call this every time your application starts up. Defaults that you set in your application (see "Setting Preferences" on page 213) are saved, however.

Accessing Preferences

Once you have a reference to one, an `NSUserDefaults` object can be treated much like a dictionary, with a few restrictions. You can retrieve a value from the defaults object by using the `objectForKey` method:

```
// Retrieve a string with the key "greeting" from the defaults object
let greeting = defaults.objectForKey("greeting") as? String
```

Only a few kinds of objects can be stored in a defaults object. The only objects that can be stored in a defaults object are *property list objects*, which are:

- Strings
- Numbers
- NSData
- NSDate
- Arrays and dictionaries (as long as they only contain items in this list)

If you need to store any other kind of object in a defaults object, you should first convert it to an `NSData` by archiving it (see "Serialization and Deserialization" on page 58 in Chapter 2).

Additional methods exist for retrieving values from an `NSUser Defaults` object. For more information, see the *Preferences and Settings Programming Guide*, available in the Xcode documentation (*http://bit.ly/abt_prefs_and_settings*).

Setting Preferences

In addition to retrieving values from a defaults object, you can also set values. When you set a value in an `NSUserDefaults` object, that value is kept around forever (until the application is removed from the system).

To set an object in an `NSUserDefaults` object, you use the `setObject(_,forKey:)` method:

```
let newGreeting = "hi there"
defaults.setObject(newGreeting, forKey: "greeting")
```

Working with the Filesystem

Most applications work with data stored on disk, and data is most commonly organized into files and folders. An increasing amount of data is also stored in cloud services, like Dropbox and Google Drive.

All Macs and iOS devices have access to iCloud, Apple's data synchronization and storage service. The idea behind iCloud is that users can have the same information on all the devices and computers they own, and don't have to manually sync or update anything—all synchronization and updating is done by the computer.

Because the user's documents can exist as multiple copies spread over different cloud storage services, it's now more and more the case that working with the user's data means working with one of potentially many copies of that data. This means that the copy of the data that exists on the current machine may be out of date or may conflict with another version of the data. iCloud works to reduce the amount of effort required to solve these issues, but they're factors that your code needs to be aware of.

Cocoa provides a number of tools for working with the filesystem and with files stored in iCloud, which is discussed later in this chapter in "iCloud" on page 222.

 This chapter deals with files in the filesystem, which is only half the story of making a full-fledged, document-based application. To learn how to create an application that deals with documents, turn to Chapter 13.

Files may be stored in one of two places: either inside the application's bundle or elsewhere on the disk.

Files that are stored in the application's bundle are kept inside the *.app* folder and distributed with the app. If the application is moved on disk (e.g., if you were to drag it to another location on your Mac), the resources move with the app.

When you add a file to a project in Xcode, it is added to the current target (though you can choose for this not to happen). Then, when the application is built, the file is copied into the relevant part of the application bundle, depending on the OS—on OS X, the file is copied into the bundle's *Resources* folder, while on iOS, it is copied into the root folder of the bundle.

Files copied into the bundle are mostly resources used by the application at runtime—sounds, images, and other things needed for the application to run. The user's documents aren't stored in this location.

 If a file is stored in the application bundle, it's part of the code-signing process—changing, removing, or adding a file to the bundle after it's been code-signed will cause the OS to refuse to launch the app. This means that files stored in the application bundle are read-only.

Retrieving a file from the application's bundle is quite straightforward, and is covered in more detail in "Using NSBundle to Find Resources in Applications" on page 67. This chapter covers how to work with files that are stored elsewhere.

 Some files are processed when they're copied into the application bundle. For example, .xib files are compiled from their XML source into a more quickly readable binary format, and on iOS, PNG images are processed so that the device's limited GPU can load them more easily (though this renders them unopenable with apps like Preview). Don't assume that files are simply copied into the bundle!

Using NSFileManager

Applications can access files almost anywhere on the system. The "almost anywhere" depends on which OS your application is running on, and whether the application exists within a sandbox.

 Sandboxes, which are discussed later in this chapter in "Working with the Sandbox" on page 219, restrict what your application is allowed to access. So even if your application is compromised by malicious code, for example, it cannot access files that the user does not want it to.

By default, the sandbox is limited to the application's private working space, and cannot access any user files. To gain access to these files, you make requests to the system, which handle the work of presenting the file-selection box to the user and open *holes* in the sandbox for working with the files the user wants to let your application access (and only those files).

Your interface to the filesystem is the NSFileManager object, which allows you to list the contents of folders; create, rename, and delete files; modify attributes of files and folders; and generally perform all the filesystem tasks that the Finder does.

To access the NSFileManager class, you use the shared manager object:

```
let fileManager = NSFileManager.defaultManager()
```

 NSFileManager allows you to set a delegate on it, which receives messages when the file manager completes operations like copying or moving files. If you are using this feature, you should create your own instance of NSFileManager instead of using the shared object:

```
let fileManager = NSFileManager()

// we can now set a delegate on this new file manager to be
// notified when operations are complete
fileManager.delegate = self
```

You can use NSFileManager to get the contents of a folder, using the following method: contentsOfDirectoryAtURL(_,includingPropertiesForKeys:options:error:). This method can be used to simply return NSURLs for the contents of a folder, but also to fetch additional information about a file:

```
let folderURL = NSURL.fileURLWithPath("/Applications/")

var error : NSError? = nil

let folderContents = fileManager.contentsOfDirectoryAtURL(folderURL!,
    includingPropertiesForKeys:nil, options:NSDirectoryEnumerationOptions(),
    error:&error)
```

After this call, the array folderContents contains NSURLs that point to each item in the folder. If there was an error, the method returns nil, and the error variable contains an NSError object that describes exactly what went wrong.

You can also ask the individual NSURL objects for information about the file that they point to. You can do this via the resourceValuesForKeys(_,error:) method, which returns a dictionary that contains the attributes for the item pointed to by the URL:

```
// anURL is an NSURL object

// Pass in an array containing the attributes you want to know about
let attributes = [NSURLFileSizeKey, NSURLContentModificationDateKey]

// In this case, we don't care about any potential errors, so we
// pass in 'nil' for the error parameter.
let attributesDictionary = anURL.resourceValuesForKeys(attributes, error: nil)

// We can now get the file size out of the dictionary:
let fileSizeInBytes = attributesDictionary?[NSURLFileSizeKey] as NSNumber

// And the date it was last modified:
let lastModifiedDate =
    attributesDictionary?[NSURLContentModificationDateKey] as NSDate
```

Checking each attribute takes time, so if you need to get attributes for a large number of files, it makes more sense to instruct the `NSFile Manager` to pre-fetch the attributes when listing the directory's contents:

```
let attributes =
    [NSURLFileSizeKey, NSURLContentModificationDateKey]
fileManager.contentsOfDirectoryAtURL(folderURL,
    includingPropertiesForKeys: attributes,
    options: NSDirectoryEnumerationOptions(), error: nil)
```

Getting a temporary directory

It's often very convenient to have a temporary directory that your application can put files in. For example, if you're downloading some files, and want to save them somewhere temporarily before moving them to their final location, a temporary directory is just what you need.

To get the location of a temporary directory that your application can use, you use the `NSTemporaryDirectory` function:

```
let temporaryDirectoryPath = NSTemporaryDirectory()
```

This function returns a string, which contains the path of a directory you can store files in. If you want to use it as an `NSURL`, you'll need to use the `fileURLWithPath` method to convert it.

Files in a temporary directory are subject to deletion without warning. If the operating system decides it needs more disk space, it will begin deleting the contents of temporary directories. Don't put anything important in the temporary directory!

Creating directories

Using `NSFileManager`, you can create and remove items on the filesystem. To create a new directory, for example, use:

```
let newDirectoryURL = NSURL.fileURLWithPath(temporaryDirectoryPath +
    "/MyNewDirectory")

var error : NSError? = nil
var didCreate = fileManager.createDirectoryAtURL(newDirectoryURL!,
    withIntermediateDirectories: false, attributes: nil, error: &error)
if (didCreate) {
    // The directory was successfully created
} else {
    // The directory wasn't created (maybe one already exists at the path?)
    // More information is stored in the 'error' variable
}
```

Note that you can pass in an NSDictionary containing the desired attributes for the new directory.

 If you set a YES value for the withIntermediateDirectories parameter, the system will create any additional folders that are necessary to create the folder. For example, if you have a folder named *Foo*, and want to have a folder named *Foo/Bar/Bas*, you would create an NSURL that points to the second folder and ask the NSFileManager to create it. The system would create the *Bar* folder, and then create the *Bas* folder inside that.

Creating files

Creating files works the same way. You provide a path in an NSString, the NSData that the file should contain, and an optional dictionary of attributes that the file should have:

```
// Note that the first parameter is the path (as a string), NOT an NSURL!
fileManager.createFileAtPath(newFilePath!,
    contents: newFileData,
    attributes: nil)
```

Removing files

Given a URL, NSFileManager is also able to delete files and directories. You can only delete items that your app has permission to delete, which limits your ability to write a program that accidentally erases the entire system.

To remove an item, you do this:

```
fileManager.removeItemAtURL(newFileURL!, error: nil)
```

 There's no undo for removing files or folders using NSFile Manager. Items aren't moved to the Trash—they're immediately deleted.

Moving and copying files

To move a file, you need to provide both an original URL and a destination URL. You can also copy a file, which duplicates it and places the duplicate at the destination URL.

To move an item, you do this:

```
fileManager.moveItemAtURL(sourceURL!, toURL: destinationURL, error: nil)
```

To copy an item, you do this:

```
fileManager.copyItemAtURL(sourceURL!, toURL: destinationURL, error: nil)
```

Just like all the other file manipulation methods, these methods return `true` on success, and `false` if there was a problem.

File Storage Locations

There are a number of existing locations where the user can keep files. These include the Documents directory, the Desktop, and common directories that the user may not ever see, such as the Caches directory, which is used to store temporary files that the application would find useful to have around but could regenerate if needed (like downloaded images).

Your code can quickly determine the location of these common directories by asking the `NSFileManager` class. To do this, you use the `URLsForDirectory(_,inDomains:)` method in `NSFileManager`, which returns an array of `NSURL` objects that point to a directory that matches the kind of location you asked for. For example, to get an `NSURL` that points to the user's *Documents* directory, you do this:

```
let URLs = fileManager.URLsForDirectory(NSSearchPathDirectory.DocumentDirectory,
    inDomains: NSSearchPathDomainMask.UserDomainMask) as [NSURL]

let documentURL = URLs[0]
```

You can then use this URL to create additional URLs. For example, to generate a URL that points to a file called *Example.txt* in your *Documents* directory, you can use `URLByAppendingPathComponent`:

```
let fileURL = documentURL.URLByAppendingPathComponent("Example.txt")
```

Working with the Sandbox

An application that runs in a sandbox may only access files that exist inside that sandbox, and is allowed to read and write without restriction inside its designated sandbox container. In addition, if the user has granted access to a specific file or folder, the sandbox will allow your application to read and/or write to that location as well.

 If you want to put your application in the Mac App Store, it must be sandboxed. Apple will reject your application if it isn't. All iOS apps are automatically sandboxed by the system.

Enabling Sandboxing

To turn on sandboxing, follow these steps.

1. Select your project at the top of the navigation pane.

2. In the Capabilities tab, scroll to App Sandbox.

3. Turn on App Sandboxing.

Your application will then launch in sandboxed mode, which means that it won't be able to access any resources that the system does not permit it to.

 To use the sandbox, you need to have a Mac developer identity. To learn more about getting one, see Chapter 1.

In the sandbox setup screen, you can specify what the application should have access to. For example, if you need to be able to read and write files in the user's Music folder, you can change the Music Folder Access setting from None (the default) to Read Access or Read/Write Access.

If you want to let the user choose which files and folders should be accessible, change User Selected File Access to something other than None.

Open and Save Panels

One way that you can let the user indicate that your app is allowed to access a file is to use an NSOpenPanel or NSSavePanel. These are the standard open and save windows that you've seen before; however, when your application is sandboxed, the panel being displayed is actually not being shown by your application, but rather by a built-in system component called *Powerbox*. When you display an open or save panel, Powerbox handles the process of selecting the files; when the user chooses a file or folder, it grants your application access to the specified location and then returns information about the user's selection to you.

Here's an example of how you can get access to a folder that the user asks for:

```
let panel = NSOpenPanel()

panel.canChooseDirectories = true
panel.canChooseFiles = false

panel.beginWithCompletionHandler() {
    (result : Int) in

    let theURL = panel.URL

    // Do something with the URL that the user selected;
    // we now have permission to work with this location
}
```

Security-Scoped Bookmarks

One downside to this approach of asking for permission to access files is that the system will not remember that the user granted permission. It's a potential security hole to automatically retain permissions for every file the user has ever granted an app access to, so OS X instead provides the concept of *security-scoped bookmarks*. Security-scoped bookmarks are like the bookmarks in your web browser, but for files; once your application has access to a file, you can create a bookmark for it and save it. On application launch, your application can load the bookmark and have access to the file again.

There are two kinds of security-scoped bookmarks: *app-scoped bookmarks*, which allow your application to retain access to a file across launches, and *document-scoped bookmarks*, which allow your app to store the bookmark in a file that can be given to another user on another computer. In this book, we'll be covering app-scoped bookmarks.

To use security-scoped bookmarks, you need to explicitly indicate that your app uses them in its entitlements file. This is the file that's created when you turn on the Enable Entitlements option: it's the file with the extension *.entitlements* in your project. To enable app-scoped bookmarks, you open the Entitlements file and add the following entitlement: `com.apple.security.files.bookmarks.app-scope`. Set this entitlement to YES.

You can then create a bookmark file and save it somewhere that your application has access to. When your application later needs access to the file indicated by your user, you load the bookmark file and retrieve the URL from it; in doing this, your application will be granted access to the location that the bookmark points to.

To create and save bookmark data, you do this:

```
// Get the location in which to put the bookmark;
// documentURL is determined by asking the NSFileManager for the
// user's documents folder; see earlier in this chapter
var bookmarkStorageURL =
    documentURL.URLByAppendingPathComponent("savedbookmark.bookmark")

// selectedURL is a URL that the user has selected using an NSOpenPanel
let bookmarkData = selectedURL.bookmarkDataWithOptions(
    NSURLBookmarkCreationOptions.WithSecurityScope,
    includingResourceValuesForKeys: nil, relativeToURL: nil, error: nil)

// Save the bookmark data
bookmarkData?.writeToURL(bookmarkStorageURL, atomically: true)
```

To retrieve a stored bookmark, you do this:

```
let loadedBookmarkData = NSData(contentsOfURL: bookmarkStorageURL)

var loadedBookmark : NSURL? = nil

if loadedBookmarkData?.length > 0 {
```

```
var isStale = false
var error : NSError? = nil

loadedBookmark = NSURL(byResolvingBookmarkData:loadedBookmarkData!,
    options: NSURLBookmarkResolutionOptions.WithSecurityScope,
    relativeToURL: nil, bookmarkDataIsStale: nil, error: nil)

// We can now use this file

}
```

When you want to start accessing the file pointed to by the bookmarked URL, you need to call startAccessingSecurityScopedResource on that URL. When you're done, call stopAccessingSecurityScopedResource.

You can find a full working project that demonstrates this behavior in this book's source code.

iCloud

Introduced in iOS 5, iCloud is a set of technologies that allow users' documents and settings to be seamlessly synchronized across all the devices that they own.

iCloud is heavily promoted by Apple as technology that "just works"—simply by owning a Mac, iPhone, or iPad, your documents are everywhere that you need them to be. In order to understand what iCloud is, it's worth taking a look at Apple's advertising and marketing for the technology. In the ads, we see users working on a document, and then just putting it down, walking over to their Macs, and resuming work. No additional effort is required on the part of the user, and users are encouraged to think of their devices as simply tools that they use to access their omnipresent data.

This utopian view of data availability is made possible by Apple's growing network of massive data centers, and by a little extra effort on the part of you, the developer.

 iCloud also supports syncing Core Data databases. However, Core Data and iCloud syncing is a huge issue, and implementing and handling this is beyond what we could cover in this chapter. If you're interested in learning more about this, take a look at Marcus S. Zarra's excellent *Core Data, 2nd Edition* (Pragmatic Bookshelf).

In this chapter, you'll learn how to create applications that use iCloud to share settings and documents across the user's devices.

What iCloud Stores

Simply put, iCloud allows your applications to store files and key-value pairs on Apple's servers. Apps identify which file storage container or key-value pair database they want to access, and the operating system takes care of the rest.

In the case of files, your application determines the location of a container folder, the contents of which are synced to the network. When you copy a file into the container or update a file that's already in the container, the operating system syncs that file across all other applications on devices that have access to the same container.

For settings, you access an instance of `NSUbiquitousKeyValueStore`, which works almost identically to `NSUserDefaults` with the exception that it syncs to all other devices.

The word "ubiquitous" appears a lot when working with iCloud. So often, in fact, that it's used instead of the marketing term "iCloud." This is intended to reinforce what iCloud should be used for—it's not just a storage space on the Internet, like Box.net or similar "cloud file storage" services, but rather a tool for making users' data ubiquitous, so they can access it from anywhere.

Users are limited in the amount of data they can store. By default, iCloud users get 5 GB of space for free, and can pay for more. There aren't any per-application limits on the amount of data that your application can store, but the user isn't allowed to exceed their total limit (though they can purchase more space). For the key-value store, you can store 64 KB of information per application.

This means that when you're working out how iCloud fits into your application, you have to choose where you're going to put the data. Storing files in an iCloud container is a good option if your application works with documents—image editors or word processors are good examples. Files are also useful for storing more structured information, such as to-do lists or saved game files. If you want to store simple, application-wide state, such as the most recently opened document, then the key-value store works well.

More than one application can access the same iCloud container or key-value store. All that's required is that the same developer writes both, and that the bundle IDs have the same team prefix.

 iCloud works on both the Mac, iOS devices, and on the iOS Simulator. However, when you're developing using the iOS Simulator, you need to manually indicate when iCloud should synchronize the local data with the data stored on the server.

You do this by opening the Debug menu, and choosing Trigger iCloud Sync. You can also do this by pressing Command-Shift-I.

Setting Up for iCloud

In order to use any of Apple's online services, an application needs to identify itself and the developer who created it. This means that if you want to work with iCloud, you must have a paid developer account for each platform that you want to develop on. So if you want to make iCloud apps for the Mac, you need a paid Mac developer account. And if you want to make iOS apps at all, of course, you need a paid iOS developer account.

To get started, we'll create an application in Xcode, and then configure it so that it has access to iCloud:

1. Create a new Cocoa application and name it Cloud. When you create the application, write down the application's bundle identifier somewhere.

2. When Xcode has finished creating the application, select the project at the top of the project navigator. In the application's Capabilities tab, scroll down to iCloud.

3. Turn on the switch next to iCloud. Xcode will begin configuring the application, by creating files that indicate that the app needs access to iCloud, as well as by letting Apple know that the app needs access.

4. Turn on the "Key-value storage" checkbox, as well as the "iCloud documents" checkbox.

To access iCloud storage and store files, you indicate which iCloud container your application should use. The examples in this chapter will cover both the key-value store and iCloud file containers, and both are identified with the same style of identifier. For now, leave the Container setting as "Use default container":

 By default, Xcode configures your application to use an iCloud container with the same identifier as your application. If you have multiple apps that should share data through iCloud, they need to be configured to use the same iCloud container. This will become important later in the chapter, when we create an iOS app that uses iCloud.

The application is now set up to use iCloud. To get started working with the system, we'll first make sure that everything's working as it's supposed to.

Testing Whether iCloud Works

In order to determine whether the application has access to iCloud, we'll run a quick test to make sure that our setup is working. To do this, we'll ask the NSFileManager class for the "ubiquity container" URL. This is the location on the filesystem that is used for storing iCloud files; if the system returns the URL, we're in business. If it returns nil, then the app hasn't been set up for iCloud properly.

 The ability of the app to access the ubiquity container isn't affected by the device's ability to talk to the iCloud servers. If you're offline, you can store information in iCloud—it just won't get synced until you're back online.

To add the test, replace `applicationDidFinishLaunching` in *AppDelegate.swift* with the following code:

```
// We run this on a new background queue because it might take some time
// for the app to determine this URL

let backgroundQueue = NSOperationQueue()

backgroundQueue.addOperationWithBlock() {
    // Pass 'nil' to this method to get the URL for the first iCloud
    // container listed in the app's entitlements
    let ubiquityContainerURL = NSFileManager.defaultManager()
        .URLForUbiquityContainerIdentifier(nil)

    println("Ubiquity container URL: \(ubiquityContainerURL)")
}
```

Run the application. Take a look at the console output. If you see a URL, then iCloud is configured correctly. If the app reports that the ubiquity container URL is nil, then iCloud isn't set up correctly, and you should double-check your code signing and settings.

Storing Settings

The first thing that we'll do is use the key-value store to cause a setting to be stored in iCloud, which will be accessible via both an iOS application and a Mac application.

The key-value store, accessed via NSUbiquitousKeyValueStore, works very much like the NSUserDefaults object. You can store strings, numbers, arrays, and dictionaries in the store. As we mentioned before, the total amount of data that your app can store in the key-value store is 64KB, and each item can be no larger than 64KB.

In this example, we're going to start by storing a single string in iCloud. First, we'll update the AppDelegate object to store and retrieve this value from the key-value store. To accomplish this, open *AppDelegate.swift* and add the following computed property to the AppDelegate class:

```
var cloudString : String? {
    get {
```

```
    return NSUbiquitousKeyValueStore
        .defaultStore()
        .stringForKey("cloud_string")
}
set {
    NSUbiquitousKeyValueStore.defaultStore()
        .setString(newValue, forKey: "cloud_string")
    NSUbiquitousKeyValueStore.defaultStore().synchronize()
}
}
```

The getter of this computed property retrieves the value from the ubiquitous key-value store, while the setter stores the value and then immediately syncs the in-memory local copy to the disk. This also indicates to iCloud that there are new changes to push up.

> When you synchronize the key-value store, your changes aren't immediately uploaded to iCloud. In fact, iCloud limits the upload rate to several per minute.
>
> This means that you can't assume that your changes will appear immediately—iCloud might decide to just wait a while before sending your changes. This is on top of any delays caused by the network.

Handling External Changes

This method here works fine when we're the only application accessing the data, but the whole point of iCloud is that it's designed for multiple applications accessing the same data. It's therefore possible that, while the application is running, another instance of the application (perhaps running on another device that the user owns) changes the same value. Our application needs to know that the change has taken place, so that both apps show the same information.

When the key-value store is changed externally (i.e., by another application) the notification NSUbiquitousKeyValueStoreDidChangeExternallyNotification is posted. So to be informed of these changes, we'll make the AppDelegate class receive this notification, and then let the rest of the application know that the cloudString property changed (which will in turn make the UI update).

First, we'll add a property that stores the observer for the notifications, and then we'll register to run a block when the key-value store is changed:

1. Add the following property to the AppDelegate class:

   ```
   var storeChangeObserver : AnyObject? = nil
   ```

2. Add the following method to *AppDelegate.swift*:

   ```
   storeChangeObserver =
   NSNotificationCenter.defaultCenter()
   ```

```
            .addObserverForName(
                NSUbiquitousKeyValueStoreDidChangeExternallyNotification,
                object: self,
                queue: NSOperationQueue.mainQueue()) {
            (notification) in
            self.willChangeValueForKey("cloudString")
            self.didChangeValueForKey("cloudString")
        }
    }
```

We're now done with the code. It's time to create the interface, which will consist of a text field that's bound to the application delegate's `cloudString` property. This way, whenever the user changes the contents of the text field, the setter for the `cloudString` property will be run, which stores the new string in iCloud. Additionally, because the store change observer calls `willChangeValueForKey` and `didChangeValueForKey`, the text field will automatically get updated when new data is received from iCloud:

3. Open *MainWindow.xib*, and open the window.

4. Drag in an `NSTextField`.

5. With the text field selected, open the Bindings Inspector, which is the second tab to the right at the top of the Utilities pane.

6. Open the `Value` property and choose App Delegate in the "Bind to" drop-down menu. Set the Model Key Path to `self.cloudString`.

We're all set—the interface is prepared and will show the value stored in iCloud. Go ahead and run the app: you can enter text, and it will be saved.

The iOS Counterpart

This is all well and good, but iCloud only gets impressive when there's more than one device that has access to the same information. We'll now create an iOS application that shows what you type in the Mac application; the app will also allow you to make changes, which will automatically show up in the Mac app.

You can develop iCloud applications on both the iOS Simulator as well as a real device. In either case, you need to make sure your *device* is signed into an iCloud account—your phone is probably signed into one already, but your iOS Simulator almost definitely isn't.

Signing into the simulator is easy, though: simply go to the Settings application, scroll down to "iCloud," and sign in, just as you would on a real phone.

To keep the project manageable, we're going to make the iOS app be an additional part of the Mac app's project. Instead of creating a new project, we'll create a new *target* for the iOS app. This will keep everything in the same window, and has some additional advantages like making it easier to share source code between the two apps:

1. Create a new target by choosing File→New→Target. Name it Cloud-iOS.

2. Make the new target a single view iOS application. Make sure the bundle identifier is the same as the app ID that you just created for the iOS application.

Once the project is created, the application needs to be configured to use iCloud, just like the Mac application. Specifically, the iOS app must be configured to use the same iCloud resources as the Mac app, which will make it possible for the two apps to share data. Here are steps you'll need to follow:

1. Select the project at the top of the project navigator. Select the iOS application that you just added. Open the Capabilities tab.

2. Scroll down to the iCloud section and turn on the switch.

3. Turn on the "Key-value storage" checkbox, as well as the "iCloud documents" checkbox.

The iOS application needs to access the same key-value store, as well as the same iCloud documents container. To set this up, follow these steps:

1. Change the Containers option to "Specify custom containers." Then, make sure that only one iCloud container is selected (i.e., the container used by the OS X application).

2. Next, open the *.entitlements* file, which Xcode should have just created for you. Change the iCloud Key-Value Store setting to read `$(TeamIdentifierPrefix)` followed by the bundle ID of your OS X application. This will ensure that both apps are accessing the same key-value store.

The iOS application is now ready to work with iCloud, just like the Mac app. We'll now set up its interface, which will consist of a single text field.

In order to be notified of when the user is done editing, we'll make the view controller used in this iOS application a `UITextFieldDelegate`. When the user taps the Return key (which we'll convert to a Done button), the application will store the text field's contents in iCloud:

1. Open *Main.storyboard*. Drag in a `UITextField` and place it near the top of the screen.

2. Select the text field and open the Attributes Inspector. Scroll down to the "Return key" drop-down item, and choose Done.

The interface is done, but we still need to make it so the view controller is notified when the user taps the Done button:

1. Control-drag from the text field to the view controller, and choose "delegate" from the pop-up menu that appears.

2. Open *ViewController.swift* in the inspector.

3. Control-drag from the text field into the ViewController class. Create a new outlet called textField.

4. Make the class conform to UITextFieldDelegate by changing its class definition line to look like this:

```
class ViewController: UIViewController, UITextFieldDelegate {
```

Now we can make the application draw its data from iCloud. We'll do this by setting the text of the textField to whatever's in the iCloud key-value store when the view loads.

We'll also register the ViewController class as one that receives notifications about when the key-value store is updated externally.

 iCloud updates its contents both when the application is running and when it's not. This means that if you make a change to a setting in the key-value store on your iPhone and then later open the same app on your iPad, the data may have already arrived.

1. Add the following property to the ViewController class:

```
var keyValueStoreDidChangeObserver : AnyObject?
```

2. Next, add the following code to the viewDidLoad method:

```
self.textField.text =
    NSUbiquitousKeyValueStore.defaultStore()
    .stringForKey("cloud_string")

keyValueStoreDidChangeObserver = NSNotificationCenter.defaultCenter()
    .addObserverForName(
        NSUbiquitousKeyValueStoreDidChangeExternallyNotification,
        object: nil, queue: NSOperationQueue.mainQueue()) {

    (notification) in

    self.textField.text =
        NSUbiquitousKeyValueStore.defaultStore()
            .stringForKey("cloud_string")

}
```

Next, we'll add the method that runs when the user taps the Done button. This works because the class is the delegate of the text field; `textFieldShouldReturn` is called by the text field to find out what happens when the Return button is tapped.

In this case, we'll make the keyboard go away by making the text field resign first-responder status, and then store the text field's contents in iCloud.

Add the following method to `ViewController`:

```
func textFieldShouldReturn(textField: UITextField!) -> Bool {
    self.textField.resignFirstResponder()
    NSUbiquitousKeyValueStore.defaultStore(
    ).setString(self.textField.text,
        forKey: "cloud_string")
    return false;
}
```

We can now see this in action! Run the iOS app and the Mac app together. Change a value on one of the apps and watch what happens.

 Be patient—it might take a few seconds before the change appears on the other device.

iCloud Storage

Storing keys and values in iCloud is extremely useful for persisting user preferences across all their devices, but if you want to make the user's files just as ubiquitous through iCloud, you need to use *iCloud storage*.

In this section, we'll make an app that allows the user to store stuff in iCloud storage. The Mac app will let you add items to iCloud and list everything in storage. Its iOS counterpart will be simpler and show a list of files currently in iCloud storage, which updates as files are added or removed.

iCloud Storage on OS X

Before we can get to work, we need to give the Mac application permission to access the user's files. By default, when you enable iCloud, Xcode helpfully marks the application as sandboxed.

Sandboxing an application restricts what it's allowed to access. Before sandboxing, all applications were allowed to access any file that belonged to the user, which caused problems if the app was compromised by a remote attacker. Apple requires any application that's submitted to the Mac App Store to be sandboxed. (All iOS applications are sandboxed—it's a requirement of running on the device.)

By default, the application will be sandboxed to the point where it can't access any user files at all. Because we're making an application that lets the user take files and move them into iCloud, we'll need access to those files:

1. Open the project settings for the Mac application and open the Capabilities tab.
2. Scroll to the App Sandbox section, and turn on the switch next to it. Next, change the User Selected File setting from "None" to "Read/Write" (you'll find this setting in the File Access section).

With that out of the way, we can begin working with iCloud storage in the Mac app.

The way that our implementation will work is this: we'll have a property on the App Delegate class that is an array containing NSURLs of each path of the files in the storage container. This array will be displayed in a table view so that you can see what's included. We'll also add a button that, when clicked, will prompt the user for a file to move into iCloud storage.

In real life, you'd likely do something more interesting with the files than just show that they're there, but this will get us started.

Open *AppDelegate.swift* and add the following code to the AppDelegate class:

```
dynamic var filesInCloudStorage : [NSURL] = []
```

Marking a property as dynamic allows Cocoa bindings to work with it.

Next, we'll create and set up the table view that displays the list of files. To keep things simpler, we'll use bindings to make the table view show its content:

1. Open *MainWindow.xib* and drag in an NSTableView into the main window. Make it fill the rest of the window.
2. Select the table view and make it have one column.
3. Drag in an NSButton and change its label to Add File....

With the interface laid out, we can begin to connect it to the code. We'll start by making the button run an action method when clicked, and then bind the table view to the application. Because we're working with an array, we'll use an array controller to manage the link between the array of files stored in the app delegate and the table view:

1. Open *AppDelegate.swift* in the assistant.

2. Control-drag from the button into `AppDelegate` and create a new action called `addFile`.

We'll now bind the table to the app delegate via an array controller:

1. Drag an array controller into the outline.

2. Select the array controller and open the Bindings tab.

3. Open the Content Array property, and choose App Delegate from the "Bind to" drop-down menu.

4. Set the Model Key Path to `self.filesInCloudStorage`.

5. Select the table view column, and bind its Value to the Array Controller. Set the controller key to `arrangedObjects` and the model key path to `description`.

We're using `description` because it's a convenient way to simply display a string version of the contents of the array.

Next, we need to load the list of files that are in iCloud into the array, and then keep an eye out for new things arriving. To check the contents of the iCloud container, we first get its URL with this code:

```
let documentsDirectory = NSFileManager.defaultManager()
    .URLForUbiquityContainerIdentifier(nil)?
    .URLByAppendingPathComponent("Documents", isDirectory: true)
```

The ubiquity container is the folder that contains all of the information that's synced to iCloud. Inside this is another folder called Documents, which is where your application should put all synced documents. It's technically possible to store information outside this folder, but the advantage of using the Documents folder is that, on iOS, the user can delete individual documents in order to free space, whereas anything outside that folder is considered internal data and can't be individually deleted by users—they can only remove it by deleting the entire iCloud container.

To work out what's inside the iCloud container and to be informed of when its contents change, we use the `NSMetadataQuery` class. This class, once configured with information about what you're looking for, runs continuously and sends notifications whenever its contents change.

To use this, we'll add an instance variable to store the query object, and when the application launches, we'll configure and start the query:

1. Open *AppDelegate.swift* and add the following properties to the class:

```
var metadataQuery : NSMetadataQuery!
var metadataQueryDidUpdateObserver : AnyObject?
var metadataQueryDidFinishGatheringObserver : AnyObject?
```

2. Add the following code to the end of the `applicationDidFinishLaunching` method:

```
metadataQuery = NSMetadataQuery()
metadataQuery.searchScopes =
    [NSMetadataQueryUbiquitousDocumentsScope]
metadataQuery.predicate =
    NSPredicate(format: "%K LIKE '*'", NSMetadataItemFSNameKey)

self.metadataQueryDidUpdateObserver =
    NSNotificationCenter.defaultCenter()
        .addObserverForName(NSMetadataQueryDidUpdateNotification,
            object: nil, queue: NSOperationQueue.mainQueue()) {

    (notification) in
    self.queryDidUpdate()
}

self.metadataQueryDidFinishGatheringObserver =
    NSNotificationCenter.defaultCenter()
        .addObserverForName(NSMetadataQueryDidFinishGatheringNotification,
            object: nil, queue: NSOperationQueue.mainQueue()) {

    (notification) in
    self.queryDidUpdate()
}

metadataQuery.startQuery()
```

This code starts by creating the metadata query object, and instructs it to limit its results to only include items found inside the Documents folder in the ubiquity container. We also give it a *predicate*, which is a description of what to look for—in this case, we're saying "find all objects whose filenames are anything," which translates to "all files in the Documents folder."

We then register the app delegate to receive notifications whenever the metadata finishes its initial sweep of the folder, and also whenever the folder changes contents. In both cases, the same method will be called.

Finally, the query is started.

We now need to add the `queryDidUpdate` method, which will prepare the `filesIn CloudStorage` property and fill it with the paths that it found.

Add the following method to `AppDelegate`:

```
func queryDidUpdate() {
    var urls : [NSURL] = []
```

```
        for item in metadataQuery.results {

            if let metadataItem = item as? NSMetadataItem {
                let url =
                    metadataItem
                        .valueForAttribute(NSMetadataItemURLKey) as NSURL
                urls.append(url)
            }

        }

        self.filesInCloudStorage = urls
    }
```

This code loops over every result in the query and retrieves the path for it. The paths
are then stored in an array, which is used to update the filesInCloudStorage property.
Because we're using bindings, the act of updating this property will update the contents
of the table view.

Next, we add the method that actually adds an item to iCloud storage. This method
presents a file-open panel that lets the user choose which item to move into storage.

The process of moving a file into storage is the following. First, you work out the URL
of the file you want to move. Then, you ask the NSFileManager to generate a destination
URL. Finally, you perform the move by asking the file manager to make the file ubiquitous, passing in the source and destination URLs.

 Moving files into storage is just that—moving the file. If you want to
copy a file into storage, duplicate it and move the copied file.

Add the following method to AppDelegate:

```
@IBAction func addFile(sender : AnyObject?) {
    let panel = NSOpenPanel()
    panel.beginSheetModalForWindow(self.window) {

        (result) in

        if (result == NSOKButton) {
            let containerURL = NSFileManager.defaultManager()
                .URLForUbiquityContainerIdentifier(nil)?
                .URLByAppendingPathComponent("Documents",
                                                isDirectory: true)

            if let sourceURL = panel.URL {
                let destinationURL = containerURL?
```

```
            .URLByAppendingPathComponent(
                sourceURL.lastPathComponent)

        var error : NSError?

        // Move the file into iCloud (AKA "ubiquitous storage")
        NSFileManager.defaultManager().setUbiquitous(true,
            itemAtURL: sourceURL,
            destinationURL: destinationURL!,
            error: &error)

        if error != nil {
            println("Couldn't make the file ubiqitous: \(error)")
        }
    }
}
}
}
```

Run the app. You can now add stuff to iCloud.

iCloud Storage on iOS

Now we'll make the same thing work on iOS. First, we'll update the UI to include a text field that displays the list of files, and then we'll add the same NSMetadataQuery that lets the app know what's in the container:

1. Open the main storyboard and add a text view. Make it not editable.

2. Open *ViewController.swift* in the assistant.

   Control-drag from the text field into the ViewController class section, and connect it to a new outlet called fileList.

Now we'll make the code work. This is almost identical to the Mac version—we create the metadata query, prepare it, and set it running. When the query finds files, we'll update the text field and display the list of items.

We first need to create properties that store the NSMetadataQuery, along with observers for notifications that will fire when the contents of the iCloud container get updated.

1. Add the following properties to the ViewController class:

```
var queryDidFinishGatheringObserver : AnyObject?
var queryDidUpdateObserver: AnyObject?
var metadataQuery : NSMetadataQuery!
```

2. Next, add the following code to the end of the `viewDidLoad` method:

```
metadataQuery = NSMetadataQuery()
metadataQuery.searchScopes =
    [NSMetadataQueryUbiquitousDocumentsScope]
metadataQuery.predicate = NSPredicate(format: "%K LIKE '*'",
                                            NSMetadataItemFSNameKey)

queryDidUpdateObserver = NSNotificationCenter.defaultCenter()
    .addObserverForName(NSMetadataQueryDidUpdateNotification,
        object: metadataQuery,
        queue: NSOperationQueue.mainQueue()) {
    (notification) in

    self.queryUpdated()
}

queryDidFinishGatheringObserver = NSNotificationCenter.defaultCenter()
    .addObserverForName(NSMetadataQueryDidFinishGatheringNotification,
        object: metadataQuery,
        queue: NSOperationQueue.mainQueue()) {
    (notification) in

    self.queryUpdated()
}

metadataQuery.startQuery()

self.fileList.text = ""
```

This code is pretty much identical to the Mac version. The only difference is that we're directly updating the text view instead of using bindings.

Next, we'll add the method that updates when the metadata query finds files.

Add the following method to `ViewController`:

```
func queryUpdated() {

    var files : [NSURL] = []

    for item in metadataQuery.results {
        if let metadataItem = item as? NSMetadataItem {
            let url =
                metadataItem
                    .valueForAttribute(NSMetadataItemURLKey) as NSURL
            files.append(url)



        }
    }
```

```
        self.fileList.text = files.description

    }
```

Now run the app, and add a file to iCloud via the Mac app. It'll appear in the iOS app.

It's important to note that items that show up in the iCloud container aren't necessarily fully downloaded, particularly if the file is large. Likewise, an item that's uploading to iCloud might take some time.

You can determine the status of a file at a given URL by using NSURL's `valueForAttri bute` method. For example, to work out if a file is completely available, you do this:

```
// metadataItem is an NSMetadataItem describing an item in the
// ubiquity container
var downloadStatus =
    metadataItem.valueForAttribute(
        NSMetadataUbiquitousItemDownloadingStatusKey) as NSString

if downloadStatus == NSMetadataUbiquitousItemDownloadingStatusDownloaded {
    // it's downloaded!
}
```

Document Pickers

Document pickers are an iOS feature that allow the user to select files, either from iCloud or from an external provider (such as a cloud file storage service). Document pickers allow your app to work with any files that the user wants to access, including files stored in other applications.

Document pickers are a fairly large topic, and we don't have room to go into them in very much detail here. We'll be covering how to set up a document picker, and how to configure it to let the user select a file, and to make your app create a copy of that file for its own use.

However, document pickers can go beyond this. For example, you can make a document picker that opens a file that's stored in another app's container, make changes, and save it back to that container. For more information on how to do this, see the *Document Picker Programming Guide* (*http://bit.ly/abt_doc_picker*), located in the Xcode documentation.

A document picker works like this: the user lets your app know that she wants to access a document, and your app creates and configures a `UIDocumentPickerViewControl ler`, and then presents it. The user navigates to the file they want—which may be inside another application's container—and selects it. Once that happens, your app is granted temporary permission to access that file, and can do some work with it. This work can include things like making a copy of the file, or opening the file and presenting it to the user for editing.

When you create a `UIDocumentPickerViewController`, you specify two things:

- The *types* of the files you want to select
- What *mode* the picker should operate in

The type of the file is a Uniform Type Identifier, which is a standard string that defines file types. For example, *public.text* means any file that contains text, while *org.gnu.gnu-zip-archive* means a gzipped archive. To indicate what kinds of files you want the user to select, you provide an array of these strings.

The mode of the document picker defines what the app intends to do with the file that the user has selected. There are four available modes:

Open
The app intends to open the file for editing, and will put it back when changes are done.

Move
The app intends to move the file from its current location into the app's container.

Import
The app intends to make a new copy of the file, and store that copy in its container.

Export
The app has a new file to place in a third-party storage provider.

This chapter discusses the *import* mode, because it's the easiest and most direct way to get data into your app. However, the other three modes have their own uses, and you should check out the documentation (*http://bit.ly/abt_doc_picker*) to see more about how they're used.

Before we get started in building an app that uses document pickers, it's good to ensure that there's actually content in iCloud for you to use.

To quickly add a file to iCloud, follow these steps:

1. Open the TextEdit application on your Mac.
2. Write some text—go on, it can be anything.
3. Save the file. When prompted for a location, choose iCloud. The file will now be stored in iCloud storage.

To implement document pickers, we first need to add a button that triggers the appearance of one:

1. Open your iOS application's storyboard. Add a button to the screen, and make its label read `Select File`.

2. Connect the button to a new action method in `ViewController`, called `selectFile`.

3. Add the following property to the `ViewController` class:

   ```
   var documentSelector : UIDocumentPickerViewController?
   ```

4. Make the `ViewController` class conform to the `UIDocumentPickerDelegate` protocol, by adding it to the list of protocols at the top of the class.

When the button is tapped, we need to create and configure the document picker, and then present it to the user.

5. Implement the `selectFile` method using the following code:

   ```
   @IBAction func selectFile(sender: UIButton) {

       // We want to select any file; 'public.data' means 'any data'
       documentSelector = UIDocumentPickerViewController(documentTypes:
           ["public.data"],
           inMode: UIDocumentPickerMode.Import)
       documentSelector?.delegate = self

       // Show the picker
       self.presentViewController(documentSelector!,
                                      animated: true,
                                      completion: nil)

   }
   ```

   The `public.data` type identifier means *any item that has data*—in other words, any file. (This type excludes folders, which don't actually contain data themselves—they're just containers.)

When the user selects a file, the document picker contacts its delegate, and provides it with an `NSURL` object that points to the file that the user selected.

What you do with this `NSURL` depends on the mode of the document picker. In the case of importing a file, the file pointed to is a temporary file, which will go away when the app closes. In this example, we want to copy any file that the user selects into the app's iCloud container. This means that we need to first copy the file into a temporary position, and then use the `NSFileManager` class to move that copy into ubiquitous storage.

There's one potential snag, though—if the file that was selected happens to be inside another app's iCloud container, the app must first indicate to the system that it wants

permission to access the file. You do this using the `startAccessingSecurityScopedRe`
`source` and `stopAccessingSecurityScopedResource` methods, which were discussed
in "Security-Scoped Bookmarks" on page 221.

When you're done working with the URL, you then need to dismiss the document picker.

There's one last thing to note: if the user doesn't select a file, and instead dismisses the
picker without picking anything, your application also needs to handle this. Usually, all
you need to do is to just dismiss the picker, but you might have some additional logic
that you need to run. Add the following methods to *ViewController.swift*:

```
func documentPicker(controller: UIDocumentPickerViewController,
    didPickDocumentAtURL url: NSURL) {

    // This picker was set up to use the UIDocumentPickerMode.Import mode
    // That means that 'url' points to a temporary file that we can move
    // into our container

    // Let the system know that we're about to start using this—it might
    // be in some other app's container, which means we need to get the
    // system to temporarily unlock it
    url.startAccessingSecurityScopedResource()

    let fileName = url.lastPathComponent

    // Copy it to a temporary location
        let temporaryURL = NSURL.fileURLWithPath(NSTemporaryDirectory(),
                                                        isDirectory:true)?
        .URLByAppendingPathComponent(fileName)

    var copyError : NSError? = nil

    NSFileManager.defaultManager().copyItemAtURL(url,
        toURL: temporaryURL!, error: &copyError)

    if let theError = copyError {
        println("Error copying: \(theError)")
    }

    // We're done—let the system know that we don't
    // need access permission anymore
    url.stopAccessingSecurityScopedResource()

    // Now, move that item into ubiquitous storage

    let destinationURL = NSFileManager.defaultManager()
        .URLForUbiquityContainerIdentifier(nil)?
        .URLByAppendingPathComponent("Documents")
        .URLByAppendingPathComponent(fileName)

    var makeUbiquitousError : NSError? = nil
```

```
NSFileManager.defaultManager().setUbiquitous(true,
    itemAtURL: temporaryURL!,
    destinationURL: destinationURL!,
    error: &makeUbiquitousError)

if let theError = makeUbiquitousError {
    println("Error making ubiquitous: \(theError)")
}

// Finally, dismiss the view controller
self.dismissViewControllerAnimated(true, completion: nil)
}

func documentPickerWasCancelled(controller: UIDocumentPickerViewController!)
{
    // Nothing got selected, so just dismiss it
    self.dismissViewControllerAnimated(true, completion: nil)
}
```

You're all done. Run the application, and tap the Select File button. Find the file you want to add, and select it. If you have the OS X application running as well, you'll see the file you just added on your iOS device appear in the file list.

Using iCloud Well

In order to be a good citizen in iCloud, there are a number of things that your application should do in order to provide the best user experience:

- Don't store some documents in iCloud and some outside. It's easier for users to choose to store all their data in iCloud or to not store anything there.

- Only store user-created content in iCloud. Don't store caches, settings, or anything else—iCloud is meant for storing things that cannot be re-created by the app.

- If you delete an item from iCloud, the file is removed from *all* the user's devices and computers. This means that you should confirm a delete operation with the user before performing it, as users might not understand the implications and may think that they're only deleting the local copy of the file.

Cocoa Bindings

So far in this book, we've talked at length about how the model-view-controller paradigm works in Cocoa and Cocoa Touch, and how dividing up your application's code into these separate areas of responsibility leads to easier-to-manage codebases.

However, sometimes it may seem like overkill to write separate models, views, and controllers, especially when all the controller needs to do is pass information directly from the model to the view and vice versa. In many cases, the only behavior you want is for a label to display information stored in a model object.

To solve this problem, Apple introduced *bindings* in OS X. Bindings are connections between views and objects, where the contents of the object are used to directly drive what the view displays. Bindings mean you can write less code for the same excellent features.

In this chapter, you'll learn how to use bindings to connect your interface directly to data. You'll also learn how to use the built-in controller classes that Apple provides to manage collections of objects. By the end of the chapter, you'll have created a sophisticated note-taking application while writing minimal code.

 Bindings are only available on OS X. Sorry, iOS developers!

Binding Views to Models

A binding is simply an instruction that you give to a view about where its content comes from. The instruction is along the lines of, *OK, text field, the text that you should show comes from this object over here. If it ever changes, update yourself. Likewise, when you change, tell the object to update the text it's storing.*

You bind views to objects by indicating which property on the object the view should show. For example, imagine that the app delegate has a property called `myString`. If you bound a label to that object's property, the two would be linked—whatever the `my String` property contains, the label would display.

Bindings know about what data to display. More importantly, they also know about *when* that display should be updated. When the value of a property is changed, the bindings system informs every view bound to it that they should update themselves.

Bindings also work in reverse. If you have an editable view, such as a text field, the bindings system updates the object with updated content when the user makes changes.

You can bind many different properties of views to model object properties. The most common property you bind is the view's value, which in most cases is the text that the view displays (for labels, text, views, etc.). You can also bind properties to things like whether the view should be enabled or hidden, what font or color the view should use, which image should be used, and so on. The specific view properties that can be bound vary from view to view.

Because bindings largely remove the work of mediating between your model code and your views, you can focus on simply building the user-facing features of your app. Simply put, using bindings means writing less code, which means that you get to make your end product faster and also reduce the potential for bugs.

A Simple Bindings App

To demonstrate how to bind views directly to model objects, let's build a simple application that connects a slider and a text field to a property that we'll add to the app delegate object:

1. Create a new Cocoa application and call it `SimpleBindings`.

2. We'll start by adding the property to the `AppDelegate` object. This property will simply store a number. Open *AppDelegate.swift* and add the following property to it:

   ```
   var numberValue : Int = 0
   ```

We're now ready to create the interface. This application will show both a text field and a horizontal slider:

1. Open the interface and add the interface components.

   First, open *MainMenu.xib* and then open the main window.

Drag in a text field and place it on the lefthand side of the window.

Next, drag in a horizontal slider, and place it on the right of the text field.

When you're done, the interface should look like Figure 11-1.

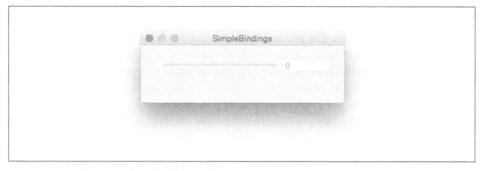

Figure 11-1. The interface for this application

2. Next, we need to make both controls continuous (i.e., we want both views to update the application as the user works with them). The controls will send their information out to the application the moment the user moves the mouse or types a key. If a control isn't continuous, it waits until the user is done interacting with it before sending its new value (which can save work for the application).

   To make the controls continuous, select both the text field and the slider and then open the Attributes Inspector, which is the fourth tab from the left in the Inspector pane. Turn the Continuous checkbox on.

Now that the interface has been set up, it's time to create bindings.

 Remember that the AppDelegate object now has a property, called numberValue, which stores an integer. We're going to bind both of these controls to this property, which will cause the property's value to be displayed in the controls. Having both controls bound to the same thing also has the effect of making them control each other— by dragging the slider from left to right, the text field will update.

Here are the steps you'll need to follow:

1. To bind the text field to the app delegate, you'll need to start by selecting the text field and then the Bindings Inspector (it's the second tab from the right, at the top of the Inspector pane—its icon looks like a little knot).

The Bindings Inspector displays the list of all possible bindable properties in the text field. In this case, we want to bind the text field's value, which is the text that is displayed, so open the Value property.

When binding to an object, we need to provide two things: the object that we are binding to, and the *key* that we want to bind to. The key is simply the name of the property, method, or instance variable that has the content that we want to display.

In this case, the object that we want to bind to is the app delegate. The Bindings Inspector lists all top-level objects in the nib as things that you can bind to, which means you can easily select it. The key that we want to bind to is numberValue, because that's the name of the property in the app delegate object.

 You'll notice that there are two "key" fields shown: the *controller key* and the *model key path*. The controller key refers to the property exposed by the object that you're binding to, while the model key path refers to the property inside the object that's returned by accessing the controller key from the bound object. Because we're not working with a controller object in this case, we provide a model key path that points directly to the property we want.

2. Next, bind the text field's Value.

   To accomplish this, select App Delegate in the "Bind to" drop-down list and set the model key path to numberValue.

 A little red alert icon may appear next to the word numberValue. This is because the text field usually expects a string to be provided, and the numberValue property is an Int. This is fine, because the bindings system knows how to convert integers to strings. However, if you see the red alert icon appear, double-check to make sure that you're binding properties of the correct data types.

3. Just as the text field updates continuously, we want the binding to also update the rest of the application continuously.

   To do this, turn on the Continuously Updates Value checkbox.

4. Now that the text field has been bound, we'll do the same thing for the slider. Keep the Bindings inspector open and select the horizontal slider.

   Open the Value binding.

Select App Delegate in the "Bind to" drop-down list, and set the model key path to numberValue.

You can now see the binding in action. Run the app, and note what happens when you drag the slider back and forth—the text field updates to show the current value of numberValue. If you change the text in the text field, the slider will update.

Binding to Controllers

In the previous example, we've bound views directly to properties that are stored in an object, bypassing a controller object. This works just fine for simple cases, but bindings are also capable of much more powerful work.

For example, it's possible to bind views to data stored in the user defaults system (i.e., within the NSUserDefaults database). This has a number of useful results, such as being able to quickly and easily build a "settings" screen that binds the controls directly to the data stored in the user preferences system.

However, NSUserDefaults is simply a data storage system, and you can't bind directly to it because its content isn't directly observable by the key-value observing system that bindings rely on. To work with it, you need an object mediating between your views and the model. Sound familiar? That's right—you need a *controller object*!

Apple provides just such an object to let you work with NSUserDefaults in bindings: NSUserDefaultsController. This object provides mechanisms for binding views to defaults stored in NSUserDefaults. It also provides a few more advanced features, such as the ability to make changes and then let the user cancel or apply them—so if you want the user to be able to cancel his changes in your preferences window, you can!

Because NSUserDefaultsController is such a common control, you don't even need to create one to start using it. Simply binding a control to the defaults makes it appear in the Interface Builder's outline.

To demonstrate how you can use this controller in your app, we'll adapt our application to store user preferences:

1. First, we'll add a checkbox whose value is stored in the user defaults system, which will also control whether the text field and horizontal slider are enabled (i.e., whether the user can interact with them). To do this, simply add a checkbox to the window and change its label to Enabled.

2. Next, bind the checkbox to the user defaults. You'll need to select the checkbox and open the Bindings Inspector.

   Bind its value to the Shared User Defaults Controller, which appears in the list of bindable objects.

Set the controller key to values and the model key path to controlsEnabled.

We haven't set up a property in the code called controlsEnabled, but that's OK—remember, when you use NSUserDefaults, you just set values for preferences you want to store.

3. Now that the checkbox has been set up, we'll make the text field and horizontal slider become enabled or disabled based on the value of the controlsEnabled property stored in the user defaults. To accomplish this, we'll bind the controls' Enabled property.

   To do this, select the text field and bind the Enabled property to the Shared User Defaults Controller. Set the controller key to values and the model key path to controlsEnabled.

   Repeat this process for the horizontal slider.

   When you're done, the interface should looks like Figure 11-2.

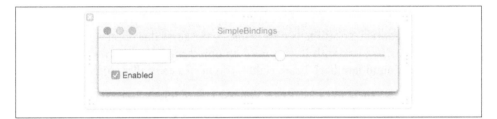

Figure 11-2. The updated interface, with the checkbox and text field added

We can now see it in action. Launch the app, and note that changing the state of the checkbox makes the text field and slider become enabled and disabled. Quit and relaunch the application, and note that the checkbox remembers its state.

Quietly marvel at the fact that you wrote no code at all for this feature!

Array and Object Controllers

As we've seen, controllers mediate between views and models, and allow you to make bindings that keep you from having to write lots of laborious code.

We've just seen NSUserDefaultsController in action, which allows you to bind views to the user preferences system. In this case, the model object is the NSUserDefaults object.

Other controllers exist, which you can use to mediate access to other data in your application. If you want your application to display a collection of data, you need parts of your interface to display the entire collection and other parts to display specific information about the currently selected item in the collection.

This is where NSArrayController comes in. NSArrayController is a controller object that manages an array, and provides access to the contents of the array. The array controller also provides the concept of "selected" objects, meaning that your code can display content relevant for only the items that have been selected by the user. Finally, the NSArrayController is also capable of adding and removing items from the array that it manages.

Another example of a controller object is NSObjectController, which acts as a controller for a single object. The typical use case for this class is where you bind your interface to the NSObjectController, and then your code gives an object to that controller. The moment the content object of the controller changes, the interface updates.

A More Complex Bindings App

Controllers allow you to create extremely sophisticated applications with minimal code. To demonstrate how this works, we're going to create an application that lets the user create, edit, view, and delete small text notes, all while doing most of the work with bindings.

The application will work with a class that we'll create called Note. This class will contain a number of properties: the note's title, the text contained within it, and the date and time that the note was created and edited. The application will display a list of all notes that the user has created, as well as displaying and allowing the user to edit notes. When the user edits a note, the note will update itself to reflect the date and time that the note was changed.

Let's get started on our app:

1. Create a new Cocoa application and call it ControllerBindings.
2. Create a new class by choosing File→New→File or by pressing ⌘-N.

   Create a new Cocoa class called Note. Make this class a subclass of NSObject.
3. Now that the class has been created, we'll add the following properties:

   - title, a String
   - text, an NSAttributedString
   - created, an NSDate
   - edited, an NSDate

Additionally, we want sensible defaults to be set when a new note is created. Specifically, the title should be "New Note," the text should be the text "New Note," and the created and edited date should both be the current date.

Additionally, when either the title or the text is changed, we want the edited date to be updated to be the current date. This can be done with Swift's didSet syntax, which lets you add code that should run when a property changes.

 NSAttributedString is a type of string that stores additional information like font, style, and color. You can use NSAttributedString to store rich text.

Open *Note.swift*, and add the following code to the Note class:

```
class Note: NSObject {

    // Created date is a constant—it's set upon creation, and never changes
    var created : NSDate = NSDate()

    // Edited date defaults to the current date
    var edited : NSDate = NSDate()

    // Title is a string that, when changed, updates the edited date
    var title : String = "New Note" {
    didSet {
        edited = NSDate()
    }
    }

    // Text is an NSAttributed string that does a similar thing
    var text : NSAttributedString = NSAttributedString(string: "New Note") {
    didSet {
        edited = NSDate()
    }
    }

}
```

We're now done with the Note class. It contains the data that we need it to, and will behave the way we want when it's created and updated.

We now need a place to store the instances of the Note class. Because we don't want to deal with the challenges of storing content on disk, this example project will simply store the Note objects in an array inside the application delegate object. This means that no information will be kept around when the app exits.

The array will be stored in a property. This is important because it means that the array controller object that we'll create later will be able to bind to it.

To add the notes property to AppDelegate, open *AppDelegate.swift*. Add the following code to the AppDelegate class:

```
// An empty array of Note objects
var notes = [Note]()
```

 This syntax, where a property is defined as the result of a constructor, effectively tells the compiler two things:

- The property is an array of Notes.
- The array should be created when the instance is created.

We're now completely done with all the code for this application. From here on out, it's bindings all the way.

The first thing that we want to do is display a list of notes that the user has created, and provide a way to add and remove notes from the list. We need a way to provide access to the Note instances. Unlike in our first application, we can't bind the controls directly to the notes property in the app delegate because that's an array, and we want to be able to display individual notes.

To enable this, we use an NSArrayController. This class acts as the gateway to the contents of the array. It will be bound to the notes property, and other views will be bound to it.

The list view itself will be an NSTableView. This class is traditionally tricky to set up and requires that your code act as a data source, implementing several methods and providing all kinds of information to the class. Not so with bindings—in this case, we'll be binding the table view's contents directly to the array controller that manages the notes collection.

First, let's create and set up the array controller:

1. Open *MainWindow.xib*. We're going to start by adding the NSArrayController instance, which lives in the object library. Search for *array controller*, and you'll find it. Drag one into the outline.

2. We'll now instruct the array controller to access the notes property when it wants to know where the data it's managing is stored.

   Select the array controller, and open the Bindings Inspector.

   Open the Content Array property, and bind it to the App Delegate. Set the model key path to notes.

3. We also need to let the array controller know about what class of object the array will contain. This is important because when the array controller is asked to add a new item to the array, it needs to know which class to instantiate.

With the array controller selected, open the Attributes Inspector. Set the Class Name to `ControllerBindings.Note`.

 When you set the Class Name in an array controller, you have to specify both the class's name as well as the name of the module that the class can be found in. Because this example is called Controller-Bindings, you set the Class Name to `ControllerBindings.Note`, but if the project was named something else, you'd change the part of the class name before the dot.

When you provide a content array to an array controller, the array controller can be bound to other objects. Some useful bindable properties include:

`arrangedObjects`
    The total collection of objects in the array, arranged based on the array controller's settings (such as any filters or sorting options that may have been applied).

`selection`
    The currently selected object.

`canAdd` *and* `canRemove`
    `Bool` properties that indicate whether the array controller is currently able to add or remove items. For example, `canRemove` will be false if there is no object selected.

These properties can be accessed by using them as controller keys in the Bindings Inspector.

The array controller is now set up, and we can start creating the interface. We'll begin by adding the table view that lists all notes, as well as buttons that allow adding and removing items:

1. Drag in a table view and place it on the lefthand side of the window. Resize it so that it's about a third of the width of the window.

    When you add a table view, it's placed inside a scroll view. We're going to want to set up several different aspects of the table view, so expand the entire tree by holding down the Option key and clicking the arrow next to Scroll View—Table View in the outline. Select Table View in the items that appear.

    Set the Columns counter in the Attributes Inspector to 1.

2. We want the table view controller to display note titles in the list. Select the Table Column in the outline and open the Bindings Inspector.

Bind the Value property to the array controller. Set the controller key to arrangedObjects and the model key path to title.

The table view will now show the value of the title property for all items in the notes array. Additionally, the table view will control which item is selected.

3. We'll now add two buttons to the view to allow adding and removing items.

Drag in a gradient button from the object library. Resize it to a smallish square shape, and place it underneath the table view.

In the Attributes Inspector, set the button's title to nothing (i.e., delete all the text). Set the image to NSAddTemplate, which will make the button show a plus icon.

Hold down the Option key and drag the button to the right. A copy will be made; place it next to the first button. Set the image of this new button to NSRemoveTem plate, which shows a minus icon.

4. We can now make these buttons instruct the array controller to add and remove items.

Control-drag from the add button to the array controller. Choose add: from the menu that appears.

Control-drag from the remove button to the array controller. Choose remove: from the menu that appears.

Now when these buttons are clicked, the array controller will add a new item to the array that it's managing or delete the currently selected item.

5. For a finishing touch, we're going to disable the remove button if there's nothing to remove or if there's no selected object. The array controller exposes a property called canRemove, to which we can bind the button's Enabled property.

Select the remove button and open the Bindings Inspector.

Bind the Enabled property to the array controller, using the controller key canRemove.

When you're done, the app's interface should look like Figure 11-3.

You can now see this in action by launching the app. Clicking on the add and remove buttons will add and remove items from the list, and when nothing is selected, the remove button is disabled.

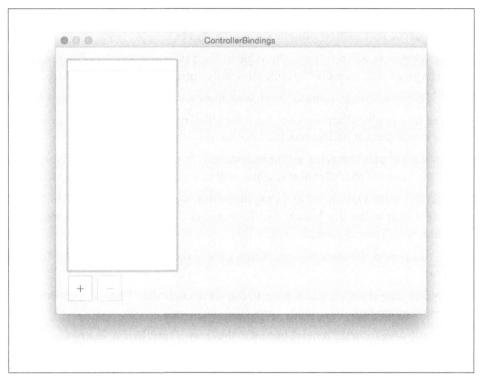

Figure 11-3. The initial interface for the new controller-based application

We'll now make the notes work. All we need to do here is set up views and bind them to the selected object, which is provided to us by the array controller:

1. To create the interface, add a text field to the right side of the window and place it at the top. This text field will show the `title` property in the notes.

   Add a text view underneath the text field. Make it rather tall to allow for plenty of room for adding text. This text view will show the `text` property.

2. Next, bind the controls: select the text field and bind its *value* to the array controller. Set the controller key to `selection` and the model key path to `title`. Turn Continuously Updates Value on.

   Select the text view (note that it's kept inside a scroll view, so you'll need to expand it in the outline to get to it), and bind its *attributed string* to the array controller. Set the controller key to `selection` and the model key path to `text`. Turn Continuously Updates Value on here, too.

3. Finally, we'll create the interface that shows the date and bind it. Add a label to the window. Set its text to `Created:` and place it under the text view.

Add another label and set its text to Edited:. Place it under the Created label.

Add a third label and put it to the right of the Created label. Resize it to the right edge of the window. This label will display the date that the note was created on.

Add a fourth label to the right of the Edited label. Resize it like the last one.

When you're done, the user interface should look liker Figure 11-4.

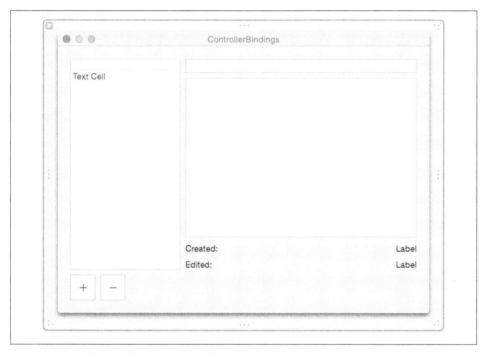

Figure 11-4. The completed user interface

4. Select the empty label to the right of the Created label and bind it to the array controller. Set the controller key to selection and the model key path to created.

   Select the other label and bind it similarly, but with the model key path set to edited.

5. By default, when you bind a label to an NSDate property, that label will show the *full* date—down to the seconds and time zone. This can get a little huge, and it'd be better if we showed this as a shorter, more succinct version. You can do this by adding a *date formatter* to the label, which gives you control over how the date that's being shown in the label is represented.

   Search for "date formatter" in the object library, and drag one from the library to the Created date label.

A Date Formatter will appear in the outline. Select it, and configure it so that the Date Style is set to Medium Style, and the Time Style is set to Short Style. This will result in the label showing the date along the lines of "7 Jul 2014 3:21 pm."

Repeat the same process with the Edited date label.

We're done. You can now see the entire app in action! You can add and remove items, and store any text you like in the text field. Renaming the note updates live in the list, and changing the note's contents updates the Edited label.

CHAPTER 12

Table Views and Collection Views

One of the most common tasks for any app, regardless of platform, is displaying lists or collections of data. iOS and OS X provide a number of tools for viewing data, and in this chapter you'll learn how to use them.

Both iOS and OS X feature table views and collection views. A *table view* is designed to provide a list of data, while a *collection view* is designed to show a grid of data. Both table views and collection views can be customized to provide different layouts.

Table views are used all over OS X—Finder and iTunes both use it to show lists of files and songs. Table views are used even more heavily in iOS—any time you see a vertically scrolling list, such as the list of messages in Messages or the options in Settings, you're seeing a table view.

Collection views are used a little less frequently, as they're a newer addition to both platforms. Collection views can be seen (again) in Finder and iTunes, as well as in Launchpad. On the iPad, a collection view appears in the Clock application, which was added in iOS 6.

Data Sources and Delegates

Despite their differences in layout, table and collection views have very similar APIs. When a data display view prepares to show content, it has to know the answers to at least two questions:

- How many items am I showing?
- For each item, what do I need to do to display it?

These questions are asked of the view's *data source*, which is an object that conforms to the table view's *data source protocol*. The data source protocol differs based on the type of view that you're using.

There are other questions that a data view may need to know the answer to, including "How tall should each row in the list be?" and "How many sections should the list contain?" These questions are also answered by the data source, but the view can fall back to some default values in case the data source isn't able to provide this information.

Sometimes displaying information is all you want, but your application usually needs to respond to the user interacting with the view's content. The specific things that the user can do vary depending on the platform, the kind of data view, and how you've configured the view. Some possible interactions include:

- Clicking (or tapping) on an item
- Rearranging content
- Deleting or modifying content

These actions are sent by the view to its *delegate*.

Table Views

Table views are designed for showing lists of information. On OS X, a table view shows data with multiple columns, which can be rearranged and resized, and is generally used to show data. On iOS, table views only show one column and are useful for any kind of vertically scrolling list, as seen in the Settings application.

UITableView on iOS

Table views are implemented on iOS using the UITableView class. This is one of the most versatile view classes on iOS: with it, you can create interfaces that range from simple lists of data to complex, multipart, scalable interfaces.

On iOS, the term "table view" is somewhat of a misnomer. The word "table" usually brings to mind a grid with multiple rows and columns, but on iOS the table view is actually a single column with multiple rows. The reason for this is that the size of the iPhone's screen is too narrow for more than one column to make sense, but the API design for UITableViewController was based on NSTableViewController, which we'll discuss later in this chapter.

 If you want to create a multiple-column table view on iOS, you either need to build it yourself, or use a UICollectionView (which we discuss in "Collection Views" on page 272).

Table views on iOS present a scrolling list of *table view cells*, which are views that can contain any data you like. UITableView is designed for speed: one of the most common gestures that the user performs on an iOS device is to flick a finger up and down a scrolling list, which means that the application needs to be able to animate the scrolling of that list at high frame rates (ideally, 60 frames per second, which is the maximum frame rate of iOS).

Sections and Rows

Table views can be divided into multiple *sections*, each of which contains one or more *rows*. Sections allow you to divide your content in a manner that makes sense to you. For example, the Contacts application uses a table view that divides rows by surname, and the Settings application uses a table view that divides rows into categories.

Because table views are divided into sections, specific locations in the table view are identified not by row, but by *index path*. An index path is nothing more complex than a section number and a row number, and is represented using the NSIndexPath class:

```
let indexPath = NSIndexPath(forRow: 2, inSection: 1)
```

(Note that you don't usually create NSIndexPath's yourself—this example just shows how they're composed.)

Let's imagine that we've got a table view that's divided into two sections: the first section has two rows, and the second section has three (Figure 12-1).

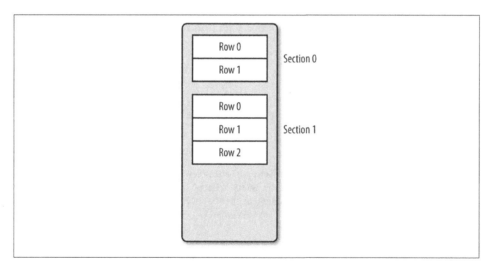

Figure 12-1. A table view, divided into sections

Using index paths, you can refer to the very first cell as section 0, row 0. The second cell is section 0, row 1, and the third cell is section 1, row 0. This allows row numbers to be independent of their sections, which can be very handy indeed.

Table View Controllers

If you add a `UITableView` to an interface without doing any additional work, you'll see an empty list. By default, `UITableView`s rely on a *data source* object to provide them with information on what content to show.

Any object can be a data source for a `UITableView`; the only requirement is that it must conform to the `UITableViewDatasource` protocol (for more information on protocols, see "Protocols" on page 46).

The object is almost always a `UIViewController`, and almost always the view controller of the view that contains the table view. There's nothing stopping you from doing it differently, though.

The two critical methods that the `UITableViewDatasource` protocol defines are:

```
func tableView(tableView: UITableView!,
    numberOfRowsInSection section: Int) -> Int

func tableView(tableView: UITableView!,
    cellForRowAtIndexPath indexPath: NSIndexPath!) -> UITableViewCell!
```

The first, `numberOfRowsInSection`, returns the number of rows in the specified table section (see "Sections and Rows" on page 259). The second, `cellForRowAtIndexPath`, returns a `UITableViewCell` for the specified index path.

For example, here's how to indicate that every section in the table has two rows:

```
func tableView(tableView: UITableView!,
    numberOfRowsInSection section: Int) -> Int {
    return 2
}
```

This method is the easier of the two. Here's an example of an implementation of `table View(_, cellForRowAtIndexPath:)` (we'll talk about exactly what it does in the next section):

```
override func tableView(tableView: UITableView,
cellForRowAtIndexPath indexPath: NSIndexPath) -> UITableViewCell {
    let cell = tableView.dequeueReusableCellWithIdentifier("StringCell",
forIndexPath: indexPath) as UITableViewCell

    cell.textLabel.text = "Hello!"

    return cell
}
```

Table View Cells

A table view cell represents a single item in the table view. Table view cells are UITable ViewCells, a subclass of UIView. Just like any other UIView, table view cells can have any other UIViews included as subviews.

When the table view needs to show data, it needs the answer to two questions: how many rows are there to show, and what should be shown for each row. The first question is answered by the numberOfRowsInSection method; the second is answered by table View(_, cellForRowAtIndexPath:).

cellForRowAtIndexPath is called for every visible row in the table view *as it comes into view*. This last part is important because it enables the table view to not have to worry about displaying content that isn't visible. If, for example, you have a table view that contains 1,000 objects, fewer than 10 of those objects are likely to be visible. Because it makes no sense for the table view to attempt to display table view cells for rows that may never be shown, tableView(_, cellForRowAtIndexPath:) is called only as a cell is about to come onto the screen.

tableView(_, cellForRowAtIndexPath:) is responsible for returning a configured UITableViewCell. "Configured," in this case, means making sure that the table view cell is displaying the right content. That content depends on what the table view is being used for: if you're making a shopping list application, each table view cell would contain an item in the shopping list.

Cell reuse. As the user scrolls the table view, some items in the list will go off screen while others come on screen. When a table view cell in the list scrolls off screen, it is removed from the table view and placed in a *reuse queue*. This reuse queue stores UITableView Cell objects that have been created but are not currently visible. When a cell is scrolled into view, the table view retrieves an already created UITableViewCell object from the reuse queue.

The advantage of this method is that the time taken to allocate and set up a new object is completely removed. All memory allocations take time, and if the user is quickly scrolling through a long list, he would see a noticeable pause as each new cell appeared.

UITableViewCell objects are automatically placed into the reuse queue by the table view as the cells scroll off screen; when the table view's data source receives the table View(cellForRowAtIndexPath:) message, it fetches a cell from the reuse queue and prepares that, rather than creating an entirely new cell.

A table view can have many different kinds of cells—for example, you might have a table view with two sections that show entirely different cells in each section. However, there's only one tableView(cellForRowAtIndexPath:) method, which is called for all rows in all sections. To differentiate, you can use the index path that is passed to this method to figure out which section and row the table view wants a cell for.

Anatomy of a UITableViewCell. A table view cell is a UIView, which can contain any additional UIView s that you want to include. In addition to this flexibility, UITableView Cell objects also support a few basic *styles*, which are similar to the table view cells seen in other parts of iOS. There are four basic table view styles:

Default
> A black, bold, left-aligned text label, with an optional image view. As the name suggests, this is the default style for table view cells.

Right Detail
> A black, left-aligned text label, with a smaller, blue-colored, right-aligned text label on the righthand side. This cell style can be seen in the Settings application.

Left Detail
> A blue, right-aligned label on the lefthand side, with a black, left-aligned label on the righthand side. This cell style can be seen in the Phone and Contacts applications.

Subtitle
> A black, left-aligned label, with a smaller, gray label underneath it. This cell style can be seen in the Music application.

The common theme is that all table view cells have at least one primary text label, and optionally a secondary text label and an image view. These views are UILabel and UIImageView objects, and can be accessed through the textLabel, detailTextLabel, and imageView properties of the table view cell.

You can see examples of all four built-in table view cell styles in Figure 12-2.

Preparing table views in Interface Builder. Prior to iOS 5, constructing table views and table view cells was a largely programmatic affair, with developers writing code that manually instantiated and laid out the contents of any nonstandard table view cells in code. This wasn't a great idea, because layout code can get tricky. So, from iOS 5 onward, table views and their cells can be designed entirely in Interface Builder.

When you add a table view to an interface, you can also create *prototype cells*. The contents of these cells can be designed by you and completely customized (from changing the colors and fonts to completely changing the layout and providing a custom subclass of UITableViewCell). These prototype cells are marked with a *cell identifier*, which allows your code to create instances of the prototypes.

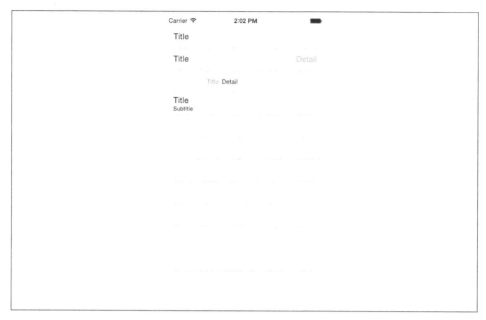

Figure 12-2. The different table view cell styles (from top to bottom: Basic, Right Detail, Left Detail, and Subtitle)

Analyzing tableView(_, cellForRowAtIndexPath:). With all of this in mind, we can now take a closer look at the `tableView(_, cellForRowAtIndexPath:)` implementation that we looked at earlier. Here it is again:

```
override func tableView(tableView: UITableView,
cellForRowAtIndexPath indexPath: NSIndexPath) -> UITableViewCell {
    let cell = tableView.dequeueReusableCellWithIdentifier("StringCell",
forIndexPath: indexPath) as UITableViewCell  ❶

    cell.textLabel.text = "Hello!"  ❷

    return cell  ❸
}
```

The method performs three actions:

❶ The table view is asked to dequeue a table view cell that has a cell identifier of `StringCell`. This causes the table view to either create an instance of the prototype cell that has this identifier, or dequeue one from the reuse queue if a cell with this identifier has been previously created and is not currently visible.

❷ The cell's primary text label is set to display the text "Hello!"

❸ Finally, the cell is returned to the table view, which will display it to the user.

Responding to actions. The most common thing that the user does with table view cells is to tap them. When this happens, the table view will contact its *delegate* and inform it that a cell was selected.

An object must conform to the `UITableViewDelegate` protocol in order to be a delegate. The table view's delegate can be different from its data source, but in practice the delegate is the same object as the data source (i.e., the view controller that manages the table view conforms to both the `UITableViewDelegate` and `UITableViewDatasource` protocols).

There are several methods that `UITableViewDelegate` specifies, all of which are optional. The most important and commonly used method is `tableView(_, didSelectRowAtIndexPath:)`, which is called when a row is tapped. This is the delegate's opportunity to perform an action like moving to another screen:

```
override func tableView(tableView: UITableView, didSelectRowAtIndexPath
                        indexPath: NSIndexPath)  {
    println("Selected \(data[indexPath.row])")
}
```

Implementing a Table View

To put it all together, we'll build a simple table view application that displays the contents of an array of `NSString` objects:

1. Create a new, single view iOS application named iOSTableView.

2. Delete the *ViewController.swift* file. We'll be creating a replacement for it shortly.

3. Create and set up the table view. In this example, the view controller will be a `UITableViewController`, which is a subclass of `UIViewController` that manages a single `UITableView`.

   Open *Main.storyboard* and delete the existing view controller. Then drag in a table view controller from the objects library. Select the new view controller, and open the Attributes Inspector. Turn on the Is Initial View Controller checkbox.

4. Set up the prototype cell. By default, a `UITableViewController` that's been dragged into the storyboard contains a single prototype cell. We're going to configure that to be the cell that we want.

   Select the single cell that appears at the top of the table view.

   Make sure the Attributes Inspector is open, and change its identifier to `StringCell`.

   Change the cell's style from Custom to Basic, by using the drop-down menu at the top of the Attributes Inspector.

The table view is fully configured; it's now time to write the code that will provide the table view with the information it needs:

---

1. Create the new table view controller class. Create a new Cocoa Touch class by choosing File→New→File… and selecting Cocoa Touch class. Name it `TableView Controller` and make it a subclass of `UITableViewController`.

2. Make the table view controller use the new class. Go back to the storyboard and select the view controller.

   Note that clicking on the table view won't select the view controller—it'll select the table *view*. You can select the table view controller itself from the Outline view on the lefthand side of the Interface Builder.

   Go to the Identity Inspector and change the class from `UITableViewController` to `TableViewController`.

3. Open *TableViewController.swift* and add the array of strings.

   We can now write the code that drives the table view. First, we need to create an array that contains the strings that will be displayed.

   Add the following property to `TableViewController`:

   ```
   var data = ["Once", "upon", "a", "time"]
   ```

4. Make the table view data source return one section. The table view will contain one section, and this section will contain as many rows as there are entries in the `data` array.

   To determine how many sections are present, the table view sends its data source object the `numberOfSectionsInTableView` message. This method is already implemented in the template code, but returns zero. We just need to change this to return 1.

   Find the `numberOfSectionsInTableView` method in *TableViewController.swift* and replace it with the following code:

   ```
   override func numberOfSectionsInTableView(tableView: UITableView)
       -> Int {
       return 1
   }
   ```

5. Make the table view data source indicate the correct number of rows for the section. We need to tell the table view that the section has as many rows as there are objects in the `data` array. This is handled by the `tableView(_, numberOfRowsInSec tion:)` method.

   Find the `tableView(_, numberOfRowsInSection:)` method in *TableViewController.swift* and replace it with the following code:

   ```
   override func tableView(tableView: UITableView,
       numberOfRowsInSection section: Int) -> Int {
       return data.count
   }
   ```

6. Implement the `tableView(_, cellForRowAtIndexPath:)` method. We need to prepare the table view cells for each of the rows that the table view will ask for.

   Find the `tableView(_, cellForRowAtIndexPath:)` method in `TableViewControl ler.swift` and replace it with the following code:

   ```
   override func tableView(tableView: UITableView,
       cellForRowAtIndexPath indexPath: NSIndexPath) -> UITableViewCell {

       let cell = tableView.dequeueReusableCellWithIdentifier("StringCell",
                       forIndexPath: indexPath) as UITableViewCell

       let string = data[indexPath.row]

       cell.textLabel.text = string

       return cell


   }
   ```

7. Implement the `tableView(_, didSelectRowAtIndexPath:)` method. Finally, we'll make the code log the string corresponding to the text that was selected.

   Add the `tableView(_, didSelectRowAtIndexPath:)` method in *TableViewController.swift*:

   ```
   override func tableView(tableView: UITableView, didSelectRowAtIndexPath
                       indexPath: NSIndexPath)  {
       println("Selected \(data[indexPath.row])")
   }
   ```

NSTableView on OS X

The process of displaying tables of data on OS X is slightly more complex than on iOS. Tables on OS X are capable of displaying multiple columns of data, which can be rearranged and resorted by the user. Table views on OS X are instances of the `NSTable View` class. However, the fundamental idea behind table views on OS X is the same as on iOS—a table view uses a data source object to determine how many rows exist and what content should be shown for each row.

The only significant difference in terms of programming for `NSTableView` is that the method that returns the content that should be shown for a table view cell needs to take into account both the row number and column for the data.

The method for returning the view that should be shown in a cell is `tableView(view ForTableColumn:row:)`. This method's parameters are the `NSTableView` that wants to show content, and the column and row number that are being displayed. The row number is represented as a simple integer, while the table column is an

NSTableColumn. This is because columns can be rearranged, and it therefore doesn't make sense to have "column numbers." Rather, NSTableColumn objects have *identifiers*, which are used by your code to figure out what specific piece of information needs to be shown.

To demonstrate how table views work on OS X, we'll build an application that displays multiple columns of data. This app will display a list of songs, along with their running times.

1. Create a new Cocoa application called CocoaTableView.

2. Create the Song class. The first thing we'll do is create the data source. Each song that the application displays will be an instance of the class Song, which we'll create ourselves. Each Song object has a title string, as well as a duration represented as an NSTimeInterval (which is just another way of saying float—it's a typedef defined by Cocoa).

   To create the class, go to File→New→File... and choose Cocoa class. Create a new class called Song and make it a subclass of NSObject.

   Once it's been created, open *Song.swift* and make it look like the following code:

   ```
   class Song: NSObject {

       var title : String = "A Song"
       var duration : NSTimeInterval = 0.0

   }
   ```

   This class only contains properties and no methods—it's only for storing data.

3. Next, we'll make AppDelegate store a list of Song objects. This list will be an NSMutableArray, which is managed by an NSArrayController.

   This controller won't be used immediately, but instead will be used as part of the bindings used to drive the table view, later in this chapter.

   Open *AppDelegate.swift* and add the following properties to the class:

   ```
   var songs : [Song] = []
   @IBOutlet var songsController: NSArrayController!
   ```

4. Finally, we need to make the object populate this list when it appears.

   Add the following method to the `AppDelegate` class:

```
override func awakeFromNib() {
    if self.songs.count == 0 {
        var aSong : Song!

        aSong = Song()
        aSong.title = "Gaeta's Lament"
        aSong.duration = 289

        self.songsController.addObject(aSong)

        aSong = Song()
        aSong.title = "The Signal";
        aSong.duration = 309

        self.songsController.addObject(aSong)

        aSong = Song()
        aSong.title = "Resurrection Hub";
        aSong.duration = 221

        self.songsController.addObject(aSong)

        aSong = Song()
        aSong.title = "The Cult of Baltar";
        aSong.duration = 342

        self.songsController.addObject(aSong)
    }
}
```

 Bonus points for those who get the reference!

We'll now prepare the interface for the application:

1. Open *MainMenu.xib*, and drag an array controller into the outline.

   Open the Bindings Inspector, and bind the Content Array to the App Delegate. Set the model key path to `self.songs`.

   Hold down the Control key and drag from the app delegate to the array controller. Choose `songsController` from the menu that appears.

2. Create the table view. Open *MainMenu.xib* and select the window. It's empty, but we'll soon fix that.

   Drag a table view from the objects library into the window. Make it fill the window.

   Select the table header view at the top of the table view. Double-click the first column's header and rename it `Title`. Rename the second column header `Duration`.

3. We now need to set up the columns to have the correct identifiers, and to use `NSViews` as their content rather than old-style `NSCells` (which was the previous method prior to OS X 10.7 Lion).

   Select the "Title" table column object in the outline. Switch to the Identity Inspector and set the Restoration ID to "Title."

   Then, select the "Duration" table column in the outline and change its Restoration ID to "Duration."

   Finally, select the table view in the outline and change its content mode from Cell Based to View Based.

4. Next, we need to set up the table view's data source and delegate. Control-drag from the table view to the app delegate, and choose "dataSource" from the menu that appears. Then Control-drag from the table view to the app delegate again, and choose "delegate."

5. The `AppDelegate` class needs to conform to the `NSTableViewDataSource` and `NSTableViewDelegate` protocols in order to satisfy the compiler.

   Open *AppDelegate.swift*, and make the class conform to two new protocols:

   ```
   class AppDelegate: NSObject, NSApplicationDelegate,
                   NSTableViewDelegate, NSTableViewDataSource {
   ```

6. Add the `numberOfRowsInTableView` method to `AppDelegate`. This method indicates to the table view how many rows should appear:

   ```
   func numberOfRowsInTableView(tableView: NSTableView!) -> Int {
       return self.songs.count
   }
   ```

7. Add the `tableView(viewForTableColumn:row:)` method to `AppDelegate`. This method returns an `NSView` that will appear in the table view cell, based on the row number and column used:

   ```
   func tableView(tableView: NSTableView!, viewForTableColumn
               tableColumn: NSTableColumn!, row: Int) -> NSView!  {

       let cell =
                   tableView.makeViewWithIdentifier(tableColumn.identifier,
                       owner: self) as NSTableCellView

       let textField = cell.textField
       let song = self.songs[row]
   ```

```
            if tableColumn.identifier == "Title" {
                textField?.stringValue = song.title
            } else if tableColumn.identifier == "Duration" {
                let durationText = NSString(format: "%i:%02i",
                                            Int(song.duration) / 60,
                                            Int(song.duration) % 60)
                textField?.stringValue = durationText
            }

            return cell
        }
```

In this method, the table view is asked to dequeue a reusable view based on the identifier of the table column. This is returned as a NSTableCellView, which will contain the text field that should show the text.

Then, depending on the specific column, the text of the text field is set to either the song's title or a string representation of the song's duration.

Finally, run the application. Behold the songs!

Sorting a Table View

When you click a table view header, you're indicating to the table view that it should re-sort the contents of the table. To do this, the table columns need to know what specific property they're responsible for showing.

This is implemented by providing *sort keys* to each of the columns. Sort keys indicate what property should be used for sorting.

To add sort keys, select the "Title" table column in the outline. Open the Attributes Inspector and set the sort key to title. Leave the selector as compare: and the order as Ascending. Then, select the "Duration" table column in the outline, and change the sort key to duration.

When a table column header is clicked, the table view's data source receives a table View(sortDescriptorsDidChange:) message. A *sort descriptor* is an instance of the NSSortDescriptor class, which provides information on how a collection of objects should be sorted.

To sort an array using sort descriptors, you take the array, and use the sort method. This method takes a closure that it uses to work out how a pair of objects is ordered; you can simple take each sort descriptor, and use its compareObject(toObject:) method to work out this ordering.

To implement the tableView(sortDescriptorsDidChange:) method, add the following method to AppDelegate:

```
func tableView(tableView: NSTableView!,
               sortDescriptorsDidChange oldDescriptors: [AnyObject]!) {

    // Apply each sort descriptor, in reverse order

    for sortDescriptor in tableView.sortDescriptors.reverse()
        as [NSSortDescriptor] {
        songs.sort() {
            (item1, item2) in
            return sortDescriptor.compareObject(item1, toObject: item2)
                == NSComparisonResult.OrderedAscending
        }
    }

    tableView.reloadData()
}
```

Now launch the application. Click one of the headings, and note the table view re-sorting.

NSTableView with Bindings

The NSTableView class is quite straightforward to use with a code-driven data source, but it's often a lot simpler to use Cocoa bindings (see Chapter 11). So to cap off our coverage of NSTableView, we're going to adapt the code to use Cocoa bindings.

When using bindings, we bind both the table view and the specific views in each table view cell. The table view is bound to the array controller so that it knows how many rows exist, and the views in the cells are bound to the specific property that should be displayed.

To bind the table view to the array controller:

1. Select the table view in the outline. Go to the Connections Inspector and remove the dataSource and delegate links.

2. Go to the Bindings Inspector, and bind the table view's Content to Array Controller.

3. Select the text field in the table view cell in the Title column. Bind its value to Table Cell View and set the model key path to objectValue.title. This will make the cell display the title of the Song object that this row is displaying.

4. Select the text field in the table view cell in the Title column. Bind its value to Table Cell View" and set the model key path to objectValue.durationString. This a method that we're about to create.

We want to display a human-readable representation of the Song object's duration property, and the best way to do that is to add a durationString method that formats the underlying NSTimeInterval appropriately. To add this method to the Song class, add the following to *Song.swift*:

```
func durationString() -> String {
    return NSString(format: "%i:%02i", Int(self.duration) / 60,
                          Int(self.duration) % 60)
}
```

Now run the application; you can continue to see the songs.

Collection Views

A collection view is a tool for displaying a collection of objects. While table views are great for tabular displays of data, you often want to display a collection of items in a way that isn't a list.

Collection views exist on both iOS and OS X, though the implementation is better on iOS. In this section, you'll learn how to use UICollectionView, the iOS class that allows you to display a collection of views.

We aren't covering NSCollectionView, the OS X counterpart to UI CollectionView, in this book, mostly because the API is a little cumbersome and also because there aren't as many use cases for it. If you need more information on NSCollectionView, take a look at the *Collection View Programming Guide* (*http://bit.ly/abt_collection_views*), included as part of the Xcode developer documentation.

UICollectionView on iOS

UICollectionView lets you present a collection of items in a way that doesn't require each item to know how it's being positioned or laid out. UICollectionView behaves rather like UITableView, but it doesn't just lay content out in a vertical list—rather, it supports customizable layout handlers called *layout objects*.

The UICollectionView class makes use of a data source and delegate, much like the UITableView and NSTableView classes. The UICollectionView displays a collection of UICollectionViewCell objects, which are UIViews that know how to be laid out in a collection view. Generally, you create subclasses of these cells and fill them with content.

By default, a UICollectionView displays its content in a grid-like fashion. However, it doesn't have to—by creating a UICollection ViewLayout subclass and providing it to the collection view, you can lay out the UICollectionViewCell objects in any way you want. UI CollectionViewLayout subclassing is a little beyond the scope of this chapter, but there's plenty of interesting discussion in the documentation for this class.

To demonstrate collection views in use, we're going to create an application that displays a collection of numbers in a grid:

1. Create a single view application for iPad called AwesomeGrid.

2. Create the collection view controller. Delete the *ViewController.swift* file. We'll be replacing it shortly.

   Create a new `UICollectionViewController` subclass by choosing File→New→File... and creating a new Cocoa Touch object named `GridViewCon troller`. Make it a subclass of `UICollectionViewController`.

3. Prepare the collection view. Open *Main.storyboard* and delete the view controller. Drag in a collection view controller. With the new view controller selected, open the Identity Inspector and change its class from `UICollectionViewController` to `GridViewController`.

We'll now create our own subclass of the `UICollectionViewCell` class, which will contain a label. Unlike `UITableViewCell` objects, the `UICollectionViewCell` doesn't provide standard styles for cells, as it doesn't make assumptions about the content your application will be showing.

The actual contents of the `UICollectionViewCell` will be designed in the Interface Builder.

Create the collection view subclass and use it in the collection view. Create a new `UI CollectionViewCell` subclass by choosing File→New→File... and creating a new Cocoa Touch object named `GridCell`. Make it a subclass of `UICollectionViewCell`.

Go back to *Main.storyboard* and select the collection view cell at the upper left of the collection view. Go to the Identity Inspector and change its class from `UICollection ViewCell` to `GridCell`.

Go to the Attributes Inspector and change the collection view item's identifier to `Cell`.

Resize the cell to be about twice the size. Drag a label into the cell. Using the Attributes Inspector, make its font larger, and change its color to white. Resize the label to fill the cell and make the text centered. Add constraints to center it horizontally and vertically within the cell.

Open *GridCell.swift* in the assistant. Control-drag from the label into the `GridCell` class, and create a new outlet called `label`.

Having set up the collection view, we can now set up the view controller to display the content. The actual "content" to be displayed will be the numbers from 1 to 200, which will be stored as numbers objects in an array. For each `GridCell` that the collection view needs to display, the view controller will convert the number to an string and display it in the `UILabel`.

The first step in this process is to store the array of numbers:

1. Prepare the data. Open *GridViewController.swift*.

   Add the following property to the `GridViewController` class:

   ```
   var numbers : [Int] = []
   ```

   Next, replace the `viewDidLoad` method with the following code (removing all other code):

   ```
   override func viewDidLoad() {
       super.viewDidLoad()

       for i in 1...200 {
           numbers.append(i)
       }

   }
   ```

2. Add the methods that indicate the number of items in the collection view. The methods for providing data to a `UICollectionView` are very similar to those for working with a `UITableView`: you provide the number of sections, the number of items in each section, and a `UICollectionViewCell` object for each item.

   Add the following methods to `GridViewController`. If they already exist, replace the code for them:

   ```
   override func numberOfSectionsInCollectionView
                   (collectionView: UICollectionView) -> Int {
       return 1
   }

   override func collectionView(collectionView: UICollectionView,
               numberOfItemsInSection section: Int) -> Int {
       return self.numbers.count
   }
   ```

3. Implement the `collectionView(cellForItemAtIndexPath:)` method. Displaying a cell in a collection view is just as simple. Because we have already prototyped the `GridCell` in the Interface Builder, the only thing that needs to happen is for the view controller to prepare the cell when it appears in the collection view.

   Add the following method to `GridViewController`:

   ```
   override func collectionView(collectionView: UICollectionView,
           cellForItemAtIndexPath indexPath: NSIndexPath)
                                           -> UICollectionViewCell
   {
       let cell =
           collectionView.dequeueReusableCellWithReuseIdentifier(reuseIdentifier,
                       forIndexPath: indexPath) as UICollectionViewCell

       if let gridCell = cell as? GridCell {
   ```

```
            gridCell.label.text = String(self.numbers[indexPath.row])
        }

        return cell
    }
```

Run the application—you should see a scrolling grid of numbers.

Note that when you rotate the iPad (if you're using the simulator, use the ⌘-← and ⌘-→ keys), the collection view lays itself out correctly.

CHAPTER 13

Document-Based Applications

For the user, a computer and its applications are simply ways to access and work with their documents (e.g., their spreadsheets, images, music, etc.). The designers of OS X and iOS understand this, and provide a number of tools for making apps designed around letting the user create, edit, and work with documents.

The idea of a document-based application is simple: the application can create documents, and open previously created documents. The user edits the document and saves it to disk. The document can then be stored, sent to another user, duplicated, or anything else that a file can do.

While both OS X and iOS provide technologies that allow you to make document-based applications, the way in which documents are presented to the user differs.

On OS X, as with other desktop-based OSes, users manage their documents through the Finder, which is the dedicated file management application. The entire filesystem is exposed to the user through the Finder.

On iOS, the filesystem is still there, but the user rarely sees it. Instead, all documents are presented to the user and managed by the application. All the tasks involved in managing documents—creating new files, renaming files, deleting files, copying files, and so on—must be done by your application.

 The user has some access to the filesystem through *document picker* view controllers, which are discussed in "Document Pickers" on page 237.

More than one application may be able to open a document. For example, JPEG images can be opened by both the built-in Preview application and by Photoshop for different purposes. Both OS X and iOS provide ways for applications to specify that they are able to open certain kinds of documents.

In this chapter, you'll learn how to create apps that work with documents on both iOS and OS X.

The NSDocument and UIDocument Classes

In iOS and OS X, documents are represented in your application with the UIDocument and NSDocument classes, respectively. These classes represent the document and store its information. Every time a new document is created, a new instance of your application's NSDocument or UIDocument subclass is created.

Document Objects in MVC

Document objects participate in the model-view-controller paradigm. In your app, document objects are model objects—they handle the reading and writing of information to disk, and provide that information to other parts of the application.

All document objects, at their core, provide two important methods: one to save the information by writing it to disk, and one to load the information by reading it from disk. The document object, therefore, is in charge of converting the document information that's held in memory (i.e., the objects that represent the user's data) into a data representation that can be stored on disk.

For NSDocument, the methods are these:

```
func dataOfType(typeName: String?,
    error outError: NSErrorPointer) -> NSData?

func readFromData(data: NSData?,
    ofType typeName: String?, error outError: NSErrorPointer) -> Bool
```

And for UIDocument, the methods are these:

```
func contentsForType(typeName: String!,
    error outError: NSErrorPointer) -> AnyObject!

func loadFromContents(contents: AnyObject!,
    ofType typeName: String!, error outError: NSErrorPointer) -> Bool
```

The first set of methods is responsible for producing an object that can be written to disk, such as an NSData object. The second is the opposite—given an object that represents one or more files on the disk, the document object should prepare itself for use by the application.

Kinds of Documents

OS X and iOS support three different ways of representing a document on disk:

- *Flat files*, such as JPEG images and text documents, which are loaded into memory wholesale.
- *File packages*, which are folders that contain multiple files, but are presented to the user as a single file. Xcode project files are file packages.
- *Databases*, which are single files that are partially loaded into memory as needed.

All three of these methods are used throughout OS X and iOS, and there's no single "correct" way to represent files. Each one has strengths and weaknesses:

- A flat file is easy to understand from a development point of view, where you simply work with a collection of bytes in an NSData object. It is also very easy to upload to the Web and send via email. However, a flat file must be read entirely into memory, which can lead to performance issues if the file is very large.
- File packages are a convenient way to break up a large or complex document into multiple pieces. For example, Keynote presentations are file packages that contain a single file describing the presentation's contents (its slides, text, layout, etc.), and include all images, movies, and other resources as separate files next to the description file. This reduces the amount of data that must be kept in memory, and allows your application to treat each piece of the document as a separate part.

  The downside is that other operating systems besides OS X and iOS don't have very good support for file packages. Additionally, you can't upload a file package to a website without first converting it to a single file (such as by zipping it).

- Databases combine the advantages of single-file simplicity with the random-access advantage of file packages. However, making your application work with databases requires writing more complex code. Some of this is mitigated by the existence of tools and frameworks like SQLite and Core Data, but your code will still be more complex.

The current trend in OS X and iOS is toward flat files and databases, because these are easier to archive and upload to iCloud.

 In this book, we'll be covering flat files, because they're simpler to work with. The same overall techniques apply to file packages and databases, however, and if you want to learn more about using them, check out the *Document-Based Programming Guide* (*http://bit.ly/ abt_cocoa_doc_architecture*) in the Xcode documentation.

The Role of Documents

A document object (i.e., a subclass of NSDocument or UIDocument) is both a model and a model-controller in the model-view-controller paradigm. For simpler applications, the document object is simply a model—it loads and saves data, and provides methods to let controller objects access that information.

For more complex applications, a document object may operate as a model-controller (i.e., it would be responsible for loading information from disk and creating a number of subobjects that represent different aspects of the document). For example, a drawing and painting application's documents would include layers, color profiles, vector shapes, and so on.

Document-Based Applications on OS X

OS X was designed around document manipulation, and there is correspondingly strong support for building document-based applications in Cocoa and Xcode.

When creating a document-based application, you specify the name of the NSDocu ment class used by your application. You also create a nib file that contains the user interface for your document, including the window, controls, toolbars, and other views that allow the user to manipulate the contents of the document.

Both the document class and the document nib file are used by the NSDocumentCon troller to manage the document-related features of your app:

- When you create a new document, a new instance of your document class is created, and copies of the view objects in the document nib file are instantiated. The new document object is placed in charge of the view.

- When the user instructs the application to save the current document, the document controller displays a dialog box that asks the user where she wants to save her work. When the user selects a location, the document controller asks the frontmost document object to store its contents in either an NSData or NSFileWrapper object (for flat files and file packages, respectively; if the document is a database, it saves its contents via its own mechanisms). The document controller then takes this returned object and writes it to disk.

- When the application is asked to open a document, the document controller determines which class is responsible for handling the document's contents. An instance of the document class is instantiated and asked to load its data from disk; the controls are also instantiated from the nib as previously discussed, and the user starts working on the document.

Autosaving and Versions

Starting with OS X 10.7 Lion and iOS 5, the system autosaves users' work as they go, even if they haven't previously saved it. This feature is built into the NSDocumentCon troller class (and on iOS, the UIDocument class), which means that no additional work needs to be done by your application.

Autosaving occurs whenever the user switches to another application, when the user quits your application, and also periodically. From your code's perspective, it's the same behavior as the user manually saving the document; however, the system keeps all previous versions of the document.

The user can ask to see all the previous versions, which the system handles for you automatically. The user is then able to compare two versions of the document, and copy and paste content from past versions.

Representing Documents with NSDocument

To demonstrate how to make a document-based application in OS X, we'll make an application that works with its own custom document format. This application will start out as a simple text editor, and we'll move on to more sophisticated data manipulation from there.

The first thing to do is create a new Cocoa app for OS X. Name it CocoaDocuments, and make sure that Use Core Data is off.

Turn Create a Document-Based Application on, and set the document extension to sampleDocument. When you create the application, it will load and save files named along the lines of *MyFile.sampleDocument*.

When you create a document-based application in Xcode, the structure of the application is different from non-document-based applications. For example, Xcode assumes that the majority of your application's work will be done in the document class, and therefore doesn't bother to create or set up an application delegate class.

It does, however, create a Document class, which is a subclass of NSDocument. This is used as the document class for the "sampleDocument" type. By default, the Document class does nothing except indicate to the application that the interface for manipulating it should be loaded from the *Document* nib file (see the windowNibName property in *Document.swift*), which Xcode has also already created when setting up the application.

Stubs of dataOfType(typeName:error:) and readFromData(data:ofType:error:) are also provided, although they do nothing except create an NSError object, which lets the document system gracefully display an alert box that lets the user know that there was a problem working with the data.

If you open *Document.xib*, you'll find the window that contains the interface that will represent each document that the user has open. If you select the file's owner in the outline and go to the Identity Inspector (the third button from the left at the top of the Utilities pane), you'll note that the object that owns the file is a Document object (Figure 13-1). This means you can create actions and outlets between your Document class and the interface.

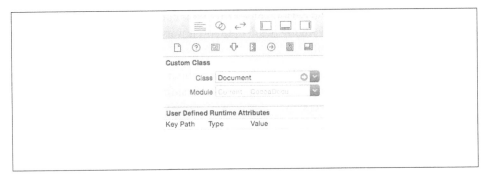

Figure 13-1. The class of the file's owner object can be set using the Identity Inspector

Saving Simple Data

The first version of this application will be a plain text editor. We'll now modify the interface for the document to display a text field, and make the Document class save and load plain text:

1. Open *Document.xib* and delete the label in the window.

   By default, the interface contains a window that has a label inside it. We'll keep the window, but lose the label.

2. Add a wrapping text field to the window.

   Open the objects library and scroll until you find "Wrapping text field." Alternatively, search for "wrapping" at the bottom of the library.

   Drag the text field into the window and resize it to make it fill the entire window.

   When you're done, the interface should look like Figure 13-2.

3. Open the assistant and connect the text field to the class. Once the interface has been built, you need to connect the interface to the document class. Open the assistant and *Document.swift* should open. If it doesn't, use the jump bar at the top of the assistant editor to select it.

   Control-drag from the text field into the Document class, and create a new outlet called textField.

In addition to having a variable that connects the document class to the text field, we need a variable that contains the document's text. This is because the document loading and interface setup take place at different times. When your readFromDa ta(data:ofType:error:) method is called, the textField won't yet exist, so you must store the information in memory. This is also a better design as far as model-view-controller goes, because it means that your data and your views are kept separate.

4. Add a string property called text by adding the following code to Document:

```
var text = ""
```

Figure 13-2. The final UI for the document window

5. Now we'll update the loading and saving methods, and make them load and save the text. We'll also update the windowControllerDidLoadNib method, which is called when the interface for this document has been loaded and is your code's opportunity to prepare the interface with your loaded data.

Replace methods dataOfType(type:, error:), readFromData(data:, ofType:, error:), and windowControllerDidLoadNib with the following code:

```
override func windowControllerDidLoadNib(aController: NSWindowController) {

    // The window has loaded, and is ready to display.
    // Take the text that we loaded earlier and display
    // it in the text field
    super.windowControllerDidLoadNib(aController)
```

```
            self.textField.stringValue = self.text
        }

        override func dataOfType(typeName: String?,
            error outError: NSErrorPointer) -> NSData? {

            // Convert the contents of the text field into data,
            // and return it
            self.text = self.textField.stringValue

            return self.text.dataUsingEncoding(NSUTF8StringEncoding,
                allowLossyConversion: false)
        }

        override func readFromData(data: NSData?, ofType typeName: String?,
            error outError: NSErrorPointer) -> Bool {

            // Attempt to load a string from the data; if it works, store it
            // in self.text
            if data?.length > 0 {
                let string = NSString(data: data, encoding: NSUTF8StringEncoding)
                self.text = string
            } else {
                self.text = ""
            }

            return true
        }
    }
```

Now run the application and try creating, saving, and opening documents. You can also use Versions to look at previous versions of the documents you work with. If you quit the app and relaunch it, all open documents will reopen.

Saving More Complex Data

Simple text is easy to read and write, but more complex applications need more structured information. While you could write your own methods for serializing and deserializing your model objects, it's often the case that the data you want to save is no more complex than a dictionary or an array of strings and numbers.

JavaScript Object Notation (JSON) is an ideal method for representing data like this. JSON is a simple, human-readable, lightweight way to represent arrays, dictionaries, numbers, and strings, and both OS X and iOS provide tools for converting certain useful objects into JSON and back.

The NSJSONSerialization class allows you to provide a *property list class*, and get back an NSData object that contains the JSON data that describes that class. A property list class is one of these classes:

- Strings
- Numbers
- NSDate
- NSURL
- NSData
- Arrays and dictionaries, as long as they only contain objects in this list

In the case of the container classes (dictionaries and arrays), these objects are only allowed to contain other property list classes.

To get JSON data for an object, you do this:

```
let dictionary = ["One": 1, "Two":2]

var error : NSError? = nil

let serializedData = NSJSONSerialization.dataWithJSONObject(dictionary,
    options: NSJSONWritingOptions(), error: &error)

// After this call, 'serializedData' is either nil or full of JSON data.
// If there was a problem, the 'error' variable is set to point to an
// NSError object that describes the problem.
```

You can pass other values for the options parameter as well—check the documentation for NSJSONSerialization. If you don't want to pass an option in, just provide an empty NSJSONWritingOptions().

To load JSON data in and get back an object, you do this:

```
let loadedDictionary =
    NSJSONSerialization.JSONObjectWithData(serializedData,
        options: NSJSONReadingOptions(), error: &error) as? [String:Int]

// loadedDictionary is now either a dictionary that maps
// strings to ints, or is nil
```

We'll now modify the application to store both a block of text and a Boolean value in a JSON-formatted document. To do this, we'll include a checkbox control in the application's UI, and a Bool property in the Document:

1. Open *Document.xib*.
2. Resize the text field to make some room at the bottom of the window.
3. Drag a checkbox into the window. The interface should now look something like Figure 13-3.

Figure 13-3. The updated interface, with the checkbox at the bottom of the window

4. Open *Document.swift* in the assistant.

5. Control-drag from the checkbox into the Document class, and create a new outlet called checkbox.

6. Add a Bool property called checked to Document.

7. Replace the methods dataOfType(type:error:), readFromData(data:ofType:error:), and windowControllerDidLoadNib with the following code:

```
override func windowControllerDidLoadNib(aController: NSWindowController) {

    // The window has loaded, and is ready to display.
    // Take the text that we loaded earlier and display
    // it in the text field
    super.windowControllerDidLoadNib(aController)

    self.textField.stringValue = self.text
    self.checkbox.integerValue = Int(self.checked)
}

override func dataOfType(typeName: String?,
    error outError: NSErrorPointer) -> NSData? {

    self.text = self.textField.stringValue
    self.checked = Bool(self.checkbox.integerValue)

    let dictionary = ["checked": self.checked,
                      "text": self.text]
```

```
var error : NSError? = nil

let serializedData = NSJSONSerialization.dataWithJSONObject(dictionary,
    options: NSJSONWritingOptions.PrettyPrinted, error: &error)

if serializedData == nil || error != nil {

    outError.memory = error

    return nil;
} else {
    return serializedData
}

}

override func readFromData(data: NSData, ofType typeName: String?,
    error outError: NSErrorPointer) -> Bool {

    var error : NSError? = nil

    let data = NSJSONSerialization.JSONObjectWithData(data,
        options: NSJSONReadingOptions(), error: &error) as? NSDictionary

    if data == nil || error != nil {
        outError.memory = error
        return false
    }

    if let text = data!["text"] as? String {
        self.text = text
    }

    if let checked = data!["checked"] as? Bool {
        self.checked = checked
    }

    return true
}
```

This new code stores the document information in an NSDictionary, and returns the
JSON in the NSData.

 If you're curious, the JSON representation of this dictionary looks like
this:

```
{
  "checked" : true,
  "text" : "Hello!!"
}
```

The loading code does the same in reverse—it takes the NSData that contains the JSON, and converts it to an NSDictionary. The loaded dictionary then has the data copied out of it.

Now run the application and create, load, and save some new documents!

Document-Based Applications on iOS

In contrast to apps on OS X, apps on iOS generally only have one document open at a time. This means that the document API is simpler, as an NSDocumentController is not needed—the concept of "frontmost document" doesn't apply.

In iOS, instead of using NSDocument, you use UIDocument. However, instead of users selecting which document to open via the Finder, you instead present a list of the user's documents and allow the user to select a file. When she chooses a file, you create an instance of your document class and instruct the document object to load from the appropriate URL.

You also provide the interface for letting the user create a new document; when she does so, you again create an instance of your document class and immediately save the new document. Generally, you then immediately open the newly created file.

We're going to create an iPhone application that acts as a simple text editor. Creating document-based applications on iOS is less automated than on OS X, but is still fairly straightforward.

This application will present its interface with two view controllers: a master view controller that lists all available documents, and a detail view controller that displays the contents of the currently open document and allows the user to edit it.

The built-in master-detail application template for iOS is ideal for this, and we'll use that. We'll also have to create our UIDocument subclass manually:

1. Create a new master-detail app for iOS. Make this application designed for iPhone and name it iOSDocuments.

2. We'll start by creating the interface. Open *Main.storyboard* and locate the master view controller.

3. Update the segues. We need to replace the default segues that come with the application template that Xcode provides.

   Delete the segue that connects the master view controller.

   Then, hold down the Control key, and drag from the master view controller to the detail view controller, and choose Push from the menu that appears.

   Finally, select the newly created segue, and set its identifier to showDetail.

4. Add a bar button item to the navigation bar.

 This button will be the "create new document" button. Select it and set its identifier to Add to make it display a + symbol.

5. Open *MasterViewController.swift* in the assistant.

6. Connect the button. Control-drag from the button to the MasterViewController class, and create an action named createDocument.

7. Update the prototype cell. Select the prototype cell that now appears in the table view. Set its style to Basic and its identifier to FileCell. Set its accessory to Disclosure Indicator.

8. Open the detail view controller and delete the label in the middle of the view.

9. Add a text view. Drag a UITextView into the view controller's view. Make the text view fill the entire screen.

10. Open *DetailViewController.swift* in the assistant.

11. Connect the text view to the detail view controller. Control-drag from the text view into the DetailViewController class. Create a new outlet called textView.

12. Add a Done button to the navigation bar in the detail view controller. Drag a bar button item into the lefthand side of the navigation bar and set its identifier to Done. (We'll make the code not display the Back button.)

    When you're done, the interface should look like Figure 13-4.

13. Make the view controller the delegate for the text view. We want the detail view controller to be notified when the user makes changes. Control-drag from the text view to the view controller, and select "delegate" from the menu that pops up.

We'll now make the code for our UIDocument subclass, called SampleDocument. This document class will manage its data in a flat file, which means that it will work by loading and saving its content in an NSData:

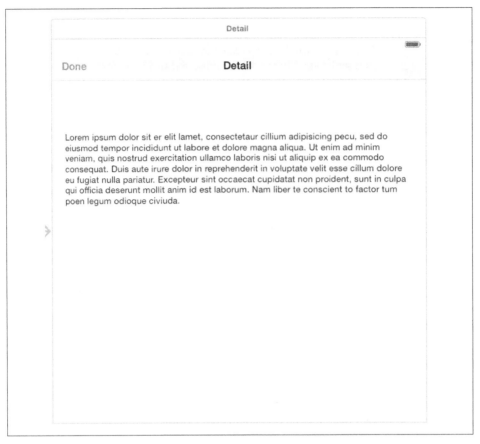

Lorem ipsum dolor sit er elit lamet, consectetaur cillium adipisicing pecu, sed do eiusmod tempor incididunt ut labore et dolore magna aliqua. Ut enim ad minim veniam, quis nostrud exercitation ullamco laboris nisi ut aliquip ex ea commodo consequat. Duis aute irure dolor in reprehenderit in voluptate velit esse cillum dolore eu fugiat nulla pariatur. Excepteur sint occaecat cupidatat non proident, sunt in culpa qui officia deserunt mollit anim id est laborum. Nam liber te conscient to factor tum poen legum odioque civiuda.

Figure 13-4. The application's interface

1. Create a new Cocoa Touch class. Name the new class `SampleDocument` and make it a subclass of `UIDocument`.

2. Update *SampleDocument.swift* so that it reads as follows:

```
import UIKit

class SampleDocument: UIDocument {

    var text = ""

    // Called when a document is opened.
    override func loadFromContents(contents: AnyObject,
        ofType typeName: String, error outError: NSErrorPointer) -> Bool {

        self.text = ""

        if let data = contents as? NSData {
```

```
            if data.length > 0 {
                // Attempt to decode the data into text; if it's successful
                // store it in self.text
                if let theText =
                    NSString(data: data, encoding: NSUTF8StringEncoding) {
                        self.text = theText
                }
            }

        }

        return true

    }

    // Called when the system needs a snapshot of the current state of
    // the document, for autosaving.
    override func contentsForType(typeName: String,
        error outError: NSErrorPointer) -> AnyObject? {

        return self.text.dataUsingEncoding(NSUTF8StringEncoding)

    }

}
```

We'll now update the code for *MasterViewController.swift* to display a list of files:

```
import UIKit

class MasterViewController: UITableViewController {

    var documentURLs : [NSURL] = []

    func URLForDocuments() -> NSURL {
        return NSFileManager.defaultManager()
            .URLsForDirectory(NSSearchPathDirectory.DocumentDirectory,
                inDomains: NSSearchPathDomainMask.UserDomainMask).last as NSURL
    }

    func updateFileList() {
        documentURLs = NSFileManager.defaultManager()
            .contentsOfDirectoryAtURL(self.URLForDocuments(),
                includingPropertiesForKeys: nil,
                options: NSDirectoryEnumerationOptions(), error: nil) as [NSURL]

        self.tableView.reloadData()
    }

    override func viewWillAppear(animated: Bool) {
        self.updateFileList()
```

```swift
}

override func numberOfSectionsInTableView(tableView: UITableView) -> Int {
    return 1
}

override func tableView(tableView: UITableView,
    numberOfRowsInSection section: Int) -> Int {
    return documentURLs.count
}

override func tableView(tableView: UITableView,
    cellForRowAtIndexPath indexPath: NSIndexPath) -> UITableViewCell {

    let cell = tableView
        .dequeueReusableCellWithIdentifier("FileCell") as UITableViewCell

    let URL = documentURLs[indexPath.row]

    cell.textLabel.text = URL.lastPathComponent

    return cell
}

override func tableView(tableView: UITableView,
    didSelectRowAtIndexPath indexPath: NSIndexPath) {

    let URL = documentURLs[indexPath.row]

    let documentToOpen = SampleDocument(fileURL: URL)
    documentToOpen.openWithCompletionHandler() {
        (success) in
        if success == true {
            self.performSegueWithIdentifier("showDetail",
                                            sender: documentToOpen)
        }
    }

}

override func prepareForSegue(segue: UIStoryboardSegue, sender: AnyObject!) {

    if segue.identifier == "showDetail" {
        let detailViewController =
            segue.destinationViewController as DetailViewController

        let document = sender as? SampleDocument
        detailViewController.detailItem = document

    }
}
```

```
@IBAction func createDocument(sender: AnyObject) {

    let dateFormatter = NSDateFormatter()
    dateFormatter.dateFormat = "yyyy-MM-dd HH:mm:ssZZZ"

    let dateString = dateFormatter.stringFromDate(NSDate())

    let fileName = "Document \(dateString).sampleDocument"

    let url = self.URLForDocuments().URLByAppendingPathComponent(fileName)

    let documentToCreate = SampleDocument(fileURL: url)
    documentToCreate.saveToURL(url,
        forSaveOperation: UIDocumentSaveOperation.ForCreating) {

        (success) in

        if success == true {
            self.performSegueWithIdentifier("showDetail",
                                            sender: documentToCreate)
        }
    }

}

}
```

Finally, we'll update the code for `DetailViewController` to make it display the content from the loaded `SampleDocument` object and send the user's changes to the document. The `DetailViewController` will also notice when the user taps the Done button that was added earlier, and signal to the document that it should be saved and closed.

We also want to make the class conform to the `UITextViewDelegate` protocol, so that we receive changes from the user as she types them.

To make `DetailViewController` conform to `UITextController`, go to *DetailView-Controller.swift* and update it with the following code:

```
import UIKit

class DetailViewController: UIViewController, UITextViewDelegate {

    @IBOutlet weak var textView: UITextView!

    @IBAction func done(sender: AnyObject) {
        if let document : SampleDocument = self.detailItem {
            document.saveToURL(document.fileURL,
                forSaveOperation: UIDocumentSaveOperation.ForOverwriting)
            {
                (success) in

                self.navigationController?.popViewControllerAnimated(true)
```

```
            return
        }
    }
}

var detailItem: SampleDocument? {
    didSet {
        self.configureView()
    }
}

func configureView() {
    if let document: SampleDocument = self.detailItem {
        self.textView?.text = document.text
    }
}

func textViewDidChange(textView: UITextView!) {
    if let document : SampleDocument = self.detailItem {
        document.text = self.textView.text
        document.updateChangeCount(UIDocumentChangeKind.Done)
    }
}

override func viewDidLoad() {
    super.viewDidLoad()

    self.configureView()

    self.navigationItem.hidesBackButton = true
}


}
```

In this code, the DetailViewController object has received the SampleDocument object loaded by the MasterViewController, and makes the text view display the text that it contains. Every time the user makes a change to the text field, the text in the SampleDocument is updated; the SampleDocument will automatically save the document's contents in order to prevent data loss if something bad happens (like a crash or the device running out of battery).

When the Done button is tapped, the document is told to close, which saves any unsaved changes. Once this process is complete, the view controller dismisses itself.

CHAPTER 14

Networking

Many chapters in books like this begin with something like, "The ability to talk to computers over the network is an increasingly popular feature." We won't bore you with that. Suffice to say—it's the 21st century, networking is huge, and your app needs to send and receive data. Let's learn how.

In this chapter, you'll learn how to make connections over the network and access resources with URLs. You'll also learn how to use Bonjour to discover nearby network services so that you can connect to them. Finally, you'll learn how to create your own network service and receive connections from other devices.

All of the content in this chapter applies to both OS X and iOS.

Connections

At the lowest level, network connections in Cocoa are the same as in every other popular OS. The Berkeley sockets API, the fundamental networking and connectivity API used on Windows and Unix OSes (which includes OS X and iOS), is available, allowing you to make connections to any computer on the network and send and receive data.

However, working with such a low-level API can be cumbersome, especially when you want to use popular, higher level protocols like HTTP. To make things more fun for developers like us, Cocoa provides a higher level API that provides a simple interface for accessing content via URLs on the Internet.

A URL is a *uniform resource locator*. It's a location on the Internet, and specifies the location of the server to connect to, the protocol to use, and the location of the resource on the server. Consider the following URL: *http://oreilly.com/iphone/index.html*.

In this case, *oreilly.com* is the location of the computer on the Internet, *http* is the scheme (here, the *Hypertext Transfer Protocol*), and */iphone/index.html* is the location of the specific resource hosted by this computer.

When working with web-based network requests, there are three primary classes that you interact with: NSURL, NSURLRequest, and NSURLSession.

NSURL

The NSURL class represents a URL. NSURLs are just model objects—they contain information about the location of the resource they point to, and provide a number of useful methods for retrieving specific components of the URL, as well as creating URLs relative to other URLs.

The easiest way to create an NSURL is to use a string, like this:

```
let myURL = NSURL(string: "http://oreilly.com")
```

If you use NSURL(string:), the string you provide must be a well formed URL. If it isn't well formed, you'll get a nil value.

Because calling NSURL's constructor can result in nil, it always returns an optional. You'll need to use ? and ! to unwrap it.

You can also create URLs that are relative to other URLs:

```
let relativeURL = NSURL(string: "resources/index.html",
    relativeToURL: NSURL(string: "http://oreilly.com/"))
```

Once you have an NSURL, you can retrieve information about it. For example, to retrieve the host (the computer name), you can do the following:

```
let host = relativeURL?.host // = "oreilly.com"
```

NSURL is an immutable class. If you want to create a URL object that you can later modify the properties of, use NSMutableURL.

URLs are also useful for indicating the location of a file or folder on the local disk, and both iOS and OS X are increasingly trending toward using them instead of strings that contain paths.

A file URL is a regular NSURL, but uses the scheme file:. A file URL, therefore, looks like this:

```
file://localhost/Applications/
```

There are special methods in NSURL that make it easier to create file URLs. For example, you can create one using the fileURLWithPath: method:

```
let myFileURL = NSURL(fileURLWithPath:"/Applications/")
```

NSURLRequest

Once you have an NSURL object that points to where your resource is located, you construct an NSURLRequest. While NSURL points to *where* the resource is on the network, NSURLRequest describes *how* it should be accessed.

NSURLRequest takes an NSURL and adds information about things like how long the request should go without an answer before timing out, whether (and how) to use caching, and, if the request is an HTTP request, which request method (GET, POST, PUT, etc.) to use and what the HTTP request's body should be.

For most cases, you can use the NSURLRequest(URL:) method to create an NSURLRequest given an NSURL:

```
let urlRequest = NSURLRequest(URL:myURL!)
```

If you want to have more control over how the request is performed, you can use NSURLRequest(URL:cachePolicy:timeoutInterval:). This method is the same as the previous one, but you specify how the request should cache content that it downloads and how long the request should wait before giving up.

 NSURLRequest(URL:) creates a request that caches content according to the default caching policy of the protocol you're using (e.g., HTTP caches depending on whether the server instructs it to, while FTP never caches) and times out after 60 seconds.

If you want to send a POST request or make changes to the request, you can use NSMutableURLRequest. This is the mutable version of the NSURLRequest class, and allows you to configure the request after you create it. To create a POST request, for example, you use the HTTPMethod property:

```
let mutableRequest = NSMutableURLRequest(URL: myURL!)
mutableRequest.HTTPMethod = "POST"
```

NSURLSession

Once you have an NSURLRequest to use, you can go ahead and execute that request on the network. Because network requests aren't instant, your code needs to be able to manage the life cycle of the connection. This is done for you by the NSURLSession object, which represents a connection in progress.

NSURLSession was introduced into OS X 10.9 and iOS 7 as a replacement for the older NSURLConnection API, and is the new and recommended way to handle any URL-related tasks, both uploading and downloading. It is comprised of four major objects: NSURLSession, NSURLSessionDelegate, NSURLSessionConfiguration, and NSURLSessionTask.

NSURLSessionConfiguration is the object representing a configuration to be used by a session. An NSURLSessionConfiguration handles, among other things, cache, cookie policy, proxies, and timeouts. Each configuration object created is mutable and designed to be shared by multiple sessions. Apple has also provided some predefined configurations for common situations.

NSURLSessionTask represents an individual task to be handled by the session. In some ways, it is the closest object to NSURLConnection in that it contains the state of the task being performed. The NSURLSessionTask also has methods to let you cancel, suspend, and resume the task.

Finally, NSURLSession and its delegate NSURLSessionDelegate is responsible for performing any tasks sent to it. In general, when using an NSURLSession you will not need to deal with its delegate; just use completion blocks when the session finishes a task. When you wish to use NSURLSession for background downloading in iOS in your application, you will have to handle the session delegate methods as well as implement the application(_, handleEventsForBackgroundURLSession:, completionHandler:) in your application's delegate.

NSURLSession is a large and complex class; however, to get it up and running is generally quite straightforward. We'll cover how it works in the sample code in the section "Building a Networked Application" on page 299.

NSURLResponse and NSHTTPURLResponse

The response classes describe the initial response from the server about the request. This information includes the expected size of the downloaded file (in bytes) and the suggested filename that the server wants to call it. If you're making an HTTP request, the server response is an instance of the NSHTTPURLResponse, which also includes the HTTP status code and the headers that the server sends down.

You don't generally create your own NSURLResponse instances, but rather get them from an NSURLSession or NSURLConnection object when it first successfully gets a response from the server and starts downloading content.

Think of it like this:

- NSURL is a finger pointing at the moon.
- NSURLRequest is a blueprint for a Saturn V rocket.
- NSURLSession is an Apollo mission to the moon.

Building a Networked Application

To put all of this together, we'll build a simple application that downloads an image from the Internet and displays it in an NSImageView.

The exact same networking code will work on iOS, but using UIImageView rather than NSImageView.

This application downloads an image from Placekitten, the world's most adorable placeholder image service. Of course, web services come and go, so if you're living in the World of Tomorrow and Placekitten is long since history, find another image URL to use instead. And then eat another meal in pill form and catch a space-taxi to the moon.

1. Make a new Cocoa application called Networking.
2. Build the interface. Open *MainWindow.xib*, and select the main window. Drag in an NSImageView.
3. Connect the interface. Open *AppDelegate.swift* in the assistant.

   Control-drag from the image view to AppDelegate's interface. Create a new outlet called imageView.
4. Add the code that performs the network request. Replace the applicationDidFinishLaunching method with the following code:

   ```
   func applicationDidFinishLaunching(aNotification: NSNotification?) {

       // PlaceKitten.com URLs work like this:
       // http://placekitten.com/<width>/<height>

       let width = self.imageView.bounds.size.width
       let height = self.imageView.bounds.size.height
   ```

```
let urlString = "http://placekitten.com/\(Int(width))/\(Int(height))"

if let url = NSURL(string:urlString) {

    // Using this URL, make an NSURLSesssion and then create a data
    // request task.
    let session = NSURLSession(
        configuration: NSURLSessionConfiguration
                        .defaultSessionConfiguration())

    let dataTask = session.dataTaskWithURL(url) {
        (data: NSData?,
        response: NSURLResponse?,
        error: NSError?) in

        if data == nil {
            self.imageView.image = nil
        } else {
            if let image = NSImage(data: data!) {
                self.imageView.image = image;
            }
        }


    }

    // Call resume() on the data request to start it
    dataTask.resume()
}
```

 It is very important to call `resume` on any `NSURLSessions` after giving them a task. As `NSURLSession` is designed to handle enqueing of
multiple tasks, it needs to be told to start.

This code creates a URL based on the size of the image view, and then creates and
configures an `NSURLSession` (using the predefined `defaultSessionConfiguration`
class) to handle the URL. Finally, the code asks the `NSURLSession` to download the URL;
the completion block then takes the loaded data, converts it to an `NSImage`, and provides
the image to the image view.

Now test the application. Run the app, and feel free to squeal in delight when you see a
cute kitten.

Bonjour Service Discovery

If you're writing networking code that deals with resources on the local network, your code needs a way to figure out where they are.

Bonjour is a protocol based on multicast DNS that allows a network service to advertise its presence on a network, and provides a method for clients to find services. Bonjour doesn't handle the actual connection, just the discovery.

When you want to find local services via Bonjour, you use an `NSNetServiceBrowser` object. This object, once created and started, looks for network services that match the description that you provide it. Because network services come and go, the `NSNet` `ServiceBrowser` continuously notifies its delegate object when services become available and when they stop being available.

Once `NSNetServiceBrowser` locates a network service, you can ask for additional information about the service such as the hostname of the computer providing the service and the port number that the service is running on. This is called *resolving* the service, and takes a bit of extra time (which is why the service browser doesn't do it for every service it discovers). When the service resolves (or fails to resolve), the `NSNetService` object informs its delegate.

To be notified of when `NSNetServiceBrowser` notices when services appear and disappear, your object needs to conform to the `NSNetServiceBrowserDelegate` protocol. To be notified of when an `NSNetService` resolves, your object also needs to conform to the `NSNetServiceDelegate` protocol.

Browsing for Shared iTunes Libraries

If you have "Share my library on the local network" turned on in iTunes, iTunes will broadcast the library via Bonjour. Specifically, it will advertise that your computer is hosting a DAAP (Digital Audio Access Protocol) server.

To discover services of this type, you get an `NSNetServiceBrowser` to search for `_daap._tcp` services. We'll make a simple application that browses for, resolves, and logs any shared iTunes libraries it finds.

All you need to do is create a new Cocoa application called iTunesDetector and update *AppDelegate.swift* so that it looks like the following code:

```swift
import Cocoa

class AppDelegate: NSObject, NSApplicationDelegate, NSNetServiceDelegate,
    NSNetServiceBrowserDelegate {

    @IBOutlet var window: NSWindow!
```

```
        let browser = NSNetServiceBrowser()
        var services = [NSNetService]()

        func applicationDidFinishLaunching(aNotification: NSNotification?) {

            browser.delegate = self;

            // Search for DAAP services that use TCP, in the default domains
            browser.searchForServicesOfType("_daap._tcp", inDomain:"")

        }

        func netServiceBrowser(aNetServiceBrowser: NSNetServiceBrowser,
            didFindService aNetService: NSNetService, moreComing: Bool) {

            services.append(aNetService)

            println("Found a service: \(aNetService)")

            aNetService.delegate = self
            aNetService.resolveWithTimeout(5.0)
        }

        func netServiceBrowser(aNetServiceBrowser: NSNetServiceBrowser,
            didRemoveService aNetService: NSNetService, moreComing: Bool) {

            services = services.filter({ $0 != aNetService})

            println("A service was removed: \(aNetService)")

        }

        func netServiceDidResolveAddress(sender: NSNetService) {
            let serviceURL = NSURL(string:"http://\(sender.hostName):\(sender.port)")

            println("Resolved address for service \(sender): \(serviceURL)")
        }

        func netService(sender: NSNetService,
                          didNotResolve errorDict: NSDictionary) {
            println("Couldn't resolve address for service \(sender), \(errorDict)")
        }
    }
```

This code does the following things:

1. It adds a class extension to the AppDelegate class, which makes the class conform
   to the NSNetServiceBrowserDelegate and NSNetServiceDelegate protocols, and
   adds two instance variables: an NSNetServiceBrowser and an NSMutableArray.
   The net service browser variable is needed to keep the net service browser in mem-

ory while it does its work; the array will be used to keep the discovered network services around.

2. In the `applicationDidFinishLaunching` method, the `NSNetServiceBrowser` is created and told to start browsing for `_daap._tcp` services.

3. The rest of the methods handle the cases of services being discovered, removed, resolved, or failing to be resolved.

Now run the application and watch the log to see your iTunes library get discovered. If you don't see anything appear, make sure that iTunes is open and that you're sharing your library. Do this by opening Preferences, going to Sharing, and turning on "Share my library on my local network."

Multipeer Connectivity

Multipeer Connectivity is a means of identifying and connecting services together, and allows for very easy passing back and forth of data with minimal setup. If you are thinking that this seems similar to Bonjour, you are correct; however, Bonjour is for service discovery, not connection or transmission. Multipeer Connectivity handles everything in one neat package.

Multipeer Connectivity is comprised of a few different components, but it works by having applications advertise their services and asking if anyone is available to connect. The service browser listens for these advertisements and can request to create a connection between the devices. If the connection is accepted, a session is created with everyone inside the session being represented by a peer object.

To demonstrate how this works, we'll make a simple chat application (this exercise is written for iOS, but the Multipeer Connectivity framework also works on OS X):

1. Create a new, single view iPhone application called MultipeerChat.

2. Open the project in the project navigator and the add the Multipeer Connectivity framework into the project from the Linked Frameworks and Libraries section.

3. Open the *Main.storyboard*, and add a `UITextView`. Make it take up most of the space, and set its editable field to be false in the Atrributes Inspector.

4. Add a `UITextField` and add two buttons. Label one `Browse` and the other `Send`.

5. Connect the `UITextView` up to a property called `chatView`.

6. Connect the `UITextField` up to a property called `messageField`.

7. Connect the browse button up to an action called `showBrowser`, and the Send button up to an action called `sendChat`.

When complete, your interface should look like Figure 14-1.

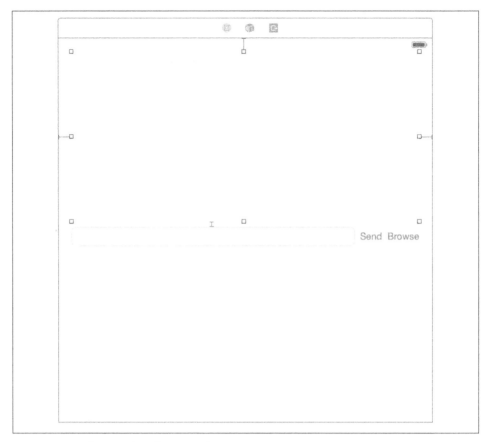

Figure 14-1. The interface for your chat program

Modify the ViewController so that it looks like the following:

```
import UIKit
import MultipeerConnectivity

class ViewController: UIViewController, MCBrowserViewControllerDelegate,
    MCSessionDelegate {

    let serviceType = "LCOC-Chat"

    var browser : MCBrowserViewController!
    var assistant : MCAdvertiserAssistant!
    var session : MCSession!
    var peerID: MCPeerID!

    @IBOutlet var chatView: UITextView!
    @IBOutlet var messageField: UITextField!
```

```swift
override func viewDidLoad() {
    super.viewDidLoad()

    self.peerID = MCPeerID(displayName: UIDevice.currentDevice().name)
    self.session = MCSession(peer: peerID)
    self.session.delegate = self

    // create the browser view controller with a unique service name
    self.browser = MCBrowserViewController(serviceType:serviceType,
        session:self.session)

    self.browser.delegate = self;

    self.assistant = MCAdvertiserAssistant(serviceType:serviceType,
        discoveryInfo:nil, session:self.session)

    // tell the assistant to start advertising our fabulous chat
    self.assistant.start()
}

@IBAction func sendChat(sender: UIButton) {
    // Bundle up the text in the message field, and send it off to all
    // connected peers

    let msg = self.messageField.text.dataUsingEncoding(NSUTF8StringEncoding,
        allowLossyConversion: false)

    var error : NSError?

    self.session.sendData(msg, toPeers: self.session.connectedPeers,
        withMode: MCSessionSendDataMode.Unreliable, error: &error)

    if error != nil {
        print("Error sending data: \(error?.localizedDescription)")
    }

    self.updateChat(self.messageField.text, fromPeer: self.peerID)

    self.messageField.text = ""
}

func updateChat(text : String, fromPeer peerID: MCPeerID) {
    // Appends some text to the chat view

    // If this peer ID is the local device's peer ID, then show the name
    // as "Me"
    var name : String

    switch peerID {
    case self.peerID:
        name = "Me"
```

```
            default:
                name = peerID.displayName
        }

        // Add the name to the message and display it
        let message = "\(name): \(text)\n"
        self.chatView.text = self.chatView.text + message

    }

    @IBAction func showBrowser(sender: UIButton) {
        // Show the browser view controller
        self.presentViewController(self.browser, animated: true, completion: nil)
    }

    func browserViewControllerDidFinish(
        browserViewController: MCBrowserViewController!) {
        // Called when the browser view controller is dismissed (i.e., the Done
        // button was tapped)

        self.dismissViewControllerAnimated(true, completion: nil)
    }

    func browserViewControllerWasCancelled(
        browserViewController: MCBrowserViewController!) {
        // Called when the browser view controller is cancelled

        self.dismissViewControllerAnimated(true, completion: nil)
    }

    func session(session: MCSession!, didReceiveData data: NSData!,
        fromPeer peerID: MCPeerID!) {
        // Called when a peer sends an NSData to us

        // This needs to run on the main queue
        dispatch_async(dispatch_get_main_queue()) {

            if let msg = NSString(data: data, encoding: NSUTF8StringEncoding) {
                self.updateChat(msg, fromPeer: peerID)
            }

        }
    }

    // The following methods do nothing, but the MCSessionDelegate protocol
    // requires that we implement them.
    func session(session: MCSession!,
        didStartReceivingResourceWithName resourceName: String!,
        fromPeer peerID: MCPeerID!, withProgress progress: NSProgress!) {

        // Called when a peer starts sending a file to us
    }
```

```
func session(session: MCSession!,
    didFinishReceivingResourceWithName resourceName: String!,
    fromPeer peerID: MCPeerID!,
    atURL localURL: NSURL!, withError error: NSError!) {
    // Called when a file has finished transferring from another peer
}

func session(session: MCSession!, didReceiveStream stream: NSInputStream!,
    withName streamName: String!, fromPeer peerID: MCPeerID!) {
    // Called when a peer establishes a stream with us
}

func session(session: MCSession!, peer peerID: MCPeerID!,
    didChangeState state: MCSessionState) {
    // Called when a connected peer changes state (e.g., if it goes offline)

}

}
```

This code does the following things:

1. It adds a class extension to the ViewController class, which makes it conform to
   the MCBrowserViewControllerDelegate and MCSessionDelegate protocols, as
   well as creating four new properties, including one to handle the multicast peer
   components:

   - The MCBrowserViewController is a prebuilt view controller that handles and
     negotiates browsing for connections.

   - The MCAdvertiserAssistant is another prebuilt class that advertises and nego-
     tiates creating a connection and session.

   - The MCSession is the object holding the sessions once it has been negotiated.

   - MCPeerID represents your peer ID for the session.

2. In the viewDidLoad method, the code initializes all the multicast peer objects before
   telling the advertiser to start advertising its availability.

3. In the sendChat method, the sendData(toPeers:error:) message on the session
   is the real meat of the application. This is the method used to send data—in our
   application, a string from the text field.

4. Finally, session(didReceiveData:fromPeer:) is the delegate method that is called
   when the session receives any data—in the case of our application, it appends the
   new data to the text view, showing the received text to the text view.

Now if you and another friend both run the application, you should have an amazing
chat app!

CHAPTER 15

Working with the Real World

Desktops, laptops, iPhones, and iPads are all physical devices existing in the real world—either on your desk, on your lap, or in your hand. For a long time, your apps were largely confined to your computer, and weren't able to do much with the outside world besides instructing a printer to print a document.

Starting with iOS and OS X 10.6, however, things began to change, and your code is now able to learn about the user's location, how the device is moving and being held, and how far away the computer is from landmarks.

In this chapter, you'll learn about how your programs can interact with the outside world. Specifically, you'll learn how to use Core Location to determine where your computer or device is on the planet, how to use MapKit to show and annotate maps, how to use Core Motion to learn about how the user is holding the device, how to use the printing services available on OS X and iOS to work with printers, how to connect game controllers into your apps, and how to make sure your apps don't excessively drain the user's battery.

 Most of the technology discussed in this chapter works on both OS X and iOS. Some of the technologies have identical APIs on both platforms (Core Location, MapKit, and Game Controllers), some have different APIs on the two platforms (print services), and some are only available on iOS (Core Motion) or OS X (App Nap). We'll let you know which technology is available where.

Working with Location

Almost every user of your software will be located on Earth.[1]

---

1. Unless, of course, you're taking your iPhone to space (*http://bit.ly/phones_on_iss*).

Knowing where the user is on the planet is tremendously useful because it enables you to provide more relevant information. For example, while the business review and social networking site Yelp works just fine as a search engine for businesses and restaurants, it only becomes truly useful when it limits its results to businesses and restaurants near the user.

Location awareness is a technology that is at its most helpful on mobile devices (like an iPhone or iPad), because their locations are more likely to change. However, it's also applicable to a more fixed-location device (like a desktop) to know where it is in the world. A great example of this is the time-zone system in OS X—if you move your computer from one country to another, your time zone will have likely changed, and OS X uses its built-in location systems to work out how to set the clock to local time.

Location Hardware

There are a number of different techniques for determining where a computer is on the planet, and each requires different hardware. The ones in use by iOS and OS X are:

- GPS, the Global Positioning System
- WiFi base station lookups
- Cell tower lookups
- iBeacons

GPS

GPS devices first became popular as navigation assistants for cars, and later as features built into smartphones. Initially developed by the U.S. military, GPS is a constellation of satellites that contain extremely precise clocks and continuously broadcast time information. A GPS receiver can listen for these time signals and compare them to determine where the user is.

Depending on how many satellites the GPS receiver can see, GPS is capable of working out a location to less than one meter of accuracy.

The GPS receiver is only included on the iPhone, and on iPad models that contain 3G or 4G cellular radios. It's not included on any desktop, laptop, or iPod touch, or on WiFi-only iPads.

Since the introduction of the iPhone 4S and later models, iOS devices capable of receiving GPS signals are also capable of receiving signals from GLONASS,[2] a Russian

---

2. Because you asked, it stands for *GLObalnaya NAvigatsionnaya Sputnikovaya Sistema*.

satellite navigation system, all transparently handled and combined with GPS to give you a better location.

WiFi base station lookups

While a device that uses WiFi to access the Internet may move around a lot, the base stations that provide that connection generally don't move around at all. This fact can be used to determine the location of a user if a GPS receiver isn't available.

Apple maintains a gigantic database of WiFi hotspots, along with rough coordinates that indicate where those hotspots are. If a device can see WiFi hotspots and is also connected to the Internet, it can tell Apple's servers, "I can see hotspots A, B, and C." Apple's servers can then reply, "If you can see them, then you must be near them, and therefore you must be near location X." The device keeps a subset of this database locally, in case a WiFi lookup is necessary when the device has no access to the Internet.

Usually, this method of locating the user isn't terribly precise, but it can get within 100 meters of accuracy in urban areas (where there's lots of WiFi around). Because it uses hardware that's built into all devices that can run OS X and iOS, this capability is available on every device.

Cell tower lookups

If a device uses cell towers to communicate with the Internet, it can perform a similar trick with the towers as with WiFi base stations. The exact same technique is used, although the results are slightly less accurate—because cell towers are less numerous than WiFi stations, cell tower lookups can only get within a kilometer or so of accuracy.

Cell tower lookups are available on any device that includes a cell radio, meaning the iPhone, and all models of the iPad that have a cell radio. They're not available on iPods, because they don't have any cell radio capability.

iBeacons

iBeacons are a new means of determining location using low-energy Bluetooth devices. By constantly broadcasting their existence via a unique identifier, they can be detected by an iOS device, allowing you to determine where you are based on the iBeacon's location. iBeacon location and accuracy is much more subjective than any of the other location methods: instead of pinpointing your position on the planet, iBeacons can tell you when you are near or far from them. iBeacons are designed more to determine the store you're near in a shopping mall or the artwork you're close to in a museum, rather than to work out where you are for navigation or tracking.

iBeacons are available on any device capable of running iOS 7 or later. Additionally, these devices can also be set up to act as an iBeacon themselves.

The Core Location Framework

As you can see, not every piece of location-sensing hardware is available on all devices. Because it would be tremendously painful to have to write three different chunks of code for three different location services and then switch between them depending on hardware availability, OS X and iOS provide a single location services API that handles all the details of working with the location hardware.

Core Location is the framework that your applications use to work out where they are on the planet. Core Location accesses whatever location hardware is available, puts the results together, and lets your code know its best guess for the user's location. It's also able to determine the user's altitude, heading, and speed.

When you work with Core Location, you work with an instance of CLLocation Manager. This class is your interface to the Core Location framework—you create a manager, optionally provide it with additional information on how you want it to behave (such as how precise you want the location information to be), and then provide it with a delegate object. The location manager will then periodically contact the delegate object and inform it of the user's changing location.

CLLocationManager is actually a slightly incomplete name for the class, because it doesn't just provide geographic location information. It also provides heading information (i.e., the direction the user is facing relative to magnetic north or true north). This information is only available on devices that contain a magnetometer, which acts as a digital compass. At the time of writing, all currently shipping iOS devices contain one, but devices older than the iPhone 3GS, iPod touch 3rd generation, and iPad 2 don't.

To work with Core Location, you create the CLLocationManager delegate, configure it, and then send it the startUpdatingLocation() message. When you're done needing to know about the user's location, you send it the stopUpdatingLocation() message.

> You should always turn off a CLLocationManager when you're done, as location technologies are CPU-intensive and can require the use of power-hungry hardware. Think of the user's battery!

To work with Core Location, you provide it with an object that conforms to the CLLocationManagerDelegate protocol. The key method in this protocol is location Manager(manager: didUpdateLocations:), which is sent periodically by the location manager.

This method receives both the user's current location (as far as Core Location can tell) and his previous location. These two locations are represented as CLLocation objects, which contain information like the latitude and longitude, altitude, speed, and accuracy.

Core Location may also fail to get the user's location at all. If, for example, GPS is unavailable and neither WiFi base stations nor cell towers can be found, no location information will be available. If this happens, the `CLLocationManager` will send its delegate the `locationManager(manager: didFailWithError:)` message.

Working with Core Location

To demonstrate Core Location, we'll create a simple application that attempts to display the user's location. This will be an OS X application, but the same API applies to iOS.

To get started with Core Location, create a new Cocoa application called Location.

Now that we have a blank application we'll build the interface. The interface for this app will be deliberately simple—it will show the user's latitude and longitude coordinates, as well as the radius of uncertainty that Core Location has about the user.

No location technology is completely precise, so unless you're willing to spend millions of dollars on (probably classified) technology, the best any consumer GPS device will get is about 5 to 10 meters of accuracy. If you're not using GPS, which is the case when using a device that doesn't have it built in, Core Location will use less-accurate technologies like WiFi or cell tower triangulation.

This means that Core Location is always inaccurate to some extent. When Core Location updates its delegate with the location, the latitude and longitude provided are actually the center of a circle that the user is in, and the value of the `CLLocation` property `horizontalAccuracy` indicates the radius of that circle, represented in meters.

The interface of this demo application, therefore, will show the user's location as well as how accurate Core Location says it is:

1. Open *MainMenu.xib* and select the window.
2. Now add the latitude, longitude, and accuracy labels. Drag in three labels and make them read `Latitude`, `Longitude`, and `Accuracy`. Lay them out vertically.
3. Drag in another three labels, and lay them out vertically next to the first three.
4. Finally, drag in a circular progress indicator and place it below the labels.

When you're done, your interface should look like Figure 15-1.

You'll now connect the interface to the app delegate. Open *AppDelegate.swift* in the assistant and Control-drag from each of the labels on the right. Create outlets for each of them called `longitudeLabel`, `latitudeLabel`, and `accuracyLabel`, respectively. Control-drag from the progress indicator, and create an outlet for it called `spinner`.

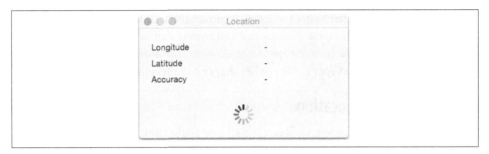

Figure 15-1. The completed interface for our Location app

Now make the app delegate conform to the CLLocationManagerDelegate protocol and finally, but very importantly, import the Core Location framework. When you're done, the top of *AppDelegate.swift* should look like the following code:

```
import Cocoa
import CoreLocation

class AppDelegate: NSObject, NSApplicationDelegate,CLLocationManagerDelegate {

    @IBOutlet weak var window: NSWindow!
    @IBOutlet weak var longitudeLabel: NSTextField!
    @IBOutlet weak var latitudeLabel: NSTextField!
    @IBOutlet weak var accuracyLabel: NSTextField!
    @IBOutlet weak var spinner: NSProgressIndicator!

    var locationManager = CLLocationManager()
```

Now we need to tell the CLLocationManager to start finding the users location. Update the applicationDidFinishingLaunching method in *AppDelegate.swift* to look like the following:

```
func applicationDidFinishLaunching(aNotification: NSNotification?) {
    self.locationManager.delegate = self
    self.locationManager.startUpdatingLocation()
    self.spinner.startAnimation(nil)
}
```

This code does the following things:

- Sets the delegate for the CLLocationManager; in this case we are setting the delegate to be the app delegate.

- Tells the location manager to start updating the user's location.

- Finally, it instructs the progress indicator to start animating.

Now we need to implement two CLLocationManagerDelegate methods—location
Manager(manager: didUpdateLocations:) and locationManager(manager: did
FailWithError:)—to handle when we get a location and when we fail to get a location.

Add the following code to the app delegate:

```
func locationManager(manager: CLLocationManager!,
    didUpdateLocations locations: [AnyObject]!)
{
    // collecting the most recent location from the array of locations
    if let newLocation = locations.last as? CLLocation
    {
        self.longitudeLabel.stringValue = NSString(format: "%.2f",
            newLocation.coordinate.longitude)
        self.latitudeLabel.stringValue = NSString(format: "%.2f",
            newLocation.coordinate.latitude)
        self.accuracyLabel.stringValue = NSString(format: "%.1fm",
            newLocation.horizontalAccuracy)
        self.spinner.stopAnimation(nil);
    }
    else
    {
        println("No location found")
    }
}

func locationManager(manager: CLLocationManager!,
    didFailWithError error: NSError!)
{
    // locationManager failed to find a location
    self.longitudeLabel.stringValue = "-"
    self.latitudeLabel.stringValue = "-"
    self.accuracyLabel.stringValue = "-"
    self.spinner.startAnimation(nil)
}
```

These two methods do the following:

- Inside locationManager(manager: didUpdateLocations:), a CLLocation object
  holding all the user's location information is created from the array of locations the
  location manager found. Then the labels are updated with the relevant information
  and the spinner is stopped.

- Inside locationManager(manager: didFailWithError:), the labels are updated
  to show dashes, and the spinner is started again.

It's possible for the location manager to successfully determine the user's location and
then later fail (or vice versa). This means that a failure isn't necessarily the end of the
line—the location manager will keep trying, so your application should keep this
in mind.

Now run the application. On its first run, it will ask the user if it's allowed to access his location. If the user grants permission, the application will attempt to get the user's location. If it can find it, the labels will be updated to show the user's approximate location, and how accurate Core Location thinks it is.

Geocoding

When you get the user's location, Core Location returns a latitude and longitude coordinate pair. This is useful inside an application and great for showing on a map, but isn't terribly helpful for a human being. Nobody looks at the coordinates "-37.813611, 144.963056" and immediately thinks, "Melbourne, Australia."

Because people deal with addresses, which in America are composed of a sequence of decreasingly precise place names[3] ("1 Infinite Loop," "Cupertino," "Santa Clara," "California," etc.), Core Location includes a tool for converting coordinates to addresses and back again. Converting an address to coordinates is called *geocoding*; converting coordinates to an address is called *reverse geocoding*.

Core Location implements this via the CLGeocoder class, which allows for both forward and reverse geocoding. Because geocoding requires contacting a server to do the conversion, it will only work when an Internet connection is available.

To geocode an address, you create a CLGeocoder and then use one of its built-in geocoding methods. You can provide either a string that contains an address (like "1 Infinite Loop Cupertino California USA") and the geocoder will attempt to figure out where you mean, or you can provide a dictionary that contains more precisely delineated information. Optionally, you can restrict a geocode to a specific region (to prevent confusion between, say, Hobart, Minnesota and Hobart, Tasmania).

We're going to add reverse geocoding to the application, which will show the user her current address. To do this, we'll add a CLGeocoder to the AppDelegate class. When Core Location gets a fix on the user's location, we'll ask the geocoder to perform a reverse geocode with the CLLocation provided by Core Location.

When you reverse geocode, you receive an array that contains a number of CLPlacemark objects. An array is used because it's possible for the reverse geocode to return with a number of possible coordinates that your address may resolve to. CLPlacemark objects contain a number of properties that contain address information. Note that not all of the properties may contain information; for example, if you reverse geocode a location that's in the middle of a desert, you probably won't receive any street information.

The available properties you can access include:

---

3. This is the case in most Western locales, but isn't the case everywhere on the planet. Japanese addresses, for example, often go from widest area to smallest area.

- The name of the location (e.g., "Apple Inc.")
- The street address (e.g., "1 Infinite Loop")
- The locality (e.g., "Cupertino")
- The sublocality—that is, the neighborhood or name for that area (e.g., "Mission District")
- The administrative area—that is, the state name or other main subdivision of a country (e.g., "California")
- The subadministrative area—that is, the county (e.g., "Santa Clara")
- The postal code (e.g., "95014")
- The two- or three-letter ISO country code for that country (e.g., "US")
- The country name (e.g., "United States")

Some placemarks may contain additional data, if relevant:

- The name of the inland body of water that the placemark is located at or very near to (e.g., "Derwent River")
- The name of the ocean where the placemark is located (e.g., "Pacific Ocean")
- An array containing any additional areas of interest (e.g., "Golden Gate Park")

You can use this information to create a string that can be shown to the user.

We'll start by creating a label that will display the user's address.

Open *MainMenu.xib* and drag in a new label under the current set of labels. The updated interface should look like Figure 15-2. Then open *AppDelegate.swift* in the assistant and Control-drag from the new label into the app delegate. Create a new outlet for the label called addressLabel.

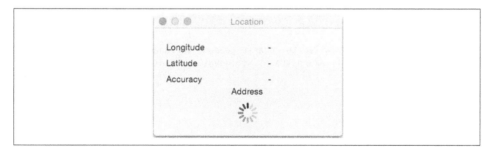

Figure 15-2. The completed interface for our Location app with geocoding

Then add CLGeocoder to the app delegate by updating *AppDelegate.swift* to have the following property:

```
@IBOutlet weak var addressLabel: NSTextField!
var geocoder = CLGeocoder()
```

When the user's location is determined, perform a reverse geocode by updating the locationManager(manager: didUpdateLocations:) method with the following code:

```
func locationManager(manager: CLLocationManager!,
    didUpdateLocations locations: [AnyObject]!)
{
    // collecting the most recent location from the array of locations
    if let newLocation = locations.last as? CLLocation
    {
        self.longitudeLabel.stringValue = NSString(format: "%.2f",
            newLocation.coordinate.longitude)
        self.latitudeLabel.stringValue = NSString(format: "%.2f",
            newLocation.coordinate.latitude)
        self.accuracyLabel.stringValue = NSString(format: "%.1fm",
            newLocation.horizontalAccuracy)
        self.spinner.stopAnimation(nil);

        self.geocoder.reverseGeocodeLocation(newLocation)
        {
            (placemarks, error) in
            if error == nil
            {
                let placemark = placemarks[0] as CLPlacemark
                let address = NSString(format: "%@ %@, %@, %@ %@",
                    placemark.subThoroughfare,
                    placemark.thoroughfare,
                    placemark.locality,
                    placemark.administrativeArea,
                    placemark.country)

                self.addressLabel.stringValue = address
            }
            else
            {
                // failed to reverse geocode the address
                self.addressLabel.stringValue = "Failed to find an address"
            }
        }
    }
    else
    {
        NSLog("No location found")
    }
}
```

Now run the application. Shortly after the user's location is displayed, the approximate address of your location will appear. If it doesn't, check to make sure that you're connected to the Internet.

Region Monitoring and iBeacons

Depending on what your app's goals are, it might be more useful to know when your user enters an area as opposed to knowing their precise location. To help with this, Core Location provides region monitoring.

There are two types of region monitors: geographical and iBeacon. Region monitoring lets you set up virtual boundaries around the Earth and be informed via delegate callbacks when the user enters or exits one of the regions; iBeacon monitoring lets your app be informed when a user is near an iBeacon region represented by a low energy Bluetooth signal.

Currently iBeacons are only available on iOS. Sorry, Mac developers.

Monitoring when the user enters and exits a geographical region is straightforward. If you wanted to add region monitoring to our existing location app, all you'd need to do is add the following to the bottom of the `applicationDidFinishLaunching` method:

```
let location = CLLocationCoordinate2DMake(-42.883317, 147.328277)
let region = CLCircularRegion(  center: location,
                                radius: 1000,
                              identifier: "Hobart")
locationManager.startMonitoringForRegion(region)
```

This does several things: first, it creates a location to use as the center of the region (in this case, the city of Hobart, in Australia). It then creates a region around this center point with a radius of 1,000 meters, and gives it an identifier to help you differentiate it later. Finally, it tells the location manager to start monitoring whether a user has entered or exited a region.

The way `CLRegion` works on OS X is a little bit different than on iOS. `CLRegion` is an abstract class in iOS that is meant to be subclassed for the specific different types of regions. So to get the same functionality in iOS, we would instead use the `CLRegion` subclass `CLCircular Region`, the region subclass designed for monitoring circular regions.

To know when a user has entered or exited a region, there are two delegate methods: `locationManager(manager: didExitRegion:)` and `locationManager(manager: didEnterRegion:)`. Both of these callbacks pass in a `CLRegion` with a string identifier property that you can use to determine the region that the user has entered or exited:

```
func locationManager(manager: CLLocationManager!, didEnterRegion
    region: CLRegion!) {
    // have entered the region
    NSLog("Entered %@", region.identifier)
}
func locationManager(manager: CLLocationManager!, didExitRegion
    region: CLRegion!) {
    // have exited the region
    NSLog("Exited %@", region.identifier)
}
```

iBeacon regions function a little bit differently when working with circular regions. Because of the nature of Bluetooth radio devices, you will never be able to guarantee a radius for each beacon. Additionally, a device might encounter multiple beacons within a single area that might not all be relevant to your app. Therefore, a radius and an identifier are not enough to be able to use iBeacons. The principle is the same though —you create a region to represent the beacon and you tell your `CLLocationManager` to start looking for that region. Say you wanted to create an iBeacon region for a particular painting in a gallery:

```
// the UUID string was generated using the uuidgen command
let uuid = NSUUID(UUIDString:"F7769B0E-BF97-4485-B63E-8CE121988EAF")

let beaconRegion = CLBeaconRegion(proximityUUID: uuid,
    major: 1,
    minor: 2,
    identifier: "Awesome painting");
```

This code does several things. First, it creates a `CLBeaconRegion` with both an identifier string that works exactly the same as it does in the circular region, and a proximity UUID. The proximity UUID is a unique identifier to be used by all the beacons in your app. In the case of a gallery, the UUID would be the same for all iBeacons in the gallery or any other gallery that your app works in. The major and minor properties are numbers that can be used to help identify exactly which beacon the user is near. In the case of a gallery, the major property could represent a section of the museum and the minor property a particular artwork.

> The UUID and major and minor properties of the beacon region must match the settings you put into your actual hardware iBeacons. How to set these will change from iBeacon to iBeacon.

Just like with geographical regions, your app gets delegate callbacks for any beacon regions that your app enounters. Unlike geographical regions, however, you have a couple of options when using iBeacons; your app can receive the delegate callbacks for circular regions `locationManager(manager: didEnterRegion:)` and `locationManager(manager: didExitRegion:)` by calling the standard `startMonitoringForRegion(region:)` on your `CLLocationManager`. Alternatively, you can call `startRangingBeaconsInRegion(region:)` on your location manager. This will result in the delegate method `locationManager(manager: didRangeBeacons: inRegion:)` being called, with all the beacons in range being passed in as an array of `CLBeacon` objects as well as the region object that was used to locate the beacons. The closest beacon will have a proximity property equal to the system-defined `CLProximityNear` value.

When testing your iBeacon apps, you need an iBeacon to make sure that your app is doing what it needs to do when it finds a beacon. Buying lots of iBeacons just for testing is going to be a bit expensive, but Apple has thankfully provided a way to turn your iOS devices into iBeacons. It is quite easy to do this, but first you need to add a `CBPeripheralManager`, an object for managing Bluetooth peripherals, to your app and make your app conform to the `CBPeripheralDelegate` protocol:

```
import CoreLocation
import CoreBluetooth

class ViewController: UIViewController,CBPeripheralManagerDelegate{
    var bluetoothManager : CBPeripheralManager?

    override func viewDidLoad() {
        super.viewDidLoad()

        self.bluetoothManager = CBPeripheralManager(delegate: self, queue: nil)
    }
```

Then to create an iBeacon for a specific region, you need to create a `CLBeaconRegion` that matches the beacon you want to simulate. Finally you need to tell the Bluetooth manager to start advertising the iBeacon:

```
    func peripheralManagerDidUpdateState(peripheral: CBPeripheralManager!) {

        if (self.bluetoothManager?.state == CBPeripheralManagerState.PoweredOn)
        {
            // the UUID string was generated using the uuidgen command
            let uuid = NSUUID(UUIDString:"F7769B0E-BF97-4485-B63E-8CE121988EAF")

            let beaconRegion = CLBeaconRegion(proximityUUID: uuid,
                major: 1,
                minor: 2,
                identifier: "Awesome painting");

            var beaconData = beaconRegion.peripheralDataWithMeasuredPower(nil)
            self.bluetoothManager?.startAdvertising(beaconData)
```

```
        }
    }
```

Locations and Privacy

The user's location is private information, and your application must be granted explicit permission by the user on at least the first occasion that it tries to access it.

People are understandably wary about software knowing where they are—it's a privacy issue and potentially a safety risk. To avoid problems, follow these guidelines in your application:

- Be very clear about what your application is using location information for.
- Never share the user's location with a server or other users unless the user has explicitly given permission.
- The user can always see when an application is accessing location information because a small icon appears at the top of the screen (on both iOS and OS X). Once your app has performed the task that location information is needed for, turn off Core Location—both to save power and to let the user know that they are no longer being tracked.

Maps

The MapKit framework provides an everything-but-the-kitchen-sink approach to maps, allowing you to create, annotate, overlay, and adjust maps as needed for your applications. It plays very well with the location tracking and region monitoring technology that Apple provides.

Previously, MapKit was only available on iOS, but since the release of OS X 10.9, MapKit is now available on OS X as well and the framework functions in virtually the same way on both platforms.

The base of all maps is the MKMapView, which is the actual view containing map data that your application can use. The map data that the map view displays comes from Apple Maps data, although in the past the view used Google Maps data.

Using Maps

Getting a map up and running is quite straightforward, so let's get cracking!

1. Create a new, single view iPhone application and call it Maps.
2. Next, create the interface. Open the *Main.storyboard* file. Drag in a map view and make it take up the entire view.

---

3. Then connect the interface. Open *ViewController.swift* in the assistant. Control-drag from the map view to the view controller and make a new outlet for the map view. Call it `mapView`.

4. You then need to extend the view controller. Open *ViewController.swift*, import the MapKit framework, and set the controller to be a map view delegate. Finally, add the MapKit framework into the project.

   When you are done, *ViewController.swift* should look like this:

   ```
   import MapKit

   class ViewController: UIViewController,MKMapViewDelegate {

       @IBOutlet weak var mapView: MKMapView!
   ```

5. Finally, configure the map. By default, the map view will be centered over Apple's headquarters in Cupertino, so we want to move that somewhere a bit different. Update `viewDidLoad()` to look like this:

   ```
   override func viewDidLoad() {
       super.viewDidLoad()

       self.mapView.delegate = self;
       let center = CLLocationCoordinate2DMake(-37.813611, 144.963056)
       let span = MKCoordinateSpanMake(2, 2);
       self.mapView.region = MKCoordinateRegionMake(center, span)
   ```

Now if you run the app, your map should be centered over Melbourne. The span is how many degrees of longitudinal and latitudinal delta the view should cover.

Annotating Maps

Just having a map all by itself isn't a lot of fun. What if we want to see where something interesting is? Luckily for us, Apple has included an easy way of annotating the map, which you may have seen in the built-in Maps app as little red, green, and purple pins. These additions to the map are called *annotations*.

The annotations are broken up into two object types: `MKAnnotation`, which represents the annotation data, including its location and any other data such as a name; and `MKAnnotationView`, which will be the view that the map displays when needed.

Apple has provided a built-in annotation class for when all you need is a simple pin called MKPointAnnotation. This class has built-in properties for a title and subtitle, and will automatically draw a pin view when needed, making it very easy to use. MapKit on both OS X and iOS supports custom annotation and custom views for the annotations, but for this example we will stick to the built-in pin annotations.

So let's start dropping those little pins. Open *ViewController.swift* and add the following to the bottom of the viewDidLoad method:

```
// creating an new annotation
var annotation = MKPointAnnotation()
annotation.coordinate = center
annotation.title = "Melbourne"
annotation.subtitle = "Victoria"
// adding the annotation to the map
self.mapView.addAnnotation(annotation);
```

This code creates a new point annotation at Melbourne, sets a title and subtitle string, and then finally adds it to the map. If you run the app, a red pin will be on top of Melbourne and if you tap it, you'll get a little window with the title and subtitle strings.

Maps and Overlays

Annotations are good and all, but sometimes you need a bit more than what a pin can provide. This is where overlays come in handy. Unlike an annotation, they don't represent a single point but instead cover an area on the map.

Overlays, much like annotations, are broken up into two parts: an MKOverlay object representing the data, and a view object called MKOverlayRender. Also much like annotations, Apple has provided some prebuilt overlays to make life simpler, including overlays and associated renderers for circles, lines, and polygons—and if you want, you can build your own.

With that understood, let's add a 100 km circle around the pin we dropped before. Add the following to the bottom of the viewDidLoad() method:

```
// creating and adding a new circle overlay to the map
var overlay = MKCircle(centerCoordinate: center, radius: 50000)
self.mapView.addOverlay(overlay)
```

This creates a circular region with a radius of 50 km around the same location where we added the pin, and then it adds the overlay to the map. Nothing will be displayed, though, until the map view's delegate provides an appropriate renderer for that overlay.

Add the following map view delegate method to *ViewController.swift*:

```
func mapView(
    mapView: MKMapView!, rendererForOverlay
    overlay: MKOverlay!) -> MKOverlayRenderer! {
    if (overlay.isKindOfClass(MKCircle))
    {
        var circleRenderer = MKCircleRenderer(overlay: overlay)
        circleRenderer.strokeColor = UIColor.greenColor()
        circleRenderer.fillColor = UIColor(
            red: 0,
            green: 1.0,
            blue: 0,
            alpha: 0.5)

        return circleRenderer
    }
    return nil
}
```

Terra, as you might know, is a sphere, and your screen is a rectangle, so there are going to be some issues when trying to squish the planet into a rectangle. Apple has used what is known as the Mercator projection to overcome this. The Mercator projection is just one of many different projections, and they all have their own strengths and weaknesses.

One of the side effects of the Mercator projection is if you add a lot of overlays spread all over the place, they might look different if you zoom the map all the way out than they do up close. Thankfully, most of the time you are using maps, you will likely be zoomed close enough in that you won't notice this.

Now if you run the app, you should see a rather large green circle hovering ominously over Melbourne, as seen in Figure 15-3.

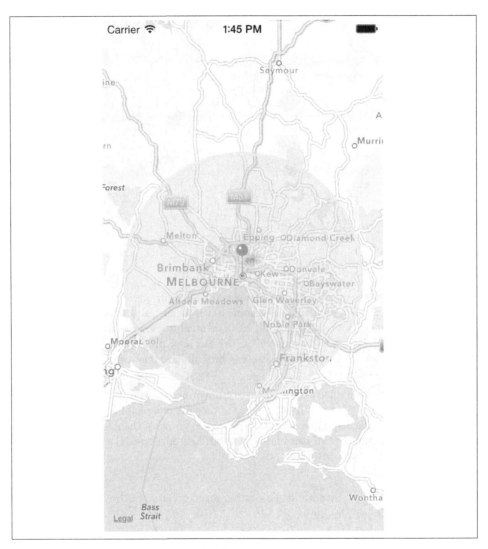

Figure 15-3. The map, with an overlay drawn over it

Device Motion

An iOS device is often held in the user's hands, which means that it's subject to movement and rotation. iOS allows your code to receive information about how the device is moving, how it's being rotated, and how it's oriented. All of this information is available through the Core Motion framework, which provides a unified interface to the various relevant sensors built into the device.

Core Motion is only available on iOS, as laptops and desktops don't generally get shaken around while being used. While some Mac laptops include an accelerometer, it isn't available to your code through any publicly accessible APIs.

Core Motion provides *device motion* information to your application by measuring data from the sensors available to the device:

- The accelerometer, which measures forces applied to the device
- The gyroscope, which measures rotation
- The magnetometer, which measures magnetic fields

The first iOS devices only included an accelerometer, which is actually sufficient for getting quite a lot of information about device motion. For example, based on the forces being applied to the device over time, you can determine the direction of gravity, which gives you information about how the device is being held, as well as determine if the device is being shaken. If a gyroscope is available, you can refine this information and determine if the device is rotating around an axis of gravity. If a magnetometer is available, it's possible to determine a frame of reference, so that it can determine which way north is—something that's not possible when all you have is relative rotation information.

Core Motion collects data from all the available sensors and provides direct access to the sensor information. You can therefore ask Core Motion to give you the angles that define the device's orientation in space, as well as get raw accelerometer information.

 Raw sensor data can lead to some very cool tricks. For example, the magnetometer measures magnetic fields, which means that the device can actually be used as a metal detector by measuring changes in the magnetic field.

Working with Core Motion

Core Motion works in a very similar manner to Core Location: it uses a manager object that provides periodic updates on device motion. However, the means by which the manager object provides these updates differs from how CLLocationManager does—instead of providing a delegate object, you instruct the motion manager to call a block that you provide. In this block, you handle the movement event.

The iOS Simulator doesn't simulate any of the motion hardware that Core Motion uses. If you want to test Core Motion, you need to use a real iOS device.

The motion manager class is called `CMMotionManager`. To start getting motion information, you create an instance of this class and instruct it to begin generating motion updates. You can also optionally ask for only accelerometer, gyroscope, or magnetometer information.

You can also get information from the `CMMotionManager` by querying it at any time. If your application doesn't need to get information about device motion very often, it's more efficient to simply ask for the information when it's needed. To do this, you send the `CMMotionManager` object the `startDeviceMotionUpdates()` method (or the `startAccelerometerUpdates()` or `startGyroUpdates()` methods), and then, when you need the data, you access the `CMMotionManager`'s `accelerometerData`, `gyroData`, or `deviceMotion` properties.

The fewer devices that Core Motion needs to activate in order to give you the information you need, the more power is saved. As always, consider the user's battery!

Core Motion separates out "user motion" from the sum total of forces being applied to the device. There's still only one accelerometer in there, though, so what Core Motion does is use a combination of low- and high-pass filtering to separate out parts of the signal, with the assistance of the gyroscope, to determine which forces are gravity and which forces are "user motion"—forces like shaking or throwing your device. (Note: The authors do not recommend throwing your device, no matter how much fun it is. The authors specifically do not recommend making an awesome app that takes a photo at the peak of a throw. You will break your phone.)

You can also configure how often the `CMMotionManager` updates the accelerometer and gyro—the less often it uses it, the more power you save (and, as a trade-off, the more imprecise your measurements become).

To work with Core Motion, you'll need to add the Core Motion framework to your project. We'll now build a small iPhone app that reports on how it's being moved and how the device is oriented:

1. Create a new, single view iPhone application and call it Motion.

2. Add the Core Motion framework. Select the project at the top of the project navigator. The project settings will appear in the main editor; select the `Motion` target.

   Scroll down to Linked Frameworks and Libraries, and click the + button.

   The frameworks sheet will appear; browse or search for `CoreMotion.framework` and add it to the project.

3. Once the framework has been added, we'll begin building the interface for the app. This will be similar to the Core Location app: it will report on the numbers being sent by Core Motion. However, you can (and should!) use the information for all kinds of things—game controls, data logging, and more. The authors once used Core Motion to build an app that tracks human sleeping activity. It's a tremendously flexible framework.

   Open *Main.storyboard*. First, we'll create the labels that display the user motion.

   Drag in three labels and lay them out vertically on the lefthand side of the screen. Make their text X, Y, and Z, respectively.

   Drag in another three labels and lay them out vertically to the right of the first three. Next, we'll create the labels that display orientation.

   Drag in another three labels and lay them out vertically on the lefthand side of the screen, under the existing set of labels. Make their text `Pitch`, `Yaw`, and `Roll`, respectively.

   Drag in a final set of three labels and lay them out vertically and to the right.

   Once you're done, your interface should look like Figure 15-4.

4. Connect the interface to the view controller. Open *ViewController.swift* in the assistant.

   Control-drag from each of the labels on the right and create outlets for each of them. From top to bottom, the labels should be called `xLabel`, `yLabel`, `zLabel`, `pitchLabel`, `yawLabel`, and `rollLabel`.

   While you have *ViewController.swift* open, import `CoreMotion`.

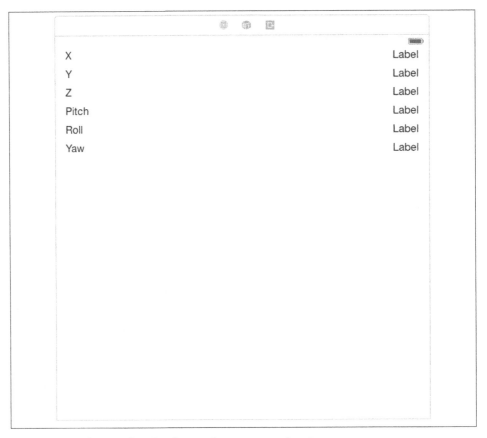

Figure 15-4. The interface for the accelerometer application

When you're done, the top of *ViewController.swift* should look like the following:

```swift
import UIKit
import CoreMotion

class ViewController: UIViewController {

    @IBOutlet weak var xLabel: UILabel!
    @IBOutlet weak var yLabel: UILabel!
    @IBOutlet weak var zLabel: UILabel!
    @IBOutlet weak var pitchLabel: UILabel!
    @IBOutlet weak var yawLabel: UILabel!
    @IBOutlet weak var rollLabel: UILabel!
```

5. Now that the view controller's header file has been set up, we'll write the code that actually creates the motion manager and then starts updating the labels as device motion updates arrive.

We'll store a reference to the CMMotionManager as an instance variable in the class, and start and stop the device motion updates when the view controller appears and disappears.

Update *ViewController.swift* so that it looks like the following code:

```
override func viewDidAppear(animated: Bool) {
    self.motionManager.startDeviceMotionUpdatesToQueue(
        NSOperationQueue.mainQueue(),
        withHandler: { (motion: CMDeviceMotion!, error: NSError!) -> Void in
            let xString = NSString(format:"%.1f", motion.userAcceleration.x)
            let yString = NSString(format:"%.1f", motion.userAcceleration.y)
            let zString = NSString(format:"%.1f", motion.userAcceleration.z)

            self.xLabel.text = xString
            self.yLabel.text = yString
            self.zLabel.text = zString

            //convert the pitch, yaw and roll to degrees
            let pitchDegrees = motion.attitude.pitch * 180 / M_PI
            let yawDegress = motion.attitude.yaw * 180 / M_PI
            let rollDegress = motion.attitude.roll * 180 / M_PI

            let pitchString = NSString(format: "%.1f", pitchDegrees)
            let yawString = NSString(format: "%.1f", yawDegress)
            let rollString = NSString(format: "%.1f", rollDegress)

            self.pitchLabel.text = pitchString
            self.yawLabel.text = yawString
            self.rollLabel.text = rollString
    })
}
```

Finally, connect an iOS device and run the application on it. Watch the numbers on the screen change as you shake and rotate the device.

Using the Built-in Altimeter

Some iOS devices have a built-in barometer, which can be used to get information about the current atmospheric pressure. This data can be analyzed to work out *relative altitude* (i.e., the change in altitude since recording began).

Not all devices have the hardware needed to use the altimeter. To find out, you ask the CMAltimeter class whether altitude data is available, using the isRelativeAltitudeAvailable method:

```
if CMAltimeter.isRelativeAltitudeAvailable() {
    println("Altimeter is available")
} else {
    println("Altimeter is not available")
}
```

To use the altimeter, you create an instance of the `CMAltimeter` class:

```
let altimeter = CMAltimeter()
var currentAltitude : Float = 0.0
```

Once that's done, you ask it to begin sending you information about changes in the user's altitude:

```
let mainQueue = NSOperationQueue.mainQueue()
altimeter.startRelativeAltitudeUpdatesToQueue(mainQueue) { (data, error) in

    // data.relativeAltitude is the change in
    // altitude since the last time this closure
    // ran, measured in meters.

    // For example, you can keep track of the total
    // change in altitude, relative to where we started:
    self.currentAltitude += Float(data.relativeAltitude)

    self.altitudeLabel.text = "\(self.currentAltitude)m"
}
```

Using the Pedometer

A pedometer is a piece of hardware that keeps track of the number of steps the user has walked or run. Your apps can access live updates from the pedometer (i.e., they can be updated in near real time as the user moves around) or they can ask the system for information about how the user has moved around over the last seven days.

Before you can access the pedometer, you need to first check to see if pedometer information is available:

```
if CMPedometer.isStepCountingAvailable() {
    println("Pedometer is available")
} else {
    println("Pedometer is not available")
}
```

If the pedometer is available, you create an instance of the `CMPedometer` class:

```
let pedometer = CMPedometer()
```

To query the system to find information about how many steps the user has taken over a date range—for example, in the last day—you use the `queryPedometerDataFromDate(_,toDate:)` method, and provide the date range as well as a handler closure that runs when data is available:

```
// Create NSDate objects that refer to 1. right now
// and 2. one day ago
let calendar = NSCalendar.currentCalendar()
let now = NSDate()
let oneDayAgo = calendar.dateByAddingUnit(NSCalendarUnit.DayCalendarUnit,
```

```
                                         value: -1,
                                         toDate: now,
                                         options: NSCalendarOptions())

    // Ask the pedometer to give us info about that date range
    pedometer.queryPedometerDataFromDate(oneDayAgo, toDate: now) {
        (pedometerData, error) in

        // This closure is called on a background queue,
        // so run any changes to the GUI on the main queue
        NSOperationQueue.mainQueue().addOperationWithBlock() {
            if let data = pedometerData {

                self.stepsSinceLastDayLabel.text =
                    "\(data.numberOfSteps) steps"

            }
        }
    }
```

If you want to receive live updates on the user's step count, use the startPedometerUp
datesFromDate method instead:

```
    // Start getting live updates on step count, starting from now
    pedometer.startPedometerUpdatesFromDate(now) { (pedometerData, error)  in

    if let data = pedometerData {

        // Run the update on the background
        NSOperationQueue.mainQueue().addOperationWithBlock() {

            self.stepsSinceAppStartLabel.text =
                "\(data.numberOfSteps) steps"

        }
    }
}
```

Printing Documents

Despite decades of promises, the "paperless office" has never really materialized. Users
like having documents on paper, and both OS X and iOS provide ways of getting stuff
printed on dead trees.

The APIs and methods for printing on OS X and iOS are completely different. On OS
X, individual NSViews are printed, either directly or via an intermediary system. On
iOS, you print via a separate system of print renderer and formatter objects.

We'll build two demo apps that show how to print documents on OS X and iOS.

Printing on OS X

One of the happy quirks of OS X's development is that the entire graphics system traces its lineage to PostScript, the language of printers. On OS X, drawing graphics is very easily translatable to printer commands—so much so, in fact, that the translation is done for you by the OS.

Given any NSView, you can print it by sending it the print() message. OS X takes over from that point—the print panel appears, the user chooses which printer to use and how, and the printer prints the document.

When a view is printed, its drawRect() method is called—however, the graphics context that is prepared before the method is called is designed for generating printer commands (specifically EPS or PDF content). This means that any custom NSView subclass that you make is already set up for printing.

To demonstrate printing, we'll build a small sample application that prints an NSTextView:

1. Create a new Cocoa application named OSXPrinting.

2. Then create the interface. Open *MainMenu.xib*.

   Drag an NSTextView into the app's main window. Make it fill the window, but leave some room at the bottom.

   Drag in an NSButton and place it at the lower right of the window. Change its label to Print.

3. Next, connect the interface. We don't need to write any code for this, since the button can be directly connected to the print function of the view.

   Select the text view.

   Open the Connections Inspector in the righthand sidebar.

   Drag from the print: in Received Actions onto the button.

4. Finally, test the application. Run the application and type some text into the text view. Click the Print button and try printing the document. (If you don't want to waste paper, you can print to PDF by choosing "Save as PDF" in the PDF menu, just like in all applications on OS X.)

 You can also choose Print from your application's File menu, or press ⌘-P. The reason this works without having connected the views is that the Print menu item is connected to the First Responder, which is the object that corresponds to whichever view is currently responding to user input.

Printing on iOS

While OS X machines are often permanently connected to a printer (usually via USB, and sometimes over the network), iOS printing is much more ad hoc and on the fly. In iOS, all printing is done over AirPrint, the WiFi-based printer discovery system. When you print a document, iOS shows you a list of nearby printers, and you send your document to the printer you want to use.

The printing system is more complex than on OS X, but more flexible. When you want to print a document, you ask iOS for the shared instance of the UIPrintInteraction Controller, which is a view controller that allows the user to configure the print job and works in the same way as the print panel on OS X. You then provide the print interaction controller with the items you want to have printed.

There are several ways you can indicate to the print interaction controller what should be printed. If you have a UIImage, or an NSData that contains PDF or image data, you can give it directly to the print controller. You can also provide an NSArray of these objects if you have multiple things you want to print.

If you want to print content like text, markup, or custom views, you create a UIPrint Formatter object for each piece of content. For example, if you have a block of text, you can create an instance of UISimpleTextPrintFormatter, give it the NSString that contains your text, and then provide the print formatter to the print controller.

If you want to have total control over what gets printed, you can also use the UIPrint PageRenderer class, which allows for advanced customization and drawing.

In this section, we'll create a simple iOS application that does the same thing as the OS X application in the previous section—a simple text box, plus a print button:

1. Create a new single view application for iOS named PrintingiOS.

2. Next, we'll create the inteface. Open *Main.storyboard*.

   Drag a UINavigationBar into the window and place it at the top.

   Drag a UIBarButtonItem into the navigation bar. Change its label to Print.

   Finally, drag in a UITextView and make it fill the rest of the space.

3. Now, we'll connect the interface to the view controller. Open *ViewController.swift* in the assistant.

   Control-drag from the text view into ViewController, and create an outlet called textView.

   Control-drag from the Print button into ViewController, and create an action called print.

We're done with the interface. The next step is to make the Print button actually print.

4. Add the printing code. Open *ViewController.swift*. Replace the `print:` method with the following code:

```
@IBAction func print(sender: AnyObject) {
    var printInteraction =
            UIPrintInteractionController.sharedPrintController()

    var textFormatter =
        UISimpleTextPrintFormatter(text: self.textView.text)
    printInteraction?.printFormatter = textFormatter

    printInteraction?.presentAnimated(true,
        completionHandler: {
            (printController:UIPrintInteractionController!,
            completed:Bool!,
            error:NSError!) -> Void in
    })
}
```

In order to test the printing system without using actual paper, Xcode provides a tool called the Printer Simulator that simulates printers on the network. It's not a substitute for actually printing on paper—if you're doing anything with graphics, for example, the colors will likely be quite different, and a simulated printer won't demonstrate effects like ink bleed—but it's sufficient for demonstrating that it actually works.

5. Launch the Printer Simulator. To do so, open the iOS Simulator if it isn't open already, and choose Open Printer Simulator from the File menu.

6. Finally, test the application. Launch the application and hit the Print button. Choose one of the simulated printers and tap Print. The Print Simulator will simulate printing and show you the final result.

Game Controllers

Game Controller is another new framework included with the release of iOS 7 and OS X 10.9 and the implementation is the same on both platforms. Each controller is represented by a `GCController` object and the operating system handles the discovery and connection of controllers automatically, leaving you free to just use them.

Apple requires you to make controllers an optional interface of a game. You must provide a fallback option of mouse and keyboard in OS X, or touch controls in iOS if the user doesn't have a game controller.

There are two profiles for game controllers, called gamepad and extendedGamepad. The standard gamepad has a four-way directional pad, four front-facing buttons in a diamond pattern, and two shoulder buttons. The extendedGamepad not only has all the elements of a gamepad (and can be detected as one by the application), but also has a left and right trigger to accompany the shoulder buttons and two joysticks to go along with the d-pad.

To demonstrate how to connect to and use the controllers, we'll create a simple OS X application (it is worth noting that if you don't have a controller, this app will be a little unexciting):

1. Create a new Cocoa application and call it Controllers.

2. Include the framework. Open the project inside the project navigator. In the General tab, scroll down to the Linked Frameworks and Libraries section and add the Game Controller.framework into the project.

3. If you haven't already done so, now would be a great time to connect any controllers you have—either plug it into your device, or pair it over Bluetooth as per the instructions that come with the controller.

Open applicationDidFinishLaunching() and add the following:

```
var controllers = GCController.controllers()

if (controllers.count != 0)
{
    // grabbing a reference to the first controller
    self.myController = controllers[0] as GCController

    // un-set the player number
    self.myController.playerIndex = GCControllerPlayerIndexUnset

    if ((self.myController.extendedGamepad) != nil)
    {
        NSLog("This is an extended controller")
        // adding a callback handler for when a value has changed
        var profile = self.myController.extendedGamepad
        profile.valueChangedHandler =
            {(  gamepad: GCExtendedGamepad!,
                element:GCControllerElement!) -> Void in
                if (element == gamepad.rightTrigger)
                {
                    if (gamepad.rightTrigger.pressed)
                    {
                        NSLog("Right trigger pressed")
                    }
                }
            }
    }
    profile.leftTrigger.valueChangedHandler =
        {(  input:GCControllerButtonInput!,
```

```
                    value:Float!,
                pressed:Bool!) -> Void in
                  if((pressed) != nil)
                  {
                      NSLog("left trigger pressed")
                  }
              }
          }
          else
          {
              NSLog("controller is a simple controller")
          }
      }
      else
      {
          NSLog("There are no controllers connected")
      }
```

This code does a few things. First, it creates a property to hold the controller as soon as we can access one. Then applicationDidFinishLaunching() uses the class method on GCController to get access to all currently connected controllers. We then store the first controller in our previously defined property and set its player index to be unset, as we are not going to be using more than one player at a time.

Then we set up two callback handlers: one that responds to every element on the controller and one that responds only to the left trigger.

If you run the application and have an extended game controller connected when you press in either of the triggers, you will get a log message.

App Nap

App Nap is a feature for OS X apps that's designed to improve battery life without impinging upon an app's responsiveness. It accomplishes this through a bunch of different heuristics to determine what apps should be suspended. The heuristics that determine if your app may be suspended by the OS are as follows:

- The app is not visible.
- The app is not making any noise.
- The app has not disabled automatic termination.
- The app has not made any power management assertions.

When asleep, your app is put in a scheduling queue that rarely gets any processing time. Any user activity that brings your app to the foreground or the receipt of an OS event will awaken your app and return it to normal processing priority. App Nap is essentially trying to keep your computer's CPU idling for a long as possible, only leaving the idle state when necessary before returning to the idle state as quickly as possible. With this goal in mind, Apple has provided three new APIs:

Application visibility

Application visibility is a simple idea: when your app isn't visible, it is likely that it doesn't need to be doing as much as if it were in the foreground. Since the release of 10.9, a new application delegate method is called when your app's visibility changes. To detect this change, add something similar to the following in your application's delegate:

```
func applicationDidChangeOcclusionState(notification: NSNotification!)
{
    if (NSApp.occlusionState & NSApplicationOcclusionState.Visible != nil)
    {
        println("You are in the foreground, go nuts")
    }
    else
    {
        println("You are in the background, best slow down")
    }
}
```

Timer tolerance

Timers are a great source of causing the system to leave idle state—even two timers mere milliseconds apart cause the system to switch to normal running from idle. Timer tolerances allows the OS to slightly shift your timers to be in sync with other timers that are also running, which allows the system to keep itself idle longer. To use timer tolerance, simply call the setTolerance method on your timers before starting them. Apple recommends a default of 10% of a timer's interval, but this will need to change on an app-by-app basis.

User actvities

User activities are a way of declaring to the system what you are doing and how important it is. When your app declares these activities, the system can begin to optimize the heuristics it uses to know when to nap apps. To declare one of these activities, implement code similar to the following:

```
let queue = NSOperationQueue.mainQueue()

var token = NSProcessInfo.processInfo()
token.beginActivityWithOptions(NSActivityOptions.UserInitiated,
                               reason: "Important stuff")

queue.addOperationWithBlock { () -> Void in
    // do important stuff in here
}
NSProcessInfo.processInfo().endActivity(token)
```

The `option` parameter allows you to declare to the system what kind of work it is. This example is saying that it is user-initiated activity, and as such is very important and should stop the app from being napped while it is occurring. By contrast, specifying the option `NSActivityBackground` indicates to the system that it is low priority, and napping the app won't affect the user.

Authenticating Using Touch ID

Many apps need to ensure that the user has given permission to do certain things. The most common example is purchasing—an app needs to make super-sure that the users really *do* want to spend their money on a virtual kitten app. Other examples include password managers, where you need to ensure that the user attempting to look at the stored information is the owner of the device.

Several iOS devices, starting with the iPhone 5S, include the *Touch ID* sensor, which is a fingerprint scanner that iOS uses to unlock the device. The Touch ID sensor stores its fingerprint information in a secure area of the device's CPU, where it cannot be directly accessed—the device may only store new information and query whether a scan matches the existing data. Additionally, because scanned fingerprint information can never be read from the chip, the device has no way to send fingerprint information to a third party.

Your app has access to the Touch ID sensor, through the Local Authentication framework. This framework is designed to provide a general way to ask the system to authenticate the user.

 As of iOS 8, the only authentication system available through Local Authentication is the Touch ID fingerprint scanner. However, the API is designed so that additional methods can be added in future releases of iOS.

To use the LocalAuthentication framework, you first import `LocalAuthentication`:

```
import LocalAuthentication
```

Once you've done that, create and store an `LAContext` object. The context is the environment in which you check to see whether the user is authenticated or not:

```
let authenticationContext = LAContext()
```

When your code needs to determine whether the device's owner has granted authorization, you need to do two things. First, you need to determine whether the app has the ability to authenticate the user or not. For example, your app may be running on a device that doesn't have the Touch ID sensor, which means that Local Authentication won't be able to authenticate the user at all.

Local Authentication refers to the different methods of authenticating the user as *policies*. Asking the system to authenticate the user via a policy is referred to as *evaluating* the policy.

As of iOS 8, Local Authentication currently only supports a single policy: the Touch ID scanner. Local Authentication refers to this policy as `LAPolicy.DeviceOwnerAuthenticationWithBiometrics`.

Using Local Authentication means doing three things:

1. Selecting a policy to use (in iOS 8, this will always be `LAPolicy.DeviceOwnerAuthenticationWithBiometrics`).
2. Asking the `LAContext` if it's possible to evaluate that policy.
3. If it is possible, evaluate the policy, and proceed from there.

 If a policy isn't available, your app will need to use an alternative method of authenticating the user. The specifics will depend on your app—if you're making an app that's tied to a web-based login system, ask the user to enter a username and password manually. Never rely on just Local Authentication, because it might not be available.

In order to check to see whether Local Authentication can evaluate a policy, you call the `canEvaluatePolicy` method. This method returns `true` or `false` to indicate whether evaluating the policy is possible, and also supports passing back detailed information on *why* it's not possible through an `NSError`:

```
// Specify how we want to authenticate. (As of iOS 8.0, the only option
// is with the Touch ID biometric fingerprint scanner.)

let policy = LAPolicy.DeviceOwnerAuthenticationWithBiometrics

// Ask the system if it's possible for this authentication check to
// succeed. (The device might not have a fingerprint scanner, or
// the user may not have enrolled their fingerprints, for example.)
var error : NSError? = nil

let canAuthenticate =
    authenticationContext.canEvaluatePolicy(policy, error: &error)

if canAuthenticate == false {
    // If we can't use it, bail out and present an alternative way of
    // authenticating.
    println("Can't use the authentication system! \(error)")
    return
}
```

The LAPolicy.DeviceOwnerAuthenticationWithBiometrics policy is not available on the iOS Simulator. Calling canEvaluatePolicy when running on the iOS Simulator will always return false.

If Local Authentication indicates that it's possible to evaluate a policy, you can then proceed to the third and final stage: actually evaluating it.

To evaluate the policy, you call the evaluatePolicy method. You provide the policy you want to evaluate, a string of text that explains to users *why* you want them to authenticate themselves, and a closure to run when the evaluation is done:

```
// Explain why they need to authenticate; for example:
let authenticationReason = "You're about to spend money."

// Fire off the authenticator!
authenticationContext.evaluatePolicy(policy,
    localizedReason: authenticationReason) {
        (succeeded, error) -> Void in

    if succeeded {

        // We're in! Go ahead and perform the sensitive transaction.

        println("Authenticated!")

    } else {

        // Didn't work! This can happen for a number of reasons,
        // including the user canceling an incoming phone call,
        // or choosing to enter a password instead.

        // Check the error code in the 'error' variable to determine
        // what the app should do next.

        println("Not authenticated! \(error)")

        // Some possible error codes:
        if error.code == LAError.UserFallback.rawValue {
            // The user decided to enter a password instead of scanning
            // her fingerprint; present a different way to authenticate.
        }

        if error.code == LAError.UserCancel.rawValue {
            // The user cancelled authentication.
        }
    }

}
```

This is the stage at which users are presented with instructions on how to authenticate themselves: the Touch ID window will appear, and they'll be prompted to scan their fingerprint (see Figure 15-5)

Figure 15-5. The Touch ID window, which is presented when you call evaluatePolicy; the user may either scan her fingerprint, enter a password, or cancel

It's important to note that users can choose to *not* scan their fingerprint, and enter a password instead. They might do this for several reasons: it might be impractical or impossible to scan their finger, or the fingerprint scanner might not be working properly (wet fingers are a lot more difficult to scan, for example.)

If the user decides to manually enter a password, the closure provided to the `evaluate Policy` method will receive a `false` value, to indicate that scanning failed, and the `NSError` passed to the closure will have an error code that indicates that choice.

Handoff

Handoff is a feature available from iOS 8 that allows the user to begin an activity on one device, and continue it from another. One of the simplest examples of how this can be useful is in email: imagine you start writing an email on your iPhone, and decide that you want to finish writing it on your laptop. When you look at your laptop's screen, a little icon appears on the dock—when you click it, Mail appears, with your half-finished draft all ready for you to finish up and send.

The Handoff system is designed to make it simple for your app to make this kind of story possible. Handoff works by getting apps to tell the operating system when they're doing an activity that can be handed off to another device, such as drafting an email, or looking at a web page. In addition, the Handoff system uses the multipeer connectivity system (discussed in "Multipeer Connectivity" on page 303) to make the operating system aware of nearby computers that have the ability to have the activity handed off to them.

To demonstrate Handoff, we'll build an app for iOS that allows the user to hand off an activity from one device to another.

 This example app is designed for iOS. However, handoffs work on OS X as well—you can hand off activities from one Mac to another, as well as handing off from a Mac to an iOS device and back. For information, see the Handoff Programming Guide in the Xcode documentation (*http://bit.ly/handoff_programming_guide*).

Handoff doesn't work in the iOS Simulator. To use Handoff, you need at least two iPhones, iPads, iPod touches, or Macs. Additionally, all of the devices need to be using the same iCloud account.

The app's "activity" will be a collection of switches; you can flip them on and off, and if you have another device in range, you can hand off the state of the switches to that device. You can see the app in action in Figure 15-6.

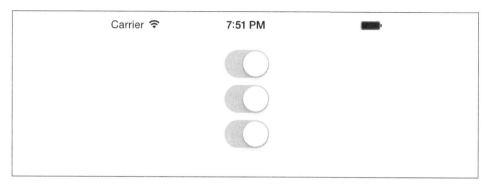

Carrier 🛜   7:51 PM

Figure 15-6. The Handoff demo app

Here are the steps you'll need to follow:

1. Create a new, single view iOS application and call it Handoffs.

2. Create the interface, which will consist of three switches, all connected to their own outlets.

   Open *Main.storyboard*, and drag in three UISwitches.

3. Connect the interface to the code.

   Open *ViewController.swift* in the assistant editor. Then hold down the Control key, and drag from each of the switches into the ViewController class. Create a new outlet for each one. Name the first one switch1, the second switch2, and the third switch3.

   We also want to know when each of the switches changes state, so that we can let the Handoff system know. Control-drag from the first switch into the View Controller class, and make a new action. Make sure that the Event is "Value Changed." Name the action switchUpdated.

   Once you've done that, Control-drag from the other two switches onto the newly created switchUpdated method.

The interface is now complete. The rest of the work is accomplished via the code.

In Handoff, the state of the activity that the user is performing is stored inside an NSUserActivity object. This object is responsible for both broadcasting to nearby devices that the user is performing an activity that can be handed off, as well as storing all of the information that another device would need to resume the activity. For example, if the activity was drafting an email, the NSUserActivity object would store the text of the draft.

In order for the Handoff system to work, you need to tell the system what *type* of activity you're dealing with. Activity types are string that look like a reverse domain name, much like bundle identifiers. For example: `com.oreilly.MyAmazingApplication.writing-email`. Your app needs to register each different activity type that it supports with the system.

To do this, you add each activity type to your application's *Info.plist* file (in this example, the app will have a single activity type: `com.oreilly.Handoffs.switches`):

1. Register the activity type. Select the project at the top of the project navigator.

   Select the Info tab, and insert a new row into the list of "Custom iOS Target Properties." Set the name of the new row to be `NSUserActivityTypes`, and set its type to be Array.

   With the new row selected, press Enter. A new entry in this array will appear. Set the new row's type to String, and set its value to be `com.oreilly.Handoffs.switches`.

The application will now register with the operating system that it's capable of accepting incoming activities with the `com.oreilly.Handoffs.switches` type. The next step is to make the application actually broadcast these.

To do this, we'll create a property on the `ViewController` class that stores an instance of the `NSUserActivity`.

2. Open the *ViewController.swift* file.

3. Add the `NSUserActivity` property to the `ViewController` class:

   ```
   var activity : NSUserActivity?
   ```

The next step is to add a method that takes the current state of the switches, and stores it in a dictionary. This will be used a couple of times in the app, so it pays to make it a method that can be called repeatedly.

4. Add the `activityInfoDictionary` method to *ViewController.swift*:

   ```
   // Creates and returns a dictionary containing the state of the activity
   func activityInfoDictionary() -> [String: Bool] {
       return [
           "switch1": switch1.on,
           "switch2": switch2.on,
           "switch3": switch3.on
       ]
   }
   ```

Next, the activity itself will be created and set up. This is done inside the `viewWillAppear` method, so that when the view appears, it indicates to the system that the user is participating in an activity.

5. Add the `viewWillAppear` method to *ViewController.swift*:

```
override func viewWillAppear(animated: Bool) {
    // When the view appears, create and set up the activity
    activity =
        NSUserActivity(activityType: "com.oreilly.Handoffs.switches")
    activity?.userInfo = activityInfoDictionary()
    activity?.title = "Switches"
    activity?.delegate = self

    // Becoming current means that this activity will be broadcast
    // to all other nearby devices that have the same iCloud account
    activity?.becomeCurrent()
}
```

We also need to make sure that the activity is turned off if the view disappears. This frees up system resources that are used by the `NSUserActivity`, and stops the app from broadcasting. We'll do this by calling the `invalidate` method on the activity when the view disappears.

6. Add the `viewWillDisappear` method to *ViewController.swift*:

```
override func viewWillDisappear(animated: Bool) {
    // When the view disappears, turn off the activity
    activity?.invalidate()
    activity = nil
}
```

As part of being set up, the activity is told to use `self` as the delegate. This is important, because it allows the activity to contact the view controller when it needs to get the most recent state of the activity. To make this work properly, you need to make the class conform to the correct protocol.

7. At the top of the class's definition, add the `NSUserActivityDelegate` protocol, like so:

```
class ViewController: UIViewController, NSUserActivityDelegate {
```

When the user changes the state of the switches, we need to indicate to `NSUserActivi ty` that the activity's state has changed. However, you don't update the activity directly. Instead, you indicate to the activity that something's changed, and that it needs to get in touch with its delegate (in this example, the view controller) to get the latest state.

Doing this means that the system can be more efficient. Instead of updating every time the user does anything, which could be as often as every time the user types a new character on the keyboard, the system can check in every so often and get the latest information.

You indicate to the activity object that new information is available by setting its needs Save property to true. Later, the activity will call the userActivityWillSave method, which is responsible for actually giving the activity new information.

8. Notify the activity when the state changes. To do that, add the following code to the switchUpdated method:

```
// A switch has changed state, so we need to update activity
@IBAction func switchUpdated(sender: UISwitch) {
    self.activity?.needsSave = true
}
```

9. Store the activity information by adding the following method to the View Controller class:

```
// Called at some point after you set needsSave on the activity to true
func userActivityWillSave(userActivity: NSUserActivity) {
    userActivity.userInfo = activityInfoDictionary()
}
```

If you run your app on two devices, and then lock one of them, you'll see a small icon in the lower-left corner of the screen. If you swipe up from this icon, your app will launch. You're half done!

Unfortunately, the app isn't actually handing information about the activity off from one device to the next. The final piece is to implement the functionality that *receives* the Handoff.

You do this by implementing a method in the application delegate, called application(_, continueUserActivity:, restorationHandler:). This method is called when the user swipes up from that icon on the lock screen, and receives both the NSUserActivity object that contains the activity state, as well as a closure that needs to be run.

10. Implement the continuation method by opening *AppDelegate.swift* and adding the following method to the AppDelegate class:

```
func application(application: UIApplication,
            continueUserActivity userActivity: NSUserActivity,
            restorationHandler: ([AnyObject]!) -> Void) -> Bool {

    // Any objects we pass to the restorationHandler function will
    // have restoreUserActivityState called on them, in which they'll
    // get data out of the activity and make themselves ready for the
    // user to resume the activity

    // In this example, we only have a single view controller,
    // so pass that in

    if let rootViewController = self.window?.rootViewController {
```

```
            restorationHandler([rootViewController])

            return true
        } else {
            return false
        }

    }
```

The last step is to add the `restoreUserActivityState` method, which is called by the system to restore the state from the activity object.

11. Open *ViewController.swift*, and add the `restoreUserActivityState` method to the `ViewController` class:

```
// Called by the system when we need to
// restore from an incoming activity
override func restoreUserActivityState(activity: NSUserActivity) {

    if activity.activityType == "com.oreilly.Handoffs.switches" {
        let userInfo = activity.userInfo as [String : Bool]

        switch1.on = userInfo["switch1"] as Bool!
        switch2.on = userInfo["switch2"] as Bool!
        switch3.on = userInfo["switch3"] as Bool!
    }
}
```

You're done! You can now hand off the state of the activity from one device to another.

CHAPTER 16

EventKit

The user's life isn't confined to the use of computers and phones, and many people even use technology to manage real-life interactions with other human beings. One capability of Apple devices is calendaring and scheduling, which is usually managed through built-in applications (the Calendar app on iOS and OS X).

However, it can be very useful for third-party applications to be able to access the calendar, either to create new appointments or to view what the user has lined up for the day. This information is exposed via EventKit, the calendar data store API.

In this chapter, you'll learn how to work with EventKit to access the user's calendar. The same API applies to both OS X and iOS; in this chapter, the sample code will be written for OS X.

Understanding Events

All of the information that relates to the user's calendars comes from the *EventKit event store*. This is the database of the user's calendars, which themselves contain *calendar events*. The event store is represented by the EKEventStore class, and you create an instance of this class to begin working with the calendar.

The event store contains multiple calendars, which are EKCalendar objects. Each calendar has information like its name, whether it's editable, whether it's a subscribed calendar, and so on.

An "event" is an entry in the user's calendar, and is represented as an EKEvent object. Events contain several key pieces of information, including:

- A text label describing what the event is
- The date and times that the event begins and ends
- The location of the event

- When the event was created and last modified

EKEvent is actually a subclass of the EKCalendarItem class, because EKCalendars can contain not only events, but also reminders, which are scheduled alerts.

 Reminders are available only on OS X and iOS 6 and later.

Events can also be set to repeat, and the rules for this repetition can be complex. For example, you can have an event that repeats every day, every second day, on the second Tuesday of every month, and so on.

In addition to this repeating behavior, it's possible to *detach* a specific instance of a repeating event. For example, imagine you have an event on the calendar that repeats every week on Monday morning, and one week you need to push it back. However, you only want to move this one instance, not the entire repeating set. When you move the event, your calendaring application asks if you want to move all future events, or just the specific one you just moved. Your answer indicates to the system whether you want to create a detached event or modify the entire repeating event.

Accessing the Event Store

To get access to the calendar system, you create an instance of EKEventStore, indicating what kinds of calendar items you want to get from the store (either events or reminders).

To connect to the store, you create an EKEventStore object:

```
var store = EKEventStore()
```

Once you create the EKEventStore, you must ask the user for permission to access the calendars by using the requestAccessToEntityType(entityType:completion:) method. If the user hasn't already granted permission to access calendar events of that type, an alert box will pop up asking the user if it's OK for your application to access the calendar. Until the user grants permission, any requests for data will return nil.

The second parameter of the requestAccessToEntityType(entityType:completion:) method is a closure, which takes two parameters of its own: a Bool that indicates whether the user granted permission or not, and an optional NSError that, if the Bool is false, describes why permission wasn't granted. This could be for a variety of reasons, including the user having parental permissions that disallow calendar access, or the user simply saying no:

```
store.requestAccessToEntityType(EKEntityTypeEvent) {
    (success: Bool, error: NSError!) in
    println("Got permission = \(success); error = \(error)")
}
```

The alert box is only shown once. When you run the app for a second time, the system will remember the user's decision. When you call `requestAccessToEntityType(entityType:completion:)`, the completion handler will be called immediately.

On the first launch, the event store might not have permission at the moment you create the `EKEventStore` object, but it might gain permission later. When the user grants (or revokes) permission, an `EKEventStoreChangedNotification` is broadcast by the object. This notification is also sent when the contents of the event store changes; in both cases, it's a signal to refresh whatever views you have that are displaying the contents of the calendar.

The alert box is only presented once. If the user revokes access later, the next time `requestAccessToEntityType` is called, it will immediately fail.

The alert box will only be displayed again if the user deletes and then reinstalls the app. The idea behind this is that the app should never pester the user for permission through the alert box—if your app really, really needs access to the calendar, then tell them that through your app's interface.

Accessing Calendars

To get the list of calendars available to the user, simply ask the event store. Because a calendar can support only events, or only reminders, you need to specify what you want the calendars that you get back to support.

To get the calendars that support storing events, you use the `calendarsForEntity Type` method, and pass in the `EKEntityTypeEvent` value as the type parameter:

```
var eventCalendars =
    store.calendarsForEntityType(EKEntityTypeEvent) as [EKCalendar]
```

This returns an array of `EKCalendars`, which you can get events out of.

Getting the array of calendars that support reminders is just as easy—you just pass in the `EKEntityTypeReminder` parameter:

```
var reminderCalendars =
    store.calendarsForEntityType(EKEntityTypeReminder) as [EKCalendar]
```

Once you have a calendar, you can start working with events inside it.

Accessing Events

A calendar is a potentially infinitely large collection of data. If a calendar contains any repeating events that don't have an end date, such as a weekly meeting or someone's birthday, then it's not possible to ask for "all events," as that collection is of an infinite size. Instead, you need to specify the date range that you're interested in receiving events for.

While you're filtering based on date range, it's also useful to filter based on other properties as well, including time of day, event name, and so on. The standard filtering tool in Cocoa and Cocoa Touch is NSPredicate, which allows you to specify parameters for finding events in a data set.

 NSPredicate is also useful outside of EventKit. For example, you can use an NSPredicate to filter an array to only contain objects that match certain parameters. For more information on this useful class, check out its Xcode documentation (*http://bit.ly/nspredicate*).

To construct an event-finding predicate, ask your EKEventStore to provide you with a predicate that finds events between a start date and an end date, as well as the calendars that the events should be in. This is done with the predicateForEventsWithStart Date method:

```
var startDate : NSDate = ...
var endDate : NSDate = ...

var predicate = self.store.predicateForEventsWithStartDate(self.date,
                                             endDate: endDate,
                                             calendars: eventCalendars)
```

 The startDate and endDate variables in the preceding code are placeholders. We'll be working with dates in "Building an Events Application" on page 356.

Once you have this NSPredicate, you can give it back to the EKEventStore and it will retrieve all matching calendar items:

```
var events = store.eventsMatchingPredicate(predicate) as [EKEvent]
```

This array contains all matching events, from which you can extract information.

Working with Events

Modifying an event or reminder is as simple as modifying its properties. For example, to modify an event's title, you just change its `title` property:

```
var event : EKEvent = events[0]
event.title = "Party Times"
```

> `title` is actually a property on `EKCalendarItem`, the superclass of `EKEvent`. This means that it exists in both `EKEvent` and `EKReminder`.

However, changing properties on an event or reminder does not update the shared calendar system immediately. When the calendar item has finished being modified, it must be explicitly saved back to the event store. You do this by using the method `saveEvent`, which takes as its parameters the event that you're saving, the span of time that the changes should apply for, and a reference to an `NSError` variable that the method will store error information in if anything goes wrong.

The span of time is represented as an `EKSpan`, which is simply an enumeration with two options: this event or future events. When you modify a repeating event and choose to make those changes apply only to one specific instance, the instance will become detached:

```
var theEvent = EKEvent()
var error : NSError? = nil
store.saveEvent(theEvent, span: EKSpanThisEvent, commit: true, error: &error)
```

> The `EKEventStore` that you use to save the event needs to be the same as the one you got the event from. If you get an `EKEvent` from one `EKEventStore` and try to save it in a different one, your app will throw an exception.
>
> If you want to copy an event from one place to another, you need to create your own new `EKEvent`, provide it with the information you want (from another `EKEvent`), and then save it into the destination event store.

It's possible that an `EKEvent` that you're working with might have changed while your code was modifying it. Whenever the calendar changes, the `EKEventStore` that you're working with posts an `EKEventStoreChangedNotification` to let you know that the contents of the event store have been modified. To ensure that an `EKEvent` is up to date with the most recent information inside the calendar, use the `refresh` method:

```
var event : EKEvent = ...
event.refresh()
```

Refreshing an event means that properties that have changed since you got the event from the event store will be updated to match the most recent version. Note that any properties that *you* have changed will *not*.

For example, say you get an EKEvent and change its title to "Excellent Party Times," but don't save it. You then modify the title of that same event using the Calendar application, and *then* save your modified EKEvent object. In this case, it will be *your* version that is written to the event store.

 This means that if you want to revert any changes that you've made to an EKEvent, all you have to do is not save them.

You can also call the reset method on your EKEventStore to reset the entire event store to its last saved state.

You can also delete events. Removing an event is straightforward: all you need to do is call the removeEvent method on your EKEventStore. This behaves much like the method used for saving events—you simply provide the event to be removed, indicate whether you want to remove a single event or all future events (if the event is a repeating one), and provide a reference to a variable for an NSError to be placed in if something goes wrong:

```
var theEvent : EKEvent = ...
var error : NSError? = nil
store.removeEvent(theEvent, span: EKSpanFutureEvents,
    commit: true, error: &error)
```

Building an Events Application

To wrap things up, we're going to build an app that displays events for the user, depending on which day they've selected.

This app presents a date picker and a list of events. When the date picker's selected date changes, the list updates to show the user's events for that day:

1. Create a new Cocoa application called Events.

    To work with EventKit, we need to add the EventKit framework.

2. Add EventKit.framework to the project. Open *AppDelegate.swift*, and add the following code at the top:

    ```
    import EventKit
    ```

First, we'll write the code that will expose the calendar information. We're going to create several properties, some of which will be backed by instance variables and some of which will not.

Specifically, the application will keep track of the following information:

- The currently selected date
- The event store used to access the calendar
- The available calendars
- The events for the currently selected date

The event store and date properties will be backed by an instance variable, while the available calendars and events properties will be dynamically computed when needed (based on the selected date and event store).

When the user selects a date, the app will query the calendar and ask for all events that fall between that date and one day following that. This means that the *time* of that first date should be midnight, in order to catch all events that happen within one day after that.

We'll first set up the event store, and then add the properties for the date, the list of events, and the list of calendars that contain those events:

1. Set up the EKEventStore. The next step is to set up the event store, which is kept in the store property, which will be lazily loaded. That is, the first time the property is accessed, an EKEventStore object will be created and assigned to the property. This keeps us from having to do any deliberate setup in the application's init or awakeFromNib methods.

   This can be done through Swift's support for *lazy* properties. By declaring a property as lazy, the object will only be created when the property is accessed for the first time by your code:

   ```
   lazy var store : EKEventStore = EKEventStore()

   func applicationDidFinishLaunching(notification: NSNotification!) {
       self.store.requestAccessToEntityType(EKEntityTypeEvent) {
           (success: Bool, error: NSError!) in
           println("Got permission = \(success); error = \(error)")
       }
   }
   ```

2. Add the date property, by adding the following code to AppDelegate:

   ```
   var date : NSDate = NSDate() {
       willSet {
           // Convert the provided date to one at midnight on the same day
           var dateComponents =
   ```

```
NSCalendar.currentCalendar().components(NSCalendarUnit.DayCalendarUnit |
NSCalendarUnit.MonthCalendarUnit |
NSCalendarUnit.YearCalendarUnit, fromDate: newValue)

        if let dateResult =
        NSCalendar.currentCalendar().dateFromComponents(dateComponents) {
            self.date = dateResult
        }


    }
}
```

NSDateComponents is a class that can perform calculations on dates, given a calendar. In this case, we're asking the class to get the day, month, and year from a date, and then create a date from that—thereby creating an NSDate object on the same date as the provided one, but with a time value set to midnight on that day.

Additionally, we want to disregard the time information from the date; when you ask NSDate for the current date, it returns an NSDate corresponding to the current date *and time*. We don't want that, so we need to do some calendar calculation to make the time value correspond to midnight on the provided day, thus ensuring that the time value is consistent no matter which date we select.

We can now add the calendars and events properties. These don't have any instance variables, because all they'll do is retrieve information from the event store.

3. First, to add the calendars property, add the following code to AppDelegate:

```
var calendars : [EKCalendar] {
get {
    return self.store.calendarsForEntityType(EKEntityTypeEvent)
    as [EKCalendar];
}
}
```

Next, add the following code to add the events property:

```
var events : [EKEvent] {
get {
    var endDate = date.dateByAddingTimeInterval(24 * 60 * 60)

    var predicate =
    self.store.predicateForEventsWithStartDate(self.date,
    endDate: endDate, calendars: self.calendars)

    return self.store.eventsMatchingPredicate(predicate) as [EKEvent]
}
}
```

The calendars method simply returns the array of calendars that support events.

The events method is a little more complex. Because a request to the event store requires that we provide a start date and an end date for our query, we need to create an end date that's one day after our start date (which we'll set up in a moment).

Because there are 24 hours in a day, 60 minutes in an hour, and 60 seconds in a minute, we can create an NSDate that's one day after the start date with the dateByAddingTimeInterval method on NSDate. This method takes as its sole parameter the number of seconds in the future that the new date should be; thus, we want a date that's 86,400 seconds in the future, which is 24 times 60 times 60.

Given these two dates, we call predicateForEventsWithStartDate and provide the start date, end date, and the calendars to check. We then get the array of events that matched that predicate, and return it.

There's one last method to create: one that will be used to indicate to the system that when the date changes, the list of events will also change.

4. Add the keyPathsForValuesAffectingEvents method to AppDelegate:

```
class func keyPathsForValuesAffectingEvents() -> NSSet! {
    return NSSet(object: "date")
}
```

This method returns an NSSet containing the list of properties that, when modified, cause the events property to change. This method is checked by the Cocoa bindings system whenever a property changes on the AppDelegate object, and helps us bind the code to the view with minimal additional work.

With all of that out of the way, it's finally time to create the interface. Fortunately, because of the work we've done in the code, it's very simple to set up.

1. Open *MainMenu.xib*. Drag an array controller into the outline. Bind its content array to the app delegate, with the model key path self.events. Open the Identity Inspector, and change its label to Events.

   Drag in a date picker and a table view. Select the date picker, and change its style to Graphical. This creates a nice calendar control.

   When you're done, the finished interface should look something like Figure 16-1.

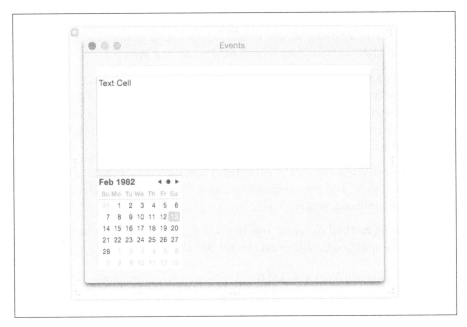

Figure 16-1. The finished interface

2. Bind the date picker. The date picker needs to control the date property on the app delegate. To make this happen, select the date picker, open the Bindings Inspector, and bind the Value property to the app delegate, with the model key path self.date.

All we need to do now is bind the table view to the list of events for the selected date. Because this is exposed as the events property on the app delegate, and this property will automatically update its contents as the date is changed, the table view will always show the events for the selected date, even as the user changes it.

3. Bind the table view. Select the table view in the outline (it's inside the scroll view), and bind its content to the Events array controller that you set up earlier. Set the controller key to arrangedObjects.

   Select the table column (inside the table view in the outline), and bind its Value to the Events array controller. Set the controller key to arrangedObjects and the model key path to self.title.

You're done! Run the app, and try selecting different dates in the date picker.

If nothing is appearing in the table view, you should double-check to make sure that there is actually an event on the date you're trying to look at. One of the authors, who shall remain nameless (although it was Jon), spent more than 10 minutes trying to debug the app before realizing his mistake.

User Privacy

Just like a user's location (see "Working with Location" on page 309) and contacts, the events on the user's calendar are considered private and sensitive information. Apps aren't allowed to access the calendar unless the user explicitly grants them permission, and they are expected to behave properly when they don't receive this permission—if your app can't access the calendar, it should handle this gracefully. Additionally, the user can revoke access to the calendar (or any of the other private data stores) at any time.

This means that you can't write code and assume that you'll get access to the information your application needs. Instead, your code needs to gracefully fail—if your app can get any useful work done without access to the calendar, it should go ahead and do so, and if it is rendered inoperable by not having access, it should tell the user in a friendly manner (don't pop up a scary "error!" dialog box).

If you're writing an application to be submitted to the App Store, you can expect that whoever reviews your application will disallow calendar access to determine how the app behaves without it. If your application doesn't cope, expect it to be rejected.

CHAPTER 17

Instruments and the Debugger

As anyone who's written software knows, designing and implementing the features of an application is only a fraction of the work. Once the app's done and performs all the tasks it's meant to do, you need to make sure that it runs *well*.

Performance is a feature that many developers neglect, but it's something that influences people's decisions to use your software or not. Many of our friends and family prefer to use Pages instead of Microsoft Word, because despite the relative lack of features in Pages, it's a more nimble and zippy application.

Not paying attention to performance also has more tangible implications for your code. For example, an application that is careless with memory will end up being force-quit by the system on iOS, and an app that consumes lots of CPU time will exhaust your user's battery and make the system run hot. There are other resources as well that your application needs to be careful with, including network bandwidth and disk space.

To help monitor your application's performance and use of resources, the developer tools include *Instruments*, an application that's able to inspect and report on just about every aspect of an application.

Instruments works by inserting diagnostic hooks into a running application. These hooks can do things like analyze the memory usage of an application, monitor how much time the app spends in various methods, and examine other data. This information is then collected, analyzed, and presented to you, allowing you to figure out what's going on inside your application.

In this chapter, you'll learn how to get around in Instruments, how to analyze an application, and how to spot and fix memory issues and performance problems using the information that Instruments gives you. You'll also learn how to use Xcode's debugger to track down problems and fix them.

Getting Started with Instruments

To get started with Instruments, we'll load a sample application and examine how it works.

The application that we'll be examining is *TextEdit*, which is the built-in text editor that comes with OS X. TextEdit is a great sample app to modify because it's a rather complex little app—it's effectively an entire word processor, with support for images, Microsoft Word import and export, and a lot more. You've probably used it before; if you haven't, you can find it by either searching Spotlight for "TextEdit" or by looking in the Applications folder.

The source code to TextEdit is available from the Apple Mac Developer site and you can find it by going to *http://bit.ly/textedit_src*.

 TextEdit is written in Objective-C, not Swift. The reason we're including it in a book about Swift is that this is one of the more complex pieces of sample code available, as well as being a real-world application that millions of people use every day.

The Developer site also contains a great deal of other example code and resources in the Mac Developer Library (*https://developer.apple.com/library/mac/navigation*).

Here are the steps you should follow:

1. Double-click the *TextEdit.xcodeproj* file to open it in Xcode.
2. Run the application. Click the Run button or press ⌘-R.

    The app will launch. Play around with it by writing some text, and saving and opening some documents.

We'll now use Instruments to examine what TextEdit is doing in memory as it runs.

3. Quit TextEdit. You can do this by pressing ⌘-Q or choosing Quit from the TextEdit menu.

4. Tell Xcode to profile the application. To do this, choose Profile from the Product menu. You can also press ⌘-I.

   Xcode will rebuild the application, and then launch Instruments. When Instruments launches, it presents a window that lets you choose which aspects of the app you'd like to inspect (Figure 17-1).

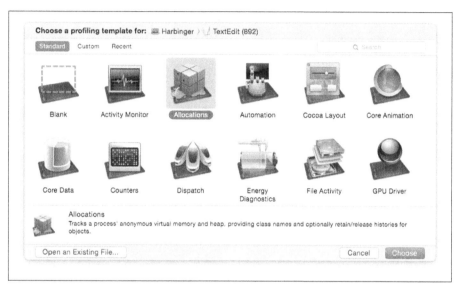

Figure 17-1. The Instruments template chooser

5. Select the Allocations instrument, and click Choose. Instruments will launch TextEdit; you can start recording memory usage information from the application by clicking the Record button. You can also press ⌘-R or choose Record Trace from the File menu.

   At this point, you're in Instruments proper, so it's worthwhile to stop and take a look around (Figure 17-2).

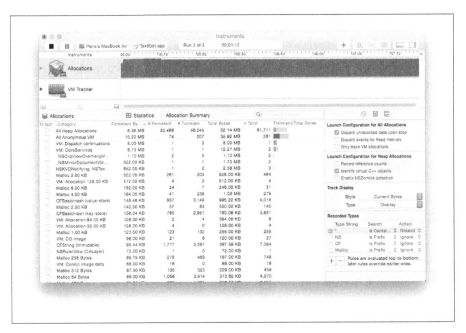

Figure 17-2. The Instruments window

The Instruments Interface

When you work with Instruments, you're working with one or more individual modules that are responsible for analyzing different parts. Each module is also called an instrument—so, for example, there's the Allocations instrument (for measuring memory performance), the Time Profiler instrument (for measuring runtime performance), the VM Tracker instrument (for measuring memory consumption), and so on.

Each instrument is listed in the Instruments pane at the top of the window. As an application runs, information from each instrument is shown in the Track pane. If you select an instrument in the Instruments pane, more detailed information is shown in the Detail pane at the bottom of the window. The Track pane is useful for giving you a high-level overview of the information that is being reported, but the majority of useful information is kept in the Detail pane.

The Detail pane shows different kinds of information, depending on the instrument. To choose which information to present, you can use the navigation bar, which separates the window horizontally.

To configure how an instrument collects its data, you can change options in the Inspector at the bottom-right of the window. From there, you can set the various options that affect what information the instrument collects.

In addition to allowing you to control how an instrument works, you can access additional information about any selected information through the Inspector. You do this by clicking the rightmost icon at the top of the Inspector to open the Extended Detail Inspector. This pane, as its name suggests, displays extended detail information on whatever is selected in the Detail pane. For example, if you're using the Allocations instrument, the Detail pane could be showing the objects currently active in your application. You could then select a specific object, and the Extended Detail Inspector would show exactly where that object was created in your code.

You can also control what Instruments is doing through the Record buttons. The large red button in the center is the main one that we care about—clicking on it will launch the application that's currently under investigation, and start recording data. Clicking it again will quit the application and stop recording, though the data that was collected remains. If you click Record again, a new set of data will be recorded—if you want to see past runs, you can navigate among them by clicking on the arrows in the display in the middle of the toolbar.

To open and close the various panes, click on the view buttons at the righthand side of the toolbar.

Observing Data

We'll now do some work inside TextEdit and watch how the data is collected:

1. Start recording, if the app isn't open already. If TextEdit isn't running, hit the Record button to launch it again.

   When the application starts up, it immediately allocates some memory as it gets going. When it needs to store more information, it allocates more. We'll now cause the app to start allocating more memory by adding text to the document.

2. Enter some text in the document. Go to the TextEdit window and start typing. Because text isn't very large, we won't see much of a difference in what's being displayed unless we enter quite a lot of text.

   So, to quickly enter lots of text, type something, select it all, copy, and paste. Then select all again, and copy and paste again. Repeat until you've got a huge amount of text in the document.

3. Observe the memory usage of TextEdit climbing. Go back to Instruments, and you'll notice that the amount of memory used by the application has increased quite a lot (Figure 17-3).

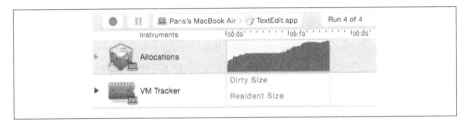

Figure 17-3. Instruments records an increase in memory usage as the application is used

Here, the consumption of memory is OK, because we deliberately stress-tested the application. However, if you see similar spikes in memory usage in your application from regular use, you probably have a problem to solve.

Adding Instruments from the Library

While Instruments provides a selection of templates that you can use to get started (such as the Allocations template we used earlier), you can add more instruments to your trace to help hunt down issues.

To add an instrument to your trace document, select the instrument you want to use from the Library. To open the Library, click the Library button, choose Library from the Window menu, or press ⌘-L (see Figure 17-4).

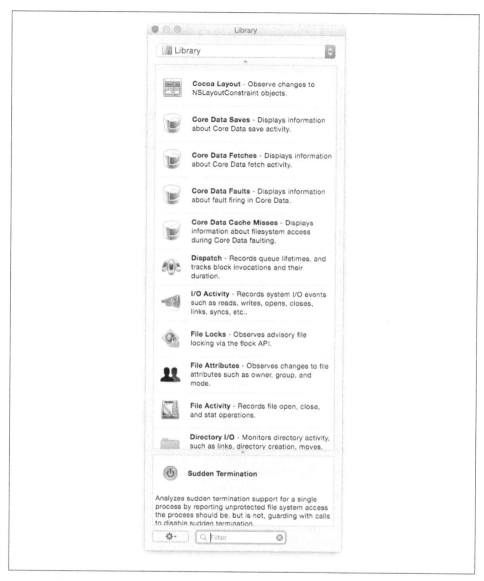

Figure 17-4. The Instruments Library

The Library lists all of the available instruments that you can use, as well as information on what each one does. To add an instrument to your trace, drag and drop an instrument into the Instruments pane, or double-click the instrument.

Not all instruments work on all platforms. For example, the Open-GL ES analyzer instrument only works on iOS.

Combining different kinds of instruments allows you to zoom in on specific problems. For example, if your application is being slow and you think it's because it's loading and processing lots of information at once, you can use a Reads/Writes instrument alongside a Time Profiler. If the slowdowns occur while both of these instruments indicate heavy activity, then your slowdowns are being caused by your application working the disk too hard while using lots of CPU time.

Fixing Problems Using Instruments

To demonstrate how to detect and solve problems using Instruments, we'll create an application that has a large memory problem, and then use Instruments to find and fix it.

This iOS application will create and display a large gallery of images and let the user smoothly scroll between them. We'll develop and run it on the iOS Simulator, and then see how well it does on a real device.

The application will consist of a single scroll view, which will have a number of image views added to it. The user will be able to scroll around inside the view to see the different images. Here are the steps you should follow to create the application:

1. Create a new, single view iOS application and call it MemoryDemo.
2. Open *Main.storyboard* in the project navigator.
3. Add a scroll view to the window. Make it fill the entire screen. While you have it selected, turn Paging Enabled on. This means that the scroll view will behave much like the home screen on the iPhone, where all scrolling snaps to the width of the scroll view.
4. Connect the scroll view to the view controller class. Open the assistant, and Control-drag from the scroll view into ViewController. Create a new outlet called imagesContainer.
5. Add the code that sets up the application. Add the following code to *ViewController.swift*:

```
func loadPageWithNumber(number:NSInteger) {

    // If an image view already exists for this page, don't do anything
    if self.imagesContainer.viewWithTag(number) != nil {
        return
```

```
    }

    // Get the image for this page
    let image = self.imageWithNumber(number)

    // Create and prepare the image view for this page
    let imageView = UIImageView(image: image)
    var imageViewFrame = self.imagesContainer.bounds
    imageViewFrame.origin.x = imageViewFrame.size.width * CGFloat(number - 1)
    imageView.frame = imageViewFrame

    // Add it to the scroll view
    self.imagesContainer.addSubview(imageView)

    // Mark this new image view with a tag so that we can
    // easily refer to it later
    imageView.tag = number
}
func imageWithNumber(number: Int) -> UIImage {

    // Inset the image by 30px so that we can see the rounded corners
    var imageRect = self.imagesContainer.frame
    imageRect.inset(dx: 30, dy: 30)

    UIGraphicsBeginImageContext(imageRect.size)

    // Draw a rounded rectangle
    let path = UIBezierPath(roundedRect: imageRect, cornerRadius: 10)

    path.lineWidth = 20

    UIColor.darkGrayColor().setStroke()
    UIColor.lightGrayColor().setFill()

    path.fill()
    path.stroke()

    // Draw the number
    let label = "\(number)"

    let font = UIFont.systemFontOfSize(50)
    let labelPoint = CGPoint(x: 50, y: 50)

    UIColor.whiteColor().setFill()

    let labelAttributes = [NSFontAttributeName: font]
    label.drawAtPoint(labelPoint, withAttributes:labelAttributes)

    // Get the finished image and return it
    let returnedImage = UIGraphicsGetImageFromCurrentImageContext()

    UIGraphicsEndImageContext()
```

```
        return returnedImage
    }

    override func viewDidLayoutSubviews () {

        // Create 10,000 images
        let pageCount = 10000

        // Load them into the scroll view
        for i in 1...pageCount {
            self.loadPageWithNumber(i)
        }

        // Tell the scroll view about its new content size
        var contentSize = CGSize()
        contentSize.height = self.imagesContainer.bounds.size.height
        contentSize.width = self.imagesContainer.bounds.size.width
            * CGFloat(pageCount)

        self.imagesContainer.contentSize = contentSize
    }
```

6. Run the application. The application runs fine on the simulator, but if you try to run it on the device, it will appear to hang for a while and finally exit without showing the app.

To find out why this happens, we'll run this inside Instruments:

1. Set the Scheme to launch on your iOS device. We want Instruments to run on the device, not the simulator. (If you don't have an iOS device to test on, that's OK—you can still use the simulator, but the numbers you see in Instruments won't be representative of how it would work on a real iPhone or iPad.)

2. Launch the application inside Instruments. Do this by choosing Profile from the Product menu, or pressing ⌘-I.

3. Select the Allocations template. We want to keep an eye on how memory is being used. Select the Allocations template, and click Choose.

4. Click the Record button, and watch the results. Instruments will plot the memory usage of the application as it attempts to start up (and then crashes).

As the application launches, you'll notice that the amount of memory used by the app steadily increase. After a while, the app will start receiving memory warnings (you'll see a bunch of black flags pop up in the timeline), and will then quit.

Clearly, the problem is that the application consumes too much memory. There's an additional problem—the number of images being drawn during startup is causing a huge slowdown. The application is creating and inserting a thousand image views onto

---

the screen. Each image displayed by the image views needs to be kept in memory, which means that the app rapidly runs out of space and is forced to exit.

A better way to handle this is to only display the images that the user can see, rather than loading all of them at once. At minimum, there are only three images that need to be present—the one currently being shown, and the two on either side of it. Because of the size of the image views, it's possible for this app to be showing one or two images at the same time, but never three.

To fix the problem, therefore, we need to make the application update the image views while the user is scrolling. If an image view isn't visible by the user, the app should remove it from the screen, which frees up memory.

To do this, we'll add a method that makes sure that the image views for the previous, current, and next pages are present, and then removes all other image views. This method will be called every time the scroll view scrolls, meaning that as far as the user is concerned, every image is on the screen when she needs to see it.

First, we'll set up the view controller to be notified when the scroll view scrolls, and then add the code that checks the image views. Finally, we'll update the viewDidLoad method to make it only display the first set of image views:

1. Open the storyboard and make the scroll view use the view controller as its delegate.

   Control-drag from the scroll view onto the view controller's icon. Choose "delegate" from the list that pops up.

2. Open *ViewController.swift*. We now need to make the class conform to the UIScrollViewDelegate protocol. Replace the class's definition with the following line of code:

   ```
   class ViewController: UIViewController, UIScrollViewDelegate {
   ```

3. Next, we'll update the code to update the collection of image views when the scroll view scrolls.

   Add the following methods to *ViewController.swift*:

   ```
   func updatePages() {

       var pageNumber = Int(imagesContainer.contentOffset.x /
       imagesContainer.bounds.size.width + 1)

       // Load the image previous to this one
       self.loadPageWithNumber(pageNumber - 1)

       // Load the current page
       self.loadPageWithNumber(pageNumber)

       // Load the next page
       self.loadPageWithNumber(pageNumber+1)
   ```

```
            // Remove all image views that aren't on
            // this page or the pages adjacent to it
            for imageView in imagesContainer.subviews {
                if imageView.tag < pageNumber - 1 ||
                    imageView.tag > pageNumber + 1 {
                    imageView.removeFromSuperview()
                }
            }
        }
    }

    func scrollViewDidScroll(scrollView: UIScrollView!) {
        self.updatePages()
    }
```

4. Replace the `viewDidLayoutSubviews` method with the following code:

```
override func viewDidLayoutSubviews () {

    // Create 10,000 images
    let pageCount = 10000

    self.updatePages();

    // Tell the scroll view about its new content size
    var contentSize = CGSize()
    contentSize.height = self.imagesContainer.bounds.size.height
    contentSize.width = self.imagesContainer.bounds.size.width
    * CGFloat(pageCount)

    self.imagesContainer.contentSize = contentSize
}
```

Once you've made these changes, try running the app on the device again. You'll find that its behavior is identical to how it used to run, with the added bonus that the application doesn't run out of memory and crash on launch.

Retain Cycles and Leaks

The Automatic Reference Counting feature built into the compiler is also great at reducing problems caused by memory leaks, but it's not foolproof.

Automatic Reference Counting releases an object from memory when the last strong reference to that object goes away. However, if two or more objects have strong references *to each other*, the number of strong references to each object will never be zero, and the objects will stay in memory—even if nothing else in the application has a reference to those objects. This is called a *retain cycle*, so named because if you were to draw a graph showing how each object refers to each other, you'd end up drawing a circle.

You can figure out if you have a retain cycle by using Instruments. When you have a retain cycle, objects will remain in memory, which means that if you repeat the process that creates the retain cycle, your app will increase in memory and never go down.

To find out if this is happening, follow these steps:

1. Launch your app in Instruments, and use the Allocations template.

2. Use your app for a bit. Go in and out of screens, tap buttons, and generally use the app as it's meant to be used.

3. Click the Mark Generation button (see Figure 17-5) in the Display Inspector, which you can access by pressing Command-2. Instruments will record how much memory is currently being used.

Figure 17-5. The Mark Generation button

4. Perform a task in the app, and then return to the point that you were at when you marked the generation. The idea here is that you've performed some task, and everything *should* have cleaned up after itself, so there shouldn't be any growth in the amount of memory that the app is using.

5. Click Mark Generation again. Instruments will again record how much memory is being used, and compare it to the previous generation. In the Growth column, Instruments shows the *difference* between this generation and the previous generation (see Figure 17-6).

   If this number is not zero, then the act of performing that task and returning to the starting point meant that the app was left with more memory.

Figure 17-6. The Growth column, showing a rise in memory since the last generation

6. Expand the generation by clicking on the arrow at the left, and you'll see the list of objects that are left behind (see Figure 17-7). You can double-click on these to see the point in your code at which they were created.

▼Generation B ⊕	03:12.389.227	6.61 MB	8,685
▶VM: CoreServices		1.86 MB	1
▶_NSClipViewOverh…		1.26 MB	2
▶< non-object >		997.57 KB	4,026
▶NSKVONotifying_N…		976.00 KB	1
▶_NSMirrorDocumen…		976.00 KB	1
▶VM: CoreUI image…		64.00 KB	14
▶NSRegularOverlayS…		60.00 KB	2
▶VM: CG image		56.00 KB	14
▶CFString (immutable)		35.00 KB	670
▶CFBasicHash (valu…		28.34 KB	172
▶CFBasicHash (key-…		23.72 KB	136
▶_NSViewAuxiliary		18.38 KB	42
▶VM: CoreAnimation		16.00 KB	4
▶CFString (mutable)		13.94 KB	223
▶NSTextFieldCell (C…		12.00 KB	1
▶__NSArrayM		11.34 KB	242

Figure 17-7. The list of objects created in this generation that are still in memory

Using the Debugger

Xcode includes a source debugger called LLDB. Like all debuggers, LLDB allows you to observe your code as it runs, set breakpoints and watchpoints, and inspect the contents of memory.

The debugger is deeply integrated into Xcode, and Xcode lets you create very specific actions to run when your code does certain things. You can, for example, ask Xcode to speak some text the third time that a specific line of code gets run.

Setting Breakpoints

There are a few ways to set a breakpoint in Xcode. The most common method is to set a breakpoint on a line of code—when execution reaches that point, the debugger stops the program.

To set a breakpoint at a line, click the gray gutter at the left of the code editor. A blue breakpoint arrow will appear (Figure 17-8).

It's easier to add breakpoints, and navigate your code in general, if you turn on line numbers in Xcode. To do this, open Preferences by pressing ⌘-, and open the Text Editing tab. Turn on the Line Numbers checkbox.

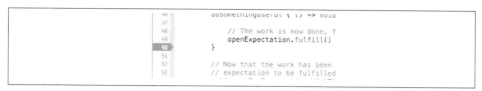

Figure 17-8. A breakpoint

After a breakpoint has been added to your code, you can drag the arrow to move the breakpoint. To remove the breakpoint, drag it out of the gutter.

When the program hits a breakpoint, Xcode shows the backtrace of all threads in the debug navigator. From there, you can see how a breakpoint was hit, and what functions were called that led to the program hitting that breakpoint.

Controlling program flow

When the program execution hits a breakpoint, you can choose to simply resume execution, or step through the code line by line.

To control program flow, you use the buttons in the debugger bar. The debugger bar is at the top of the debug area, which you can open and close by clicking the middle segment of the View control, at the top right of the toolbar (Figure 17-9).

Figure 17-9. The debugger bar

From left to right, the buttons in the debugger bar perform the following actions:

- Close the debug area
- Pause or resume execution
- Step Over (continue to the next line of code)
- Step Into (if the current line of code is a method call, continue into it)
- Step Out (continue until execution leaves the current method)

When you add a breakpoint, it appears in the breakpoints navigator. From there, you can see all of the currently set breakpoints—you can also jump directly to a breakpoint, disable it, or delete it.

Custom breakpoints

Normally, a breakpoint just pauses execution when hit. However, you can customize your breakpoints to perform specific actions.

To customize a breakpoint, right-click the arrow or the breakpoint's entry in the breakpoints navigator, and choose Edit Breakpoint. The Edit Breakpoint window will appear (Figure 17-10).

Figure 17-10. Editing a breakpoint

The Edit Breakpoint window allows you to customize when the breakpoint should trigger and what happens when it does. You can also indicate how many times the breakpoint should be ignored, what actions the breakpoint should run, and whether the breakpoint should pause the execution of the program.

Adding actions to a breakpoint allows you to run some AppleScript, speak a line of text, play a sound, or other actions. To add an action, click the "Click to add an action" button and choose the action that should be run.

This is a tremendously flexible feature, as it allows you to get additional information about how your program is running without the program stopping and starting.

Special breakpoints

The breakpoints navigator also allows you to add special breakpoints for exceptions, symbols, OpenGL ES Errors, and Test Failures.

An *exception breakpoint* stops the program when an exception is thrown. For example, if you have an NSArray with two items and you try to access the third one, an exception is thrown and your program exits. Normally, Xcode stops the program at the point where the exception is caught, which isn't often the place where it is thrown. This makes it difficult to work out where the problem is. To solve this problem, you can add an exception breakpoint that stops the program at the instant the exception is thrown.

A *symbolic breakpoint* stops the program when a specific, named function or method is entered. This is mostly useful when you want to stop execution at a function that you might not have the source code for, and then view the backtrace.

An *OpenGL ES Error breakpoint* stops the program whenever an OpenGL ES error is encountered. This is mostly useful when debugging graphics-heavy iOS applications such as games.

A *Test Failure breakpoint* stops the program when a test assertion fails. This breakpoint is designed to be used in conjunction with unit tests, letting you see exactly when, where, and hopefully why your tests are failing.

To add one of the special breakpoints, click the + button at the lower left of the breakpoints navigator. Then choose which type of breakpoint you want to add, and Xcode asks you to configure the new breakpoint (Figure 17-11).

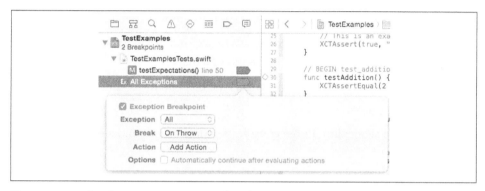

Figure 17-11. Configuring an exception breakpoint

If you're creating an exception breakpoint, you can choose whether you want to stop on exceptions thrown by Objective-C code (remember, lots of iOS and OS X is still written in Objective-C), C++ exceptions (likewise!), or both. You can also choose whether the breakpoint should stop when the exception is thrown or caught.

Inspecting Memory Contents

When the program is stopped in the debugger, you can see the current state of objects and variables in memory.

The variables view is the lefthand section of the debug area. When the program is stopped, the variables view shows the variables that exist at that point.

The variables view shows the value of the variables. If the variables are simple types like Int or Bool, their values are shown; if the variables are things like arrays, then summary information about them is shown, like the content of the string or the number of items in the array.

If you use the flow control buttons while the program is stopped, the variables view updates to show any changes. If a variable changes, it gets highlighted in blue.

The variables view also allows you to quickly send the `description` message to any object and see the results. To do this, right-click on a variable and choose Print Description.

Working with the Debugger Console

At the righthand side of the debug area is the console. The console is the command-line interface to the debugger, and allows you to directly access some of the debugger's powerful, lower-level features.

Working with LLDB via the console is a subject large enough to fill its own book, but in this section we'll talk about how to use the console for its arguably most powerful purpose: running custom code to work with your program's variables.

Let's assume that the debugger has stopped at a breakpoint in a method. In this method, `myArray` is an array, and you want to check its contents.

To see how many items are in `myArray`, you'd type this into the console:

```
print myArray.count
```

Note the lack of a semicolon. In the console, you don't put a semicolon at the end of lines.

 When you call a method in the debugger, you must specify what type of data the method will return. In the preceding example, `count` returns an `int`.

You can send arbitrary messages to objects. For example, if you wanted to get the second object in the `myArray` array, you'd do this:

```
print-object myArray.objectAtIndex(1)
```

The `print-object` command takes an object and sends it a `description` message. It then returns the string that comes back.

View Debugging

Xcode lets you debug not only your code, but also your views. Using the *view debugging* feature, you can peel back the contents of your screens to get a better understanding of how the screen is laid out.

Using the view debugging feature, you can look behind views and find out what they've covering up, find out if any views aren't visible because they're off-screen, and get information about the constraints that are defining the view's position and size. This makes them great for spotting and solving problems where you've added a view, but it isn't showing up on the screen.

To use the view debugging feature, simply run any application from Xcode.

 View debugging works on both iOS and OS X.

Once the app is running, click the View Debugging button, in the debugger controls bar (see Figure 17-12)

Figure 17-12. The debugging controls (the View Debugging button is the second from the right)

Once you click that button, the application will be paused, and you'll be presented with the view debugging screen. This screen takes a snapshot of the app's current state, but *exploded* out into each of its different views, as shown in Figure 17-13.

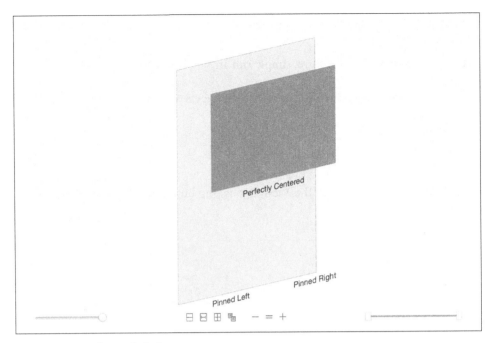

Figure 17-13. The exploded view

When you're in the view debugging screen, you can click and drag to rotate the entire scene, and get different views on how the screen is laid out.

You can also click individual views to get additional information about them, including their position and size, as well as any object-specific information (e.g., clicking a label will reveal its text). You can also use the slider at the lower left of the screen to increase and decrease separation of views.

At the bottom center of the screen, you'll find controls that determine what the view debugging screen will show you (seen in Figure 17-14.)

Figure 17-14. The view debugging options

Each of these buttons let you configure the view debugging view. From left to right:

1. Toggles whether content that's clipped by something (like another view) is shown
2. Toggles whether constraints are shown
3. Resets the view to normal

4. Lets you select whether you see view contents, wireframes, or both

The Testing Framework

Xcode comes bundled with XCTest, a full-featured testing system for iOS and OS X applications. XCTest allows you to define *unit tests* for your code—small, independent blocks of testing code that are designed to be run all at the same time, to verify that your code is behaving the way you want it to.

Testing is an incredibly important part of application development. When developing, you'll often find yourself ensuring that the current part of the app that you're working on is functioning correctly, and has no bugs; however, this can make you focus too closely on a single piece, without taking other areas in your app into consideration.

When you write tests for your code, they're kept around after you're done working on the feature you're focusing on at the moment. This means that when your tests are run, all of your old tests run as well—which means that you can ensure that your new changes didn't break anything.

Tests give you peace of mind. By automating the process of ensuring that your app works, you don't have to worry as much when releasing a view version.

On top of this, creating tests is incredibly simple. When you create a new project in Xcode, a *test suite* is also created. Test suites contain all of your application's code.

You can see this in action by following these steps:

1. Create an app. It doesn't matter whether it's an iOS app or an OS X app. Name it TestExamples.

2. Find the test suite. In the project navigator, find the *TestExamplesTests* folder, which contains the project's test files.

3. Open the test case file. Find and open the *TestExamplesTests.swift* file. Inside this file, you'll add your test methods.

Writing Tests

Writing tests using XCTest is very simple. To create tests, you create a subclass of the XCTestCase class, and then add individual test methods to that subclass. In the preceding example, Xcode has created the *TestExamplesTests* file for you, but it's straightforward to add your own.

The XCTestCase class has three special methods that you add—the setUp method, the test methods, and the tearDown method:

- The setUp method is run immediately *before* each test, and serves as the location to set up the environment needed for each test.

- Any method whose name begins with test, and takes no parameters and returns no value, is considered a *test* method. Inside this method, you write code that checks to see if your application's working the way you want it to.

- The tearDown method is run immediately *after* each test, and is your opportunity to tidy up after the test is run.

Inside test methods, you write code that exercises some part of your app—creating objects, running methods, and so on—and then verify that the results of that code matches what you expect. You verify these results using special methods called *assertion functions*.

Assertion functions are functions that check to see if a certain condition is true. If it's not, the test fails. For example, to test whether addition works as you expect, you can add a test method that looks like this:

```
func testAddition() {
    XCTAssertEqual(2 + 2, 4, "2 + 2 should equal 4")
}
```

You can also assert many other conditions, such as a Boolean value being true or false, two objects being equal, and many other states. In each case, you provide the condition as well as a short text string explaining what the test represents; if the test fails, Xcode uses this string to explain to you what went wrong. You can have multiple assertions in a single test method.

To run your tests, hit Command-U, or open the Product menu and choose Test. The app will build and start up, and all tests will run. The app will then automatically quit.

If you want to run a specific test, click the diamond shape in the sidebar that's next to the test. When you do this, the app builds and starts, and then runs that single test.

The most effective way to use tests is to write tests before you write the code itself. If you have a feature you want to implement, write a test that checks the result of your code, as well as empty methods that return fake data. When you run the tests, you're expecting the tests to fail. (If they don't fail, you have something to investigate!)

Once you have a set of failing tests, you can then begin implementing your code proper. You're done once your tests are all passing.

Writing code in this way forces you to think about how the code you're writing will be used. When you write a method, you'll spend more time writing code that uses the method than writing the method itself. If you begin your designs with usage in mind, you'll write better code.

Writing Asynchronous Tests

Some code takes time to run. For example, your app might include an animation that runs some code when complete, or it might download a file in the background and then process it. The XCTest system can handle this kind of test using *expectations*.

An expectation is an object that represents the fact that the system *expects* a certain condition to be fulfilled later. In the case of the background download example, your test might be that you want to ensure that the file downloaded correctly. In this case, you'd create an expectation just before starting the download, and then when the download is done, you'd mark the expectation is fulfilled. If the expectation as never fulfilled, then the test fails.

Here's an example of how to use expectations in your tests:

```
func testExpectations() {

    let openExpectation =
    self.expectationWithDescription("Something useful happened");

    // Perform some work that might take a bit of time
    // (This example method takes a block that runs when the work is done)
    doSomethingUseful { () -> Void in

        // The work is now done, fulfill the expectation
        openExpectation.fulfill()
    }

    // Now that the work has been kicked off, wait 1 second for the
    // expectation to be fulfilled
    self.waitForExpectationsWithTimeout(1.0) { (error) in

        println("The expectation wasn't fulfilled in time! \(error)")

    }


}
```

Performance-Testing Blocks with Tests

The `measureBlock` method allows you to test the performance of a piece of your code. When you call `measureBlock`, you provide a block of code that exercises the code you want to measure. The testing system will repeatedly run that code, and measure the amount of time taken each time. When this completes, you're given a report that indicates how much time was taken, on average:

```
func testPerformanceExample() {
    // This is an example of a performance test case.
    self.measureBlock() {
```

```
        // Do some useful work; this block will be run multiple times, and
        // the time taken to run it will be measured.

    }
}
```

Debug Gauges

The *debug gauges* allow you to quickly get information about how your app is using system resources. Specifically, you can get information about the app's CPU load, memory usage, and how heavily it's using the disk and network. In all four of these cases, the less the app is using, the better.

To see the debug gauges in action, run any application, and then open the debug navigator, which is the third button from the right in the Navigator panel (see Figure 17-15).

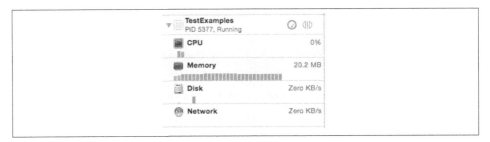

Figure 17-15. The debugging gauges

Debug gauges supplement the heavier functionality provided by Instruments. The gauges aren't as good at letting you view different kinds of usage side by side, but they save time in launching and dealing with Instruments.

Performance Optimization

When writing any application, it's vital that you consider performance. When an application performs well, it runs faster, consumes less system resources, and creates a better overall user experience. For example, if your application is CPU-heavy, you'll end up draining the user's battery, and generally ruining her day.

The specific techniques involved in ensuring that your app performs well depend on the details of what your app does; however, the following are some general tips to make your application perform well:

- Run code on background queues as much as possible, to give the system opportunites to put it on other cores. Use NSOperationQueue to let the system decide how to run the code—it's a lot more efficient to run two cores than it is to run a single core for twice that time.

- Use less memory. Reduce the number of images that your application keeps in memory, and remove items from memory when they're not needed. This is especially important on iOS, where running out of memory means that your application will be terminated by the system.

- Delay reading and writing data until it's actually needed. While pre-caching is fine in principle, there's often no reason to spend time loading data from disk into memory "just in case." Load the data that your app needs only when there's a very good chance that the user will actually need to use it.

- Performance-test your code. While performance is often a matter of *feeling* fast, using performance tests in your code allows you to be objective about whether the changes to your code are improving or worsening your performance.

CHAPTER 18

Sharing and Notifications

Just about every app these days deals with some kind of content—whether it's business documents written in an office suite, images created in an image editor, or even high scores earned in a game. Users frequently want to be able to show this content to other people, and the OS provides built-in sharing APIs that let your application send various kinds of content to services that can handle them. For example, online services like YouTube and Vimeo can receive video files and share them over the Internet, the Messages app can send text, photos, and videos, and email can send just about any file.

In addition to sending content to other locations, the OS is also capable of receiving *notifications*. These are short messages sent from a server to an iOS device, which are received regardless of whether the app is running or the phone is awake.

In this chapter, you'll learn how to share data from your application using the built-in sharing APIs, and how to send and receive both push and local notifications.

Sharing

From the user's perspective, the problem of data sharing can be rephrased as, "How can I send this to someone else?" From your application's perspective, however, the problem of data sharing is really the question, "Where can I send this data?"

Different systems are capable of accepting different kinds of data. A video, for example, cannot be sent to a printer, and plain text cannot be sent to a photo-hosting site like Flickr. Fortunately, the sharing systems on both iOS and OS X already know what different data types are supported by the sharing destinations that the OS knows about.

As of OS X 10.10, the available sharing destinations for OS X are as follows:

Email

Text, images, videos, and anything that can be copied and pasted

Messages
Same content as email

AirDrop
Files

Aperture
Photos

iPhoto
Photos

Flickr
Photos

YouTube, Vimeo, Todou, Youku
Videos

Safari Reading List
URLs

Setting the Desktop background
Images

Setting a Twitter, LinkedIn, or Facebook profile picture
Images

Twitter, Facebook, LinkedIn, Tencent Weibo, and Sina Weibo
Text, images, videos, and URLs

As of iOS 8, the available sharing destinations for iOS are as follows:

Email
Text, images, videos, and URLs (including URLs pointing to local files)

Messages
Text and images

AirDrop
Files

Flickr
Photos

YouTube, Vimeo, Todou, Youku
Videos

Twitter, Facebook, Tencent Weibo, and Sina Weibo
Text, images, videos, and URLs

Copying to the pasteboard
Text, images, URLs, colors, and NSDictionary objects

Saving to the camera roll
Images and videos

Printing
Text, images, and any of the UIPrintRenderer or related printing objects (see "Printing Documents" on page 333)

Assigning to a contact
Images

 Sina Weibo and Tencent Weibo are social media services, similar to Twitter and Facebook, based in the People's Republic of China. You-ku and Tudou are video hosting services, similar to YouTube and Vimeo, and are also based in the People's Republic of China.

As you can see, there are a number of different kinds of content that can be given to the various sharing destinations. Fortunately, the method for actually sharing is rather straightforward:

1. Make an array containing all of the things you want to share. This array should contain everything that you want to share—text, images, videos, and so on.

2. Give this array to the sharing system. The OS will figure out which sharing destinations can be used based on the content that was provided. The greater the number of different kinds of content you provide, the more sharing destinations will be offered to the user.

   For example, if you provide both text and an image on iOS, "Save to camera roll" appears, even though it doesn't support both. Only the supported content will be shared by the selected sharing destination.

3. Let the sharing system actually handle the sharing. Depending on which sharing destination was selected, the user might be prompted to provide a little more information. For example, if the user is posting an image to Twitter, he'll be presented with a Twitter share sheet, which allows him to add some text before sending the tweet.

It's a simple and elegant system, and can be a very positive thing for your apps.

To get our hands dirty, we're going to take a look at the different sharing APIs that are available on both iOS and OS X.

Sharing on iOS

Sharing content on iOS is handled by the `UIActivityViewController`. When you have some content that you want to share—some text stored in a string, say—all you need to do is create a new `UIActivityViewController` and provide it with an array containing that object:

```
let text = "Hello, world!"
let activity = UIActivityViewController(activityItems: [text],
    applicationActivities: nil)
```

The second parameter, left `nil` in the previous example, can also take an array of `UIActivity` subclasses. These can be used if you want your app to provide custom sharing destinations. Note, however, that any custom sharing destinations you include will only show up inside your own app.

When that's done, you just need to present the view controller modally as you would any other modal view controller:

```
self.presentViewController(activity, animated: true, completion: nil)
```

From there, the OS takes over, allowing the user to select the sharing destination and completing the share.

To show this in action, we'll build a simple iOS application that supports sharing both text and images:

1. Create a new single view iPhone application called iOSSharing.

2. Add an image to share. Find an image of some sort on your computer, or take one with a camera. Once you have it, drag it into the project's asset catalog.

 Apps can also capture images from the built-in camera. We cover how to make apps that do this in "Capturing Photos and Video from the Camera" on page 204.

3. Create the interface. Open *Main.storyboard*, and drag a text field into the top of the window.

   Drag in a `UIButton` just beneath the text field. Set its title to `Share Text`.

   Drag in a `UIImageView` beneath this button, and set its image to the one that you added earlier.

   Finally, drag in a second `UIButton` and place it beneath the image view. Set its title to `Share Image`.

---

4. Connect the interface. There are two actions to add: one for sharing text and one for sharing an image. We're going to connect these two actions to the appropriate buttons; we'll also use the text field and the image view as the sources for the content that will be shared:

Open *ViewController.swift* in the assistant, and Control-drag from the top and bottom buttons into the class's interface. The two actions you want to create are `shareImage` and `shareText`.

Once that's done, Control-drag from the text field into `ViewController`'s interface, and create a new outlet called `textView`. Then, Control-drag from the image view into `ViewController`'s interface and create a new outlet called `imageView`.

Finally, because we want the keyboard to go away when the user taps the Return button, Control-drag from the text field to the File's Owner in the outline, and choose "delegate" from the menu that pops up.

The final result should look like Figure 18-1.

The code for this is extremely simple. The two methods that are run when the share buttons are tapped are only two lines each.

5. Add the image sharing method. Add the following code to `shareImage`:

```
@IBAction func shareImage(sender: AnyObject) {

    if let image = self.imageView?.image {

        let activity = UIActivityViewController(
            activityItems: [image], applicationActivities: nil)

        self.presentViewController(activity,
            animated: true, completion: nil)

    } else {
        // No image to share!
    }

}
```

Figure 18-1. The connected interface

6. Add the text sharing method. Add the following code to `shareText`:

```
@IBAction func shareText(sender: AnyObject) {
    let activity = UIActivityViewController(
        activityItems: [self.textView.text], applicationActivities: nil)

    self.presentViewController(activity, animated: true, completion: nil)
}
```

7. Finally, add the code to dismiss the keyboard when the Return button is tapped. Add the following method to `AppDelegate`'s implementation:

```
func textFieldShouldReturn(textField: UITextField!) -> Bool {
    textField.resignFirstResponder()
    return false
}
```

8. Run the app. Try sharing both text and images, and see what sharing services can be used for each.

Sharing on OS X

Sharing content on OS X is very similar to sharing on iOS; the only real difference is in how the list of sharing destinations is presented.

On OS X, you create an NSSharingServicePicker, which presents a menu of available sharing destinations depending on what content you provide it. This pattern is very similar to iOS's model.

Creating an NSSharingServicePicker looks like this:

```
var text = "Hello, world!"
var share = NSSharingServicePicker(items: [text])
```

After the picker has been created, it needs to be presented to the user. Because the picker shows a menu, it needs to know where the menu should appear on screen. This information is provided when you call the showRelativeToRect(_, ofView:, preferredEdge:) method. This method receives an NSRect and an NSView that the rectangle should be considered to be in the coordinate space of, as well as information indicating which edge of the rectangle the menu should appear on.

For example, if you have an NSView called myView, you can tell the menu to appear on the far right edge of its bounds rectangle with the following call:

```
share.showRelativeToRect(aView.bounds, ofView: aView, preferredEdge: 2)
```

The behavior of the picker after this point is identical to UIActivityViewController. The user is invited to choose which sharing service to use, and the OS will ask for additional information as necessary.

Notifications

Notifications are a way for your app to send messages to the user, regardless of whether the application is currently being used or even running. Originally introduced in iOS 3, they've become an indispensable tool for many apps. Starting with OS X 10.7, notifications are also available on the Mac. Figure 18-2 shows an example of a notification.

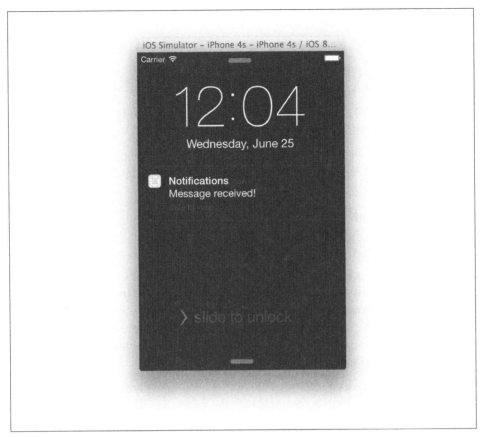

Figure 18-2. A notification

There are two kinds of notifications: *push notifications* (also known as *remote notifications*) and *local notifications*. Push notifications are sent from a server you control to the device, while local notifications are scheduled by your app to be displayed later.

Registering Notification Settings

Notifications on iOS can be intrusive. When you're using an app, it can be annoying to have your experience interrupted by another app; it's just as annoying to have your phone buzz in your pocket and disturb you when that notification isn't particularly important. As a result, before you can show either type of notification, you need to first tell iOS what kinds of notifications your app intends to show.

This section applies to iOS only. It doesn't apply to OS X.

You do this by creating a `UIUserNotificationSettings` object, which specifies which kinds of notifications your app would like to show. You then call the `registerUserNo` `tificationSettings` on the shared `UIApplication` object, which registers these settings:

```
// Indicating that we we want to deliver alerts
let notificationSettings = UIUserNotificationSettings(
    forTypes: UIUserNotificationType.Alert, categories: nil)

UIApplication.sharedApplication().registerUserNotificationSettings(
    notificationSettings)
```

When you call `registerUserNotificationSettings` for the first time, the system pops up a dialog box asking if the user wants to grant permission to display notifications, as shown in Figure 18-3.

In this example, the call to `registerUserNotificationSettings` was simply declaring that notifications were going to be sent. However, you can provide more information about what your notifications will contain, including whether your notifications should include *actions*.

Actions are simply small buttons that are attached to your notifications. When a notification arrives, you can attach actions that the user selects by swiping the notification to the left, as shown in Figure 18-4.

To set this up, you first need to create a *notification action* object, which is an instance of `UIMutableUserInteractionAction`. You then set up things like the text that should be shown to the user, an internal identifier string, and whether selecting the action should cause the app to launch or not:

Figure 18-3. When your app registers for notifications, iOS displays this alert to ask for the user's permission

```
let notificationAction = UIMutableUserNotificationAction()

// The title is shown to the user
notificationAction.title = "Save World"

// The identifier is used by your app
notificationAction.identifier = "saveWorldAction"

// When this action is selected, bring the app to the foreground
notificationAction.activationMode =
    UIUserNotificationActivationMode.Foreground

// If true, the user must enter their passcode before the action runs.
// (Always set to true when the activation mode is Foreground.)
notificationAction.authenticationRequired = false

// Should the action be highlighted as destructive? (i.e., red and
```

```
// dangerous looking)
notificationAction.destructive = false
```

Actions can also be configured as *destructive*. Destructive actions are ones that can have some kind of irreversible, destructive effect, like deleting files. When you mark an action as destructive, the only thing that changes is its appearance:

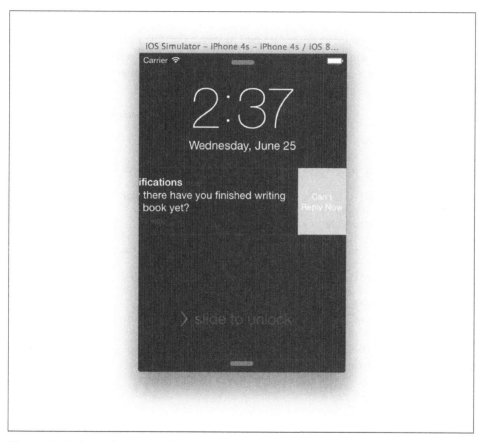

Figure 18-4. A notification with an action attached

```
// This action will be presented as destructive
let destructiveNotificationAction = UIMutableUserNotificationAction()

// Conquering the world is generally destructive
destructiveNotificationAction.title = "Conquer World"

// This action will launch the app in the background
destructiveNotificationAction.activationMode =
    UIUserNotificationActivationMode.Background
```

```
// Highlight the action as destructive
destructiveNotificationAction.destructive = true
```

Once you've defined your actions, you create a *category*. Categories are just containers of actions combined with an identifier string; the idea is that, when you send a notification, you include which category should be used, which lets the system know which action buttons to display.

When you provide the actions to the category, you also specify which *context* these actions should be displayed in. There are two contexts: the *default* context, where there's lots of space for showing buttons (in other words, the lock screen—see Figure 18-5), and the *minimal* context, where there's less space (as seen in Figure 18-6, which shows a notification that you need to pull down on to reveal):

```
var notificationCategory = UIMutableUserNotificationCategory()

// The name of the category, used by the app to tell different
// notifications apart
notificationCategory.identifier = "com.oreilly.MyApplication.message"

// Set which actions are displayed when a large amount of space is
// visible; up to 4 can be provided
notificationCategory.setActions(
    [notificationAction, destructiveNotificationAction],
    forContext: UIUserNotificationActionContext.Default)

// Set which actions are displayed when not much space is visible;
// up to 2 can be provided
notificationCategory.setActions([notificationAction],
    forContext: UIUserNotificationActionContext.Minimal)
```

 The default context has room for four actions, while the minimal context only has room for two.

Figure 18-5. The default notification context

Finally, when you're done setting up your categories, you put those categories in an
NSSet object, and use it to create your UIUserNotificationSettings:

```
// Create an NSSet containing a single object (the category
// we defined earlier)
var notificationCategories = NSSet(object: notificationCategory)

// Use that NSSet to create the notification settings
let notificationSettingsWithAction =
    UIUserNotificationSettings(forTypes: UIUserNotificationType.Alert,
        categories: notificationCategories)

// Register those notification settings
UIApplication.sharedApplication()
    .registerUserNotificationSettings(notificationSettingsWithAction)
```

Figure 18-6. The minimal notification context

Push Notifications

Every iOS and OS X machine with notifications enabled maintains a permanent connection to Apple's *push notification service*, which delivers short, infrequent messages to applications.

Push notifications work by having a server make an SSL-secured TCP connection to the Apple push notification service. When an application wants to receive push notifications, it calls the `registerForRemoteNotifications` method on the application's global `UIApplication` or `NSApplication` object.

When registering for remote notifications, it's important to know about the different kinds that can be delivered. Notifications can:

- Set a badge (i.e., a number) on the app's icon, either in the Dock on OS X or on the home screen in iOS

- Play a sound file included in the app
- Display an alert

All notifications on all platforms may also include additional application-specific information.

What Happens When a Notification Arrives

When a remote notification arrives, your application may or may not be running. If it's running, your application delegate receives the `application(_, didReceiveRemote Notification:)` message, which contains as its second parameter a dictionary containing any additional information in the notification. This is your app's opportunity to do something useful with the notification.

If the application isn't running when the notification arrives, what it's able to do depends on the platform. On OS X, the only thing a notification can do if the app isn't running is to modify the app icon's badge. This is less of a restriction than it seems, because an application that's currently running receives a message sent to its application delegate when the notification arrives, and your application can run any code you want when that happens.

On iOS, it's another matter. Because only one app is allowed to be open at the same time (all other apps are allowed to run in the background for a bit, but are eventually suspended or terminated—see "Multitasking on iOS" on page 71), a notification is more likely to arrive when the app *isn't* running.

An iOS notification can contain an alert, which is a string of text that's shown to the user. When the notification arrives, if it contains an alert, that alert text appears on the screen. (The specific presentation depends on the user's preferences, but it's generally a banner at the top of the screen, or a pop-up box if the phone was locked when the notification arrived.) When the user interacts with this alert, the application is launched (or resumed if it was already launched). At this point, your application is informed that it received a notification, and can then respond appropriately.

This is why iOS notifications can contain more than OS X applications—because an iOS app is much less likely to be able to respond to a notification at the moment it arrives, the system steps in to provide some minimal functionality (showing some text, playing a sound, etc.). On OS X, that's not necessary, because the application is much more likely to be running in the background.

Sending Push Notifications

A push notification is nothing more than a JSON-formatted dictionary. When a push notification is created, it can contain any valid JSON data that you want (i.e., strings, numbers, arrays, and dictionaries).

 For more information on JSON-formatted data, see "Saving More Complex Data" on page 284 in Chapter 13.

When your application receives the notification, it receives an NSDictionary containing whatever was sent as the push notification.

In addition to the application-specific data that can be included in the JSON dictionary, push notifications also contain a special aps dictionary. This dictionary contains information about how the push notification should be presented: its alert text, the number to display in the application icon's badge, and so on.

For example, here's a sample push notification in JSON form:

```
{
    "aps":{
        "alert":"Hello, world!",
        "badge":1,
        "sound":"hello.wav"
    },
    "foo":"bar"
}
```

This push notification, when delivered to an iOS device, does the following things:

- Displays the alert text "Hello, world!" on the screen
- Sets the badge on the application's icon to 1
- Plays the sound *hello.wav* (which must be inside the application's bundle—see "Using NSBundle to Find Resources in Applications" on page 67)

The maximum size for a push notification is 256 bytes, including the aps dictionary. If you try to send a push notification larger than this, it won't be accepted by the Apple Push Notification Service.

Additionally, delivery of push notifications is *not guaranteed*. Apple describes it as a "best effort" service, much like SMS. And the delivery mechanism for push notifications cannot be considered secure.

Therefore, your push notifications should never contain any sensitive information, and they shouldn't be used as the primary way for your application to receive data. Instead, use push notifications to let your application know that new data is available and let the application itself do the work of actually retrieving that data.

Additionally, when the *application* receives the notification (either because the notification was opened by the user or the application was running when the notification was received), the NSDictionary that the application receives will contain a value @"bar" for the foo key.

This is a book on Cocoa, not server programming, so we're not going to go into a huge amount of detail on how to set up a server that sends push notifications to Apple. For information on how to do this, see "Apple Push Notification Service" in the *Local and Remote Notification Guide* (*http://bit.ly/abt_local_and_remote_notifications*), included in the Xcode developer documentation.

Setting Up to Receive Push Notifications

Applications don't receive push notifications automatically. That's because push notifications are considered a potential intrusion on the user's device—if, as a user, you don't want an app to interrupt you, it shouldn't be able to.

In order to make your app indicate to the push notification system that it wants to receive notifications, it needs to make a method call to the global UIApplication or NSApplication object:

```
UIApplication.sharedApplication().registerForRemoteNotifications()
```

Before you call registerForRemoteNotifications, you must first indicate to the system which types of notifications you plan on receiving, just like you do for local notifications, using the registerUserNotificationSettings method.

When you register these notification types, the OS will present an alert box to the user, asking if he wants to receive notifications. If he chooses not to receive them, your application delegate receives the application(_, didFailToRegisterForRemoteNotifi

cationsWithError:) message immediately after your call to registerForRemoteNoti
fications to let your code know about it:

```
func application(application: UIApplication!,
    didFailToRegisterForRemoteNotificationsWithError error: NSError!) {
    // Called when registering for remote notifications
    // doesn't work for some reason
    println("Failed to register for notifications! \(error)")
}
```

Registering for push notifications can also fail if there's no Internet connection, if the push notification service is down, or if your code is running on a platform that doesn't support push notification.

If the user *does* want notifications, the OS contacts the Apple Push Notification service (APNs), which registers the device and application as able to receive notifications. Once this is done, the APNs sends a *device token* back to your application, which is a unique ID that acts as a "telephone number" for push notifications. When a push notification is created, the device token is included and sent to the APNs, which uses it to figure out which of the millions of devices worldwide should receive the notification.

When the application successfully registers for push notifications, it receives the appli
cation(_, didRegisterForRemoteNotificationsWithDeviceToken:) message, which takes as a parameter an NSData object containing the device token:

```
func application(application: UIApplication!,
    didRegisterForRemoteNotificationsWithDeviceToken deviceToken: NSData!) {
    // Called when we've successfully registered for remote notifications.

    // Send the deviceToken to a server you control; it uses that token
    // to send pushes to this specific device.
}
```

Once you have a device token, it needs to be sent to whatever server will actually be sending the push notifications. Without the device token, it's not possible to indicate which device should receive a push.

 If you don't want to deal with setting up your own push server, there are several existing services that can handle it for you. Most of them are based on usage—that is, the number of push notifications you send per month—and many include a free plan. We've used Urban Airship (*http://urbanairship.com*) and Parse (*http://parse.com*).

Receiving Push Notifications

Remember that a push notification may arrive when your application is open, or when it's not.

When your application is open and a push notification is received, your application delegate receives the `application(_, didReceiveRemoteNotification:)` message:

```
func application(application: UIApplication!,
    didReceiveRemoteNotification userInfo: NSDictionary!) {
    // Called when a remote notification arrives, but no action was selected
    // or the notification came in while using the app

    // Do something with the information stored in userInfo
}
```

This method receives an `NSDictionary` that contains whatever information was contained inside the JSON bundle that was originally sent.

If the user selects an action (if one is available), the application delegate instead receives the `application(_, handleActionWithIdentifier:, forRemoteNotification:, completionHandler)` message:

```
func application(application: UIApplication!,
    handleActionWithIdentifier identifier: String!,
    forRemoteNotification userInfo: NSDictionary!,
    completionHandler: (() -> Void)!) {
    // Called when a remote notification arrives,
    // and the user selected an action
}
```

If your application is *not* running and is opened from a push notification, then your application launches and your application delegate receives the `application(_, didFinishLaunchingWithOptions:)` message (on iOS). This is the same message that's sent when an application normally launches, but when opening from a push, the `launchOptions` dictionary contains the contents of the JSON dictionary:

```
func application(application: UIApplication!,
    didFinishLaunchingWithOptions launchOptions: NSDictionary!) -> Bool {

    var remoteNotification =
        launchOptions[UIApplicationLaunchOptionsRemoteNotificationKey]

    if remoteNotification? {
        // do something with the notification info
    }

    return true;
}
```

On OS X, the message received by the application delegate is a little different. On launch, the application delegate receives the `applicationDidFinishLaunching` message, which takes an `NSNotification` object as a parameter. The equivalent to iOS's `launchOptions` dictionary can be accessed thusly:

```
func applicationDidFinishLaunching(_ aNotification: NSNotification) {
    if let remoteNotification = aNotification
        .userInfo[NSApplicationLaunchRemoteNotificationKey] {

        // do something with remoteNotification, which contains
        // the notification info
    }
}
```

Finally, if your application ever needs to stop receiving push notifications, it can unregister from the Apple Push Notification service by sending the `unregisterForRemoteNotifications` message to the global `UIApplication` or `NSApplication` object:

```
UIApplication.sharedApplication().unregisterForRemoteNotifications()
```

If you unregister for notifications, you can always register again later.

Local Notifications

While remote notifications require a complex setup involving a remote computer that communicates with the Apple Push Notification service, *local* notifications are created and presented entirely on the device.

 Local notifications are only available on iOS.

A local notification looks the same as a remote notification to the user, but its delivery is controlled by the application. Local notifications are represented by the `UILocalNotification` class.

Local notifications can either be created and presented immediately (if the application is currently running and is in the background), or scheduled to appear at a certain date and time.

To construct a local notification, you simply create, configure, and schedule a `UILocalNotification`:

```
var localNotification = UILocalNotification()
localNotification.fireDate = NSDate(timeIntervalSinceNow: 3);
localNotification.category = "com.oreilly.MyApplication.message"
localNotification.alertBody = "The world is in peril!"

UIApplication.sharedApplication()
    .scheduleLocalNotification(localNotification)
```

This example code creates a local notification that displays the text "The world is in peril!" three seconds after it's created.

When a notification fires and the user chooses to open it *without* selecting an action, the application delegate receives a message very similar to the one used when a remote notification arrives, application(didReceiveLocalNotification:):

```
func application(application: UIApplication!,
    didReceiveLocalNotification notification: UILocalNotification!) {
    // Called when the user taps on a local notification (without selecting
    // an action), or if a local notification arrives while using the app
    // (in which case the notification isn't shown to the user)

    println("Received notification \(notification.category)!")
}
```

If an action was selected, your application delegate receives the application(handle ActionWithIdentifier:forLocalNotification:completionHandler:) message, which receives both the UILocalNotification object, as well as the identifier string for the action that was selected. In addition to these, you also receive a completion block, which you must call after you finish dealing with the action. The reason you do this is that this method might be called when you're in the background and because apps aren't allowed to run in the background for long, you need to let the system know when it's safe to suspend your process:

```
// This function may be called when the app is in the background, if the
// action's activation mode was Background
func application(application: UIApplication!,
    handleActionWithIdentifier identifier: String!,
    forLocalNotification notification: UILocalNotification!,
    completionHandler: (() -> Void)!) {

    // Called when the user selects an action from a local notification

    println("Received \(notification.category)! Action: \(identifier)")

    // You must call this block when done dealing with the
    // action, or you'll be terminated
    completionHandler()

}
```

If you don't call the completion block after you're done responding to the action, your application will be terminated.

Likewise, if the application isn't running when the local notification fires and the user opens the notification, the application is launched, and the launchOptions dictionary contains the notification:

```
func application(application: UIApplication!,
    didFinishLaunchingWithOptions launchOptions: NSDictionary!) -> Bool {

    var localNotification =
        launchOptions[UIApplicationLaunchOptionsLocalNotificationKey

    if localNotification? {
        // do something with the notification info
    }

    return true;
}
```

A local notification can also be presented immediately in the background. For example, if you have an application that is performing some work in the background and you want to let the user know that the work is complete, you can create a notification to that effect:

```
UIApplication.sharedApplication()
    .presentLocalNotificationNow(localNotification)
```

Once a local notification has been scheduled, you can cancel it; you can also cancel all scheduled notifications:

```
UIApplication.sharedApplication().cancelLocalNotification(aNotification)
```

or

```
UIApplication.sharedApplication().cancelAllLocalNotifications()
```

CHAPTER 19

Nonstandard Apps

For the majority of this book, we've talked about GUI applications designed to run on either OS X or iOS. These applications receive user input via the mouse, keyboard, or touchscreen, display information via the screen, and are launched by double-clicking them on OS X or tapping them on iOS.

However, not every piece of software that you write is a traditional app. In some cases, you might want to create something that the user doesn't need to interact with—for example, a background application that automatically downloads files from the Internet. Another case where you don't want to build a traditional app is when you want to create a preference pane, which the user can access via the System Preferences application.

In this chapter, you'll learn how to build apps for OS X that don't fit the mold of standard applications. Specifically, you'll learn how to build command-line tools (which don't use a GUI), system preference panes, and applications that add an item to the system-wide menu bar. Finally, you'll learn how to make apps on iOS that can use more than one screen.

This chapter mostly applies to OS X only—on iOS, you can only build apps that display a graphical interface interface, and command-line tools and daemons aren't supported.

The only exception to this is "iOS Apps with Multiple Windows" on page 419.

Command-Line Tools

The simplest possible application on OS X is a command-line tool. This kind of app never presents a GUI to the user, but instead sends and receives input and output via the command line.

The command line is a common traditional user interface for interacting with the system, and it is often the foundation that graphical user interfaces build on top of. OS X, as a Unix-based system, offers a command-line interface that your applications can use.

In fact, the command line has been involved in many of the apps that you've been developing in this book. Whenever you use NSLog or println to log some text, that text goes to the command line. (Xcode redirects it so that you can view it in the IDE, but if you were to launch the app via the Terminal, you'd see it there.)

To demonstrate how to build a command-line tool with Swift, we'll create a simple app that prints text out to the command line:

1. Create a new command-line tool project named CommandLine.

   Xcode will create a command-line application that uses the Foundation framework and is written in Swift.

    There are several types of command-line apps, which vary by the framework that your code uses. If you use Foundation, you'll be writing Swift. If you create a Core Foundation application, you'll write C.

2. Replace the main method in *main.swift* with the following code:

   ```
   import Foundation

   for var i = 10; i > 0; i-- {
       NSLog("%i green bottles, standing on the wall", i);
       NSLog("%i green bottles, standing on the wall", i);
       NSLog("And if one green bottle should accidentally fall");
       NSLog("There'll be %i green bottles, standing on the wall\n\n", i-1);
   }
   ```

3. Test the application by running it and noting what gets shown in the log.

4. Then test the application in the Terminal. Open the Terminal application, and in Xcode, scroll down to the Products group and open the folder. You'll see the CommandLine application. Drag it onto Terminal's icon in the Dock and watch the program run.

Preference Panes

For the most part, your applications should show their preferences inside the apps themselves. For example, most apps that have preferences you can change have a Preferences window, accessible via the main menu (or by pressing ⌘-,).

However, some software doesn't present a traditional interface where the preferences can be displayed—for example, background applications or device drivers. In these cases, you create *preference panes*, which are small programs hosted by the System Preferences application.

Preference panes are designed to allow the user to control features that affect the entire system (as far as the user is concerned). For example, when you install drivers for a graphics tablet, the features the drivers provide apply to all applications, which means that the drivers don't have an app to show UI in. To allow the user to configure how it works, therefore, the drivers provide a preference pane.

Preference panes are only available on OS X. On iOS, you use Settings Bundles, which are basically files that describe what settings to show to the user. You don't write any code to display them. These settings are then available to the user using the NSUserDefaults system, which is discussed in "Preferences" on page 211.

How Preference Panes Work

A preference pane is not a separate application, but is instead a bundle of code loaded by the System Preferences application. The bundle contains code and whatever resources it needs (such as images, nib files, etc.); when the preference pane is installed, System Preferences displays it as an icon in the main window. When the user selects the preference pane's icon, the bundle is loaded, its main nib is displayed, and your code begins running.

The preference pane bundle stays in memory after the user switches to another pane, until the System Preferences application exits.

Because your preference pane is a bundle that's loaded by another application, accessing resources via NSBundle's pathForResource(ofType:) method or NSUserDefaults won't work the same way as in your applications. This is because these methods access the application's bundle and preference domain, not your bundle and preference domain. If you want to set preferences, you need to specifically tell NSUserDefaults which domain the preferences should be set in.

Preference Domains

Imagine that two applications exist, both of which set a preference called `favoriteCol` `or`. These applications are by different authors and use the preference in different ways, so each assumes that it's the only one using the `favoriteColor` preference.

To prevent preferences colliding, OS X and iOS separate preferences by *domain*. When you use NSUserDefault's `setValue(forKey:)` and `valueForKey` methods (and related methods like `setBool(forKey:)`), it assumes that the preference domain you want to work in is the one with the same name as your application's bundle identifier.

So, to go back to our two example applications, as long as each has a different bundle identifier—and it should, because Apple won't allow it into the App Store unless a unique one is set—the two applications will set and retrieve preferences in their own, separate domains.

When you're building a preference pane, however, the bundle identifier of the application is that of System Preferences. This means that calling methods like `boolForKey` won't retrieve the settings you want. To solve this problem, you indicate to NSUser Defaults exactly which preference domain you want to work with.

To retrieve the preferences for a specific domain, you use the `NSUserDefaults` class's `persistentDomainForName` method. This method takes an `NSString` containing the name of the domain, and returns an `NSDictionary` containing all of the keys and values stored in that domain's preferences.

To set the preferences for this domain, you use NSUserDefaults's `setPersistentDo` `main(forName:)` method. This works in much the same way: it takes an `NSDiction` `ary` containing settings to apply, and an `NSString` containing the name of the domain to set.

This means that, instead of working with preferences on an individual basis, you work with a dictionary that contains all of the settings. When you set the values for a domain, you replace all of the settings at once.

For example, imagine that you want to work with the preferences for the domain *com.oreilly.MyAmazingApplication*.

To get the preferences as a mutable dictionary (so that you can modify it later), you do this:

```
let domainName = "com.oreilly.MyAmazingApplication"
var preferences =
    NSUserDefaults.standardUserDefaults().persistentDomainForName(domainName)
```

You can then modify that dictionary as you like, like so:

```
preferences["isChecked"] = true
```

When you're done, you set the preferences for the domain by passing in the dictionary:

```
NSUserDefaults.standardUserDefaults().setPersistentDomain(preferences,
    forName: domainName)
```

Building a Sample Preference Pane

We'll now build a preference pane that displays a single checkbox, which we'll store in the domain *com.oreilly.MyAmazingApplication*.

1. Create a new preference pane application for OS X. You'll find the template in the System Plug-in section.

    Name the project `PreferencePane`.

2. Create the interface. Open *PreferencePane.xib*. This is the nib file that contains the view that will be shown when the preference pane is selected.

    Drag in a checkbox and make its label read whatever you like.

3. Make the File's Owner of the nib file use the `PreferencePane` class. By default, the nib file created as part of the project template does not set the File's Owner object to use the main class of the project. We'll change that first.

    Select the File's Owner in the Interface Builder, and open the Identity Inspector.

    Change the class from `NSPreferencePane` to `PreferencePane` (your class).

4. Connect the interface to the code. Open *PreferencePane.swift* in the assistant.

    Control-drag from the checkbox into `PreferencePane`'s interface. Create an outlet called `checkbox`.

5. Add the code that loads the current preference. We'll first add the code that loads the current value of the setting and turns the checkbox on or off. To do this, replace the `mainViewDidLoad` method in *PreferencePane.swift* with the following code (this method is run when the preference pane finishes loading):

```
override func mainViewDidLoad() {
    var preferences = NSUserDefaults.standardUserDefaults()
        .persistentDomainForName(domainName)

    if let checked = preferences?["isChecked"] as? NSNumber {
        switch checked {
        case true:
            self.checkbox.state = NSOnState
        default:
            self.checkbox.state = NSOffState
        }
    }

}
```

6. Add the code that sets the preference when the pane is closed.

   Add the following method to *PreferencePane.swift* (this method is called after the preference pane has stopped being shown by the user—such as when the System Preferences pane quits or the user clicks the Back, Forward, or Show All button):

```swift
override func didUnselect() {
    var preferences = NSUserDefaults.standardUserDefaults()
        .persistentDomainForName(domainName) as? [String: AnyObject]

    // persistentDomainForName might return nil, because this might
    // be the first time we've ever tried to save the preferences.
    // If this is the case, set 'preferences' to be an empty
    // dictionary, so that it can be used.

    if preferences == nil {
        preferences = [:]
    }

    // Store the info in the dictionary
    switch self.checkbox.state {
    case NSOnState:
        preferences?["isChecked"] = true
    default:
        preferences?["isChecked"] = false
    }

    // Store the dictionary in NSUserDefaults
    NSUserDefaults.standardUserDefaults()
        .setPersistentDomain(preferences!, forName: domainName)
}
```

7. Test the application.

   Build the preference pane by pressing ⌘-B or choosing Build from the Product menu.

   Launch the System Preferences application.

   Open the Products group in the project navigator. Drag the *PreferencePane.prefPane* file onto the System Preferences application in the Dock. System Preferences will ask how you want to install the preference pane.

   Play around with the preference pane. If you check the checkbox, quit System Preferences, and come back to your preference pane, the checkbox will remain checked.

 You can't test preference panes like you can other applications, because preference panes aren't run like normal applications. Instead, you build the application and load it into the System Preferences application.

Status Bar Items

Another example of applications that don't present themselves with traditional GUIs are applications that exist as *status items*—items that live in the top-right corner of the screen. OS X has a number of built-in applications that live like this, such as the volume changer and clock.

Status items can display any text, image, or view when clicked, and can display either a menu or a custom view. You create a status item by asking the system's status bar to create an NSStatusItem for you; you then customize the status item by setting its title text, image, or view, and providing it with an NSMenu or other view to display when it's clicked.

You must keep a reference to the NSStatusItem object that you get from the NSStatusBar class. If you don't, the object will be released from memory and removed from the status bar.

Status items allow you to work with an application's features without requiring that the application be the foreground application. For example, Twitter for Mac shows a status item while the application is running that changes color when new messages arrive.

You can also create an application that *only* displays a status item. Such applications are generally background utility apps such as Dropbox, which use the status item to indicate the app's current status and provide an easy way to access basic settings, as well as a means to access a more complete settings UI for controlling the application.

If you're writing an application that only shows a status item, you likely don't want to show the dock icon. To implement this, set the Application is agent (UIElement) value in the application's *Info.plist* file to YES, and the app will not show a dock icon.

Building a Status Bar App

We'll now demonstrate how to build a status bar application that doesn't show a dock icon:

1. Create a Cocoa application named StatusItem.
2. Create the interface. This application will have neither a menu bar nor a window to show. The only UI will be the status item.

   Open *MainMenu.xib* and delete both the main menu and the main window.

   Drag in an NSMenu. It will contain three items—delete the second and third.

   Make the single menu item's label read Quit.

3. Connect the interface to the code. Open *AppDelegate.swift* in the assistant.

   Control-drag from the menu into `AppDelegate`, and create a new outlet called `menu`.

   Control-drag from the Quit menu item into `AppDelegate`, and create an action named `quit`.

4. Next, we'll create the status item and prepare it. We'll also add the code that gets run when the Quit menu item is chosen.

   We'll also need to add a property that stores the `NSStatusItem` object. Without this variable, the status item would be removed from memory, and therefore the status item would disappear immediately after it was added.

   Update *AppDelegate.swift* so that it looks like the following code:

   ```
   import Cocoa

   class AppDelegate: NSObject, NSApplicationDelegate {

       @IBOutlet var window: NSWindow!
       @IBOutlet var menu: NSMenu!

       var statusItem : NSStatusItem!

       @IBAction func quit(sender: AnyObject) {
           NSApplication.sharedApplication().terminate(nil)
       }

       func applicationDidFinishLaunching(aNotification: NSNotification?) {

           // Make a status bar that has variable length
           // (as opposed to being a standard square size)

           // -1 to indicate "variable length"
           statusItem = NSStatusBar.systemStatusBar().statusItemWithLength(-1)

           // Set the text that appears in the menu bar
           statusItem.title = "My Item"

           // Set the menu that should appear when the item is clicked
           statusItem.menu = self.menu

           // Set if the item should change color when clicked
           statusItem.highlightMode = true

       }

   }
   ```

5. Finally, we'll make the application not show a dock icon. The status item will remain visible no matter which application is currently active, so there's always a way to access it.

To do this, you modify the application's *Info.plist* file and indicate that it's an *agent*. "Agent" is Apple's term for a background application that doesn't present a dock icon.

Select the project at the top of the project navigator. Open the Info tab at the top of the main editor.

Add a new entry into the `Application is agent (UIElement)` property list and set the value of this entry to `YES`.

6. Run the application. Nothing will appear in the dock, but the word "Test" will appear at the top of the screen in the menu bar. You can open this menu and choose to quit the app.

iOS Apps with Multiple Windows

Sometimes, you might want to run your iOS app on more than one screen. For example, you might want to use the built-in touchscreen to receive input from the user and display the results on a television. Without the touch sensor or any of the other iOS device hardware, any second screen will be for output only, but this doesn't mean it isn't useful.

A window on an iOS device is represented by a `UIWindow` object. Inside this window are two important properties. The `rootViewController` holds the root view controller to be displayed; in the case of a standard iOS app, this will be the inital view controller from the storyboard, and in the case of an external window, it can be anything you wish. The second important property is the `screen`, which represents the actual physical screen on which the window is going to be displayed. The screen has a `bounds` property, which holds its size, and also has additional properties such as brightness, meaning that you can customize the second window to a degree.

To demonstrate how to use a second window in your iOS apps, we'll create a demo app with two different view controllers—one for the device and another for the external monitor:

1. Create a new single view iPhone application and call it MultipleWindows.
2. Create the interface. Open the *Main.storyboard* and add a second view controller to the storyboard. There is no need to hook it up to the inital view controller, but do make sure it looks different so you can see it on the second window later.

   Select the new view controller and open the Identity Inspector, and set the Storyboard ID to `secondWindowVC`.

3. Connect to the new window. Replace the *AppDelegate.swift* file with the following:

   ```
   import UIKit

   @UIApplicationMain
   ```

```
class AppDelegate: UIResponder, UIApplicationDelegate {

    var window : UIWindow!
    var secondWindow : UIWindow!

    func application(application: UIApplication!,
        didFinishLaunchingWithOptions launchOptions: NSDictionary!) -> Bool {

        // Register to be notified of when screens connect or disconnect
        var notificationCenter = NSNotificationCenter.defaultCenter()

        notificationCenter.addObserver(self,
            selector: Selector("screenDidConnect:"),
            name: UIScreenDidConnectNotification,
            object: nil)
        notificationCenter.addObserver(self,
            selector: Selector("screenDidDisconnect:"),
            name: UIScreenDidDisconnectNotification,
            object: nil)

        // We're in the middle of starting up. If the system already has
        // multiple screens, set up the second one!
        if UIScreen.screens().count >= 2 {
            var secondScreen = UIScreen.screens()[1] as UIScreen
            self.setupScreen(secondScreen)
        }

        return true
    }

    // Given a screen, prepare and display the view
    // controller for the screen.
    func setupScreen(screen : UIScreen) {

        // If we already have a second window, do nothing
        if self.secondWindow != nil {
            return;
        }

        // Create a window to display on this screen
        self.secondWindow = UIWindow(frame: screen.bounds)
        self.secondWindow.screen = screen
        self.secondWindow.hidden = false

        // Create a view controller to show in the window
        var storyboard = UIStoryboard(name: "Main", bundle: nil)
        var viewController = storyboard
            .instantiateViewControllerWithIdentifier("secondWindowVC")
                as UIViewController

        // Show the view controller in the window
        self.secondWindow.rootViewController = viewController
```

```
    }

    // Called when a screen connects
    func screenDidConnect(notification: NSNotification) {

        // Get the screen from the NSObject
        var screen = notification.object as UIScreen

        // Attempt to set it up
        self.setupScreen(screen)
    }

    // Called when a screen disconnects
    func screenDidDisconnect(notification: NSNotification) {

        // Get the screen from the NSObject
        var screen = notification.object as UIScreen

        // If we have a second window, and it uses this window...
        if self.secondWindow?.screen == screen {

            // ... remove it!
            self.secondWindow = nil
        }

    }

}
```

This code is registering to be notified when a second monitor is being connected or disconnected from the device. When it detects a connection, it creates a new UIWindow object to hold that screen and then it adds the second view controller from the storyboard onto that window.

When it detects a window being disconnected, it simply clears out the window so it doesn't take up memory.

Now if you run the app and then plug in a second monitor to your device, you should see the second view controller you created in the storyboard appearing while the initial view controller is showing on the device.

It's worth noting that if you start the application and the window is *already* connected to the device, you won't receive a notification. To find out what screens are connected when the app launches, you can query the screens property of the UIScreen class, which is a list of all screens currently attached to the device.

CHAPTER 20

Working with Text

Both OS X and iOS have tremendously powerful tools for working with text. Whether it's working with multiple languages, converting data into human-readable forms, or detecting information in text, Cocoa and Cocoa Touch contain a wide variety of useful tools for working with strings, text, and language.

In this chapter, you'll learn how to use the system's built-in internationalization and localization features to easily make your app display strings in your code in whatever language the user prefers. You'll also learn how to use NSFormatter and its subclasses to format data into strings, and how to use data detectors to detect URLs and dates in arbitrary text.

Internationalization and Localization

Your primary language may not be the one spoken by your end user. When you write strings embedded in your code for the user to see, those strings are hardcoded into the compiled executable—so if something is written in English, the user will see it in English, even if she doesn't necessarily read English.

To address this problem, Cocoa has support for *localized text*, which is text that is replaced at runtime with versions appropriate for your user. In your code, you use placeholder strings, and store the translated versions for every language that you support in a separate file. When the code that displays the text runs, it checks to see which language the user is using, and replaces the placeholder text with the appropriate version.

Strings Files

A *strings file* maps internal representations of text to localized representations. Strings files look like this:

```
"welcome message" = "Welcome to OS X!";
"quit message" = "Goodbye! Come back soon!";
```

Strings files let you keep the text used in your application separate from your code. This becomes especially useful when the text used in your application changes—for example, when running in another language.

Strings files can be localized, which means that Xcode will create multiple versions of the file based on language; at runtime, the application will use only the version of the file appropriate to the user's choice of language. If an appropriate version doesn't exist, the application will load the best one it can find.

Creating a Sample Localized Application

To demonstrate how localization works in Cocoa, we'll build an application that makes use of strings files to translate its interface.

1. Create a new Cocoa application named Localized.

   The first thing to do is to enable localization on the interface file. This will make the application automatically load the locale-appropriate version of the file, and also lets you preview the application in different languages.

2. Go to the File Inspector. This is the leftmost inspector in the Utilities pane.

   Once there, scroll down to the Localization section. You'll see two localizations available: *Base* and *English*.

   Turn on the checkbox next to English. This will enable localization on the file, because at least one localized language is now available.

3. Create the interface. Open *MainMenu.xib* and drag a label into the window. Position it at the upper left of the window and make its text read "This is a localized application for Mac OS X."

   Drag a second label into the window. Position it at the left edge of the window, underneath the first label. Make its text read "Today is 30 July 2014."[1]

   Finally, drag in a button. Place it on the right side of the window, aligned with the second label. Make its text read "Tell the World."

   Next, add the following constraints to the items in the window:

   • First label ("This is a localized application for Mac OS X"):

     — Leading space to superview: 20

     — Top space to superview: 20

---

1. You may provide any date you like for this field. The possibilities available to you in this universe are truly limitless.

— Vertical space to second label: ≥ 8
- Second label ("Today's date is 30 July 2014"):
  — Leading space to superview: 20
  — Bottom space to superview: 20
  — Trailing space to button: ≥ 20
- Button ("Tell the World"):
  — Trailing space to superview: 20
  — Align baseline to second label

When you're done, the window should look like Figure 20-1.

Figure 20-1. The user interface for the application, including its constraints

 When designing interfaces that are going to be localized (which should be all of them!), avoid creating constraints that set a fixed width on controls. A piece of text will be one width in one language and a different width in another, and if you enforce a fixed width, you'll more than likely end up with truncated text.

Instead, it's better to set up leading and trailing space constraints. The constraint system will then able to work out the width appropriately.

We can now see if the interface appropriately handles different text lengths, even before translating any of the text in the application. This is possible thanks to Xcode's built-in *pseudolocalizations*, which do things with your app's base text to test out your interface.

One of these pseudolocalizations is the Double-Length Pseudolanguage. This localization simply takes the text of your development language, and doubles it. So, for example, "Tell the World" becomes "Tell the World Tell the World." While many pieces of text won't actually *double* in length when translated to another langauge, it serves as a great way to test to see whether your interface can handle the wide variation in length.

We'll now test this interface using this pseudolocalization:

1. Select Preview from the menu at the far left of the Jump Bar at the top of the assistant.

   A copy of the main window of the app should appear in the right side of the Xcode window. If it doesn't, make sure you've selected the window on the lefthand side.

2. Change the language, at the lower-right of the window, to Double-Length Pseudo-language, as shown in Figure 20-2.

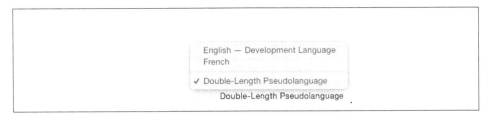

Figure 20-2. Selecting the Double-Length Pseudolanguage in the Preview assistant

The preview pane will update to show the app as it appears in the new *language*. You'll notice that it mostly works! The labels have updated to their new sizes, and the button has been pushed aside further to accomodate the width of the label next to it. However, one obvious error immediately appears: the first label (the one that reads *This is a localized application for Mac OS X*) is too long, and goes off the side of the window. You can see this in Figure 20-3.

Figure 20-3. The application, translated into the Double-Length Pseudolanguage (note that the first label is too long, and extends off the side of the window)

The cause of the error is that the first label's trailing space isn't constrained: what we want is for the trailing edge of the first label to always be 20 pixels away from the edge of the window. Fortunately, this is very easy to add:

3. Constrain the trailing edge of the first label. Hold down the Control key, and drag from the trailing edge of the label to the window. Select Trailing Space to Container.

A new constraint will appear. Select it, and open the Attributes Inspector. Change its Relation from Equal to Greater Than or Equal, and set the Constant to Standard by selecting Use Standard Value from the drop-down menu. You can see the final settings of this constraint in Figure 20-4.

Figure 20-4. The settings for the trailing space

Once the constraint is set up, the preview will update, showing that the layout flows correctly, as seen in Figure 20-5.

Figure 20-5. The double-length interface, now flowing correctly

The Double-Length Pseudolangage is a great test of your interface's ability to handle varying text length, but it's not a real language, and is only applicable to developers. Let's now translate this interface to a real language.

 In this chapter, we're using French as our demonstration language, but you can pick anything you like. Just choose a different language when adding a new localization to your app.

The first step to adding a new language is to add a new localization to the project. This makes Xcode aware that you want to start translating files into that language, which means you can do things like select that language in the Preview assistant.

1. Select the project in the project navigator. It's at the top of the list. Select the project from the menu at the top of the editor, as seen in Figure 20-6.

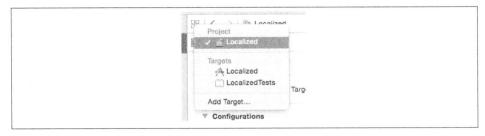

Figure 20-6. Selecting the project in the editor view

2. Add the new localization. Scroll down to the Localizations section. Click the + button, and select French from the menu that appears, as seen in Figure 20-7.

 Most languages come in a variety of different dialects. You may see a giant list that includes many different *types* of French.

3. Select the files you want to localize. Xcode will ask you which files you want to translate into the new language. At this stage, there will only be a single file: the app's interface, stored in *MainMenu.xib*. It's selected by default, so click Finish.

A new file will be created: a strings file for the *MainMenu.xib* file. It'll appear as an item *inside* the *MainMenu.xib* file, in the project navigator, as seen in Figure 20-8.

4. You can now go through the new French version of the strings file, and begin translating the interface to French. For each item in the strings file, you replace the original language with the French version.

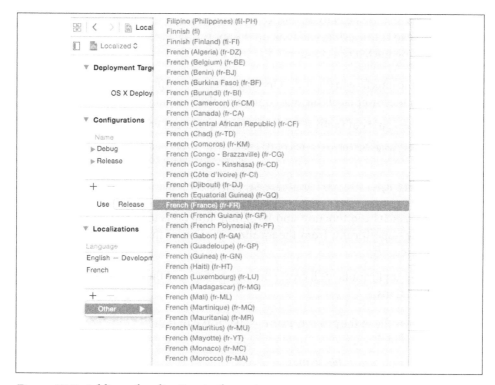

Figure 20-7. Adding a localization to the project

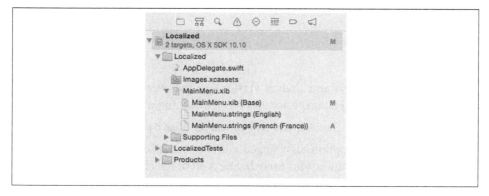

Figure 20-8. The strings files, shown in the project navigator

This application now has a mostly localized interface. However, it's not obvious how the second label will be localized, as it's going to be displaying dynamic text (i.e., the text isn't defined at compile time, but rather depends on the current date).

To localize this text, we need to be able to localize chunks of text from within code. We need to be able to take a string, and look up the appropriate localization at runtime. We can do this using the NSLocalizedString function.

5. Connect the interface to the code. Open *AppDelegate.swift* in the assistant. Control-drag from the lower label (the one containing the date) into the AppDelegate class.

6. Replace the applicationDidFinishLaunching method with the following code:

```
let languageFormat = NSLocalizedString("today's date: %@",
                          comment:"shows today's date")

self.dateLabel.stringValue = String(format: languageFormat, NSDate())
```

The NSLocalizedString function and its sibling functions load text from the *Localized.strings* file—specifically, from the localized version of that file that fits the user's current language.

To localize this application, we'll create the strings file, and then add both English and French localizations.

7. Create a new file in the project: a strings file. You'll find this in the Resource section of the file templates.

Name the file *Localizable.strings*.

 It's important to use this filename, as this file is the one the app will look for if you don't specify another name.

8. Next, add the English and French versions of the strings file. Select *Localizable.strings*. Open the File Inspector and scroll down to Localizations.

Click the Localize button. A menu will appear; choose Base and click Localize.

Now the localization option has changed, with three small checkboxes, one for Base, one for English, and the last for French. Select all of the checkboxes.

9. Add the English text. Open *Localizable.strings (English)* and add the following text:

```
"today's date: %@" = "Today's date is %@";
```

10. Then add the French text. Open *Localizable.strings (French)* and add the following text:

```
"today's date: %@"="La date d'aujourd'hui est %@";
```

It is also good practice to fill in the Base language, but in this case it is also English so we will leave it blank.

11. Run the application. Now that the localized strings files have been written, test the application in English mode.

    The text of the label will change to the more accurately written English text.

Next, we'll test the French version. To avoid having to change the language of the entire system, we'll make Xcode launch the application using the French langauge.

To do this, we'll edit the current scheme and add a parameter that is passed to the application at start time:

12. Make the application launch using the French language. Click on the Scheme at the upper left of the window (it's the drop-down list just to the right of the Stop button).

    Choose Edit Scheme… from the menu that appears.

    Make sure that the Run Localized.app option is selected. Open the Options panel.

    Change the Application Language from System Language to French.

13. Run the application like a Frenchman.

    Run the app again. Note that the text appears in French. *Quelle surprise!* (See Figure 20-9.)

    You can continue adding more localized strings and more localizations to your application. The more languages supported by your app, the more potential users you have.

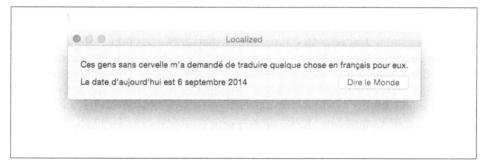

Figure 20-9. The application fully localized into French

Xcode can also export and import the localized parts of your app using XLIFF, a standard XML-based format for localized information. Using XLIFF, you can export all of the strings in your app that need translation, and hand them off to a translator who can work on it using their own tools; they can then deliver the translated XML back to you, and you can import it back into your project.

To learn more about Xcode's support for XLIFF, see the *Internationalization and Localization Guide* (*http://bit.ly/abt_internationalization*) in the Xcode documentation.

Formatting Data with NSFormatter

Many useful pieces of information need conversion to text before a human can read them. Additionally, different people expect information to be presented in different ways depending on where they live. For example, dates and times are displayed differently depending on the country. The difference could be as simple as the order of numbers and punctuation—dates are written "MM-DD-YY" in the United States, and "DD-MM-YY"[2] in Australia. However, sometimes the differences are radical—your user could be using the Muslim calendar, in which case the same point in time has a completely different date representation.

To solve this and other problems, Cocoa separates dates from their presentation. When you want to work with date and time information, you use the NSDate class. When you want to create text to display a representation of that date to the user, you use the NSDateFormatter class.

Dates aren't the only things that can be formatted. Numbers have different representations in different cultures, as well as different representations in different contexts.

For example, in the United States, the decimal marker is a period (.), while in many European countries the marker is a comma (,). Different locales also group numerals together differently—some Indian numbering systems group numerals in two and three, so that the number *one million* is represented as 10,00,000. If you're writing an application that displays monetary figures, it's common to display negative figures in parentheses (()). Additionally, the locale that your user is in will very likely have a different currency symbol than $.

NSNumberFormatter takes localization into account, and creates strings that suit what your user expects to see to what your application needs to display.

To demonstrate how formatters work, we'll extend the application that we created earlier in this chapter to format the date using an NSDateFormatter:

---

2. The authors, who are Australian, contend that this is superior.

```
let languageFormat = NSLocalizedString("today's date: %@",
                                comment:"shows today's date")

let dateFormatter = NSDateFormatter()

dateFormatter.timeStyle = NSDateFormatterStyle.NoStyle
dateFormatter.dateStyle = NSDateFormatterStyle.LongStyle

let dateString = dateFormatter.stringFromDate(NSDate())

self.dateLabel.stringValue = String(format: languageFormat, dateString)
```

 Creating an NSDateFormatter is a rather expensive operation. If you need to format a large number of dates, create one and keep it around rather than creating a new one for every time you need to format a date.

Run the application. The date will appear in the application, correctly formatted for your user's locale (Figure 20-10).

You can set the style of both the time and date in the formatter. Both timeStyle and dateStyle accept any of the following options (note that the precise format will change depending on the user's locale—read on if you want total control!):

NoStyle
  Dates and times don't appear at all.

ShortStyle
  A brief style. Usually, only numbers appear. Dates appear like "10/24/86" and times appear like "5:05pm."

MediumStyle
  Slightly more detail appears in the medium style. Dates appear like "Oct 24, 1986." Times appear like the short style.

LongStyle
  With the long style, almost every detail appears. Month names, for example, are fully spelled out. Dates appear like "October 24, 1986" and times appear like "5:05:23pm."

FullStyle
  Every detail is presented in the full style, including era and time zone information. Dates appear like "Friday, October 24, 1986 AD" and times appear like "5:05:23pm AEDT." NSDateFormatter also allows you to format dates with your own format string. A format string defines which components of the date and time should appear. For example, to render an NSDate to look like "17:05 October 24, 1986" (in that order, regardless of the locale's preference), you do this:

```
let dateFormatter = NSDateFormatter()
dateFormatter.dateFormat = "HH:mm, MMMM d"
```

 Note that the various names for months and days will be correctly presented in the user's current language. "July" in English becomes "juillet" in French, for example.

All the different letters in the format string define what parts of the date and time appear, and the number of times the symbol is repeated changes the format of the component.

For full details on the format patterns that can be used, see the Unicode specification TR35 (*http://bit.ly/unicode_spec_tr35*), which is used by both OS X and iOS.

Testing Different Locales

The language of an application is separate from the way that dates, times, and measurements are displayed. If you want to test out different locales in your application, you need to add a parameter to your application's run scheme.

To do this, choose Edit Scheme… from the menu that appears, select the Run option, and open the Options panel.

Change the Application Region to Europe → France.

You can then run your application, and the date formatter will produce a date string that's delivered in the system language, but uses French styles of dates. The differences are often subtle—things like the names of months being shorter—but add up to feeling like an app that matches what the user is comfortable with.

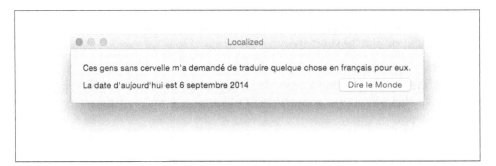

Figure 20-10. The app, with a French-formatted date

Formatting Numbers, Lengths, Mass, Energy, and Data

In addition to dates, it's often very useful to format values for the user to see. These sometimes need localization, such as in the case of formatting numbers as currency, but often you just want to display a quantity with the right unit.

This is where the NSNumberFormatter and its related classes comes in. These classes take a value along with any information on how you'd like it to be formatted, and return a string for you to display to the user.

NSNumberFormatter

The basic NSNumberFormatter is very straightforward, but also very versatile. You can use it to format numbers into decimal formats, scientific notation, currency, and as percentages.

Creating one is very easy—all you need to do is to create an instance of the class:

```
let numberFormatter = NSNumberFormatter()
```

Let's say you wanted to format a number value as some currency. In this case, you'd just need to set the formatting style as CurrencyStyle; the formatter automatically selects the locale-appropriate currency symbol:

```
// Showing currency
numberFormatter.numberStyle = NSNumberFormatterStyle.CurrencyStyle
numberFormatter.stringFromNumber(23.42) // = "$23.42"
```

 The number formatter doesn't perform currency conversions—you'll need to do that yourself. All it does is take a number and turn it into a string that can be presented to the user.

The number formatter is also capable of rounding to arbitrary intervals. For example, if you want to round to the nearest 0.5:

```
// Round to the nearest 0.5
numberFormatter.roundingIncrement = 0.5
numberFormatter.stringFromNumber(23.42) // = "$23.50"
```

NSNumberFormatter is good for more than just currency, however. When you need to render an arbitrary number, it's got you covered:

```
// Showing numbers
numberFormatter.numberStyle = NSNumberFormatterStyle.DecimalStyle
numberFormatter.stringFromNumber(2003.42) // = "2,003.42"
```

You can also feed it decimal numbers and have it render them as percentages (such as 0.43 being rendered as "43%"; this would be displayed as "45%" with rounding enabled):

```
// Showing percentages
numberFormatter.numberStyle = NSNumberFormatterStyle.PercentStyle
numberFormatter.stringFromNumber(0.95) // = "95%"
```

NSEnergyFormatter, NSMassFormatter, and NSLengthFormatter

The NSEnergyFormatter class is designed to support rendering values, measured in joules, into locale-appropriate strings. This is usually for apps that care about energy in food, such as in diet-management apps, but the concepts apply to non-food energy just the same.

NSEnergyFormatter, along with its NSMassFormatter and NSLengthFormatter cousins, allow you to keep all of your app's data in a single consistent unit (joules, kilograms, and meters), and display them to the user in units that they're familiar with, no matter where they're from.

Creating an energy formatter is just a matter of creating an instance of the NSEnergy Formatter class:

```
let energyFormatter = NSEnergyFormatter()
```

If you have a specific unit you want to display the energy value in, you can provide that unit to the formatter along with the value you want to format:

```
// Formats the value, given in joules; uses a specific unit
energyFormatter.stringFromValue(5000,
    unit: NSEnergyFormatterUnit.Kilojoule) // = "5,000 kJ"
```

If you want to use the user's default units, you can simply provide just the value, and the formatter will automatically select an appropriate unit for its size and the user's locale:

```
// Formats the value, given in joules; automatically uses a locale-specific
// unit
energyFormatter.stringFromJoules(50000) // = "11.95 kcal"
```

Mass formatters and length formatters work identically to energy formatters. First, you create the instance:

```
let massFormatter = NSMassFormatter()
```

```
let lengthFormatter = NSLengthFormatter()
```

Once you have the object, you can begin formatting values. You can format mass and lengths as specific units (you provide the values in either kilograms or meters, respectively):

```
// Formats the value, given in kilograms; uses a specific unit
massFormatter.stringFromValue(0.5,
    unit: NSMassFormatterUnit.Kilogram) // = "0.5 kg"

// Formats the value, given in meters; uses a specific unit
lengthFormatter.stringFromValue(42.3,
    unit: NSLengthFormatterUnit.Meter) // = "42.3 m"
```

Additionally, you can provide just the values, and have the formatter select the unit for you, depending on the quantity and the user's locale.

```
// Formats the value, given in meters; automatically uses a locale-specific
// unit
massFormatter.stringFromKilograms(0.5) // = "1.1 lb"

// Formats the value, given in meters; automatically uses a locale-specific
// unit
lengthFormatter.stringFromMeters(42.3) // = "46.259 yd"
```

NSByteCountFormatter

The NSByteCountFormatter class is a bit different to the previously discussed formatters. The byte count formatter is designed to take a value, measured in bytes, and convert that to a representative string that displays the number of kilobytes, megabytes, gigabytes (or more). This is very useful for indicating the size of a download, a file, and more.

Again, creating the formatter is simple:

```
let dataFormatter = NSByteCountFormatter()
```

Simple use of the byte count formatter is just as straightforward—you simply provide a number of bytes, and receive a string:

```
// Formats the value, given in bytes
dataFormatter.stringFromByteCount(200000) // = "200 KB"
```

The main way in which the byte count formatter differs from other formatters is that there are two ways that bytes can be counted: decimally, in which 1,000 bytes are counted as a kilobyte, and binarily, in which 1,024 bytes are counted as a kilobyte. The reasoning for this is boring, and filled with words like "mebibyte"; let's just leave it at the simple fact that most people think of a thousand bytes as a kilobyte, and are totally incorrect in doing so.

However, good app design is all about not surprising the user, so the default counting style is decimal: 1,000 bytes is a kilobyte. If, however, you want to change this counting style, you can very easily do so:

```
// Count style can be changed; defaults to decimal (2,000 bytes = 2KB)
// Setting this to Binary makes it treat 2,048 = 2KB
dataFormatter.countStyle = NSByteCountFormatterCountStyle.Binary
dataFormatter.stringFromByteCount(200000) // = "195 KB"
```

The byte count formatter also intelligently knows how to handle zero bytes. Zero bytes is a special case, and simply displaying the digit 0 isn't very readable. `NSByteCountFor matter`, therefore, formats zero bytes using words:

```
// Also formats zero bytes intelligently, as a word
dataFormatter.stringFromByteCount(0) // = "Zero KB"
```

Detecting Data with NSDataDetector

As far as the system is concerned, text that it receives can be literally anything. However, text frequently contains information that's useful to both the user and to the app you're writing. For example, posts to Twitter often contain links to websites, and it's a useful feature for a Twitter app to be able to quickly open a link in the tweet's text. Another example is date and time information: an email could contain the date for a meeting, and an app may want to extract that.

To extract information from text, you use the `NSDataDetector` class. This class reads through a string and looks for whatever data you tell it to keep an eye out for.

You can use data detectors to detect the following kinds of data in strings:

- Dates
- Addresses
- Links
- Phone numbers
- Transit information (like flight information)

When you create an `NSDataDetector`, you provide it with the kinds of information that you're looking for. You then provide a string to the data detector, and get back an `NSArray` that contains `NSTextCheckingResult` objects. Each `NSTextCheckingResult` contains additional information about what type each result is—a date, URL, or other kind of detectable data.

To demonstrate data detectors, we'll build a simple application that allows users to type in anything they want and see what the data detector finds.

The application will present a text field and a button. When the button is clicked, the text will be checked and the results will be presented in a label:

1. Create a new Cocoa application and call it DataDetectors.
2. Create the interface. Open *MainMenu.xib*.

    Drag in a text field, and resize it until it's a few lines high. Place it in the top half of the window.

Drag in a button and place it under the text field. Change its label to Check.

Drag in a multiline label. Place it under the button in the bottom half of the window. When you're done, the app's interface should look like Figure 20-11.

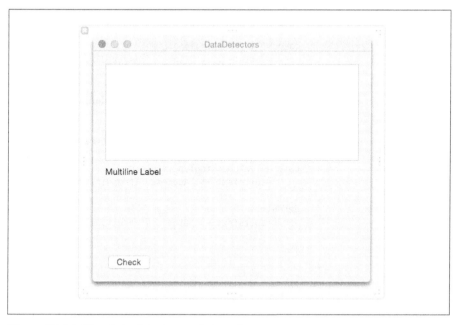

Figure 20-11. The data detector app's interface

3. Connect the interface to the code. Open *AppDelegate.swift* in the assistant.

   Control-drag from the top text field into the AppDelegate class. Create an outlet called inputTextField.

   Control-drag from the bottom text field into AppDelegate, and create an outlet called outputTextField.

   Finally, Control-drag from the button into AppDelegate, and create an action called check.

4. Replace the check() method with the following code:

```
@IBAction func check(sender: AnyObject) {

    let detector = NSDataDetector(
        types: NSTextCheckingTypes(NSTextCheckingAllTypes), error: nil)

    let inputString = self.inputTextField.stringValue
    var resultsText = ""

    if let matches = detector?.matchesInString(inputString, options: nil,
```

```
            range: NSMakeRange(0, countElements(inputString))) {

            for match in matches {

                if let result = match as? NSTextCheckingResult {

                    switch result.resultType {

                    case NSTextCheckingType.Link:
                        resultsText += "Link: \(result.URL)\n"

                    case NSTextCheckingType.Date:
                        resultsText += "Date: \(result.date)\n"

                    case NSTextCheckingType.PhoneNumber:
                        resultsText += "Phone Number: \(result.phoneNumber)"

                    case NSTextCheckingType.Address:
                        resultsText += "Address: \(result.addressComponents)"

                    default:
                        resultsText += "Other: \(result.description)\n"

                    }
                }
            }
        }


        self.outputTextField.stringValue = resultsText

    }
```

5. Run the application. Type in text like this:

    ```
    Apple's doing an event at 4pm tomorrow!
    ```

    and click the Check button. The app will display the date and time it detected.

TextKit

TextKit is a new text rendering engine, originally included in iOS 7, built on top of *CoreText*, replacing WebKit as the text engine for iOS. Technically, everything that TextKit allows you to do was possible in the past through clever use of CoreText, but it was hard and very time consuming. TextKit allows you to do text-related manipulation, including kerning, ligatures, and letterpress effects, among other features.

One of the most important features of TextKit is dynamic type, allowing your users to increase or decrease the size of fonts on the fly to better suit their own needs. Users of your app will start expecting dynamic font to be implemented and obeyed inside your app from the beginning, so be wary of ignoring it! At its most basic, dynamic fonts simply add a new method to UIFont called preferedFontForTextStyle to allow for the user's system-wide preferred font to be determined. The different text styles available are:

- Headings
- Subheadings
- Body
- Footnotes
- Captions

As a quick demonstration of TextKit and dynamic fonts, we'll create a simple iPhone app that responds to the updates in dynamic fonts.

1. Create a new single view iPhone application, and call it TextKitDemo.
2. Create the interface. Open *Main.storyboard*.

   Drag in a text view, and place it to fill the entire view.

   Select the text view, and inside the Attributes Inspector, untick Editable.

3. Connect the interface. Open *ViewController.swift* in the assistant.

   Control-drag from the text view into the ViewController class, and create an outlet called textView.

4. Add the code. Replace *ViewController.swift* with the following:

```
import UIKit

class ViewController: UIViewController {

    @IBOutlet weak var textView: UITextView!

    var observer : AnyObject?

    override func viewDidLoad() {
        super.viewDidLoad()

        self.textView.font =
            UIFont.preferredFontForTextStyle(UIFontTextStyleBody)


        observer = NSNotificationCenter.defaultCenter()
            .addObserverForName(UIContentSizeCategoryDidChangeNotification,
                object: nil, queue: NSOperationQueue.mainQueue(),
                usingBlock: { (notification) in
```

```
        self.textView.font =
            UIFont.preferredFontForTextStyle(UIFontTextStyleBody)

    })
}


}
```

Now if you run the app, it will dynamically change and update to the user's preferred dynamic font!

Index

We'd like to hear your suggestions for improving our indexes. Send email to index@oreilly.com.

About the Authors

Jonathon Manning is the cofounder of Secret Lab (*http://www.secretlab.com.au*), an independent game development studio based in Hobart, Tasmania, Australia. Jon is a game designer and programmer who's worked on all kinds of projects, ranging from iPad games for children to instant messaging clients. Jon is about to submit a PhD exploring the manipulation of online social networks. He can be found on Twitter as *@desplesda*.

Paris Buttfield-Addison is also a cofounder of Secret Lab, where he works as a mobile app engineer, game designer, and researcher with a passion for making technology simpler and as engaging as possible. Paris has a PhD in Computing and can be found on Twitter as *@parisba*.

Tim Nugent pretends to be a mobile app developer, game designer, PhD student, and now he even pretends to be an author. When he isn't busy avoiding being found out as a fraud, he spends most of his time designing and creating little apps and games he won't let anyone see. Tim spent a disproportionately long time writing this tiny little bio, most of which was spent trying to stick a witty sci-fi reference in, before he simply gave up. Tim can be found as *@The_McJones* on Twitter.

Colophon

The animal on the cover of *Swift Development with Cocoa* is an Australasian gannet. The Australasian gannet (*Morus serrator* or *Sula bassana*) belongs to the Sulidae family and has a small range or territory, though its overall numbers seem to be increasing. This bird breeds on Tasmania, Victoria, and New Zealand; and tends to live in large colonies on cliffs and beaches.

This large coastal seabird has mostly white plumage, with black lining and flight feathers, plus a yellow head and a blue beak. The young bird has darker coloring, mostly brown with light spots, but gradually becomes whiter over its first five years. Its body is around three feet long, with a wingspan of approximately five feet. Younger birds disperse to a greater extent than their mature counterparts, who tend to hang in pairs for several consecutive seasons. In breeding season, a couple lays only one egg. Flat ground surrounded by the sea seems to be the preferred nesting location for the gannet, and anchovies, mackerel, flying fish, and squid are some favorite foods.

Many of the animals on O'Reilly covers are endangered; all of them are important to the world. To learn more about how you can help, go to *animals.oreilly.com*.

The cover image is from Wood's *Natural History*. The cover fonts are URW Typewriter and Guardian Sans. The text font is Adobe Minion Pro; the heading font is Adobe Myriad Condensed; and the code font is Dalton Maag's Ubuntu Mono.

Have it your way.

Lightning Source UK Ltd.
Milton Keynes UK
UKOW07f1042210715

255559UK00003B/16/P